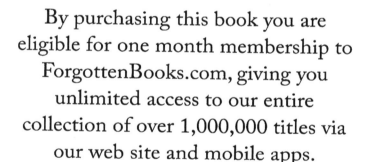

ISBN 978-1-5285-6448-9
PIBN 10058804

A SHORT HISTORY OF THE AMERICAN PEOPLE

In Two Volumes

A SHORT HISTORY OF THE AMERICAN PEOPLE

VOLUME I. (1492 TO 1789)

The Foundations of American Nationality

By *Evarts Boutell Greene*

Professor of History, University of Illinois

VOLUME II. (1783 TO THE PRESENT TIME)

The Development of American Nationality

By *Carl Russell Fish*

Professor of American History, University of Wisconsin

From Houdon's Bust

GEORGE WASHINGTON

THE DEVELOPMENT OF AMERICAN NATIONALITY

BY

CARL RUSSELL FISH

PROFESSOR OF AMERICAN HISTORY
UNIVERSITY OF WISCONSIN

AMERICAN BOOK COMPANY

NEW YORK   CINCINNATI   CHICAGO

AUG 27 1918

© Cl. A 503216

ms I

GENERAL PREFACE

THE authors hope that this " Short History of the American People " may serve the purposes of two classes of readers. They have aimed, in the first instance, to provide for college undergraduates pursuing an introductory course in American history, a general manual which will embody, in some measure at least, the enlarged knowledge and the new points of view made possible by the results of research in recent years. They believe also that this history will meet the requirements of the general reader who desires a comprehensive view of the subject within reasonable compass. For the student and the general reader alike, it is hoped that the bibliographical notes may point the way to more extended studies.

The aim of the authors is not so much to present a balanced narrative of events, as to describe those movements and forces which have left their permanent impress upon the national character and institutions. The first volume (*The Foundations of American Nationality*, 1492 to 1789) deals with the molding of the varied European nationalities and the several detached colonies into an independent and united nation ; the second (*The Development of American Nationality*, 1783 to the Present Time) deals with the development of the nation so formed. While any division of the subject matter of history occasions perplexity and disagreement, the authors believe that the character of the problems confronting the people of the time, and the character of the materials which the historian must employ, permanently differentiate the colonial period from the national, and that the two can best be treated by different men. In order, however, that each author might have full liberty to express his views, the volumes overlap for the period 1783 to 1789.

PREFACE TO VOLUME II

THE aim of the author, in writing this volume, has been to exhibit American history as a development. The central point of view has been the political, with the idea that the American people have expressed themselves more fully in their political life than elsewhere, and more so than has been the case with most other nations. To make clear this political development, the various factors, economic, social, intellectual, and moral, which from time to time have, by their interaction, contributed to it, have been treated in as much detail as the author believes their relative importance entitles them to. It cannot be hoped that any such selection of contributing factors will prove universally satisfactory, but the greater vitality which this method gives is felt to more than counterbalance the criticism that might be avoided by a more conventional treatment. With respect to military history, the author has departed from the standard of relative values, and given it less space than its real importance demands, believing that most persons possess a better knowledge of this than of other fields, owing to the interest which it seems to hold for them during their high school age.

As the chief purpose of this book is to serve as a text for use in college classes, the author calls attention to three assumptions that he has made with reference to college students: first, that they have some general knowledge of American history; second, that they will make some use of collateral reading; third, that they have somewhat more maturity of mind than students in high schools, and may be expected to grasp more fundamental ideas and to comprehend a greater complexity of causal relations. With these assumptions in mind, it has been felt possible to eliminate some of the more commonly known facts, and to disregard chronology to a greater degree than is advisable in books for the use of less mature students. In thus adapting American history, the author has been guided by a ten years' experience in presenting the period under review to students of this type.

The bibliographical notes given at the end of the chapters are not intended to supply references for extensive topic work, which must always be molded to the capacity of the libraries available; or to give authority to the text. Their sole purpose is to suggest supplementary reading. The aim has not been to make the lists long, but to give those references which have been found most useful in actual class-room work. In general, reference has not been made to rare works now out of print, but to material apt to be at hand in the average college library. With this point in mind extensive use has been made of publications of learned societies. References to the same work have seldom been repeated at the end of the several chapters, and in the absence of the articles specifically noted, many general histories might well be used to supplement other chapters than those in connection with which they are mentioned. No attempt has been made to equalize the references at the close of the several chapters, and it is the belief of the author that reading on some subjects is much more valuable than on others, and that students should not be encouraged to expect mechanical assignments of equal length to supplement the work of each subject or each week. The author believes in the value of general reading in the sources even more than in the reading of important special documents, and the source references are to such material as is readily available.

GENERAL REFERENCES

Channing, E., Hart, A. B., and Turner, F. J., *Guide to the Study and Reading of American History*, Boston, 1912. This guide in its newest edition should be in the hands of all college teachers of history. Its bibliographical references are richer than those of any textbook can be, and its pedagogical suggestions represent the latest thought with reference to college teaching.

McLaughlin, A. C., and Hart, A. B., *Cyclopedia of American Government*, N. Y., 1913.

Stanwood, E., *History of the Presidency* (to 1909), 2 vols., Boston, 1898, 1912. This contains party platforms and votes.

The following general histories are valuable through the periods mentioned:

1801–1817. Adams, H., *History of the United States*, N. Y., 1889–1891.

1492–1789. Bancroft, G., *A History of the United States*, 6 vols., N. Y., 1883–1885.

1783–1865. Curtis, G. T., *Constitutional History of the United States*, 2 vols., N. Y., 1889–1896.

1789–1900. Dewey, D. R., *Financial History of the United States*, N. Y., 1907.

1300–1907. Hart, A. B. [editor], *The American Nation: A History*, 27 vols., N. Y., 1904–1908. Each volume has a separate author, and several of them are referred to in the chapter bibliographies.

1783–1860. McMaster, J. B., *History of the People of the United States from the Revolution to the Civil War*, 8 vols., N. Y., 1884–1913.

1849–1877. Rhodes, J. F., *History of the United States*, 7 vols., N. Y., 1891–1906.

1783–1865. Schouler, J., *History of the United States*, 7 vols., N. Y., 1894–1914.

The following series are of especial value: for biography, the *American Statesmen*, edited by J. T. Morse; and for state history, the *American Commonwealths*, edited by H. E. Scudder, and the *Stories of the States*, edited by E. S. Brooks.

CONTENTS

PORTRAITS

MAPS

THE DEVELOPMENT OF
AMERICAN NATIONALITY

CHAPTER I

THE UNITED STATES IN 1783

THE history of the American people from the landing at
Jamestown to the present day is one and indivisible. It is,
moreover, indissolubly connected with the development of
European civilization. History does not occur in epochs,
and each great event is at the same time the culmination of
one line of causation and the starting point of another. For
the purposes of study as well as of writing, however, something less than the whole must be taken, and the attempt
should be made to divide at the point where fewest threads
will be broken. In a history like this, where the main interest
is political, the meeting of the first Continental Congress or the
adoption of the Constitution might seem to be more logical
dates for separation than 1783. In fact, 1789 is to serve as
the real point of departure, but to treat of the Constitution
without giving the conditions and the struggles out of which
it came seemed impossible; and so this book and the preceding volume overlap for the period 1783 to 1789. In
addition, this first chapter attempts to summarize those conditions resulting from colonial development which are most
essential for an understanding of the subsequent history.

The event which makes 1783 significant is that in that year Independ-
American independence was finally achieved and formally ence.
acknowledged in the treaty of Paris. This treaty marked
the failure of the attempt to govern the English settlements

1

on the Atlantic coast of America as a portion of the British empire. It left them free to guide their own future development, and face to face with the problem of making of themselves a new nation. The territory assigned them by the

Territory. treaty was amply sufficient for present needs, amounting to about 850,000 square miles; but the descriptions of its boundaries, owing to the lack of geographical knowledge at the time, were inaccurate, and occasioned years of controversy and sometimes danger of war. The national population amounted to less than 3,500,000, and occupied less than a third of the territory to which the treaty gave title. The remaining area was waste, or was peopled by Indians, and portions were still held by foreign powers. It was years before the actual situation was made to conform to the title we received in 1783, — before it became certain that the United States would be a great continental power.

States and sections. The lack of unity within made our title the more precarious. There were thirteen distinct and separate state governments, united by but a loose bond of confederation, and Vermont had its own local authority which defied the rest. The effort to bind these separate states into one effective government was the first great national task, and was successful; but there was another element of disunion, still more important and destined to prove more obstinate. Differences in the original stock, emphasized by different physical conditions and by the isolated life of the colonial period, had created several great sections or divisions of the country, which had sufficient similarity within themselves, and sufficient unlikeness to each other, to make them permanent entities, and to cause sectionalism to be a permanent factor in American history.

New England. In the northeast lay New England. From its mountains, the White and the Green, the land sloped away south and east to the sea. Excepting a fringe of sandy plain only a few miles wide on the south shore, the whole region had been glacier swept. The tops of the granite ridges which radiated from Mount Washington toward the coast had been ground down, and the débris covered the intervening valleys with a soil, rough, filled with bowlders, and hard to work, but inexhaustible. These valleys, widening as they approached the sea, gathered up the waters into rivers, generally not navigable for long distances, but strong and rapid. At the falls of these rivers there stood already mills to grind flour and to saw the timber which covered nearly the whole region. Where the mountain ridges breasted the ocean they formed headlands and islands, and the intervening inlets and bays, into which the rivers flowed, afforded sheltering harbors for ships of all sizes, and were rich in all kinds of fish.

The New Englanders were of nearly pure English descent, and the ancestors of a majority of them had been Puritans who came to America during the brief period between 1620 and 1640. They were, therefore, remarkably homogeneous. Religion had been an important cause of the first migration, and still played a large part in their lives. They were accustomed to look even at political matters from a religious point of view, and this tended to make them peculiarly tenacious of their opinions, and to consider their opponents not only as mistaken but as bad. This "New England conscience" was accompanied by a strong missionary spirit, under the impulse of which they tried firmly, and not always sympathetically, to impress upon others New England beliefs and usages. Their religion was Calvinistic. They held that the relations between God and man were regulated by contract, and this idea of contract they transferred to the other relations of life. Thus they had long based their political systems upon the theory, afterwards formulated by Locke and expressed in the Declaration of Independence, that government must rest on the consent of the governed, preferably expressed in the form of a written contract or constitution.

New England stock and ideas.

Owing in part to the physical characteristics of New England, the numberless little harbors of the coast and the hills of the interior, the people lived mostly in villages, rather than on farms. The village settlement was the center of the town, which was a geographical area corresponding to the modern western township. Towns differed in size and were irregular in shape, but those lately founded averaged about six miles square. The town was also the smallest unit of local government and was a very busy one. It attended to practically all government matters not managed by the state; for, although counties existed, they did little except judicial business. Moreover, the recognized functions of government were unusually extensive. The town managed nearly all church affairs, and it exercised a very close supervision over the lives of the townspeople. All this business was done in the town meeting, which all voters could attend, and, between meetings, by a committee of selectmen. New Englanders, therefore, were accustomed to a government which actively interfered in their everyday life, to a government in which they took a direct part, and as a result of this direct participation, political education was more widely diffused there than in any other part of the world at that time. In most New England town meetings, due regard was paid to family and wealth and learning. As John Cotton had said, New England was neither "meerly democratical " nor "meerly aristocratical."

This population of New Englanders in 1783 occupied the four states of Massachusetts (which included Maine), New Hampshire, Rhode Island, and Connecticut, and also the unrecognized state of Vermont. Nearly all the 900,000 inhabitants lived south of a line drawn across the middle of New Hampshire and Vermont. A desire to escape the rigid scrutiny of New England town life, combined with a restless seeking for better lands and climate, had caused many to migrate to other colonies, and now others were forced to do the same as the increasing population pressed up the narrowing valleys, where the soil became more and more difficult to cultivate. Thus a New England element was to be found in neighboring parts of New York and New Jersey, and was beginning to enter northern Pennsylvania and the Mohawk valley.

The majority depended for a living upon agriculture, Occupations. eking out the scanty returns of their rock-strewn glacial soil by weaving, or making shoes, or nails, of winter nights. A large number on the coast hoped, with the return of peace, to resume their fishing on the banks of Newfoundland. Most of those who hoped to grow wealthy engaged in commerce. They were accustomed to carry their fish to Spain and the West Indies; of West Indian molasses they made rum, with which to purchase in Africa negroes to sell in America; they served as carriers and agents for the less commercial people of the other colonies. The ships for all this trade were built in New England, where ship timber grew to the water's edge of many snug little harbors, which afforded equal security for construction, and facility for putting to sea. The economic life of the people, therefore, was varied. One man had several occupations. Mechanical skill and commercial shrewdness were developed. Many of the things to which they turned their hands, moreover, such as trading and fishing beyond the national boundaries, were of such a character as to thrive or droop according to the degree of protection and encouragement afforded by the government. Politics and industry were, therefore, closely connected. Boston, although surpassed in population by Philadelphia and New York, had the most widespread commercial connections of all the cities in the country. For years Americans were known in many parts of the world as Bostonese.

On the great Atlantic coast plain, with its sinuous, slow- The coast moving rivers, and its rich, thin, alluvial soil, a very different plain and the type of civilization had developed. The characteristic in- system.

stitution was the plantation. Back from the road or the river stood the mansion house of the owner; behind it clustered the cabins of the slaves, while beyond, the fields stretched away to the surrounding woods. This little village was the absolute possession of the master, and its object was the production of as large a crop as possible of the staple: tobacco or rice or indigo. Food was raised, and some simple trades were practiced, but these were of subsidiary interest. Its economic relations with the outside world consisted chiefly of shipping the crop to England, and receiving in return clothes, tools, and such other necessities or luxuries as might be ordered for the ensuing year. The one-crop system of cultivation used up the soil rapidly, and most plantations were surrounded by great tracts of land exhausted in the past, or reserved for future use.

Extension of plantation system.

When the land had been long used, and when there came to be great numbers of old and useless slaves, the plantation became less profitable. The planter, however, was not willing to reduce his standard of living. Many of the great families of Virginia had been founded by cavaliers, supporters of Charles I in the great English civil war, who had migrated to America during the Commonwealth, between 1648 and 1660, and who had tried to reproduce the conditions of their old English homes. The style of living they adopted became the aspiration of all planters, of whatever origin, who made money; to curtail it, was to admit defeat. Some borrowed money and increased their holdings of land and slaves. Others sold out, and, investing in new land beyond the settlements, opened new plantations. This increasing area of production constantly lowered the price of the staple, whether tobacco, rice, indigo, or, later, cotton; and this again reduced the profits of the planter on each slave and each acre. It again became necessary to enlarge the investment, or to move on. This same story continually repeated itself; the plantations growing in size, and the plantation system stretching inward from the coast, across the tidewater region, and up into the piedmont or foothills. In the old plantation area, there remained the more successful, and to them succeeded their eldest sons. The community became wealthy and conservative. To the back country went the more adventurous, the younger sons, the successful merchants, and small farmers who aspired to become planters, taking with them some little capital, represented by young and able-bodied slaves.

In the tidewater region, lawyers, doctors, and the wealthiest merchants associated with the planters, but the remainder of the white population, consisting largely of the descendants of white servants brought over under conditions of practical slavery, were, for the most part, in poverty and dependence. In the piedmont, planters like Jefferson and Patrick Henry lived on terms approaching equality with independent farmers who came down from the mountain valleys, and plantation and small farm existed peaceably side by side.

The smallest unit of government was the parish, which had civil as well as religious duties, and which was governed by a vestry composed of the wealthier planters. More important was the county, governed by a county court, composed of a number of the greater planters appointed by the governor. Members of the legislature were elected by the people, who, having come together and heard speeches and eaten and drunk at the candidates' expense, divided into two crowds to be counted. The government exercised few functions. Poor relief, education, and often road and bridge making were largely left to the individual planter. Under these conditions the planter class came to be all-powerful, and the planters came to believe strongly in democratic principles, meaning, thereby, the least government possible. In the management of their large plantations, with sometimes hundreds of souls dependent upon them, many acquired great administrative ability and a strong sense of public duty.

Government and ideals.

It was by no accident that for more than two thirds of the period before the Civil War our presidents were of this class.

Area.

In 1783 plantations occupied nearly all the Atlantic coast plains of Delaware, Maryland, Virginia, the Carolinas, and Georgia. The system had a foothold in the piedmont region of these states, and some veterans of the Revolution were planning to establish plantations in the beautiful blue-grass district along the banks of the Kentucky. The population of this area was about 1,200,000, of whom nearly half were slaves. There was only one really important city, Charleston, whither the South Carolina planters had to flee, at certain seasons, to escape the fever.

The Middle States.

The region between the plantation country and New England consisted of the valleys of three great rivers, the Hudson, the Delaware, and the Susquehanna, which ran into three great bays, and near whose mouths stood the busy cities of New York, Philadelphia, and Baltimore. Each valley had distinguishing characteristics. The Hudson had been settled by the Dutch, and although many English, New Englanders, Germans, and others had mixed with them, they were still an important factor. The Delaware region was largely occupied by English and German Quakers, whose kindly humanity had made Philadelphia a real abode of brotherly love and social betterment, but the extreme toler-ance of whose creed caused them to be less influential than the New Englanders in impressing their ideas upon others. Quaker shrewdness and honest dealing, moreover, had built up many substantial fortunes, and Philadelphia was one of the few places in the United States where capital was seek-ing investment on a large scale. The Susquehanna valley contained a large proportion of Germans, still using their native tongue. Generally known as "Pennsylvania Dutch," they constituted about one fourth the population of that state. They lived to a considerable extent in separate communities, and clung tenaciously to their national customs. It was many years before they ceased to be a distinct element, and many of their characteristics remained to their descendants long after their unity was broken up by intermarriage and dispersal. The Susquehanna valley contained also many Scotch-Irish and English. Its natural port, Baltimore, lay in Maryland, and so was affiliated politically with the plantation area.

Throughout the whole region there was a varied agriculture, producing every year a surplus for export, the handling of which supported a mercantile community in the three leading cities. This trade, although, unlike that of New England, it was confined almost entirely to the local needs of the section, was already sufficient to make New York the most cosmopolitan city in America, and Philadelphia the financial center. There were those, too, who even in 1783 foresaw unlimited possibilities of expansion. The headwaters of the three great rivers of the region are in the Appalachian mountains, where they interlace with those of the rivers of the Ohio and Great Lake systems. Where these rivers break through the mountain ridges and plateaus, some to flow eastward, some westward, they form low passes, which even in Indian times afforded routes for war and trade and migration between the coast and the Mississippi valley. It was felt that when the Middle States developed, if only the passes could be made convenient highways, these cities would become the gateways of western commerce. This, however, was a dream of the future; and, moreover, as yet the great mineral resources of the mountains had but little effect on the life of the people. *Economic conditions.*

The Dutch, the Germans, and the Scotch-Irish were comparatively inexperienced in the political institutions by which they were governed, and the Quakers largely indifferent to politics. In New York, as a result of the method of settlement, great tracts of land were held by landlords who rented *Political conditions.*

it to tenant farmers, whose votes they controlled. Self-government, therefore, did not work so smoothly as in New England and Virginia. There existed, also, well-defined interests, the mercantile, the agricultural; the German, the Dutch, and the Quakers; the city, the country. To lead such a population required men who could organize their supporters; and the germs of party organization and the spoils system were already to be found. To adjust the conflicting forces required men clever at shifting political alliances to suit the needs of the moment. These problems resembled, on a small scale, those of the nation as a whole, and many of the politicians trained in the Middle States came to exercise great influence in national affairs, harmonizing, conciliating, and manipulating the divergent sections and parties.

Local government.   The system of local government combined some of the characteristics of the sections to the east and south. In Pennsylvania, the county was all-important, but its officials were elected by the people. In New York, township and county divided the local powers, the county being governed by representatives from all the townships of which it was composed. Lying in the road between the coast and the West, the Middle States were to contribute much to the traits of that section which was yet to be developed, and among other things, one or the other of these methods of managing local affairs has been adopted by every state north of the Ohio and the Missouri. In some respects the Middle States were in 1783 the most American of the sections; the population of this region was somewhat over 700,000.

The frontier.   From central Pennsylvania to northern Georgia, southerly and southwesterly, there sweeps a broad mountain belt, one hundred and fifty miles wide, seven hundred miles long, and composed of almost unbroken parallel ridges, with valleys, now fertile with a rich limestone soil, now waste and fruitless, lying between. About 1720, pioneers began to enter these mountain troughs in Pennsylvania, where the

Susquehanna breaks through many of the ridges. Naturally this movement included many of the valley Germans; it included also adventurous or unsuccessful families from nearly all the other colonies; but the characteristic strain was furnished by that Scotch element which, attracted to northern Ireland in the early seventeenth century, now began to seek its fortunes in America. Allured by good hunting and fertile limestone bottoms, and impelled by the need of more room for their large families which clannishly clung together, this population had by 1783 pushed to the southern extremities of the valleys.

The individual settler, with his family, here met the wild single-handed, and lived a self-sustaining life; he must mend his gun, and raise his corn, and kill his meat. The community was almost cut off by lack of facilities for transportation from all the world besides, and most men within it began with the ax and plow, and sent their sons out again with the ax and plow to win a living. It was, therefore, a democratic community, and one apt to chafe under authority. It had resisted England,[1] its Revolutionary epic culminating in the battle of Kings Mountain; but it was equally ready to resist the authority of the states. A broad belt of wilderness separated this back country from the coast settlements, where government centered, and distrust was mutual. Free from the state patriotism so powerful in the older communities, the frontier possessed a strong national feeling, fostered by the Presbyterian church with which many of the Scotch-Irish settlers were connected, which was the oldest nation-wide institution in America and whose synods had for many years regularly drawn ministers and elders from the whole region to Philadelphia or New York. Life afforded no opportunity for formal education, and but a narrow range of

Character-istics.

---

[1] In accordance with common usage the words England and English are often used in this book to apply to the kingdom of Great Britain; in speaking of immigrants therefrom, however, the several racial stocks are differentiated.

experience, but it gave self-reliance, practical ability to cope with vital problems individually, or, if needs be, to organize to fight the Indians or resist interference, and it allowed only the courageous and physically fit to develop into manhood.

Area.

This population in 1783 fairly well filled the mountain valleys, and was flowing out to the eastward into the piedmont, particularly in Virginia, where it was already mingling with the first waves advancing from the coast. The greater portion of the migration, however, was westward. In 1775 Daniel Boone moved his family into Kentucky, and by 1783 steadily increasing streams were flowing into the Mississippi valley, following the courses of the Tennessee, the Cumberland, the Kanawha, and the Ohio. The total population of this area amounted to about 550,000, and closely allied to it in characteristics were about 150,000 living in Vermont, New Hampshire, and Maine, who have been already counted as belonging to New England.

Transporta-tion.

The differences between the sections, and even those between smaller localities within the greater sectional areas, were accentuated by the difficulties of transportation. The British government had discouraged trade between the several colonies, desiring each to deal directly with the mother country. Roads were few and poor except in closely settled areas, as those around Boston and Philadelphia. To go by land from one state to another was in most cases an adventure taking time, strength, and often courage. Commercial intercourse was nearly all by water, and the coasts were by no means easy of navigation. Much time and money and skill would be required before the states could be knit together by a common life.

Elements of union.

The divergencies of the sections were offset by many bonds of union. Nearly the whole population spoke English, which meant that their minds were fed by the same ideas, derived from the English literature of the time, particularly on religious, legal, and political lines. The great bulk of the population, aside from the negro slaves, was of

Teutonic stock; the Scotch, except a few living chiefly in North Carolina, being from the lowlands, where Anglo-Saxon blood predominated. In Maryland there were many Roman Catholics, but elsewhere Protestants were in overwhelming majority, and of them the greater number were Calvinists. There was a common political experience based upon the fact that all the states were confronted by much the same problems. The English common law was universally accepted. Most important of all was the similarity of practice and principle with regard to methods of government other than local. The defense of these colonial political institutions had been in large measure the object of the Revolution, and now they had been crystallized in the constitutions of the several states.

Organic unity among the states was actually represented by the Articles of Confederation. These established not so much a form of government as a method of diplomatic intercourse, and the organization took the form of a body called a Congress, a term at that time denoting a meeting of diplomatic representatives. The delegates of each state jointly cast one vote, though Rhode Island had only about 60,000 population, while Virginia had 700,000. Two or more members had to be present to cast the vote of a state, and they might, by dividing equally, nullify it. The assent of nine states was necessary to all important measures, and to amend the Articles the consent of the legislature of every state was necessary. The delegates were elected and paid by their state legislatures, and were liable to recall at any time. Their term was for one year, and they could be reelected only twice in any series of six years. *Articles of Confederation.*

The powers of Congress were adapted particularly for war. It could not collect customs, or regulate commerce, except by making treaties prohibiting discrimination against foreign goods and vessels. It could treat with those Indian tribes only which did not live wholly in any one state. Its *Powers of Congress.*

revenue was to be obtained by dividing its expenses among the states in proportion to the value of land held by individuals, but there was no method of forcing a state to pay, and during its existence the Confederation received only about $6,000,000 of the $16,000,000 for which it asked.

The judiciary.

There was no general judiciary, but Congress was given power to select certain state courts to try piracies and felonies on the high seas, and to establish courts of appeals in prize cases. One such court was established and was active, but was in 1784 discontinued, the war claims having been mostly adjudicated. Congress was authorized also to call special courts, made up according to a carefully detailed plan, to decide boundary disputes between states.

The executive.

No executive department was provided for, but Congress had power to appoint civil officers, and in 1783, as a result of hard experience during the war, executive business had been divided among three departments. The Secretary of Foreign Affairs was Robert Livingston of New York, succeeded in 1784 by John Jay of the same state, who came to be the most influential man at the seat of government. Robert Morris was Superintendent of Finance until 1784, when he gave up in despair or disgust, and was succeeded by a board of three commissioners. General Knox in 1785 followed General Lincoln as Secretary at War. A naval department was provided for, but remained unorganized. The post office was but a small affair and was not considered as a department.

Weakness of the Confederation.

The government was weak because there was no head to unite and correlate the work of the departments, because these executive officers had no powers independent of Congress, and because Congress was so dependent upon the states. The intention of those who drew up the Articles seems to have been to divide the sovereignty between the states and the national government; to make each sovereign within its own sphere. Political theorists are not in agreement as to whether such a division is possible, but however this may be, there can be little doubt that no division was accomplished by this agreement. The powers of the general government were so few that it became essentially a creature of the states, and they practically retained the whole sovereign power during the period.

BIBLIOGRAPHICAL NOTES

(As to the use of this material, see the last paragraph of the Preface, page viii.)

This chapter is but a recapitulation of physiographic and sectional factors existing in 1783, the development of which was traced in volume one. As it is becoming increasingly common, however, to begin the basic college course in American history at about this period, a few references follow, which have been found useful in expanding the students' knowledge of these subjects.

Farrand, L., *Basis of American History*, 1–22. Powell, J. W., *Physiographic Regions of the United States*. Shaler, N. S., *Physiography* (Winsor, J., *Narrative and Critical History of America*, vol. IV, pp. i–xxx). *Physiography.*

Channing, E., *Town and County Government* (*Johns Hopkins Historical Studies*, II), 437–474. Eggleston, E., *The Beginners of a Nation*, 98–188; 315–346. Fiske, J., *The Beginnings of New England*. Howard, G. E., *Local Constitutional History*, 51–99; 319–351. Low, A. M., *The American People*, vol. I. Mathews, L. K., *Expansion of New England*, chs. 1, 2. *New England.*

Bruce, P. A., *Economic History of Virginia*, vol. I, chs. I, VII; vol. II, ch. XX; *Institutional History of Virginia*, I, chs. I and III. Channing, *Town and County Government* (*Johns Hopkins Historical Studies*, II), 437–489. Commons, J. R., etc., *A Documentary History of American Industrial Society*, vol. I. Doyle, J. A., *The English Colonies in America, Virginia*, 101–184. Eggleston, E., *The Beginners of a Nation*, 1–98. Fiske, J., *Old Virginia and Her Neighbors*, II, 1–44. Jefferson, T., *Notes on Virginia* (published separately and in his Writings). *Plantation area.*

Howard, *Local Constitutional History*, 102–117; 358–387. Faust, A. B., *The German Element in the United States*, I, chs. 5, 6. *Middle States.*

The frontier.

Roosevelt, T., *The Winning of the West*, I, chs. I, V, VI. Turner, F. J., *The Significance of the Frontier in American History* (Am. Hist. Assoc., *Report*, 1893, 197–227). Faust, A. B., *German Element in the United States*, I, chs. 10, 11, 12.

Elements of union.

Frothingham, R., *Rise of the Republic*, chs. III, IV, VII. Howard, G. E., *Preliminaries of the Revolution*, ch. I. Shaler, N. S., *History of United States*, ch. I.

Articles of Confederation. Sources.

American History Leaflet, no. 20. *The Federalist* (any edition), nos. 15, 16, 21, 22.

General accounts.

Fiske, J., *Critical Period of American History*, chs. I and II. Frothingham, R., *Rise of the Republic*, 1–32, 101–157, and ch. XII. McLaughlin, A. C., *The Confederation and the Constitution*, 35–53. Small, A., *Beginnings of American Nationality* (*Johns Hopkins Historical Studies*, VIII), 1–89.

CHAPTER II

THE HISTORY OF THE CONFEDERATION

THE chief claim of the national government under the Confederation to consideration lay in its ownership and control of lands west of the mountains, and its permanent contribution to American development was the enactment of regulations for the survey and government of this area. The manner in which it became possessed of this immense territory was as follows.

Seven of the colonies, Massachusetts, Connecticut, New York, Virginia, the Carolinas, and Georgia, had claimed, on the basis of charters and of Indian treaties, land stretching westward to the Mississippi. The British government had wished to make the mountains the western boundary of the several colonies, and itself to direct the development of the Mississippi valley on imperial lines. The resulting dispute was a minor cause of the Revolution. The Continental Congress took up this claim of the British government, and the first draft of the Articles gave Congress the right of fixing state boundaries. This power was cut out before the Articles were presented to the states for adoption. Maryland, thereupon, in behalf of the landless states, fearing the size and power that its neighbors might attain if their claims were granted, refused to accept the Articles unless the western lands were granted to the central government. In 1781 New York, whose claim was the most dubious, led the way with a cession. Maryland at once accepted the Articles, and negotiations began which ended in cessions by the other states. In 1784 Virginia ceded to the national

Land cessions.

government the jurisdiction of all the land she claimed north of the Ohio, on certain conditions; but she retained the right to grant the ownership of land within a certain area, west of the Scioto, in payment of the land bounties promised her soldiers during the Revolution. Massachusetts in 1785 ceded her claims west of the western boundary of New York. Connecticut followed in 1786, reserving on the southern shore of Lake Erie a tract, about the size of the parent state, now known as the "Western Reserve." In 1800, having sold all this land, Connecticut yielded her jurisdiction to the United States government. South Carolina ceded her claims in 1787; and in 1790 North Carolina, having sold her land, handed over the jurisdiction. Georgia yielded nothing until 1802.

State boundaries.

In the meantime the power of Congress to arrange for the arbitration of state boundaries was several times resorted to. In 1782 Pennsylvania was awarded land claimed by Connecticut. In 1786 suits between Massachusetts and New York, and South Carolina and Georgia, were arranged by satisfactory compromises. Later Congress sold to Pennsylvania the triangle between New York, Ohio, and Lake Erie, which was left in its hands by the cessions, and thereafter state boundary disputes east of the Mississippi never became serious.

Land survey and sale.

One reason for the rapid settlement of these questions was the desire for securing titles on the part of many who wished to buy, some for the purpose of settlement and some for speculation. They were unwilling to invest money while titles were undetermined. Once title was clear, the demand for land became insistent, and Congress was eager to sell in the hope of increasing its revenue. It therefore became necessary to devise a system of land sale. There was no lack of experience on this subject, for the problem had existed from the beginning of colonization in America and had existed in every colony. In framing a national system practices were brought together from all sections and incorporated in an act passed in 1785. The details were worked out by Williamson of North Carolina, with Jefferson as an adviser. So satisfactory has it proved, that under it, amended as it has been from time to time, two thirds of our territory has passed from public to private ownership. The basic idea was that no land should be sold until it had been surveyed. The unit of survey was the township, six miles square, and divided into thirty-six sections, each one mile square and numbered according to a uniform system. The townships were surveyed by running a base line east and west, from which perpendiculars were drawn every six miles. The land between each two perpendiculars was called a range, and the ranges were numbered from east to west. The ranges were divided into townships by lines drawn every six miles, parallel to the base, and these townships were numbered from the base, south or north as the case might be. Section sixteen in every township was, in accordance with colonial practice, reserved for the support of education.

A beginning was made by ordering the survey of seven ranges west from Pennsylvania and the Ohio. The terms on which this land was offered for sale were unwise, Congress overreaching itself in the desire for money. It would not sell land for less than a dollar an acre, plus the cost of the survey, nor less than 640 acres, and would not allow credit. Sales, moreover, were to be held, not on the spot, but in the several states, and were by auction. This excluded the majority of those who wished actually to settle, for the bulk of the migratory population had little money or credit. States and private land companies were offering land on better terms, and so Congress derived little revenue from this source.

A satisfactory system of government was as necessary as a secure title. In 1784 a plan drawn up by Jefferson was adopted, but it was vague, and failed to satisfy a body

Northwestern Ordinance.

of Revolutionary officers, chiefly from New England, who desired to settle on the north bank of the Ohio, west of the seven ranges. They organized as the "Ohio Company of Associates," and in 1786 proposed to Congress to purchase a large tract in that region, using for the purchase money the certificates of indebtedness for five years' pay which they had received from Congress at the close of the war in place of the half pay for life which had at first been promised them. Congress, glad to sink this debt, listened readily to their suggestions; and Nathan Dane, a delegate from Massachusetts, after consultation with their agent, Dr. Manasseh Cutler, drew up an ordinance which passed July 13, 1787, and which ranks among the most important pieces of legislation ever adopted in the United States. It provided that the territory be ruled by a governor and judges, appointed by the national government, until the male population over twenty-one reached 5000. Then a legislature was to be added, and ultimately, in accordance with the repeated promises of Congress and the terms of the Virginia cession, the territory was to be admitted into the Union, divided into not less than three nor more than five states. These states were to be bound forever by certain conditions: freedom of person and of religion, security of contracts, encouragement of education, common use of rivers, and that "There shall be neither slavery nor involuntary servitude . . . otherwise than in the punishment of crimes." This ordinance applied only to the territory north of the Ohio. In 1790 the first Congress under the Constitution organized the lands ceded by North and South Carolina as the Territory South of the River Ohio, upon the same plan as the Northwest Territory, except that slavery was not prohibited. Kentucky was never a territory, remaining a part of Virginia until admitted as a state.

Settlement.   The Ordinance of 1787 satisfied the Ohio Company, which promptly purchased 1,500,000 acres southwest of the seven ranges and founded Marietta in 1788. Its members, combining with the Connecticut settlers that somewhat later occupied the Western Reserve, started a stream of New England and Middle States emigration, which balanced the Virginia veterans and the mountaineers who were occupying Kentucky and the military bounty lands of what is now southern and central Ohio. These two streams of population, representing differing traditions and political conceptions, were destined to divide the country west of the mountains, and their conflicts ultimately resulted in the great Civil War.

In 1782 Jacob Yoder, a Pennsylvania German, started down the Monongahela with a boatload of flour. Running down the Ohio and the Mississippi, he bartered it at New Orleans, sold his boat, and took ship for Philadelphia, trading at Havana on the way, and returned home across the mountains with his profits. This voyage shows the natural and, for the time, the only outlet for the crude bulky products of the frontier farms. Unfortunately Spain held its key. The United States did, indeed, claim to inherit from England the right to navigate the Mississippi, but there was also necessary a "place of deposit," where goods could be transshipped and rafts broken up. Spain denied the one with the other. This was in part because of a dispute between the two countries as to the southern boundary of the United States, this country claiming the parallel of 31°, and Spain that of 32° 30'. A more important reason was the hope of the Spanish government to use the Mississippi as a bribe to induce the western settlers to desert the United States and declare themselves either independent or subject to Spain. If the bribe failed, a lash was ready, for Spain was on good terms with the powerful southwestern Indians, and could loose the curse of frontier war. When, year after year, Congress failed to open the river or to quiet the Indians, it was not unnatural that the people of the West

The problem of the Mississippi.

lost their attachment to the Union, and many entered more or less heartily into intrigues with the Spaniards.

Diplomatic problems of the northwest. To the northwest the situation was similar. England continued to hold Niagara, Detroit, and other key points within the territory assigned the United States by the treaty of 1783, on the plea that we had not carried out certain terms of that treaty. Through these posts she controlled the fur trade, and through the fur trade, the Indians. The settlement of the lake region was prevented, and that of the north bank of the Ohio hindered. Moreover, by means of the St. Lawrence, the English controlled the prosperity of Vermont, as Spain did that of Kentucky, Tennessee, and western Pennsylvania. The Vermont legislature was treating for a separate commercial arrangement, and English officials, many of whom had been Loyalists during the Revolution, contemplated with pleasure the possibility of a dissolution of the United States. The West, as Washington said, stood "upon a pivot, the touch of a feather would turn them any way."

Commercial problems. Independence brought to the coast colonies freedom from the navigation acts, and all the nations of Europe sought the commerce which England could no longer monopolize. Treaties were made with Sweden, Prussia, France, Holland, and Morocco, and adventurous American seamen found their way into the Pacific, bartering on the northwest coast of America for furs and ginseng, which they exchanged at Canton for the teas and silks demanded in the United States. In 1788 it became necessary to appoint a commercial agent at Canton. Such new openings, however, scarcely made up for the loss of some old trade connections and the disturbance of others. British protection had previously enabled us to carry on a considerable trade in the Mediterranean, where the Barbary pirates preyed on the commerce of weaker nations. The new government was unable to make a treaty with any of these lawless little powers except Morocco,

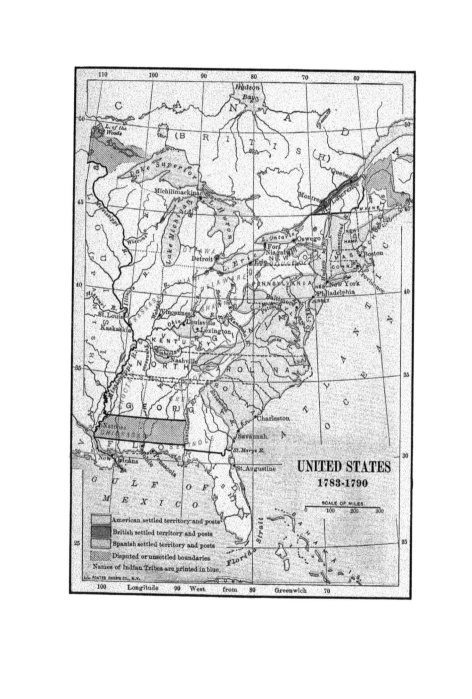

UNITED STATES
1783-1790

SCALE OF MILES
100   200   300

American settled territory and posts
British settled territory and posts
Spanish settled territory and posts
Disputed or unsettled boundaries
Names of Indian Tribes are printed in blue.

L.L. POATES ENGRG CO., N.Y.

and consequently trade beyond Gibraltar vanished. More important was the fact that Great Britain cut off most of our trade with the West Indian islands belonging to her. Previously these colonies had received most of their provisions and lumber from New England and the Middle States, and had paid for it in molasses, rum, and money. Now England allowed them to import American goods only when the other English colonies could not possibly supply the demand, and even then ordered that the importation be made only in English vessels, whereas, before the Revolution, the trade had been carried on almost entirely in American shipping. These regulations distressed American merchants, farmers, fishermen, and shipowners, and they all asked for relief. John Adams was sent as minister to England, but proved powerless. Congress had no power to threaten England with retaliation; the several states pursued varying and contradictory commercial policies, and we had nothing to offer England, for the American people still preferred English goods, and she held as large a proportion of our import trade as before the war. The Spanish trade, also, demanded attention. Spain needed American fish and flour, but merchants engaged in this trade labored under a disadvantage, owing to the absence of a treaty. Spain refused to make such a treaty unless we would give up our claim to navigate the Mississippi. In 1786 Jay arranged a treaty whereby we were to allow this claim to stand over without prejudice for twenty-five years. Congress divided on the subject; the Northeast, to which the commercial aspect appealed, favored it; the South opposed and defeated it.

The net result was that the Confederation government proved incompetent to foster American commerce, and the commercial classes came to desire a stronger central government. Washington wrote Mr. McHenry, a delegate in Congress, August 22, 1785: "We are either a united people under one head and for federal purposes, or we are thirteen independ-

ent sovereignties, eternally counteracting each other. . . .
[The nations of the world] must see and feel, that the Union
or the States individually are sovereigns, as best suits their
purposes; in a word, that we are one nation to-day and thirteen to-morrow. Who will treat with us on such terms?"

Financial
disorder.
The paper money issued by the Continental Congress
had been repudiated, but the national debt remained. This
amounted to about $45,000,000, of which about $8,000,000
was due to foreign nations and bankers. The states were
annually asked for the sums of money required, but they
seldom responded promptly, often paid in their own depreciated paper, and sometimes not at all. Altogether they
scarcely supplied the modest running expenses of the government, about half a million a year. The interest on the
domestic debt remained unpaid, and the notes and certificates which represented it fell to about fifteen cents on the
dollar; the interest on the foreign debt was met by additional loans from Dutch bankers, obtained by John Adams.
Jefferson outlined the scheme of metallic coinage with the
dollar as the unit, which has ever since been used, but during
the Confederation only copper cents were coined. In 1781
Congress, on the advice of Robert Morris, established the
Bank of North America, the first real bank in the country.
The power of Congress to grant a bank charter was questioned,
and to strengthen the bank's position a Pennsylvania state
charter was obtained in 1782. This was revoked in 1785 and
the bank remained in a questionable position until 1787, when
Pennsylvania granted a new charter under which the bank has
since operated. During this period of uncertainty the bank
was naturally of little assistance to the national government.
Conditions grew steadily worse, the requisitions of 1786 were
scarcely heeded by the states, delegates neglected to attend
Congress, and those chosen were men of smaller caliber than
in the first enthusiastic days of the Revolution. Lack of
power to accomplish results brought about lack of interest.

The real political life and interest of the people centered State legislation, legal and religious. in the state governments. Leaders like Patrick Henry, John Hancock, and George Clinton served as governors. The judiciary in nearly all the states ranked high. Under the new constitutions, established after the Declaration of Independence, it rested upon the authority of the people and not of an alien government as before the Revolution. So great was the respect for its personnel and the confidence in its honesty, that in some states it ventured to stand between the legislature and the state constitution, declaring laws unconstitutional and therefore void, thus paving the way for the high position subsequently taken by the national Supreme Court. Such cases during the Confederation were those of *Holmes* v. *Walton* in New Jersey in 1780, *Caton* v. *Commonwealth of Virginia* in 1782, *Trevett* v. *Weeden* in Rhode Island in 1786, and *Bayard* v. *Singleton* in North Carolina in 1787. In 1791 the Supreme Court of New Hampshire came to a similar conclusion in the case of *Gilman* v. *McClary*. Some attempt was made to render judicial processes more simple and less expensive. In Virginia the laws of entail and primogeniture, by which great estates were kept intact and passed on from eldest son to eldest son, were abolished. In Virginia also, after a hard fight, Madison and Jefferson succeeded in disestablishing the state church, and in most of the states some steps were taken towards the separation of church and state, though it was to be many years before officeholding was made universally independent of religious belief, and taxes for the support of religion were abolished.

Special interest attaches to the antislavery agitation of Antislavery movement. the period. The Quakers had always opposed slavery, and there had been a few other voices crying in the wilderness. The region north of the Carolinas had sufficient slaves, in fact, more than it wanted, and the colonies there had endeavored to get the consent of the English government to the prohibition of their importation. During the Revolution, many states had prohibited the trade. Slavery had, in fact, ceased to pay except in the newly exploited districts of the extreme South. Under these circumstances the equality doctrines of the Revolution were readily extended to the negroes, at least to the extent of causing the majority of the leaders of thought to condemn slavery. There began an era of abolition. Vermont led the way in 1777. The Massachusetts constitution of 1780 was later interpreted as abolishing slavery, and New Hampshire followed in 1783. Pennsylvania in 1780 began gradual emancipation, and similar laws were adopted in 1784 by Connecticut and Rhode Island. New York and New Jersey followed in 1799 and 1804. The number of slaves actually freed was small; some were sold south, and some continued to be held under the gradual emancipation acts, except in Massachusetts, Vermont, and New Hampshire, almost until the Civil War. In Virginia there was an equal disposition to free the slaves, but the property sacrifice would have been greater, and the future of the freed negroes was too uncertain. The movement, therefore, halted at the Mason-Dixon line, while the Northwest Ordinance, prohibiting slavery north of the Ohio, carried the division to the Mississippi, and a new sectionalism, ominous for the future, but by no means sharp at this time, was thus foreshadowed.

Economic problems and paper money.   Even the state governments were not able to deal with all their problems successfully. The Revolution, like all wars, left behind it much economic distress. Not only was there destruction of wealth, but also much wealth changed hands. To a great degree the rich grew richer and the poor poorer. This was intensified during the Confederation, for the coast region and the merchants recovered from the effects of the war sooner than the farmers of the interior, who found taxes heavier, but no new means of making money. In 1783 and 1784 there were large imports of long desired English goods, and many, particularly the farmers, thinking that independence would mean immediate good times, bought more than they could pay for. They became indebted to the merchants, who came to constitute a creditor class. Taxes, too, were heavier than before the Revolution, because of the state debts created to carry on the war, and they were levied chiefly upon landowners. The farmers came to hate those to whom they owed money, the lawyers who attempted to collect the debts, and the judges who insisted upon payment, or sent the debtor to prison in accordance with the law of that day. In the South, many of the merchants belonged to the debtor class. The chief political question that divided these classes was that of currency. Congress, as has been stated, had repudiated the paper money it had issued during the Revolution, and furnished only a small amount, which was speedily withdrawn, after the war. The question was, therefore, left to the states. There was undoubtedly too little money for the needs of the country. Gold and silver were sent abroad to pay for our imports, which were very heavy during the first years after the peace, really exceeding the capacity of the country to pay for them. The debtor class demanded the issuance of unlimited amounts of paper, which would make it easy to pay debts and taxes.

This desire for cheap money was not the result of dishonesty, but of lack of financial experience. The colonies generally had been a debtor community, and before the Revolution had indulged in many dangerous financial experiments, and had been kept from others only by the restraining hand of England. Moreover, the Revolution had spread the idea that a legislature was omnipotent and could do anything the people desired; that it could make value where no value was before. The paper-money party was the conservative American party; the sound-money party was a progressive element standing for ideas associated with England and composed of men interested in loaning money, a new business in America. In the Carolinas, Pennsylvania, New Jersey, and New York, the paper-money party succeeded to a degree. In Rhode Island it gained full control. Currency was issued, for the redemption of which there was little hope, and it was voted that if the creditor refused it, the debt could be absolved by depositing the amount at court and advertising the fact in the newspapers, and that the creditor in such case be deprived of the franchise. Such notices began "Know ye," and the papers were so filled with them that that phrase became the nickname of the party. Creditors fled their debtors, and were brought into court for refusing to accept payment. The state supreme court, in the case of *Trevett* v. *Weeden*, decided that the law was unconstitutional, whereupon the legislature began an attack upon the court.

While the Rhode Island government ceased to be a protection to property, that of Massachusetts was threatened with overthrow or dismemberment for protecting it. There, the debtors obtained in 1782 the right to tender, at prices to be fixed by arbitration, cattle or indeed almost any form of property as payment for debt, but paper money was refused. Taxes were high, state officers received what seemed to the farmer extravagant salaries, and lawyers, who were universally distrusted, grew rich. Under the lead of Captain Shays, the movement for relief assumed, during the fall and early winter of 1786–1787, an insurrectionary form in the western counties. Thanks to the energy of Governor Bowdoin the insurrection was put down, but the movement was not stamped out. Governor Bowdoin was defeated for reëlection, and there was widespread sympathy for Shays.

Shays's Rebellion.

The states were not only torn by politics but were threatened with dissolution. In Maine and in the Berkshires there was talk of secession from the rest of Massachusetts; Pennsylvania and North Carolina were similarly threatened with disruption; and Kentucky and Virginia were trying to agree to separate. Vermont, which was an unrecognized state, occu-

Tendencies toward dissolution.

pying territory claimed by New Hampshire, New York, and Massachusetts, at one time seemed likely to annex the New Hampshire towns in the valley of the Connecticut River; at another, to be divided by the union of all the towns in that valley to form a new state. States seemed as liable to dissolution as the Confederation. John Marshall wrote, January 5, 1787: "I fear . . . that they have truth on their side who say that man is incapable of governing himself. I fear we may live to see another revolution." It seemed that the American people, instead of founding a nation, were destined to be resolved into an indefinite number of constantly changing political units, whose conflicting interests would scarcely allow them to live forever at peace, the one with another, and that their separation from the British Empire was but a first step toward anarchy.

BIBLIOGRAPHICAL NOTES

American History Leaflets, nos. 22 and 23. Paine, Thomas, *The Public Good.* Western problems. Sources.

Adams, B. H., *Maryland's Influence in Founding a National Commonwealth* (*Johns Hopkins Historical Studies*, III, no. 1). Ford, A. C., *Colonial Precedents of Our National Land System.* Hinsdale, B. A., *Old Northwest*, chs. XV, XVI. McLaughlin, *The Confederation*, 108–138. McMaster, J. B., *People of the United States*, I, 147–167; III, 89–113. Roosevelt, T., *The Winning of the West*, II. Treat, P. J., *The National Land System.* Turner, F. J., *Western State Making* (*Am. Hist. Review*, I, 70–87; 251–269). Historical accounts.

Adams, John, *Works*, III, 353–406. Coxe, Tench, *A Brief Examination of Lord Sheffield's Observations on the Commerce of the United States.* Commerce and finance. Sources.

Bancroft, G., *United States* (1883), VI, 136–153. Fisher, S., *American Trade Regulations before 1784* (Am. Hist. Assoc., *Papers*, III, 467–496). Hill, W., *First Stages of the Tariff Policy* (Am. Econ. Assoc., *Publications*, VIII, no. 6). Lyman, T., *Diplomacy of the United States*, II, ch. IV. McLaughlin, *The Confederation*, 71–89. Sumner, W. G., *The Financier and Finances of the American Revolution*, chs. XIII–XV. Historical accounts.

Reform legislation.

Hunt, G., *Madison and Religious Liberty* (Am. Hist. Assoc., *Report*, 1901, I, 163–171). Jameson, J. F., *Introduction to the Study of the Constitutional and Political History of the United States* (*Johns Hopkins Hist. Studies*, IV, no. 5). Jameson, J. F., *Essays on the Constitutional History of the United States*, no. 5. Thorpe, F. W., *Constitutional History of the American People*, I, 60–132. Williams, G. W., *History of the Negro Race*, chs. XXVI–XXXI.

Economic conditions.

Bates, F. G., *Rhode Island and the Formation of the Union* (*Columbia University Studies in Political Science, etc.*, vol. X, no. 2). McLaughlin, *The Confederation*, 138–168. McMaster, *United States*, I, 299–354. Minot, G. R., *The Shays's Rebellion*. Warren, J. W. P., *The Confederation and the Shays's Rebellion* (*Am. Hist. Review*, XI, 42–68).

CHAPTER III

THE FORMATION OF THE CONSTITUTION

ALTHOUGH on the surface all was disorder and dissolution, during the period of the Confederation, tendencies were at work in favor of a stronger union. An illustration of such nationalizing influences was the action of various religious bodies. The Episcopalians and the Methodists adopted national constitutions. The Catholics received from the Pope a national organization, while the Presbyterians adapted their system, already national in character, to the conditions of independence and formed a partial alliance with the Congregationalists of New England. Far-sighted thinkers became more and more convinced that the only remedy for the existing political evils also lay in creating a stronger central government. Franklin had, in fact, in a preliminary draft for the Articles of Confederation, sketched a much stronger government than that adopted; and even before the Articles were in force, Hamilton had begun an attack upon them, based on their insufficiency. The leader of the strong government party, however, was Washington, who, with the difficulties of waging war in the disorganized condition of the country fresh in his mind, continued to impress upon his wide circle of personal acquaintances the need of action, and who found in young James Madison a lieutenant that spared no labor in collecting and marshaling facts and arguments. Every year there were added to these leaders, supporters from among the business, property-holding, and professional classes. Some of these thought that only a monarchy could save the country, while the disorders in

31

Rhode Island and Massachusetts convinced many, even decided Republicans, that the central government must be at least strong enough to preserve order.

Attempts to amend the Articles.

At first, in 1781, it was attempted to amend the Articles by giving Congress power to collect an import duty of five per cent to pay the debt. This was defeated by Rhode Island on the claim that "The power of the purse is the touchstone of freedom." The real reason was that Rhode Island was attracting trade by underbidding its neighbors by means of a lower tariff. Then in 1783 Congress requested power to lay certain duties for twenty-five years. This was defeated by New York, where the state treasury was growing rich from duties on goods imported to be used in other states, and there was consequently jealousy of a federal impost. A third request, to allow Congress to pass navigation acts against countries refusing favorable commercial treaties, was discussed for three years without tangible result.

Calling of the convention.

The failure of these attempts at amendment strengthened the demand for more radical action. Hamilton, Thomas Paine, Pelatiah Webster, and others called for a constitution to be drawn, as later state constitutions had been, by a convention summoned for that special purpose. The first step was taken in 1785 at Mount Vernon, where commissioners from Virginia and Maryland had met to settle a dispute as to the navigation of the Potomac River. As a result of discussion there, Virginia asked the states to send delegates to Annapolis to consider the condition of commerce generally. The meeting at Annapolis, held in 1786, was attended by delegates from only five states, and it recommended that a convention be held the next spring at Philadelphia for the purpose of devising amendments to the Articles. This call was indorsed by Congress after some hesitation, and on May 25, 1787, the convention met.

Characteristics of the convention.

The Philadelphia convention was a very different body from any that had previously assembled in America. Fifty-five members attended, and thirty-nine signed the Constitution. Of the thirty-nine, only six had signed the Declaration of Independence, and only four the Articles of Confederation. The members represented not a younger generation, but another element in the same generation. They were less democratic, many distrusted the people, and nearly all cared less about political theory than about good government. The majority of the members were well educated; there were many graduates of American colleges, four had been students of law in the Temple in London, James Wilson of Pennsylvania had attended three Scotch universities. There was much legal knowledge, and Blackstone, the expounder of the common law, was used more than Locke, the political philosopher and the guide of the Revolutionary statesmen. The great majority belonged to the rising strong government party; partly because the Revolutionary leaders, such as Clinton, Samuel Adams, and Patrick Henry, did not care to attend. The men who preached the Revolution were not to be the leaders in raising up a new government.

The constitution drawn up by this convention was not, as is often claimed, an inspiration; rather it was a compromise. There is hardly an important clause which was not the result of mutual concession, and not a member was entirely satisfied. There was a conflict of interest between the large and the small states, between the states with a large slave population and those with few or no slaves, between the commercial and the agricultural districts, between those members who wanted the central government to be as strong as possible and those who wished it to be only as strong as was necessary. Though the latter were outnumbered in the convention, they spoke with weight, for they represented those powerful leaders who were not present, and many voters whose acquiescence it would be necessary to secure before putting any plan into effect.

Conflicting interests.

Madison, as the mouthpiece of Washington and the drafter of the Virginia plan which was presented as a sort of starting point for work, was the most active leader of the strong government party. Hamilton's views were so extreme as to deprive him of some of the weight he might otherwise have possessed, and Franklin elected to play the part of peacemaker. Roger Sherman of Connecticut and James Wilson of Pennsylvania contributed much practical experience and legal knowledge, while a number of younger men, as Charles Pinckney of South Carolina, who came with a well-developed plan of his own, and Rufus King of Massachusetts, were constantly on the floor. Mason of Virginia, Luther Martin of Maryland, and Paterson of New Jersey, who also presented a model of his own, were among the most consistent representatives of the weak government party. With Washington as presiding officer, and with closed doors, which allowed the discussion to become confidential, the convention went to work to harmonize the conflicting interests.

No body of men ever worked more conscientiously or with a more sincere desire of coming to an agreement, but again and again it seemed as if their differences would prove absolutely irreconcilable ; time and again points were voted in committee of the whole only to be reconsidered and determined differently in the regular session. On June 28 Franklin referred to " the diversity of opinion that had prevailed throughout the deliberations of the convention. . . . In this situation groping as we were in the dark, how has it happened that nobody has thought of applying for light to that powerful friend who alone can supply it ? " His proposal for prayers, however, was rejected lest the public take alarm. By September the long four months' debate had cleared the minds of the delegates as to many of the fundamental problems of government, and when at length an instrument was framed the majority found more joy in its successful com-

pletion than grief at the fact that they had been forced to
compromise many of the convictions with which they had
entered the convention.

One of the most important of the compromises was with
regard to representation. The small states were unwilling
to forego the equal voice to which they had been accustomed;
the large states were determined to have a change. While
this discussion was progressing, it was decided that the
legislature should consist of two houses, and Roger Sherman
suggested the plan that was adopted: of having the states
represented by two members each in the Senate, and according to some equitable ratio in the House. The Senate
could check any legislation injurious to the small states,
and the House, any unfavorably affecting the large. A
similar compromise was made with regard to the election of
the President, who was to be voted for in the first instance
by an electoral college in which each state was to have as
many members as it had senators and representatives. In
case no person received a majority, which it was supposed
might frequently occur, the election was to be made by the
House, the delegation of each state having one vote. With
these compromises the conflict of large and small states
disappeared forever. It was, indeed, only a temporary and
artificial alignment.

There was much discussion as to what should be the
equitable ratio upon which representation in the House was
to rest. Ultimately it was decided to accept population,
and this raised the question as to whether slaves should or
should not be counted. They certainly contributed to the
wealth of the country, but on the other hand they were not
voters, and the vote of a free man in a state with slaves
would count for much more than in a state with few or no
slaves. This question was settled according to a compromise
which had been almost unanimously recommended by Congress to the states in 1783, to the effect that direct taxes be

Compromises on representation.

apportioned according to population, five slaves being counted as three free persons. Now it was agreed that both representation and direct taxes be apportioned according to this ratio. If the slave states received less representation, they also would pay smaller taxes. The fact that direct taxes were levied only three times before the freeing of the slaves removed, in practice, one of the compensating elements of this compromise, but the compromise of three for five remained, and, although both parties to it subsequently complained, it was probably the fairest arrangement which could have been made at that time.

Compromise on commercial powers.

Another compromise was between the northern commercial states that wanted Congress to have power to assist the merchant marine by passing navigation acts, and the extreme southern states. These latter feared that such legislation would increase freight rates, and particularly that the power of Congress might be used to prohibit the importation of slaves, and they, therefore, wished to forbid the passage of such acts except by a two-thirds vote; that is to say, practically, except with their consent. It was agreed, finally, that navigation laws be allowed if passed by a simple majority, and that Congress should not prohibit the slave trade for twenty years.

The question of sovereignty.

Throughout the convention there was continual conflict between those who wished the new national government to be supreme and those who wished it to be the agent of the states. In the end, the question was evaded rather than settled. As the majority of the members belonged to the national party, they inserted many clauses tending in that direction, particularly one to the effect that the Constitution, treaties, and the laws of Congress be the "supreme law of the land" and binding upon the judges of every court. Still they did not venture to be absolutely explicit, because their work had to be submitted to the people of the states, who they feared would reject a plan plainly and strongly nationalistic. The document that they drew up was, therefore, ambiguous to the extent that it did not specifically vest the sovereignty either in state or nation. The convention probably leaned toward the latter position, but, as Madison points out, in interpreting the Constitution, the ultimate authority is not the opinion of the convention that drew it up, but the understanding of the people, particularly the members of the state conventions, who made it law. It is probable that a majority of these supposed that the Constitution divided the sovereignty between state and nation; some believed that all sovereignty remained in the states, and the central government was merely an agent to perform certain functions; few, if any, conceived that the states were giving up all their sovereignty to the new government.

The majority in the Philadelphia convention hoped that they were giving enough power to the national government to make it self-dependent; and they sought to avoid friction between state and nation by reducing their relations to a minimum and allowing the nation to enforce its laws directly upon the individual, and not upon the states as had been the case in the Confederation. They laid upon the citizen a double duty and allegiance. Friction could not be altogether avoided, and ultimately the country divided in civil war over the question of sovereignty and its consequences. Yet this does not condemn the compromise arrived at. The country did not divide because the Constitution was ambiguous, but the Constitution was ambiguous because the country was already divided. In its elasticity lay its strength. Parties could differ as to its meaning and still be loyal and united in its support. If it had explicitly given the sovereignty to the nation, it would not have been accepted; if it had given sovereignty to the states, it could not have been adapted, as it has been, to the growing needs of national activity.

Elasticity of the Constitution.

Questions as to the form of government were more easily

settled. The first formal resolution presented to the convention was: "That a national government ought to be established, consisting of a supreme legislature, executive, and
judiciary." This resolution was adopted and of itself removed many difficulties. The members knew how to form
a government, and a government of three departments;
they had but to look about them at the state constitutions
framed within the last dozen years, and to recall the experience of colonial times. It was the attempt to form a league
of states, a confederation, which had proved unsuccessful
because it was a novel task. Madison's carefully analyzed
plans of confederacies, ancient and modern, which he had
brought to Philadelphia, became almost worthless. The
provisions that survived debate were practically all based
on American precedent, and in most cases upon practices running back into colonial times. In discussion,
indeed, the English constitution was often cited, but it was
the English constitution as found in Blackstone, who described it as it had existed in the seventeenth century when
its customs had been transplanted to America, and not the
actual practice in 1789. Members saw in England three
coequal departments, not the supreme legislature guided by
a cabinet which actually existed, and so their attempt to
follow English example but reënforced American tradition.

The chief discussion arose from the fear, felt by some of
the more democratic members, of intrusting the executive
power to a single man. Defeated in the attempt to secure
a multiple executive, these delegates endeavored to limit the
President by an executive council. This also was voted
down, but the Senate was given a check on his most important executive acts, its "advice and consent" being made
necessary for the making of appointments and of treaties.
The leading ideas that controlled the arrangement of details
were those of the threefold separation of powers, and of
checks and balances. The legislature was dependent upon

the people alone; the House, whose members were elected for two years, stood for the masses; the Senate, whose members were to be chosen by the legislatures of the states and to serve six years, were expected to represent wealth and influence, as well as the integrity of the states. The President was independent of the legislature, for its members could not serve as electors, and, even if he should be chosen by the House, it would be to serve a fixed term of four years unless he committed some misdemeanor so serious as to call for impeachment. The executive could raise no money or troops without the vote of the legislature; the legislature could pass a bill over the President's veto only by two-thirds majority. The Supreme Court was to be appointed by the President, by and with the advice and consent of the Senate; but as the justices were to serve for good behavior, they became practically independent on appointment. Thus, legislature, executive, and judiciary stood each uncontrolled by the others, but unable to take serious action without the others' consent. Amendments to the Constitution could be formally proposed by a two-thirds vote of both houses of Congress, and become a part of the Constitution on their acceptance by three quarters of the states. On application by the legislatures of two thirds of the states, Congress was to call a convention to propose amendments.

The Constitution, finally drawn up in the lucid English of Gouverneur Morris, was completed September 17, 1787, and it was submitted to Congress with the request that that body transmit the draft to the state legislatures. The Constitution itself, however, provided the method by which it was to receive its sanction, which was that it be submitted to conventions specially called in the several states, and go into effect on its ratification by nine states. This would give the Constitution a more direct sanction from the people than the Articles of Confederation had received, which had been simply adopted by the state

The Constitution before the people.

legislatures; it would give the federal Constitution in fact precisely the same sanction that the state constitutions had received, except in Massachusetts, where there had been a popular vote; but it would be in direct violation of the Articles of Confederation, which the convention had been called to amend, and which could be amended only by the consent of the legislature of every state.

Opposing forces.

Congress, however, transmitted the draft, September 28, 1787, to the state legislatures with its recommendation, and thereupon began the most momentous political conflict ever waged in this country. One clause of the Constitution forbade the states to issue "bills of credit," and this brought against it all the paper-money party. It was opposed by many of the established state authorities, partly because it would diminish the importance of the state and partly because those in power represented those favoring weak government. George Clinton and Patrick Henry fought it in their states, and they were aided by men like Gerry and Martin, who attended the convention but refused to sign. They characterized it as a "continental exertion of the well born of America," and scented danger of monarchy, aristocracy, and oppression.

The Federalists.

The advocates of adoption were in the awkward position that they must defend every provision. It was easier to compromise the interests of a state in the convention, where all states and interests were represented, than to defend that compromise at home, where people saw only one side of the question. Men returning from the convention, however, had the advantage of thorough familiarity with all arguments pro and con, and they kept in touch with one another by correspondence. In the war of pamphlets which followed, the most efficacious were those entitled "Federalist" and written by Hamilton, Madison, and Jay. This title was adopted by the party of the Constitution, and so they forced their opponents to assume that of Anti-Federalists.

The Constitution was, on the whole, favorable to the small states, and these were the first to accept it. First, Delaware; then Pennsylvania, which, though not small, was by its central position nationalistic; then New Jersey, Georgia, and Connecticut. In Massachusetts there was a struggle, but by clever management Samuel Adams and John Hancock were prevented from coming out against it, and on February 6, 1788, the convention accepted it by a vote of 187 to 167. Maryland, South Carolina, and New Hampshire followed, each after a hard contest. This brought the number up to nine, but the Constitution could hardly have gone into effect without Virginia and New York. In Virginia Patrick Henry led the opposition, and John Marshall, who was later to do so much toward interpreting the Constitution, was now one of its most effective supporters. The Federalists won, but it was with the understanding that they would do their best to secure certain amendments. In New York the country members still clung to the duties collected on goods imported for Connecticut and New Jersey. The city merchants thought that they would gain trade enough under the new system to more than make this up, and even proposed to secede from the state and join the new union. Hamilton, supporting the Constitution, conducted a legislative fight unequaled in American history, and forced it through a convention two thirds of whom had been opposed to it.

With the assent of these eleven states the Constitution was assured a trial. Congress, on September 13, 1788, voted that it had been ratified, that elections should be held for the officers called for under the new government, and that they meet in New York on the first Wednesday of March, 1789. This done, the old Congress practically disappears from history, though it continued to meet until the next spring.

North Carolina and Rhode Island were left in a peculiar position. Their associate states had repudiated the Articles, and they themselves had agreed to no substitute. In

North Carolina the influence of Patrick Henry was strong,
and it was decided to stay out until certain amendments
should be adopted.   As Willie Jones, the Anti-Federal-
ist leader, said: "We run no risk of being excluded from the
union when we think proper to come in.   Virginia, our next
neighbor, will not oppose our admission.   We have a common
cause with her.   She wishes the same alterations."   Five
states, in fact, when ratifying the Constitution, had proposed
amendments.   Many of these had to do with details, being
devised to hedge about authority with limitations.   The
most important, however, were to supply what many felt
to be a most serious omission, that is, a "bill of rights," such
as preceded nearly all the state constitutions, setting forth
those rights reserved by the people, and, in this case, by the
states also, to themselves inviolably forever.   This matter
was at once taken up by the new Congress when it met.
On September 25, 1789, it proposed to the states, for their
acceptance, ten amendments, constituting such a bill of
rights, and on November 21 North Carolina ratified the
Constitution.   These amendments were accepted by the
states, but even they did not satisfy Rhode Island.   There
the paper-money party was still supreme, and the legislature refused even to call a convention, in spite of threats
by the commercial element to bring about the secession of
Providence.   Congress dealt with her vigorously.   Mr.
Maclay, a Pennsylvania senator, wrote in his diary: "They
admitted on all hands that Rhode Island was independent,
and did not deny that the measures now taken were meant
to force her into the adoption of the Constitution."   These
measures, consisting of tariff regulations, were successful,
and on May 29, 1790, Rhode Island ratified the Constitution,
and the union was complete.

Thus was launched what has proved to be, up to the
present time at least, the final and successful attempt at
continental organization ; a problem which for one hundred

years had been attracting increasingly the best minds, first of the British Empire and then of America; and the importance of which merited, while the success of the solution justified, the attention devoted to it. The frame of government of no independent country, with the exception of Siam, has survived from 1789 to the present day with so few vital changes as has the Constitution of the United States.

BIBLIOGRAPHICAL NOTES

General source reading is probably more desirable and more Sources. easily possible than for any other period. The letters of Washington and Madison, Madison's *Papers*, Elliot's *Debates*, and *The Federalist* are and will remain the best reading on the subject.

Bancroft, G., *History of the United States*, VI, 207–370. Beard, General C. A., *An Economic Interpretation of the Constitution of the United* accounts. *States*. Curtis, G. T., *Constitutional History of the United States*, I, chs. XV–XXXII. Farrand, M., *Framing of the Constitution of the United States*. Jameson, J. F., *Studies in the History of the Federal Convention of 1787* (Am. Hist. Assoc., *Report*, 1902, vol. I, 89–161), containing a bibliography. McLaughlin, A. C., *The Confederation*, 221–277. Story, J., *Commentaries*, I, 470, 627–643. Thorpe, F. W., *Constitutional History of the United States*, ch. V.

Boutell, L. H., *Roger Sherman*. Brown, W. G., *Oliver Ellsworth*. Biographies. Gay, S. H., *James Madison*. Lodge, H. C., *George Washington*. Morse, J. T., *Alexander Hamilton*. Roosevelt, T., *Gouverneur Morris*. Rowland, K. M., *George Mason*.

Davis, J., *Confederate Government*, 86–103. Harding, S. B., Adoption of *Ratification of the Federal Constitution by the State of Massachusetts.* the Constitution. *Federalist* (edited by P. L. Ford), 632–651 (amendments proposed by the states). Henry, W. E., *Patrick Henry*, II, chs. XXXVI–XXXIX. Jameson, *Essays on the Constitutional History of the United States*, no. 2. Libby, O. G., *Geographical Distribution of the Vote of the Thirteen States*. McLaughlin, *The Confederation*, 277–310. McMaster, *United States*, I, 454–502. Roper, C. L., *Why North Carolina at first refused to ratify the Federal Constitution* (Am. Hist. Assoc., *Report*, 1905, vol. I, 99–108). Story, J., *Commentaries*, 308–372.

CHAPTER IV

THE ORGANIZATION AND ESTABLISHMENT OF THE NATIONAL GOVERNMENT

"Conventions of the Constitution." THE national Constitution, as compared with the usual state constitution of to-day, was brief. It but sketched the general outlines of the government, and left the filling in to those who should be elected under it. It was fortunate, therefore, that the first election brought into power those who had favored its adoption and who were consequently most interested in proving it a success. This work was done with as much care as the framing of the original provisions, and many of the practices and customs adopted in the first few years have come to have a force almost as binding as that of the Constitution itself, and are known as "conventions of the Constitution."

Organization of Congress. Congress had been called for the first Wednesday of March, 1789, but it was not until April that a quorum assembled, and it was April 6 before both houses were organized. Though it was a new government which was being founded, the majority of the members of Congress had had legislative experience. They were familiar with English parliamentary law, the ripe product of centuries of development, and they were accustomed to handling public affairs. Their methods they took, not so much from the practices of the contemporary British Parliament, though these were often quoted, as from those of the colonial and state legislatures and the Continental Congress, which were based on the older practice of the House of Commons during the Stuart period.

Committees. From the first they made extensive use of committees, and

44

in 1794 began the development of a system of appointing standing committees, to hold for the entire life of each Congress, and each to attend to some particular class of business. Gradually these committees became more important, until more work was done in the committee room than in the regular meetings of either the Senate or the House.

The presiding officer of the House is called the "Speaker," and the first occupant of the position was Frederick A. C. Muhlenberg, who had held a similar post in Pennsylvania. In the legislature of that state the speaker had been unusually powerful, and it was perhaps as a result of Mr. Muhlenberg's experience that the House voted, January 18, 1790, that committees be chosen by the Speaker "unless otherwise specially directed." Later, the Speaker was allowed to appoint the chairman of the committee of the whole, the speaker *pro tempore*, and, at first by courtesy, and in 1804 by rule, to name the chairmen of all committees. In the meanwhile, the rules of debate were developing in such a way as to increase his power. In 1789 he obtained the right to decide which of a number of members desiring to speak held the floor, and on February 27, 1811, the practice known as the "previous question" was introduced, which gives the Speaker, working with a majority of the House, power to limit debate. Thus there was a tendency from the first for the Speaker, the representative of the majority, to control the House, and he became in time the second most powerful officer of the government.[1]

The Speaker.

The Senate pursued a different course. Its presiding officer was not of its own choice, nor even a member, but was the Vice President; and there was some feeling of jealousy

Vice presidency.

[1] As is pointed out later this system reached its extreme development under Speaker Reed, 1889 to 1891, and Speaker Cannon, 1903 to 1911. In the latter year, however, the Speaker was deprived of the power to appoint standing committees, and was required to give the floor to the member who first rises.

toward him.   In spite, therefore, of the efforts of John Adams, the first Vice President, the senators kept and have maintained the right to choose their committees by ballot, and the Vice President quickly came to be one of the least powerful of national officers.

Senate *versus* House.

The Senate considered itself the upper house, and endeavored to have this claim recognized by the House of Representatives, particularly to secure for its members higher pay.   They secured one dollar a day additional for one year, 1795 to 1796.   The political weight of the two branches has varied with the ability of their members.

Choice of electors.

The President and Vice President were to be chosen by electors, each state having as many as it had senators and representatives.   The method of selecting these electors was left to the state legislatures, and there was considerable diversity in the ways they adopted.   In the first election three did so by a popular vote for a general state ticket, which later became the universal practice; two chose the several electors by districts; and in five the legislature elected them, a custom which continued in many states for forty years, and in South Carolina until the Civil War.   In 1789 New York lost its vote because of a contest as to the method of selection; North Carolina and Rhode Island had not yet joined the Union.   The electors cast their votes on the first Wednesday in February, and while they but confirmed popular opinion in voting unanimously for Washington, their selection of John Adams as Vice President was due to their own choice from among several available candidates.

President Washington.

The choice of Washington as commander in chief of the Continental Army, in 1775, was due in large measure to the fact that he came from Virginia, the largest colony, and one whose coöperation was essential for the war.   His choice as President, in 1789, was due to universal appreciation of his character.   The Revolution had tested not only his generalship but also his executive capacity. He had practically been the continental executive through that dark period, maintaining national harmony and coöperation, not by authority, but by influence. At the close of the war he not only himself resigned from office, but he persuaded the military forces to subordinate themselves to Congress, although they were smarting under injustice, and Congress was so weak that many believed it could be brought to terms at the bayonet's point. During the Confederation he had, as a private citizen, devoted himself to national undertakings, and all who had attended the constitutional convention recognized how great his influence had been in framing the Constitution and securing its adoption. Although he was not the peer of Franklin in intellectual ability, he had an active and original mind, but his distinguishing characteristic was the soundness of his judgment. He listened patiently to advice; he balanced it with his own ideas, and, in a greater proportion of instances than any other American statesman, he decided upon the course which the future proved to be the right one. He decided, moreover, in time; the crisis never passed while he hesitated. His judgment of men was as good as of policies, and he judged them for character as well as for ability. His own character was such as to give his judgments the weight that they deserved. Seemingly somewhat cold, and with a decided dignity of demeanor, he had, nevertheless, a restless and impulsive spirit. His calm was that of self-restraint, and meant force and not inertia. His sense of honesty was acute, and he had in the highest degree the feeling of honor and of public duty which were the best characteristics of the Virginia planter aristocracy to which he belonged.

Such was the man who, on April 30, after a triumphal journey from Mount Vernon, was inaugurated at New York. Some members of Congress wished to give him a sounding title calculated to inspire respect abroad and awe at home.

The presidency.

John Adams called attention to the fact that cricket clubs had presidents. Nothing was agreed upon, however, and it proved that no title was needed to dignify an officer exercising such powers as the Constitution conferred upon him, especially when Washington occupied the office. Congress gave him a salary of $25,000, sufficient to enable him to support an ample establishment; and Hamilton drew up a set of rules for social conduct, which protected him from intrusion and yet satisfied the demands of hospitality.

Executive *versus* legislature.

In his relations with Congress Washington was disposed to assert his authority to the full. On April 5, 1792, he sent in the first veto, and on March 30, 1796, he refused the request of the House to send to it certain executive papers that he thought should be kept secret. These points he successfully maintained, but his attempt to take part personally when the Senate was giving its "advice and consent" to appointments and treaties was defeated, and the precedent finally became established that all communication between the executive and the legislature be in writing. The President received compensation, however, in the decision of Congress that he should possess the full power of removing officials from office, although the Constitution might be interpreted to give the Senate the same right to advise and consent to their removal that it had in the case of their appointment. On the whole the executive and legislature proved, as the convention had intended, each to have sufficient power to maintain its independence, but not enough to control the other. Still, force of character or popular support has, from time to time, given now the one, now the other, the greater power.

The cabinet.

One of the first duties of Congress was to provide for the more extensive organization of the executive. Three departments—"Foreign affairs" (soon changed to "State"), "Treasury," and "War"—were at once established, each headed by a secretary. Independent of these secretaries were an Attorney-General to manage the legal business of the government, and a Postmaster-General to take charge of the post offices and post routes. The treasury department was modeled with peculiar care on a system largely the work of Robert Morris; several auditors, comptrollers, and registers mutually checked one another in such a way as to render misappropriation of funds practically impossible. The Constitution gave the President power to require the "Opinion, in writing, of the principal officer in each of the executive Departments, upon any subject relating to the Duties of their respective Offices." Washington from the first followed the practice of asking the advice of all the secretaries upon matters of general interest, and soon oral consultations followed. In these conferences the Attorney-General took part, but not the Postmaster-General, as his office was regarded as purely administrative. Washington showed a disposition to include the Chief Justice, John Jay, and the Vice President, John Adams, among his intimate advisers; but Jay refused on the ground that it was improper for him to express his views on matters upon which he might subsequently be obliged to give a judicial opinion, and Adams, although he sometimes wrote an opinion, did not become a regular member of the group, perhaps fearing to compromise the dignity of his position by putting himself on a level with the heads of departments. By the end of the first administration these meetings, although not provided for in the Constitution, had come to constitute an organization, to which the name "Cabinet" was applied. As its members served at the pleasure of the President and were consequently under his control, Congress resisted the attempt to allow them to appear in person before it, and so the cabinet in this country has always had less influence on the course of legislation than the cabinet in England.

To the making of appointments to fill these and the numerous subordinate positions created by Congress, Washing- *Appointments.*

ton devoted the utmost care, for he knew that the quality of the personnel was vital to the success of the Constitution. He appointed no one whom he did not consider well fitted for the duties of the office. In addition he sought men of prominence who would bring prestige to the new government. He tried to avoid sectional and state jealousies, by apportioning the offices as equally as possible among the states and sections. Where he could, he tried to retain men in positions similar to those which they had occupied under the Confederation, or under the state governments where state services, like that of the customs, had been transferred to the Union. He refused, however, to appoint men notably opposed to the Constitution, even when they had held such positions. Particularly was this true in Rhode Island and North Carolina, where opposition had been keenest. For his cabinet, he secured Thomas Jefferson for Secretary of State, Alexander Hamilton for the Treasury, and Edmund Randolph for Attorney-General, while Henry Knox continued to serve as Secretary of War.

The judiciary. With regard to the organization of the judiciary, the Constitution merely provided that there be a Supreme Court and such inferior courts as Congress might establish. Congress at once went to work upon the matter, and an act was drawn up, largely the work of Oliver Ellsworth of Connecticut, which was passed September 24, 1789. The Supreme Court was to consist of a chief justice and five associate justices. In each state, and also in Maine and Kentucky, which were not yet states, there was to be a district court, with a judge, an attorney, and a marshal. Intermediate circuit courts were provided by having two justices of the Supreme Court sit with the judge of the district. Washington put forth redoubled efforts to supply the framework with men who would inspire public confidence. John Jay was made Chief Justice, and for the other positions many distinguished judges were drawn from the benches of the states. Still, the national courts did not have much business at first, as the custom of appealing or transferring cases from state courts did not develop for some time. One of the Supreme Court decisions, that of *Chisholm* v. *Georgia*, in 1793, was to the effect that a state might be sued by a citizen of another state. The supporters of state sovereignty were so seriously alarmed at this, it being a principle of English law that the sovereign cannot be sued, that the Eleventh Amendment to the Constitution was adopted, definitely prohibiting a suit by an individual against a state. Gradually, however, the judiciary acquired respect, and, as cases arose, it blocked out some of the constitutional interpretations which later formed the basis of its power. It did not, during the Federalist period, declare any act of Congress unconstitutional, but in the case of *Hylton* v. *the United States* it discussed the constitutionality of such an act; while in *Ware* v. *Hylton* it declared a state law of Virginia void because in conflict with a treaty.

While the new government was thus working out its internal organization, it was devoting serious attention to the solution of those problems, the failure to solve which had wrecked the Confederation. First came that of revenue. Already on March 25, 1789, Fisher Ames was complaining that every day's delay in framing a tariff bill meant the loss of a thousand pounds, and under the pressure of financial necessity the first tariff bill was rushed through and passed July 4. It was entitled "An act for the encouragement and protection of manufactures," but was a haphazard affair in no true sense protective. The schedule of duties established was much lower than has ever been known since, the highest being fifteen per cent. The discussion was not political in the sense of dividing Congress into two parties, favoring high and low tariff, or any two opposing policies. It was, however, interesting in bringing out conflicting interests, as those between the Virginia producer of slaves and the

The first tariff.

Georgia consumer, and between the farming, agricultural, and commercial sections. New England manufacturers of rum objected to duties on molasses, the raw material. Fisher Ames wrote, "Another molasses battle has been fought." The question of the tariff was on the whole treated as one of administration and of local interests rather than as involving a conflict of principles.

Financial conditions.

The tariff provided a revenue unexpectedly great, but the financial problem was still a delicate one. The amount appropriated during the first session for running expenses was only $629,000. This figure did not include salaries for customs, consular, and post-office officials, as they were remunerated by fees. The largest item of expense was for interest. The foreign debt now amounted to $11,710,378, and it was expected that something would be done for the domestic debt, of which the face value was $42,414,085. Hamilton, the new Secretary of the Treasury, speedily conceived a vast scheme for solving these difficulties and at the same time building new foundations of political strength for the government. This plan he presented to Congress in a series of reports.

The excise.

He first turned his attention to the revenue, and advised Congress to raise the tariff slightly in accordance with the principle of protection. Then he recommended the passage of an excise tax on distilled spirits, not a very productive measure, but one creating a new staff of officials and increasing the prestige of the government.

Funding the debt.

These measures passed easily enough, but the next step brought a significant break between Hamilton and Madison, who was now serving as member of the House. Hamilton wished to fund the national domestic debt, giving the holders of the various forms of indebtedness a new uniform security of the same face value as that which they had held, and bearing a uniform rate of interest. Madison pointed out that much of the indebtedness was in the hands of speculators, many of whom had paid for it but fifteen cents on the dollar and who did not deserve to receive full face value. Congress supported Hamilton, the debt was funded, and the interest paid. The financial element, seeing that the new government desired and was able to meet its obligations, were soon willing to lend money at a lower rate, and the credit of the United States was speedily established.

Hamilton's next step was to extend the newly created national credit to the assistance of the states, by assuming such portion of their debts as had been incurred in support of the Revolution. He had in mind not only finance, but also politics, for he believed that the firmest support the national establishment could have would be a large body of moneyed men looking to it for interest on their bonds. If he could transfer this great mass of debt from the states to the Union, he would weaken the former and add a bulwark to the latter. His plan was opposed by those who feared just this centralization, and by members from states which had small debts or none at all. The balance hung so close that both parties feared to bring it to the touch. In the meantime Congress was agitated by the rival claims of the Delaware, the Susquehanna, and the Potomac for the location of the federal district provided for by the Constitution as the site of the federal capital. This, too, hung in the balance. One session of Congress passed without action, the next brought in North Carolina, which was for the Potomac and against assumption, and Rhode Island, which was for assumption and against the Potomac. Innumerable attempts were made to bring about a bargain between the conflicting interests by combining the two questions. At length, at a little dinner given by Jefferson, who had just arrived from France to be Secretary of State, the matter was adjusted. State debts were assumed to the amount of $21,500,000, and the federal district was located on the Potomac. Those interested in the Delaware were conciliated by making Philadelphia the seat of government for ten years, while the new city was being prepared.

The assumption of the state debts.

The national
bank.
The crown of Hamilton's plan was the creation of a national bank. It would facilitate the business of the government; it would strengthen the connection between the moneyed classes and the Union, and it could be made the means of establishing a stable national bank-note currency, — for which there was a real need. Growing business, moreover, needed banking facilities, for there were but three banks in the United States, one at each of the centers of capital: Boston, New York, and Philadelphia. The bank bill passed Congress practically as Hamilton drew it. It established the Bank of the United States, with $10,000,000 capital, four fifths to be invested in United States securities. It was to be under private management, but the government was to own one fifth of the stock. It could establish branches in the states, and could issue notes on the security of its capital. It had the privilege and duty of handling the financial business of the government and was bound to report its condition to the Secretary of the Treasury, if he asked.it, as often as once a week. The charter ran for twenty years.

Strict *versus*
broad con-
struction.
When, in February, 1791, the bank bill was presented to Washington for his signature, he asked the members of the cabinet for their opinions as to its constitutionality, that point having been raised in Congress. Jefferson, who already had begun to fear the consequences of the centralizing policy, and to regret the part he had taken in aiding the assumption of state debts, wrote an elaborate opinion against it. He could find no authorization "among the powers specially enumerated," nor "within either of the general phrases which are the two following: 'to lay taxes for the purpose of providing for the general welfare,' and 'to make all laws necessary and proper for carrying into execution the enumerated powers.'" "To take a single step beyond the boundaries thus specially drawn around the powers of Congress is to take possession of a boundless field of power, no longer susceptible of any definition." Hamilton at length, and with wonderful acumen, argued that from

the powers granted to the Union other powers could be implied, that the Union was sovereign with respect to those powers granted to it, and that, in carrying them out, it could use any means that were "proper." He was firmly persuaded that if Jefferson's strict view prevailed it would be "fatal to the just and indispensable authority of the United States." Washington signed the bill, and the administration was committed to a policy of broad construction.

These financial measures, upon which the success of the new establishment depended, were to an unusual degree the work of one man, Alexander Hamilton. Born in the West Indies, of a Scotch father and a French mother, he combined most happily the business sagacity of the one nationality with the vivacity and charm of the other. He came to New York just before the Revolution, and his precocity brought him, while still a boy in years, to the notice of the leading men of the time. He served on Washington's staff, and he married a daughter of General Philip Schuyler, head of an old New York family of great political and social weight. Combining law and politics in the manner becoming common in America, he had by 1789 attained a position of such prominence that his appointment as Secretary of the Treasury, although he was only thirty-two, was received with confidence. His success in this position was due not only to the wisdom of his proposals, but also to his ability in securing their adoption by Congress. His dominating personality soon converted the supporters of his measures into followers, and from about 1792 until his death in 1804 a great proportion of the strongest men in the country looked upon him as the surest support of rational government and held him in almost reverential affection. His qualities, however, were not such as to appeal to the mass of people who did not come into personal contact with him, and his West Indian training led him to place a reliance in the financial element as the

Hamilton.

touchstone of political strength which was unwarranted in
the United States.

Hamilton
and Jefferson.

An opposition to Hamilton's party soon developed,
centering itself about Jefferson, the Secretary of State, and
Washington saw the fading of his dream of governing without parties, even before he had completed his first term.
Nor was the Constitution at fault. The difference between
Hamilton and Jefferson was more fundamental; they represented two eternally opposed types of mind. Hamilton's
ideal was a strong government actively assisting in the progress of the nation; Jefferson wished to see a government
preserving order, but leaving to every individual the largest
possible amount of freedom for personal development. They
both read in the Constitution the expression of their views
and so could coöperate in its support, while differing as to
particular measures. This difference grew broader with
almost every policy broached, and although Washington
tried to stand between them, his judgment was so often
with Hamilton that on December 31, 1793, Jefferson left the
cabinet and became the head of a new party, professing
especially loyalty to the Constitution strictly construed,
and adopting the name Republican.

The Whisky
Rebellion.

The establishment of the financial system met with other
opposition more violent but less important. In the mountain valleys of the frontier, the lack of transportation facilities compelled the farmer to transmute corn and wheat into
commodities more easily handled. In later times much
was fed to cattle, which were then driven to the coast, but
even this was almost impossible in the eighteenth century.
In the distillation of whisky most farmers found their escape from this dilemma. Whisky served as the currency
of much of the mountain region, and upon its sale the inhabitants depended largely for what they had to buy from
other sections. Upon them, therefore, the new excise tax
fell with an especial rigor. Unaccustomed to oppression,

ALEXANDER HAMILTON

they resisted at first by concealing their distilleries, and then, when United States officers attempted to enforce the law, by arms. In 1794 western Pennsylvania and neighboring regions of Virginia broke into revolt. Liberty poles were raised, and the "whisky boys" rifled the mails and captured Pittsburgh.

This was a situation demanding the utmost tact. Other portions of the mountain region were apt to join the insurgents, and the Republicans, while disapproving their violence, sympathized with them in their opposition to the tax. Washington's handling of .this delicate situation was perfect. He assembled an army overwhelmingly large, which marched with much pomp and circumstance, but slowly, towards the disaffected district. This gave the insurgents time to deliberate, and by the time the army reached Pittsburgh moderate leaders among them had gained the upper hand, and all organized forces had disappeared, without battle and without bloodshed. Some of the leaders were arrested, but they were treated with leniency, and Congress met some of the popular demands by rendering the enforcement of the law less onerous. The tax, however, was retained, and the government had shown its ability to cope with armed resistance.

BIBLIOGRAPHICAL NOTES

Of general importance are the *Writings* of Washington and Sources. *Works* of Hamilton, the *Annals of Congress*, or T. H. Benton's *Abridgment of the Debates of Congress*, giving the debates in the House of Representatives, and *Sketches of Debate* by William Maclay, giving those in the Senate with many lively bits of local color. Callender, G. S., *Selections from Economic History of the United States*, 221–231, gives material of the financial system adopted. The following discuss the bank question: Hamilton, A., *Works* (edited by J. C. Hamilton), IV, 104–138; (edited by H. C. Lodge), II, 47–108, 294–348; III, 180–227. Jefferson, T., *Writings* (edited by H. A. Washington), VII, 555–561; (edited by P. L. Ford), V, 284–289; VI, 470–494. *McCulloch* v. *Md.,* in *United States Reports,* 4 Wheaton, 316; Thayer, I. B., *Cases,* 271–284.

Historical accounts. Organization of the legislature.

Follett, M. P., *Speaker of the House,* chs. I, XI. Jameson, J. F., *Origin of the Standing Committee System in American Legislative Bodies* (*Political Science Quarterly,* IX, no. 2). Lodge, H. C., *The Senate* (*Scribner's Magazine,* vol. 34, 541–550). Lowell, A. L., *Essays on Government,* no. 1. McCall, W. S., *The Power of the Senate* (*Atlantic Monthly,* vol. 92, 433–442). McConachie, L. G., *Congressional Committees.* McMaster, *United States,* I, 525–568. Morse, J. T., *John Adams,* ch. X. Wilson, W., *Congressional Government,* chs. II, IV.

The executive.

Fish, C. R., *Civil Service and the Patronage,* ch. I. Jameson, *Essays,* no. 3. Hinsdale, M. L., *The Colonies and Congress* (Am. Pol. Sci. Assoc., *Proceedings,* 1905), 126–149. Learned, H. B., *The President's Cabinet.* Lodge, H. C., *Washington,* 40–81. McMaster, *United States,* II, 267–275. Mason, E. C., *The Veto Power,* chs. III, VI. Salmon, L. P., *History of the Appointing Power,* 1–32. Stanwood, E., *History of the Presidency,* chs. I–IV.

The judiciary.

Baldwin, S. E., *The American System of Supreme Courts* (*International,* vol. IV, 540–557). Brown, W. G., *Oliver Ellsworth,* 180–200. Jameson, *Essays,* no. 1. McLaughlin, A. C., *The Courts, the Constitution, and Parties,* pages 4 and 5 giving a select bibliography of recent literature on the subject. Pellew, G., *J. Jay.* Willoughby, *Supreme Court* (*Johns Hopkins Historical Studies,* extra vol. VII).

The financial system.

Bassett, J. S., *The Federalist System,* 27–42. Curtis, *Constitutional History,* II, 182–190, 589–600. Dewey, D. R., *Financial History of the United States.* Lodge, H. C., *Hamilton,* chs. V, VI. Macdonald, W., *Select Documents,* nos. 6, 8–12. Taussig, F. W., *Tariff History,* 8–17.

The frontier.

Adams, H., *Gallatin,* 86–151. Bassett, *Federalist System,* 101–117. McMaster, *United States,* I, 593–604; II, 42–47, 67–72, 189–206.

CHAPTER V

PROBLEMS OF THE FRONTIER AND OF COMMERCE

Even while occupied with these fundamental tasks of organization and finance, the government could not neglect the problems of the West and of commerce. Failure to solve them had been one of the charges against the government of the Confederation, and continued failure would be fatal to that under the Constitution.

Some satisfaction was given the western settlers by the admission of Vermont in 1791, of Kentucky in 1792, and of Tennessee in 1796, as states on an equality with the original thirteen. In 1799 the Northwest Territory passed into the second stage of development provided for by the Ordinance of 1787, which called for the organization of a legislature and the election of a delegate to Congress, who could speak but could not vote. In general, the western representatives counted for little in Congress, where their roughness and lack of oratorical ability caused them to be underrated. One exception was William Henry Harrison, the Northwestern delegate, who in 1800 secured a modification of the system of land sales, which had long been regarded as unsatisfactory, but which had not been changed, owing to conflicting views. By the new act, as little as 320 acres could be purchased, and credit was allowed for part of the purchase price. Thus for $160 a year for four years the settler could secure a title, an arrangement which was decidedly more advantageous to the actual pioneer than the legislation of 1785.

The West. Land.

59

Transporta-
tion.

To the solution of the vital problem of transportation the new government contributed nothing except the opening of the Mississippi River in 1795, and this contribution was regarded with disfavor by many who feared that it would result in drawing western trade into independent channels, and so wean the affections of the people from the Union. The failure to improve and develop the routes over the mountains was certainly not due to oversight, for no one understood the problem, either politically or physically, better than Washington, who had given much time during the Confederation to the attempt being made in Virginia to connect the Potomac and the James with tributaries of the Ohio. Nor is it likely that it was due to hesitation as to the power of Congress, considering the views of Hamilton and his associates. It is more probable that it was due in part to lack of resources, and in part to the absorbing character of the problems pressing for immediate attention. While the national government did not act, some states were working at the subject, and some improvement was made by individuals and by corporations acting under state charters, which built toll roads in Pennsylvania and made possible a heavy wagon traffic between Philadelphia and Pittsburgh.

Indian
policy.

The Indian question was dealt with more promptly and effectively. In 1790 an act was passed providing that all land sales from the Indians must be made by public treaty with the United States, and that Indian trade be restricted to licensed traders, in order to prevent the friction resulting from the presence of irresponsible white men among them. In 1796 the government itself went into the business of trading with them in order to meet the competition of Spaniards and English, and to bind the Indians to the United States. None of these measures except the first were completely successful, but they all tended to improve conditions. In addition to this general legislation negotiations were carried on with the several tribes to secure peace, territorial concessions, and definite boundaries. In 1790 McGillivray, the Creek chief, was invited to New York and flattered and bribed into promising to keep the peace, a promise partly fulfilled. Yet the greater part of Georgia remained in the hands of this and other tribes. The Iroquois of New York, weakened by the Revolution, were friendly; but the Indians of the Northwest continued warlike, instigated, so the frontiersmen believed, and probably at least not strongly discouraged, by the English. In 1790 General Harmar was sent against them and was defeated; in 1791 St. Clair, governor of the Northwest Territory, went against them, and his army was almost annihilated. In 1794, however, General Wayne won a victory at Fallen Timbers, near what is now Toledo, Ohio; wasted the Indian villages and fields, and in 1795 made with them the treaty of Greenville, which secured comparative peace for fifteen years. With peace, settlement in the Northwest began to increase rapidly, and the population grew from about 4000 in 1790 to 51,000 in 1800. In the Southwest, Tennessee and Kentucky, whose Indian difficulties were less important or earlier composed, increased from 109,000 to 326,000.

The commercial community of the East felt the advantages of the new government sooner than the West. The establishment of the Constitution was coincident with a natural revival of trade, and stimulated it by giving stability to credit and by putting a stop to tariff wars between the states. Before the Revolution, trade between the several colonies had been almost prevented by the restrictions of the navigation acts ; during the Confederation the people of different states began to trade with each other in spite of vexing differences between their commercial systems ; now that a single system embraced the whole country, interstate trade at once assumed large and flourishing proportions. *Increase of trade. Domestic.*

Commerce with the East Indies and other regions closed during colonial times began to flow smoothly. American *Foreign.*

shipping was encouraged by the passage of a navigation **act**
in 1789. By this act, ships built and owned by foreigners
paid a duty of fifty cents per ton, American-built ships
owned by foreigners paid thirty cents, and those wholly
American, only six cents. The last class received also the
additional advantage of a ten per cent reduction in the duty
charged on the goods they brought in. The effect of this
legislation was immediate. In 1787 only thirty per cent of
our exports and seventeen and a half per cent of our
imports were carried in American vessels. In 1795 the figures were eighty-eight and ninety-two per cent respectively,
and they remained approximately the same for many years.
The classes which had most ardently favored the adoption
of the Constitution were, therefore, confirmed in its support.

Commercial treaties with Spain and England, however,
were still wanting. Jefferson wished to bring those nations
to terms by discriminating in favor of the goods and ships of
countries with which we had treaties, but the commercial
element doubted the efficiency of such measures and feared
they would bring even more unfavorable treatment upon us.
His policy was not adopted.

The policy
of neutrality.
The settlement of boundary and commercial questions
rested, in fact, not upon ourselves alone, but depended on
complex interrelationships among all the nations concerned.
In 1790 our two neighbors, Spain and England, seemed to
be on the point of war, and war might involve hostilities
in our own western country. The cabinet, in considering
this question, laid down the momentous principle, the basis
of all our subsequent foreign policy, that it was to our interest to remain absolutely neutral, avoiding entanglements
with either.

The French
Revolution.
This war cloud never burst, but there was already gather-
ing a storm much more serious, which resulted in 1793 in war
between England and France. Although France was not a
neighboring power, populations of French descent lived in

Louisiana and in Canada, and French statesmen had never given up their dreams of colonial empire. Moreover, American commerce used the seas on which the two nations contended, and sought the ports of both. Of most ominous significance, however, was the fact that this war became a struggle rather between parties and principles than between nations; nations were divided within themselves, and particularly was this the case in the United States. The first movements of the French Revolution had been greeted in this country with almost universal approval, but when the Louis XVI who had supported our Revolution was beheaded, when Lafayette was forced to flee from France, when the Reign of Terror established anarchy in the place of government, Washington, Hamilton, and men of their stamp first cooled, and then became hostile. Jefferson, however, saw only the triumph of the rights of man, and looked on the "Terror" as a temporary phase, soon to be replaced by sane, democratic government. The dangers then were, that the seemingly frail union of the United States would be shattered, or that the predominant party would tear the nation from its neutrality and range it on the one side or the other.

The first crisis came from the designs of the French. The treaties of 1778 and that of 1788 gave the French special privileges in our ports in time of war, and contained a clause guaranteeing the French possessions in the West Indies. Much of the money loaned by France to the United States, moreover, was still unpaid, and the French leaders hoped that the two republics thus intimately bound together might face together the "impious band of tyrants." To bring this alliance to the point, they sent, as minister to the United States, "Citizen Genêt," a young enthusiast, who **The mission** reached Charleston, April 8, 1793. There he issued com- **of Genêt.** missions to privateers to prey on English commerce, and he journeyed on to Philadelphia amid popular demonstrations of joy. On the day of his arrival in Charleston the news of the king's death had reached our government, and counsel was taken as to the policy to be adopted. Hamilton and Jefferson presented conflicting opinions, and Washington decided on a middle course. He would receive Genêt as minister of the French republic; he would not take the stand urged by Hamilton that the treaties had lapsed because made with the former government of France which was now overthrown, but he held that the guarantee of the French possessions was not binding because intended to apply only in case France was fighting a defensive war, whereas he considered that France was now the aggressor. He would interpret the clauses with regard to port privileges for French privateers and naval vessels as narrowly as possible in order not to anger England, and finally, on April 22, he issued a proclamation of neutrality. At his suggestion, too, a law was rushed through Congress, giving the government power strictly to enforce this neutral policy and especially to prevent the further launching of French privateers from our ports. Genêt, therefore, on his arrival in Philadelphia, found justified the cynical prediction of his instructions, that the Americans no longer regarded "liberty as lovers, but as married persons: . . . reflection indeed guides them, but it cools them." At least the government showed no disposition to enlist in a crusade for universal liberty.

Western projects.

Genêt was instructed, even if he failed to receive the active assistance of the government, to direct certain military operations from the United States as a base. Not without the sympathy of Jefferson, he arranged expeditions of American frontiersmen against the Spanish settlements in Florida and Louisiana. The chief expedition was to be directed against New Orleans, and Genêt's agent for the purpose was General George Rogers Clark, who during the Revolution had led the frontier soldiery against the British in Illinois. Love of adventure and the belief that this was a practical scheme for opening the navigation of the Mississippi, drew many to the French colors. Genêt's further project of separating the West from the Union and encouraging the establishment of a new republic in the Mississippi valley was not known to many of his American associates. It was, however, an essential part of the French program, as that nation was anxious to make the West Indies independent of this country for their food supply. These plans, so fraught with danger of war and disunion to the United States, did not succeed, partly through the vigilance of General Wayne in the West, and partly because Genêt, elated by the popular enthusiasm for France, put himself in the wrong by defying the government, fitting out an illegally captured English vessel as a privateer, and dispatching it for a cruise from Philadelphia itself, under the very nose of the administration. His recall was requested, and his party, the Girondists, having fallen in France, it was granted by the new French government.

While the allurements of Genêt failed to entice us into a French alliance, the policy of England seemed likely to drive us perforce into hostilities against that country. Fisher Ames, an English sympathizer, wrote: "The English are absolutely madmen. Order in this country is endangered by their hostility no less than by French friendship. They act in almost every point against their interest and their true wishes." The outbreak of the European war had at first Neutral seemed wholly beneficial to American commerce. Particularly important was the commerce of the French West Indies, which produced at that time immense quantities of sugar and coffee. The carrying of these products to France was now done almost wholly in American vessels, which received several millions yearly as freight. A great provision trade with the islands sprang up also, for the planters were too much interested in their staple crops to raise the food they needed, and the European wars left little in France to export to them. In fact, American foodstuffs were in demand in Europe, while American vessels, having the advantage of a neutral flag, found ready employment on many trade routes. In America farmers enjoyed high prices, shipbuilding increased, wages advanced, and successful merchants began to pile up fortunes.

Disputed points of international law. It became the policy of England to cut off, or at least to regulate, this neutral trade. During the two centuries in which she had been the greatest naval power, she had developed a system of international law giving belligerent nations great power over neutrals. In defense of their commerce, American statesmen resorted to the theories developed by the French and Dutch, which nations had found it to their advantage to limit the rights of belligerents and to protect the neutral. For twenty years English and American diplomats clashed over these rival systems.

England claimed the right to seize, as contraband of war, provisions destined for France, on the ground that without them the war could not be carried on. These provisions were, it is true, ultimately paid for, but England persisted in her right to take them, while the United States refused to grant the principle that foodstuffs were contraband. Moreover, England declared many French ports blockaded, and claimed the right to seize and condemn as prize any vessel whose papers showed it to be destined for them. The United States maintained that a blockade, to be legal, must be effective; that is, that a sufficient fleet must be kept off the port to render entrance practically impossible, and that seizures could be made only off the port. England also revived the "Rule of 1756," declaring that any trade closed in time of peace should remain closed in time of war. The effect of this was to make American vessels sailing between the French West Indies and France liable to capture, as they had been forbidden the trade by France before the war, when she wished the monopoly. England claimed that France should not have the advantage of monopoly when there was no danger to her own vessels, and of the protection of a neutral flag during times of war.

In executing these regulations, the English navy claimed the right of stopping and searching any vessel on the high seas. If it appeared to be engaged in a legal voyage, it was released, but even in such a case the searching officer might force into the English naval service any member of the crew born in England. The United States acknowledged the right to visit a vessel and to examine its papers, but not to examine the cargo or to impress the crew. This matter of impressment was scarcely one of the leading questions at this time, but it proved to be one of the most obstinate. If a mistake were made and a native-born American were taken, he would be ultimately returned; though it was sometimes after years of negotiation, and many died in the English service. If, however, he were an English-born, naturalized American, agreement was impossible; for England denied the right of any one to change his nationality, while the American government felt it its duty to protect all its citizens, naturalized as well as native. "Right of search" and impressment.

The attitude of the French government was actually not much more friendly. It professed the most liberal views, but claimed that if the United States could not defend its neutral rights against England, France was justified in retaliating specifically for every English regulation which interfered with neutral commerce. This somewhat curious position, which was afterwards still further developed by Napoleon, rested on the idea that neutral nations were bound to defend their neutral rights, that because the United States was not strong enough to maintain her rights against Great Britain the latter nation received certain advantages, that the United States to that extent ceased to be a neutral, and that France was justified in seeking redress by retaliation in kind. The naval predominance of England, however, enabled her to carry out her policy more Hostility of France and of England.

fully, while the brusqueness of the English officers, and
the high-handed methods of her admiralty courts in the
West Indies gave to her action a greater offensiveness.
Moreover, the French design of separating the West from the
Union was known to but a selected few, while England
openly kept the frontier posts, and was popularly supposed to
encourage the Indians in their hostility. The result was that
England received even more than her fair share of popular
ill feeling. Indignation reached its climax when the news
spread that eight Algerian corsairs had passed the straits of
Gibraltar, it was believed by the connivance of England,
and were raiding the trade routes of the Atlantic.

Conflict of
policies.

The Republicans, or the party of Jefferson, proposed to
meet this emergency by suspending all commercial intercourse with Great Britain until redress was given. The
Federalists, the party of Hamilton, felt that this would be
equivalent to a declaration of war with Great Britain,
which they were most anxious to avoid. After a vigorous
debate in Congress they were able to defeat the Republican
proposals, and to carry out their own policy. They put a
temporary embargo upon all commerce, thus avoiding discrimination; they increased the army and began the creation of a navy; and they sent a solemn final embassy
to England to test the possibility of agreement.

The Jay
treaty.

John Jay, the Chief Justice, who was appointed to undertake this delicate mission, had perhaps the best diplomatic
training of all Americans, but he was naturally timid, and
was so impressed with the critical character of his task that
he failed to take full advantage of the perilous position in
which England herself was at this time placed by the successes of the French. He had, moreover, a dangerous habit
of breaking his instructions.

The treaty which he obtained provided in the first place for
a settlement of the difficulties growing out of the treaty of
1783. The British agreed to give up the frontier posts, and

commissions were arranged to settle disputed points regarding the boundary and the claims of British merchants for pre-revolutionary debts. Commissions were also to adjudicate on the claims of American merchants, resulting from illegal maritime seizures, and of British merchants for seizures by French privateers illegally equipped in United States ports before the neutrality law began to work effectively. Disputed questions of international law were not mentioned, or were settled in favor of England, except that more effective notice of blockade was to be given. The administration of English regulations was somewhat eased, partly by the terms of the treaty and partly by an understanding between Jay and Grenville, the English foreign minister. On these points no one could have done much, if any, better than did Jay, since nothing but total defeat could have brought England to curtail her belligerent practices upon the high seas, for she considered them rights and essential to her strength. In framing the long-desired commercial treaty, however, Jay probably obtained less than another might have done. It provided for trade on the basis of the "most favored nation" between the United States and Great Britain and Ireland. It gave Americans privileges in the British East Indies, and it unbottled western Vermont, whose natural outlet was down Lake Champlain and the Richelieu River to the St. Lawrence, by legalizing trade to Montreal and Quebec. In the case of the British West Indies, however, but small concessions were allowed, and these on conditions so onerous that the Senate rejected this article of the treaty.

This treaty violated the instructions of the administration, particularly in yielding to some of the English contentions on international law. Washington, however, decided to present it to the Senate, and that body ratified it with the exception of the West Indies clause, an exception to which England consented. After much hesitation Washington signed it, and it became the law of the land. In the sum-

The Jay treaty in politics.

mer of 1795 it was made public and was greeted by a storm
of popular indignation. When Congress met in December,
the Republicans attacked it and threatened to refuse the
appropriations of money for which it called. The Federalist
leaders exerted themselves to the uttermost, and by the
first great outburst of congressional oratory Fisher Ames
secured the passage of the appropriation. Thus peace with
England was made secure, for the time at least.

Results of the treaty. The treaty worked not unfavorably. The commissions
awarded to American merchants damages much greater than
to the British. Vermont could now send her products to
Montreal, where they found a ready market. The evacuation of the posts, coming just after Wayne's victory over the
Indians, opened up the Northwest to settlement. Best of
all, as a result of the treaty in conjunction with European
events, Spain at length, in 1795, agreed to a treaty acknowledging the American claim to the parallel of 31° as a
southern boundary, opening the navigation of the Mississippi, allowing New Orleans to be used as a place of deposit
for three years, and promising to renew the privilege after
that period or to assign some other place as a port of transshipment.

Washington's second term. In 1792, when the time of the second presidential election
arrived, Washington had desired to retire, and had even
gone so far as to begin the preparation of a farewell address.
The situation still remained so critical, however, that he
consented to serve another term, and was reëlected unanimously, while Adams was again chosen Vice President by
a substantial majority. During his second administration,
in fact by the year 1795, the new government was proved
to be a success. It had established the finances, suppressed
insurrection, regulated and protected commerce, cleared the
boundaries recognized by the treaty of 1783 of European
troops, conquered peace with the Indians, opened the Mississippi, and maintained a dignified neutrality in spite of the

all-absorbing European war. Nevertheless, Washington was saddened, because during this term it was equally proved that his hope of uniting the ablest men of the country, though of differing political views, in a joint effort to govern the country, was to be disappointed. The division which had appeared in the bank controversy was widened by the French Revolution. Jefferson and his associates sympathized with France, Hamilton and his supporters with England. The division spread through the country, and in Congress the great majority of the members came to be known as Federalists or as Republicans, only a small number holding themselves independent of party. When Jefferson resigned as Secretary of State in 1793, he was succeeded by Edmund Randolph, a man of wavering views. In 1795 the latter was forced to resign, owing to improper communications with the French minister. Timothy Pickering, who succeeded him, was a thoroughgoing and partisan Federalist, and from this time the administration must be regarded as belonging to that party. Hamilton had left the cabinet in 1795 to engage in the more lucrative practice of law in New York, but he was replaced at the Treasury by a devoted follower, Oliver Wolcott, and his advice was still sought and generally taken on important questions.

Washington was deeply sensitive to the attacks which the opposition press made upon the government and upon even himself personally, and, practically all the dangers which had threatened the nation in 1784 having been averted at least for the time, he determined to carry out his plan and finally retire to Mount Vernon. In refusing a third term he established another "convention of the Constitution," or unwritten law, which has not yet been broken. In his Farewell Address he sought, with some success, to fix upon the country certain fundamental policies, calculated to keep it from danger and guide its continuous advancement. He warned his countrymen of the danger

Washington's retirement.

of sectionalism, and of the necessity of actively developing a national feeling based on a really national life; he pointed out the evils of party and factional divisions; and, finally, he urged that the United States preserve that policy of neutrality with regard to European wars which he had in-augurated. On the 4th of March, 1797, he left office. If he had been younger, he would have been happy in what he had accomplished, but although only sixty-five years of age, he was broken in the service of his country, and his fears for the future overcast his joy in his accomplishments. No man has ever done more for his fellow-citizens.

BIBLIOGRAPHICAL NOTES

Sources.
Fisher Ames's oration on the Jay treaty makes a valuable assignment. For public sentiment with regard to the French Revolution see Hart, A. B., *History told by Contemporaries*, nos. 93–95. Washington's *Farewell Address*, Richardson's *Messages and Papers of the Presidents*, I, 213–224, gives a good review of conditions.

Historical accounts. Frontier.
Hildreth, R., *United States*, IV, 498–538. Roosevelt, T., *Winning of the West*, IV, chs. I, II.

Genêt affair.
Bassett, *Federalist System*, 84–101. Foster, J. T., *American Diplomacy*, chs. IV, V. Hazen, C. D., *Contemporary American Opinion of the French Revolution* (*Johns Hopkins Historical Studies*, XVI), ch. IV. McMaster, *United States*, II, 86–191. Turner, F. J., *Genêt's Attack on Louisiana and the Floridas* (*Am. Hist. Review*, III, 650–671).

Jay treaty.
Bassett, *Federalist System*, 117–136. Conway, M. D., *Edmund Randolph*. McMaster, *United States*, II, 165–170; 213–242. Moore, J. B., *American Diplomacy*, chs. II, III. Pellew, J. Jay, ch. X.

Party alignment.
Adams, H., *Administrations of Jefferson and Madison*, I, chs. III, V. Bassett, *Federalist System*, 42–56, 136–150. Fiske, J., *Essays, Historical and Literary*, I, 99–142. Lowell, A. L., *Influence of Party on Legislation* (Am. Hist. Assoc., *Report*, 1901, vol. I, 319–542). Sumner, W. G., *Hamilton*, chs. X–XIII. Woodburn, J. A., *Political Parties*, 1–30.

Political methods.
Becker, C. L., *Parties in Colonial New York* (*Am. Hist. Review*,

VI, 260–275; VII, 56–76). Caheen, F. van A., *Society of Saint Tammany of Philadelphia* (*Pa. Mag. of Hist.*, January, 1903). Jernegan, N. W., *The Tammany Societies of Rhode Island* (Brown University Historical Seminary, *Papers*, no. 8). Luetscher, G. D., *Early Political Machinery in the United States.* Meyer, G., *History of Tammany Hall.* Walton, J. S., *Nominating Conventions in Pennsylvania* (*Am. Hist. Review*, II, 262–279).

CHAPTER VI

THE ADMINISTRATION OF JOHN ADAMS

The election of Adams.

ALTHOUGH Washington had been unanimously elected in 1792, the vote for Vice President had been on party lines. The electors of New York, Virginia, North Carolina, and Georgia had voted for George Clinton, a Republican; those of Kentucky for Jefferson; and Adams was reëlected only by seventy-seven to fifty-five. In 1796 a still closer division of the electoral college was to be expected. In anticipation of the election, conferences or caucuses were held by the members of Congress belonging to the different parties. John Adams and Thomas Pinckney, popular as the negotiator of the Spanish treaty, were selected as the Federalist candidates, and Jefferson and Burr as the Republican. These nominations were not regarded as absolutely binding upon the electors, who were still expected by many to use their own discretion. Hamilton, in fact, who distrusted the Federalism and the temper of Adams, hoped to reverse the order of the Federalist candidates. Each elector was to cast two votes, and the candidate receiving the highest number would be elected President, and the next highest, Vice President. Hamilton tried to persuade all the Adams electors to vote for Pinckney, expecting that some scattering votes would also go to him, thus bringing him the largest vote and the presidency. The result was unexpected. The plan of Hamilton became known, and so alarmed the friends of Adams that twenty-one of them declined to vote for Pinckney, and although a majority of the electors were Federalists and Adams was elected President, Jefferson received the second largest vote and became Vice President.

Adams thus became President after a contest which re- Adams's cabinet. vealed not only that two parties divided the country, but also that the Federalists were divided among themselves. He must needs fight for the leadership of his own party. Under these circumstances, his decision to retain Washington's entire cabinet was unfortunate, as its members, being friends of Hamilton, looked to the latter for advice and failed to give the new President loyal support.

The first problem that confronted the administration was French intrigues. a new phase of the foreign situation. France had been very much incensed by the Jay treaty. She held that the United States was bound, both by special treaties and by international obligation, to defend its rights as a neutral to the fullest extent; that in surrendering these rights to England it had become *de facto* the enemy of the French republic. James Monroe, a friend of Jefferson, had been sent on a mission of conciliation, but he so thoroughly sympathized with the French position that he became indiscreet and was recalled. On leaving, he intimated to the French government that there were two parties in America, that Jefferson would succeed Washington, and that, after the election, satisfaction would be given.

The French government was prompt to throw its influence on Jefferson's side. It refused to receive Monroe's successor, the Federalist, Charles Cotesworth Pinckney, and ordered Adet, its minister in the United States, to suspend his diplomatic functions. Adet announced his withdrawal in a letter, written for the public eye, which was immediately printed and had some influence on the election. While thus working for the success of the pro-French party, Adet secretly laid plans, in case of the election of Adams, to revive, on a large scale and somewhat different plan, those projects with reference to the western country which Genêt had endeavored to carry out.

The proposals of Talleyrand.   This was the situation with which Adams had to deal. He resolved to make an effort to reëstablish diplomatic intercourse, and to that end sent John Marshall and Elbridge Gerry to join Pinckney, making a special commission consisting of two Federalists and one Republican. The French government remained, on the surface, obdurate, but Talleyrand, the French foreign minister, through authorized agents, offered to negotiate if bribes were given to him and to his associates, and a large sum of money to the French treasury. William Pitt, prime minister of England, was at the time toying with an offer precisely similar, but our commissioners, less accustomed to the devious methods of continental diplomacy, emphatically refused to buy French friendship, and, finding no other way open, returned to America.

The X Y Z affair.   The correspondence of the commissioners, known from the fictitious names given Talleyrand's agents as the "X Y Z correspondence," was at once sent to Congress by Adams, with the assertion that he would "never send another minister to France without assurances that he will be received, respected, and honored as the representative of a great, free, powerful, and independent nation." Congress, although the balance in the House of Representatives was held by a few independents, passed by large majorities the measures recommended by the administration (1798). A direct tax was voted, and a large volunteer army was provided for, of which Washington consented to take command, with Hamilton as active head. The navy was largely increased, and a navy department organized. Commercial intercourse with France and the French possessions was ordered discontinued, the French treaties were declared abrogated, American warships were authorized to engage and capture French warships, and private vessels were permitted to arm both for defense and to attack any armed vessel, public or private, flying the

French flag. Hostilities existed, naval encounters occurred, and several hundred merchant vessels changed hands, but no declarations were exchanged, and it was not war to the finish.

Great popular excitement prevailed. The X Y Z cor- War feeling.
respondence was published, and Pinckney's "No, no, no, not a penny," transmuted into the ringing phrase "Millions for defense, but not one cent for tribute," raised him into a national hero; addresses of loyalty were showered upon the President, and the black cockade of Federalism was worn by many who up to this time had clung to French friendship and Republican doctrines. Joseph Hopkinson wrote *Hail, Columbia*, which became for a time the national anthem.

The Federalist leaders considered that this outburst of The Federal-'
national feeling gave them an opportunity to put a bit in the st program. i
mouth of democracy. The Constitution had done something to check what they considered the license of the Revolutionary period, but the Whisky Rebellion, the scurrilous vituperation of the press, widespread and demonstrative sympathy with the doctrines of the French revolutionists, so much more radical than those of the most extreme leaders in America twenty years before, convinced them that something more must be done to repress the demoralizing tendencies of the times. They therefore speedily adopted a program of reaction, which the momentary popular anger against France enabled them to carry through Congress. Many of the Republican leaders were of foreign birth, particularly Albert Gallatin, who had been concerned as a moderate in the Whisky Rebellion and was now leader of the opposition in Congress; and so in the spring of 1798 Congress increased the term of residence in the country required for naturalization from five to fourteen years, and passed the "Alien Law," allowing the President to remove, at his discretion, obnoxious foreigners residing in the country. No

prosecutions, however, were attempted under the law. The second step was an attack on the press. A "Sedition Act" was passed, making it a crime to libel Congress or the President; prosecutions under it promptly began, and convictions were secured, the most noteworthy being that of Callender, a friend of Jefferson. Also, Adams removed from office some few of the more active of his opponents, and was urged to make a clean sweep. "The ingrates," said the *Columbian Sentinel*, "ought not for a moment to be suffered to eat the bread of the public, when they wait only for a safe occasion to betray our country to France."

The elections of 1798–1799. In the fall of 1798 and the spring of 1799 occurred elections for Congress, and the contest was hard fought. The Federalists appealed to the people to support the administration in a time of national peril against the "Jacobins," who would sacrifice the country to France. The Republicans attacked the Alien and Sedition Laws. The Federalists were surprisingly successful; even south of the Potomac, where they had been least strong, they elected twenty-two members to fifteen Republicans. Encouraged by this popular approval, they planned to push forward their policy of increasing the power of the central government. They passed a national bankruptcy law, they adopted a more elaborate organization for the judiciary, increasing the number of judges; and Hamilton advised that a system of internal improvements be undertaken, that the people might become accustomed to look to the national government rather than to the states for beneficial legislation.

War plans. Vital to the success of the Federalists was the continuance of hostilities with France. Hamilton even thought to extend the scope of the war. France was out of our reach, but Spain was the ally of France, and "France is not to be considered as separated from her ally." "Tempting objects will be within our grasp." Largely ignoring Adams, he corresponded with Rufus King, minister to England, with Pitt, and with Don Francisco de Miranda, a Spanish American who sought coöperation in the revolutionizing of Spain's possessions in America. A plan was in process of arrangement, according to which Hamilton was to lead the army, Great Britain was to furnish the navy, and the ultimate object was to be the establishment of well-ordered, constitutional independence for Spanish America, the addition of Florida and New Orleans to the United States, and the sharing of the commercial advantages to come from the overthrow of Spain's monopolistic system by the United States and England. To this scheme the opposition of Adams proved fatal. He refused to countenance the Miranda negotiation, and he allowed trade with the French ports in the island now called Haiti, thereby preventing Hamilton's plan of starving that island until it declared its independence and threw in its fortunes with England and the United States. Finally, on receiving assurances that a minister would be properly received by France, he at once, without even consulting his cabinet, which he knew would be hostile, nominated William Vans Murray for the post.

The popular desire for peace was so great that the Senate dared not reject the opportunity, but Adams was induced to send three commissioners, Oliver Ellsworth, Governor Davie of North Carolina, and Murray, instead of a minister. The offer on the part of France did not indicate a change of heart, but a conviction that a mistake had been made. Talleyrand had not intended actual war; our merchant marine was too useful to French commerce, and our foodstuffs too vital to the French West Indies. He had hoped to frighten the United States, and had failed. On September 30, 1800, a convention was concluded at Paris which was mutually satisfactory. France renounced her claims under the treaties of 1778 and of 1788, and the United States forbore to press the claim of Americans for certain classes of illegal seizures. With the French peace, plans for an English alliance fell, and

Peace with France.

Adams's action restored to the nation that neutrality and isolation from European politics which Washington had believed to be so essential to our progress.

Hamilton and his friends were not able to oppose in public the restoration of peace, as they had not been able to reveal to the public all their plans, because an overwhelming majority of the people either sympathized with France or believed in the policy of peace, if there could be peace with honor. Among themselves, however, they execrated Adams. Theodore Sedgwick, Speaker of the House, wrote: "Had the foulest heart and the ablest head in the world been permitted to select the most embarrassing and ruinous measure, perhaps it would have been precisely the one which has been adopted." Mutual quarrels led Adams to dismiss Pickering, the Secretary of State; others of the cabinet resigned; and he appointed in their stead men whose views harmonized with his own, John Marshall becoming Secretary of State.

This breach was partly the result of a rivalry and mutual distrust between Adams and Hamilton, which was of very long standing and which was accentuated by Hamilton's attempt, in 1796, to deprive Adams of the succession, and by the reluctance with which Adams acceded in 1798 to Washington's request to make Hamilton second in command in the new army. The difference was, however, far more than personal. About Hamilton gathered a group of able, self-sufficient men who distrusted popular government more and more with every passing year. George Cabot, leading member of the "Essex Junto," as the Massachusetts group of "high-toned" Federalists was called, wrote in 1801: "There is no security for a good government without some popular mixture in it; but there will be neither justice nor stability in any system if some material parts of it are not independent of popular control." In 1804 he wrote: "I hold democracy in its natural operation to be the government of the worst." These men believed, as had John Cotton, in a government neither "meerly democratical," nor "meerly aristocratical"; and with Winthrop, that "The best part of a community is always the least, and of that least part, the wiser is still less." They deprecated the peace with France for domestic reasons, for without war, said George Cabot, "The people will not support the army; the navy will not be increased; neither taxes nor loans will be permitted beyond what may be necessary to discharge existing engagements." They felt, moreover, that the United States could not forever stand as a spectator of the world contest which was going on between the untrammeled forces of democracy represented by France, and England, the defender of authority, of law and order. They believed that if we waited until that contest was decided, we should fall a victim to whichever side was victorious. George Cabot wrote, June 9, 1798: "It is pretty certain that, if Great Britain yields, we shall have the weight of the whole European world to oppress us."

Although these leaders practically controlled the party, they realized that they could not control the country without the addition of the more moderate Federalists of the Adams type, who had somewhat more of confidence in the people and in the ability of the United States to stand alone and aloof. Consequently, Hamilton advised that in the forthcoming campaign all should loyally support Adams for the presidency, although he set forth in a pamphlet, designed for private circulation, that the latter was totally unfitted for that office by reason of his views and his temperament. The candidate agreed upon for Vice President was C. C. Pinckney, whose name would recall the intrigues and the insults of the French. With the war issue removed, divided in counsel and deprived by Washington's death in 1799 of the great prestige of his support, the Federalists realized that the campaign of 1800 would prove very much more

Federalist candidates for 1800.

difficult than that of 1798–1799. Yet they fully expected a victory, confident in their record of usefulness.

Republican program.
This record, however, was precisely the basis of the Republican campaign. The leaders of that party attacked the whole centralizing tendencies of the last twelve years, the increase of taxes, the failure to reduce the debt, the multiplication of public officers. They attacked the administration as tyrannical because of its prosecutions under the Sedition Law and its removals from office; they attacked the judiciary for partial conduct in the trial of one Fries, accused of treason for inciting armed resistance in Pennsylvania to the collection of the direct tax. But, under the skillful leadership of Jefferson, they emphasized most of all the lurking danger to liberty and popular government involved in the stretching of the Constitution by the doctrine of "implied powers." As an antidote to the policy of centralization and as a platform about which to rally the party, Jefferson's friends secured in 1798 the passage by the legislatures of Kentucky and Virginia, of resolutions condemning the Alien and Sedition Acts. Those of Kentucky, adopted almost *verbatim* as drawn up by Jefferson, stated that the Constitution was a compact, "that the government created by this compact was not made the exclusive or final judge of the extent of the powers delegated to itself . . . but that . . . each party [state] has an equal right to judge for itself, as well as of infractions, as of the mode and measure of redress." The Virginia resolutions, drafted by Madison, gave a similar interpretation to the Constitution, and added: "That in case of a deliberate, palpable, and dangerous exercise of other powers not granted by the said compact, the States who are the parties thereto, have the right, and are in duty bound, to interpose for arresting the progress of the evil, and for maintaining within the respective limits, the authorities, rights, and liberties appertaining to them." The Alien and Sedition Laws were declared to be instances of such violation. When nine of

the ten states lying to the north replied unfavorably to the constitutional interpretation presented by Virginia and Kentucky, the latter state, November 22, 1799, passed a new resolution setting forth the theory that in case of an infraction of the federal compact by the national government: "Nullification by those sovereignties [the states], of all unauthorized acts done under color of that instrument, is the rightful remedy." In Virginia John Randolph of Roanoke, John Taylor of Caroline, and others contemplated the possibility of separation from the Union, and urged that the state prepare herself for self-defense. Jefferson did not give countenance to violent action, however. Solemnly to voice a protest was all that he desired, at any rate for the present; he had confidence that under the normal conditions of peace his principles were those of a majority of the people, and he confidently expected that the election would establish his principles.

While Jefferson directed party policy, the Republican candidate for the vice presidency, Aaron Burr of New York, applied himself with equal skill to the manipulation of politics in that pivotal state. He secured and published Hamilton's letter condemning Adams; he organized and combined all the elements in any way dissatisfied with the Federalist administration, and finally succeeded in carrying the new state legislature which would choose the presidential electors. *Aaron Burr.*

The election throughout the country resulted in the choice of seventy-three Republican electors to sixty-five Federalist. This assured the defeat of the Federalists, but it did not determine who would be the next President. Jefferson and Burr received an equal vote, and the election was therefore thrown into the House of Representatives, — the House which was elected in 1798–99 and in which the Federalists retained the majority. It therefore fell to them to choose between their two opponents. The majority preferred Burr; *The elections of 1800 and 1801.*

young, brilliant, fascinating, an opportunist devoid of political principle, he might, they felt, by care and skill be made in effect a Federalist President. Burr, however, refused to commit himself by promises, and Hamilton, long the rival of Burr in law as of Jefferson in politics, urged that it would be safer to choose Jefferson, who would, though an enemy, be timid and conciliatory, rather than Burr, whom he believed to be entirely untrustworthy. Hamilton's advice was finally taken, and on February 17, 1801, by the thirty-sixth ballot, Jefferson was elected President.

The achievements of the Federalists.

The Federalists, in their twelve years of power, had given the country so good a government that the Constitution was universally accepted as a success, and there was contest only over its interpretation. They had established many supplementary practices or conventions so well devised as to last until our own day. They had preserved the neutrality of the country in the great struggles that were desolating Europe, in spite of threats and lures and internal divisions, and in so doing had laid the foundations of our foreign policy. Finally, one of the last acts of Adams was to appoint to the position of Chief Justice, John Marshall, who, in a series of decisions extending through thirty-five years, was to embody permanently in the law of the land the constitutional principles of moderate Federalism.

Causes of Federalist defeat.

The Federalists lost power because they were out of sympathy with a majority of the people. The leadership of the party came from the financial and commercial classes, whereas agriculture was the predominant interest of the country. They stood for national centralization, whereas the spirit of local independence was still more vital than that of nationality. The country had not yet grown together into a real economic unit, nor had it been fused into one by an enduring national patriotism. The Federalists, moreover, were firm believers in the subordination of the masses, while the spirit of democracy and the confidence of the people in themselves were growing daily stronger. The work of the Federalists in organizing and establishing the central government proved of permanent value, but the people now preferred to give the administration of it to men more in sympathy with their interests and ideals.

BIBLIOGRAPHICAL NOTES

For the Kentucky and Virginia resolutions, etc., *American History Leaflets*, no. 15. Ames, H. V., *State Documents on Federal Relations*, 15–26. Johnston, A., *Readings on American Constitutional History*, 228–236. Macdonald, W., *Select Documents*, 148. — Sources.

Adams, C. F., *John Adams*, II, ch. X. Allen, G. W., *Our Naval War with France.* Bassett, *Federalist System*, 204–252. Schouler, J., *United States*, I, ch. IV. — Historical accounts. French war.

Adams, H., *A. Gallatin*, 189–266. Adams, H., *John Randolph*, ch. II. Anderson, F. M., *Contemporary Opinion of Kentucky and Virginia Resolutions* (*Am. Hist. Review*, V, 45–63, 225–244). Bassett, *Federalist System*, 252–276. Holst, H. von, *United States*, I, ch. IV. Hunt, G., *J. Madison*, 259–271. Story, J., *Commentaries*, secs. 158, 1288, 1289, 1885, 1886. — Political contest.

CHAPTER VII

JEFFERSONIAN DEMOCRACY

The inaugu-
ration. ON March 4, 1801, Thomas Jefferson was inaugurated. It was the first occasion on which a President took office at Washington, although the government had moved there the year before. The city had but a small population, scattered here and there over the great area laid out by l'Enfant, the French engineer, and the public buildings were unfinished. The occasion was stripped of the pomp and dignity with which the Federalists had surrounded such functions, and Jefferson walked from his boarding house to the Capitol, instead of riding in a coach. Natural as such an act was to him, it was probably not without the design of typifying the overthrow of what he considered the aristocratic party and the incoming of democracy. Significant as is the triumph of Jefferson, however, his election did not mark so much the incoming of new principles as a return of those of the Revolution. The strong government reaction of the Federalist period had accomplished its task of reëstablishing order, but had grown irksome to the majority of the people, who now turned to the men who had held their confidence during the Revolutionary struggle, and to younger men of like mind. Jefferson himself had held office almost continuously, but is remembered chiefly for his work during the Revolution and as President. Many states, like the nation, sought veterans. In the state elections of 1799 and 1800, Thomas McKean became governor of Pennsylvania, and George Clinton of New York; and later Republican victories made John Langdon governor of New Hampshire,

The return to
the men and
principles of
the Revolu-
tion.

86

Thomas Jefferson

and Elbridge Gerry of Massachusetts. In both houses of the new Congress, the supporters of Jefferson were in the majority.

The leadership of the new party in thought and personnel was Virginian. The Virginia stock was now at its prime. The hardships of the early years had weeded out the physically weak, and the cavalier immigration had infused an element of high refinement, which served to excite the emulation of the rest. At this period the plantation system had reached its highest possible development in Virginia. As it had stretched westward into the piedmont, the plantations had become larger, and the need of administrative talent on the part of the owners greater. The next generation would be deflected by the mountains southward and into cotton culture, but now founders and administrators of the greatest plantations in the country were still living in Virginia, and were moved to public service by a desire for distinction and a sense of *noblesse oblige*. Finally, at this period the Virginia or kindred North Carolina stock controlled Kentucky, and also Ohio, which was to become a state in 1803; and so Virginia was brought into close contact with the expanding life of the West. The Virginia element.

Typically Virginian was Thomas Jefferson. He was democratic in his unwillingness to dictate or be dictated to, rather than in an unquestioned acceptance of the will of the majority. He hated form, abolished many of the social conventions of the Federalist period, and risked a war with England by taking the wrong lady in to dinner. Yet he built the most exquisite mansion in America, and ruined himself financially to maintain a lavish hospitality. He would brook no superior. Both his simplicity and his extravagance aroused the grave distrust of the more formal and exact men of the North, and he was thrice anathema because of his freedom of expression on religious matters, in a generation which was not indeed very religious, but which regarded orthodox religion as essential to the support of authority. Thomas Jefferson.

His dislike of form, perhaps, prevented his becoming an orator, but in conversation he was convincing, and he possessed one of the most persuasive pens in all America. He was not a good judge of men and was often found in association with those of questionable conduct, but he did not cherish that jealousy of men of talent which is often an accompanying trait. He combined better than any other American statesman the strength that comes from the possession of a few ineradicable convictions, such as confidence in the wisdom of mankind and the consequent supremacy of reason, with an aptitude for shifting his views on nonessential questions; and so he preserved the magnetism of the idealist while he adapted himself with ease to the changing conditions of a growing country. While he was President, this change was chiefly in the direction of an enlarging view of the functions that the national government might beneficently exercise; and in this development he was followed by his faithful collaborators: Madison, the new Secretary of State, and Albert Gallatin, the Secretary of the Treasury.

Republican conservatives.

Another group, enthusiastic Jeffersonians in 1800, clung to the views of that date: John Taylor of Caroline, the closet statesman, author of *Construction Construed and the Constitution Vindicated;* John Randolph, in 1801 chairman of the committee on ways and means, administration leader in the House, and keenest master of sarcasm among American statesmen; Nathaniel Macon, Speaker of the House from 1801 to 1807, and guardian of pure government and economy; and James Monroe, the favorite though uninspired foreign agent of the administration. These men all held strictly to the principles with which the government had come into power, while the administration drifted away. In Jefferson's second administration they came to form a third party known as the "Quids," which, however, was but short-lived.

Northern Republicans.

The northern section of the Republican party played at

first a decidedly minor part in determining party policy. In New York it was composed of a union between the factions of the Clintons, the followers of Burr, and the old manorial family of the Livingstons. Interest was mainly centered in the rivalries of these groups, and national politics were subordinated to those of the state. DeWitt Clinton resigned a United States senatorship to become mayor of New York. Pennsylvania seemed to be represented by Gallatin, who, with Madison and Jefferson, formed the inner council of the party, but his views were rather cosmopolitan than local, and he was in no sense characteristically Pennsylvanian. Leaving him aside, the Pennsylvanian democracy was not only torn by internal divisions, like that of New York, but failed to produce leaders even of any great local influence. In New England a democratic element existed, and after a few years of agitation and organization became numerically powerful, but the bulk of the ability and education remained with the Federalists, and it was many years before any New Englanders disputed with the Virginians the guidance of the Republican party.

The distinguishing feature of the northern democracy was party organization. Tammany Hall had been founded in 1789. In 1793 and 1794 this club type of party organization received great impetus from the success of the Jacobin clubs in France, and Democratic societies were formed from Maine to Charleston and Kentucky. These societies were believed to have been concerned with the Whisky Rebellion, and Washington so sternly discountenanced them that, except in New York, they lost their influence and passed away. Even Tammany Hall formed separate political and social organizations. In the meantime there had been developing the type of organization that was ultimately established. In New York, in colonial times, men had put themselves forward for office or had been brought to public notice by a few friends. About the time of the Revolution nominations were made by mass meetings of those interested. Later, these mass meetings had

Party organization.

degenerated into caucuses, where a few politicians met, often secretly, and made up a "slate" of nominations, which was then presented to the public as the choice of large and enthusiastic assemblies of voters. In the meantime, there had been developing in Pennsylvania a system which applied to candidates for more general offices, where those interested could not be expected to come together. County officials were nominated by conventions of representatives, and in 1788 the first state party convention was held. Such conventions for the sole purpose of selecting party candidates were too expensive in time and money to be held regularly, and their place was generally supplied by a legislative caucus of the members of the party. Sometimes there was a "reënforced caucus," delegates being specially sent to speak for those districts which were represented in the assembly by members of the opposing party. By controlling the local "caucuses" or "primaries," politicians were able to select the members of the legislature and the delegates, and through them to control the party policy and the selection of its general candidates.

The spoils system. The management of such party machinery had not yet become a profession upon which any considerable number of persons depended for a living, but not all these politicians were disinterested, and most of them wanted some payment for their services. The newspaper editor wanted the state printing; the wealthy man wanted, perhaps, a bank charter; others looked to some public-salaried position as their reward. It was already felt, as Josiah Quincy said, that party cohesion was strengthened by "interchange of good offices." In 1799 McKean of Pennsylvania, and in 1800 Clinton of New York, marked their entry into power by the removal of many Federalists and the appointment of Republicans in their places, and many of the most active workers for Jefferson's election looked to the distribution of the spoils as the most important result to come from their success.

Jefferson was not opposed in principle to making political appointments or removals, but he hesitated to adopt a policy of proscription, as he hoped to win to his support the bulk of the Federalist voters, leaving their leaders helpless. His inaugural breathed a spirit of universal good will. "But every difference of opinion," he said, "is not a difference of principle. We have called by different names brethren of the same principle. We are all Republicans, we are all Federalists." To satisfy his supporters and win his opponents was a difficult task, but one exactly suited to his ability and temperament. He proceeded, tentatively, à *talons* as he expressed it, beginning with cases where removal might be defended on some special ground without an appeal to general principles. He reinstated all who had been removed by Adams; he declared void certain so-called "midnight" appointments made in the last moments of the Adams administration, the commissions for which had not been delivered; he removed officers appointed by Adams after it was known that the latter was defeated for reëlection and that these appointees would serve a hostile administration. In defense of this action, he wrote an ingenious letter to the merchants of New Haven who had protested against the removal of their collector,—and then he waited. No reaction followed; the Federalist press raged, but the elections went Republican, and Jefferson proceeded to make removals generally upon the principle that more offices should be held by Republicans. As the Republicans gained one state after another, similar state proscriptions marked their victories as in Rhode Island in 1810, and Massachusetts in 1811. Appointments were, on the whole, good, being by no means given purely because of party usefulness, and those appointed kept office while their party was in power. The principle of rotation in office was not yet established. Moreover, the practice of removal was in large measure confined to the North. "Some states," said Jefferson, "require a different regimen from others." The adoption of a proscriptive policy did not, therefore, mean the introduction of a complete spoils system into national politics. Moreover, as Washington had been occupied as capital for only a year, there was no firmly rooted official class whose distresses could stir the popular imagination, as when Jackson took similar action at a later time. The proscription of Jefferson, therefore, effected no great change in the character of the civil service, and was soon forgotten.

Democratic innovations. While the personnel of the government was being changed, the general aspect of official life was assuming a simpler and more democratic tone. Jefferson discarded the official rules of etiquette which Hamilton had drawn up. He lived simply, though somewhat lavishly, as he did at home. The Federalist practice of having the two houses of Congress send the President formal addresses at their coming together, and of his replying, — a practice drawn from the custom of the British Parliament, — was done away with. On the other hand Congress sought to draw closer to the people. The House of Representatives granted better opportunities for reporters, and the Senate, against the unanimous vote of its Federalist members, provided itself with a stenographer to take down its debates.

The repeal of the judiciary act of 1801. The regular program of the party was destructive, and few administrations have so thoroughly carried out the work they were elected to accomplish. One of the earliest measures was the repeal of the judiciary act of 1801, which was regarded as creating an unnecessarily expensive system. Additional venom was given to the attack upon this law because Adams had made it a means of providing positions for Federalist congressmen who had been defeated for reëlection. John Randolph wished "to give a death-blow to the pretension of rendering the judiciary a hospital for decayed politicians." The repeal was made, in spite of the question raised as to the constitutional power of Congress thus to deprive of their offices men appointed to hold office during good behavior.

The repeal of this act was one move in a general attack on the judiciary, the only department of government in which the Federalists remained intrenched. It availed, however, comparatively little to reduce the number of judges if those that remained were still Federalists; and partly with the object of gaining control of the bench by displacing Federalist judges and putting Republicans in their places, a number of impeachments were brought. The first, against Mr. Pickering, a district judge, was successful; but in the next case, that of Samuel Chase, a justice of the Supreme Court, accused of undue political activity, the Senate failed to find him guilty, taking the position that impeachment was judicial in its nature as well as in its processes, and conviction should be based on some definite judicial offense and not on general grounds. This failure led to the abandonment of the attempt to weed out the judiciary. It was a plan discountenanced by the more moderate of the Republicans. In Pennsylvania, a similar effort to control the judiciary met with a similar result. Stung by these defeats, Randolph and others of the more radical among the Republicans proposed that judges be removable by a joint resolution of the houses of Congress, and that state legislatures have the right to recall their senators. These proposals, however, met with small response, and although an additional judge was added to the Supreme Court in 1807, it was not until 1811 that a majority owed their selection to a Republican President, and even then Marshall continued to dominate the court by his reasoning and his powerful personality.

The attack on the judiciary.

In the field of legislation there were no obstacles, and progress was rapid. The excise law fell at once, as Gallatin sympathized with the frontier whisky makers, of whom he had been in 1794 a leader, and Jefferson disliked the for-

Repeal of Federalist laws.

midable corps of officials which its enforcement required. The bankruptcy act was easily repealed. The residence requirement for naturalization was again reduced to five years, while the Alien and Sedition Acts expired by limitation. The Bank, having a charter for twenty years, could not be overthrown during Jefferson's administration, but when in 1811 its charter expired, it was forced to go out of existence.

The pursuit of simplicity. Still in the pursuit of simplicity, the diplomatic service was curtailed, and the standing army reduced. "For defense against invasion," said Jefferson of the latter, "their number is as nothing. . . . Uncertain as we must ever be of the particular point in our circumference where an enemy may choose to invade us, the only force which can be ready at every point and competent to oppose them is the body of neighboring citizens as formed into a militia." In the same way, the regular navy was reduced by laying up many of the frigates, while a multitude of small gunboats were built, which might be manned by naval militia and act as a coast guard in time of war.

Financial administration. Upon Gallatin, the Secretary of the Treasury, lay the burden of proving that a simple government could be also efficient, and it was hoped that he might do something to remove that last remaining instrument of Hamiltonian consolidation, the national debt. In pursuit of these aims Gallatin showed great skill and was assisted by great good luck. In the first place, he brought the finances more closely under the control of Congress, by securing the adoption of the system of specific appropriation, in the place of the general appropriation of lump sums for civil service, war, and so forth, that it had previously been customary to make. Expenses he pared down, with almost too severe an economy. At the same time the increase of the customs revenue was unparalleled. Sir William Scott, the English admiralty judge, decided in 1799, in the cases of the *Emmanuel* and the

Polly, that American vessels might carry on the trade between France and her colonies, if the goods were first brought to the United States and paid duty. The result was that in some years during the Napoleonic wars sixty million dollars' worth of products of the West Indies paid duty in American ports. The revenue advanced, surpluses piled up, and when Jefferson retired in 1809, $33,000,000 of debt, all that had matured and was payable, had been wiped out.

When Jefferson became President, the war in Europe was drawing to a close, but the peace bid fair to be more dangerous than the war. Napoleon, now in control of France, found in the colonial policies of his predecessors an outlet for his tremendous energies. His foreign minister and leading supporter, Talleyrand, was well acquainted with American affairs and urged them upon his attention. On September 30, 1800, the peace with the United States removed one obstacle to the enterprise; the next day the secret treaty of San Ildefonso, by which Spain ceded Louisiana to France, gave the field for exploitation; October 1, 1801, preliminary articles with Great Britain were signed, and in March, 1802, the treaty of Amiens established peace ·with that country and opened the ocean to French exploits. Before France actually took possession of New Orleans, and while the treaty of cession was still in fact a secret, the right of deposit at that place accorded Americans by the treaty of 1795 was withdrawn. Nor was another place of deposit designated as the treaty required. Thus, when the French should occupy Louisiana, they would have all the strings of western intrigue in their hands, and the future of the Mississippi valley might be at their disposition. *New dangers from France.*

The news of the withdrawal of the right of deposit, coupled with well-authenticated information regarding the secret treaty of cession, created a panic in public circles at Washington. Every one realized what it would mean to have France as a neighbor, instead of decrepit Spain, one of whose heirs *Jefferson's Mississippi policy.*

we had intended to become. Just what Napoleon's next step would be was unknown at the time, and cannot be stated with certainty even to-day. It was sufficiently evident, however, that he would strive to reëstablish the French colonial empire in America on the broadest scale, and that his plans would necessarily conflict with the aspirations of far-seeing Americans. The struggle for the Mississippi valley, which had seemed won by the peace of 1763, appeared now to be on the point of reopening, under very different conditions: in the earlier period the conflict was for the opportunity to expand over an unoccupied territory, but now the territory was occupied by tens of thousands of Americans whose livelihood would be dependent upon the French, since the latter might, by keeping the Mississippi closed, cut them off from all commercial intercourse with the outside world. The Federalists lamented the peace with France, and again urged war. Jefferson saw clearly the peril of the times, but he had confidence in the reasonableness of the French government. He wrote on April 18, 1802 : "The day that France takes possession of New Orleans fixes the sentence which is to restrain her forever within her low-water mark. It seals the union of two nations, which in conjunction can maintain exclusive possession of the ocean. From that moment we must marry ourselves to the British fleet and nation." He talked peace, and he sent Monroe, as special commissioner to France, instructed to buy New Orleans. If France would not sell, or grant us full navigation rights on the Mississippi, we would delay until the next war between France and England, and then ally ourselves with the latter. Meantime he extended courtesies to the English minister.

Jefferson's policy would have been perfect if, in addition to what he did and did not do, he had also prepared for the emergency of war ; but it was neither to his skill nor to the efforts of Monroe that success was due. The key to the

French plan was the island of Santo Domingo, perhaps at that time the richest colony in the world. The negroes on the island had revolted, and Napoleon's first work was to reduce them. On January 7, 1803, news reached Paris that the expedition intended to accomplish the reduction had been virtually destroyed. At once Napoleon dropped his whole project and devoted himself to European affairs. He threw over Talleyrand; he prepared for war with England and Austria; and he decided to sell, not New Orleans alone, but all Louisiana, to the United States in order to prevent its falling into the hands of England, to replenish his coffers, and to secure the effective gratitude of this country. Purchase of The offer was made to Robert R. Livingston, our regular Louisiana. minister, before Monroe arrived, and the bargain was concluded April 30, 1803, for $15,000,000, $3,750,000 of which was to be paid our own citizens for claims against the French government.

The treaty was received in America with astonishment, Constitu- and not with unmingled pleasure. Jefferson realized its tional con- troversies. value, perhaps more clearly than any one else, but it conflicted with his idea of strict construction, as the Constitution nowhere explicitly gave the right to annex territory. It was, however, so easy to imply such a right from the treaty-making power, that his followers swept aside even his suggestion of a constitutional amendment to legalize the treaty, and thus they started on the broad path that was to lead them to stretch the Constitution almost as much as the Federalists had done.

The Federalists could not object to the treaty on this ground, but based their opposition on the clause providing that "The inhabitants of the ceded territory shall be incorporated in the Union of the United States, and admitted as soon as possible, according to the principles of the Federal Constitution, to the enjoyment of all the rights, advantages, and immunities of citizens of the United States."

This clause obviously implied the admission of the new
territory into the Union as a state or states. Foreseeing the
diminished consequence of the eastern states, if this great
addition were made to the southern and western sections,
many Federalists contended that we could acquire territory to
govern as a colony, but that to enlarge the Union, to admit
new states, was to change the character of the government,
and required the consent of all or at least three quarters of
the states. Defeated in Congress, some Federalists, such
as Pickering, discussed the advisability of secession by the
New England states. George Cabot urged patience:
"We shall go the way of all governments wholly popular,
from bad to worse, until the evils, no longer tolerable, shall
generate their own remedies." The Republicans were
forced to maintain the implied power to add to the Union
as well as to annex territory.

Territorial organization of Louisiana.   The question of the government of the newly acquired
territory was not without difficulties, as the population was
very largely alien in law and language. It was found inconvenient to apply to it at once all the rights and privileges customary in the other territories, and the first territorial act was, therefore, based on the idea that Congress has
absolute power over the territories, unrestricted by the guarantees of individual rights contained in the amendments to
the Constitution. George W. Campbell said: "It really
establishes a complete despotism; it does not evince a single
trait of liberty." This act, passed in 1804, divided the
region by the parallel of 33°; the Territory of Orleans lying
to the south, the District of Louisiana to the north. In
1805 the latter division was made a territory, and both sections were given governments modeled on that laid down in the
Northwestern Ordinance. The constitutional importance of the
Louisiana purchase controversies, in committing the Republicans, the party of strict construction, to such decided
principles of broad construction, cannot be overestimated.

The annexation of Louisiana settled at once and finally the allegiance of the West to the Union. The government which could secure an outlet for their products deserved and received the full support of the western settlers. The work partly accomplished by the Spanish treaty of 1795 was now complete. Jefferson aimed also, though less successfully, Indian policy. at the solution of the Indian problem. He hoped by civilizing them to attach them to the whites, abolish war, and do away with the need of extensive hunting grounds. He continually extended the purchases of Indian land in Georgia, in Tennessee, and all along the northern bank of the Ohio, and up the Mississippi and the Wabash.

At the same time, Jefferson's insatiate scientific curiosity Exploration. made it a pleasant public duty for him to direct the exploration of the new territory to the west. In 1785, when minister to France, he had conversed with and encouraged John Ledyard, who was endeavoring to establish American possession and trade on the northwest coast of the continent. He never lost interest in the project, and he firmly believed that American civilization would reach across to the Pacific. The most important of Jefferson's exploring expeditions was, in fact, organized before the purchase. Led by the President's private secretary, Meriwether Lewis, and by William Clark, it ascended the Missouri in 1804, and wintered in what is now North Dakota; the next summer it crossed the Rocky Mountains and wintered near the Pacific coast. Returning in 1806, it brought back masses of invaluable information, which, popularized by Nicholas Biddle, made Louisiana known to the people. Other expeditions under Zebulon Pike during 1805–1807 explored the upper Mississippi, and also the region as far westward as Pikes Peak, and far enough to the southward to get into trouble with the Spaniards.

The reëlection of Jefferson caused scarcely a ripple of The reëlection of Jefferson caused scarcely a ripple of The reëlection of Jefferson caused scarcely a ripple of The reëlection of Jefferson. excitement, so content and prosperous was the country. The Twelfth Amendment had now been adopted, requiring each elector to cast one vote for President and one for Vice President, preventing such a deadlock as that of 1800. The growth of democratic feeling was evinced by the fact that ten states out of seventeen chose their electors by popular vote. The Republican caucus dropped Burr, and nominated George Clinton for Vice President. The Federalists supported C. C. Pinckney and Rufus King, but secured for them only 14 electoral votes to 162 for Jefferson, carrying only Connecticut, Delaware, and two districts in Maryland.

The Hamilton-Burr duel, and Burr's fall.

Jefferson had almost succeeded in his object of winning the Federalist voters from their leaders, and the same year saw the disappearance of his two most conspicuous rivals. Burr, his ambition thwarted in the Republican party, ran for governor of New York, counting on Federalist support. Hamilton opposed him, and he was defeated; whereupon he challenged Hamilton, shot, and killed him. The profound and generous grief for the loss of Hamilton, whose high ability and character were now almost universally admitted, and the circumstances of the duel, ended Burr's hope of political advancement through the ordinary channels. He turned to the West, thinking, with his address and skill, to weave some great project from the maze of frontier intrigue, but he was too late. The securing of the Mississippi valley had contented the frontiersmen, and Burr's plans, whatever they may have been, fell flat. He was arrested and tried for treason, and while acquitted, found public sentiment so strongly turned against him that he left the country for many years.

Jefferson's plans for an extension of national activities.

Secure in his power, Jefferson began to take a more genial view of government. His fertile mind saw so many ways in which he could benefit the country that he began to chafe under the restrictions which his strict view of the Constitution put upon him. In his second inaugural he looked forward to the time when the debt should be paid, "and that redemption once effected, the revenue thereby liberated may, by a just repartition of it among the states and a corresponding amendment of the Constitution, be applied in time of peace to rivers, canals, roads, arts, manufactures, education, and other great objects within each of the states." By the time he wrote his sixth annual message he was sure that the people would find no advantage in a reduction of the tariff, but would prefer the application of the surplus "to the great purposes of the public education, roads, rivers, canals, and such other objects of public improvement as it may be thought proper to add to the constitutional enumeration of Federal powers. By their operations new channels of communication will be opened between the states, the lines of separation will disappear, their interests will be identified, and their union cemented by new and indissoluble ties." Gallatin made a careful report on practicable internal improvements, and Congress appropriated money for a survey of the coast, and of a national road to run from Cumberland, Maryland, westward, connecting Washington with the Ohio; but it preferred to find its power by implication, rather than by amendment to the Constitution as Jefferson proposed.

This movement of the administration toward centraliza- Republican factions. tion led to a breach in the Republican party. The main issue was as to whether Jefferson's successor should be the ever faithful Madison, or Monroe, whose views were less elastic. John Randolph, however, at the head of the "Quids," carried the campaign into many matters and harassed the administration on every side. Particularly bitter was his attack on Gallatin who had proposed — as part of the agreement by which Georgia in 1802 ceded to the national government her claims to all territory west of what is now her western boundary — to reimburse the Yazoo claimants for their losses caused by the revocation of grants they had corruptly obtained from the Georgia legislature. This plan he defeated, although the proposition was repeatedly renewed, and although in 1811 the Supreme Court, in the case of *Fletcher* v. *Peck*, declared that the original contract was binding. An appropriation to pay the claim was secured only in 1814, when Randolph was not in Congress. On the whole, however, the honors of war were with the administration, for Randolph's friend Macon was defeated for the speakership in 1807, and as a consequence Randolph lost the chairmanship of the committee on ways and means.

The Barbary wars. It was in the field of foreign affairs that Jefferson encountered his chief difficulties. Peace was his passion, but in one instance he overcame his repugnance to war. The utter barbarity and unreasonableness of the Barbary pirate states had always disgusted him, and even during the Confederation he had opposed the policy of placating them with bribes in order to open up the Mediterranean to our trade. Now, as President, he made war on Tripoli, and in 1805 secured a peace without payment, meanwhile saving the navy from the extinction to which the policy of economy seemed destined to condemn it. An American squadron remained in the Mediterranean, and that sea continued open to American merchant vessels until the war of 1812.

England's policy toward neutral trade. The foreign questions of greatest difficulty, however, arose from the renewal of the war in Europe, and the necessity of protecting our trade as a neutral nation. The battle of Trafalgar in 1805 gave England a naval supremacy that she had not had in the previous war, and with this renewed power to enforce her demands, she revived the practices to which we had then objected. The British mercantile interests, jealous of the prosperity of the American marine, called for action, and in 1805, in the case of the *Essex*, Sir William Scott reversed his previous decision in the case of the *Polly*, and declared liable to seizure French colonial products, even though landed and paying duty in American ports, unless it could be shown that they had actually become the property of American merchants, and that the intention was to keep them in America. In 1807 the protective clauses of the Jay treaty expired, and the substitute treaty which William Pinkney, as special commissioner, and Monroe, the regular minister in England, secured, was so unsatisfactory that Jefferson refused to present it to the Senate. England was, therefore, left free to adopt such policy as pleased her, and her program for the regulation and control of the trade of neutrals was made continuously more complete. In May, 1806, the coast of Europe from Ostend to Brest was declared blockaded by England, and the British Orders in Council of January 7, 1807, and November 11, 1807, had the effect of extending this blockade to every port of Europe from which the British flag was excluded. England declared that this policy was retaliatory, her Orders being in answer to Napoleon's Decrees, which will be subsequently mentioned. Napoleon stated that his first Decree was in answer to the Brest blockade. To neutrals the question of which belligerent was primarily at fault was of small moment compared with the practical fact that neutral trade was hampered and vexed.

The manner in which the officers of the British navy actually exercised these so-called belligerent rights was not less obnoxious than the claims themselves. It was found more convenient to blockade the American coast than that of Europe; and two frigates were therefore stationed off New York to examine the papers of vessels leaving port, and if their destination or cargoes appeared contrary to the Orders, they were sent to Halifax for judgment by the admiralty court there. In performing this police duty, in 1806, the English accidentally shot and killed an American sailor, John Pierce. *Blockade of New York.*

Still more troublesome was the matter of impressment. The increase of American trade, which, adjusting itself to conditions, continued to grow until 1808, called every year for four thousand new sailors, and high wages and good *Impressments.*

treatment induced many to desert the English service, both public and private, for the American. This whetted the zeal of English naval officers in making impressments. It was estimated that 2500 sailors deserted the British marine, public and private, every year, and that impressments amounted to 1000 a year. This difficulty culminated when, on June 22, 1807, the *Leopard* fired on, stopped, and took men from the United States frigate *Chesapeake*. Such an insult was even more distressing than the impressment of men from private merchant vessels. England, indeed, did not venture to defend the act, but made difficulties about the form of apology, and a call to war swept over the country as it had in 1794, when England was reported to have unleashed the Algerian pirates.

French policy toward neutral trade.

The policy of France was as disastrous to neutrals as that of England. After Trafalgar, Napoleon despaired of reaching England directly, and saw that he could conquer her only by cutting off her trade, the source of her wealth. He planned to close the continent to English goods, and until his fall this was the predominant idea in his wars and alliances. He professed to be the champion of the freedom of the seas, but his policy took the form of declaring England beyond the range of law, and of stamping as English allies all neutrals who did not maintain their rights against her. On November 21, 1806, he issued the Berlin Decree, declaring the British Isles in a state of blockade. As the French had no men-of-war, but only privateers at sea, this decree would not materially affect neutral vessels on their way to England, but any vessel coming from the ports of England could be seized on entering a French port. On December 7, 1807, he followed this with the Milan Decree, which declared any vessel that should submit to be searched by an English vessel, or should enter a port of England or her colonies, denationalized and liable to capture.

With the two belligerents equally maltreating us, it was

difficult indeed to formulate a policy for the United States. One party, after the *Chesapeake* affair, clamored for war with England. The majority of the Federalists would have preferred war with France. Jefferson would war with neither, but would bring both to reason by arguments addressed to their self-interest. In his youth he had been much impressed with the efficacy of the nonimportation agreements directed against England. As Secretary of State he had submitted a report to Congress, advising that we coerce foreign nations into a liberal policy toward us by commercial discrimination. He argued that we exported things absolutely necessary to foreign nations, such as food and raw materials; that we received luxuries and things that we could do without; and that, therefore, our trade was more important to them than theirs to us.

He first directed this policy against England, and had introduced into Congress a nonimportation bill, excluding such British goods as could be replaced by goods from other nations or could be produced at home. This was passed in March, 1806, to go into effect on November 15, if England did not come to terms before that date. It was subsequently suspended and went into operation only on December 14, 1807. It was intended as a threat only, not to be enforced. "What is it?" said Randolph, "a milk and water Bill! A dose of chicken broth to be taken nine months hence." Eight days after the nonimportation act went into effect, it was replaced by the more vigorous measure of an embargo, utterly prohibiting all foreign intercourse and requiring coasting vessels to give bond to go only to domestic ports. While the embargo was nominally directed equally against France and England, it was really upon the latter country that it fell hardest. It was, in fact, an extension of Napoleon's continental system of exhausting England by depriving her of her markets. So true was this, that one of the French ministers said, "The Emperor applauds the em-

Marginal notes:

Jefferson's policy of commercial coercion.

Nonimportation and embargo.

bargo," and many Federalists believed that it was dictated by Jefferson's French sympathies. This charge was unjust, for the embargo was, in fact, a particular hobby of Jefferson's, who believed that he had discovered in it a substitute for war.

The effects of the embargo.

Like war, the embargo was not one-sided. It substituted a test of passive endurance for one of active conflict. England, indeed, suffered severely, but the government remained firm, its aristocratic structure enabling it to resist popular discontent. In the United States the embargo was a greater blow to the mercantile interests than any measure yet taken by the belligerents, or than war itself would have been. Some of the Federalist leaders again talked of a secession of the states of New England, and in practice the act was very generally evaded by smuggling. Smuggling led to the passage of various enforcement acts of great rigor. These, the legislature of Massachusetts declared, February 15, 1809, "in many respects unjust, oppressive, and unconstitutional, and not legally binding on the citizens of this state." It, however, counseled obedience and remonstrance to Congress.

Repeal of the embargo.

In the meantime, the embargo was proving even more disastrous to the agricultural interests and particularly to the planters, who could not dispose of their crops, although they had to continue to support their slaves. The Federalists, led in the House of Representatives by Josiah Quincy of Massachusetts, were joined by dissatisfied Republicans like Joseph Story and John Randolph, and the embargo was brought to an end March 1, 1809. Thus, three days before his retirement, Jefferson was forced to see the failure of his favorite experiment in international relations, and to submit to almost his only defeat from Congress, which, most largely through the democratic weapon of argument, he had ruled more completely than any President before or after.

BIBLIOGRAPHICAL NOTES

Every student should read Jefferson's inaugural, Richardson's *Messages*, I, 321–324. The *Writings* of Jefferson and the *Works* of Gallatin are generally interesting and useful. If available, *An Inquiry into the Principles and Policy of Government in the United States*, by John Taylor (of Caroline), 530–571, gives a clear view of Virginia constitutional theories. *Sources.*

Adams, H., *Administrations of Jefferson and Madison*, I, chs. V–VII, is the best account of the intellectual condition of the country for the period. In general, however, and particularly for narrative, this invaluable work is not usable for class work, as it is long and is too well knit to break up easily into selections. Channing, E., *The Jeffersonian System*, is distinctly workable. See also Trent, *Southern Statesmen of the Old Régime*. *Historical accounts. General.*

Fish, C. R., *Civil Service*, chs. II and III. *Civil service.*

Allen, G. W., *The Barbary Wars*. *Barbary policy.*

Adams, H., *Randolph*, ch. IV. Cox, I. J., *Exploration of Louisiana Purchase*, 1803–1806 (Am. Hist. Assoc., *Report*, 1904, vol. I, 149–174). Ogg, F. A., *The Opening of the Mississippi*. Story, J., *Commentaries*, §§ 1277–1288, 1317–1321. Sparks, J., *John Ledyard* (Library of American Biography, vol. XIV). Turner, F. J., *Diplomatic Contest for the Mississippi Valley* (*Atlantic*, vol. 93, 676–691). *Louisiana.*

Callender, G. S., *Economic History*, 239–260. Foster, J. W., *Century of American Diplomacy*. Moore, J. B., *American Diplomacy*, chs. III and V. Schouler, J., *United States*, II, ch. VI, secs. 1, 2. See also Adams as noted above. *Diplomacy.*

Other valuable biographies are: Adams, H., *Gallatin;* Dodd, W. E., *Statesmen of the Old South*, and *Macon;* Roosevelt, T., *Morris;* Quincy, E., *Quincy*. *Biography.*

CHAPTER VIII

The election of 1808.

THE election of 1808 occurred during the stress of the debate over the embargo. It was understood that Madison represented the administration policy, although Jefferson professed to stand neutral between the Republican candidates. Monroe was the candidate of Randolph and the "Quids," who attacked the growing consolidation of the government, and would have limited the embargo to American vessels, a measure which would have relieved the southern planter by allowing him to export his crops, but would not have benefited the maritime interests. The Vice President, George Clinton, felt that he deserved promotion, and that the northern democracy should be recognized. The contest was practically settled by the first public congressional caucus, which selected Madison and Clinton as the candidates; but in spite of this selection, Monroe was run for President in Virginia and Clinton in New York. The Federalists at first thought of supporting Monroe or Clinton, but in a secret meeting of the leaders in New York decided to repeat the ticket of 1804, presenting C. C. Pinckney and Rufus King. The Federalist candidates received the votes of all New England except Vermont, and, in addition, those of Delaware, and 5 in Maryland and North Carolina, 47 in all. Madison received 122, and Clinton 6 for President. The vote for Vice President was a little more scattering, but Clinton was reëlected.

The domestic policy of the new administration.

Madison had been a most efficient assistant. He had proved invaluable to Washington during the movement for the formation of the Union, and to Jefferson during the struggle for religious liberty in Virginia, and afterwards during the conflict with the Federalists and the establishment of the Republican régime. He was, however, a weak leader, and at once encountered congressional opposition. Fear of his opponents deterred him from promoting Gallatin from the treasury to the state department, and caused him to appoint to the latter Robert Smith, the weakest man who ever filled the office. Gallatin remained at the treasury, and Madison made up for Smith's incompetence by writing many of his dispatches. Probably no administration ever came into office with so few intentions; in fact, absence of intent was naturally its policy. The destruction of Federalist legislation had been almost completed under Jefferson; the party policy now demanded an administration without a history. There was a growing demand for internal improvements, such as Jefferson had favored, and this movement was fostered by Gallatin, but the majority were as yet so true to the principles of 1800 that the only thing accomplished was the granting of various small appropriations for the Cumberland Road. In 1811, though by a close vote, the National Bank was discontinued.

Foreign affairs, therefore, absorbed the main attention, and here Madison seemed at first to score a victory. The embargo had been succeeded by a nonintercourse act, prohibiting all trade with England and with France, but allowing it with the rest of the world. If, however, England would withdraw her "Orders," or Napoleon revoke his "Decrees," the prohibition would cease against the compliant power. Canning, the British minister of foreign affairs, proposed to take advantage of this offer, if he could at the same time secure other advantages, and so instructed Erskine, the English minister in the United States. The latter was a young man, with an American wife and American sympathies, and he consented to a treaty more favorable to America than

Nonintercourse.

Canning had intended. Madison promptly withdrew the prohibition of intercourse with England, and 1200 ships sailed for that country. Canning, however, promptly rejected the treaty, claiming that Erskine had exceeded his authority; nonintercourse was revived, and Madison's seeming victory was turned into defeat. Erskine was succeeded by Francis James Jackson, a disagreeable man, whom Madison was easily able to worst diplomatically, but whose year in America meant practically a cessation of negotiations.

Prosperity of American trade.

In the meantime, American trade was rapidly reviving; the mercantile marine of Massachusetts in 1809 was larger than ever before. Losses from seizures were guarded against by high freight rates and insurance. Neutral ports were utilized, as is shown by the growth of exports to Russia, from about $12,000 in 1806 to about $4,000,000 in 1810. Moreover, the laws of the United States were disobeyed, and many vessels sailed for England and France, while those countries issued many special licenses permitting the violation of their own regulations. This prosperity, however, was in spite of the restrictive commercial system of the Republicans and not because of it. This system had no victory to its credit, and it became steadily more unpopular. The result of this growing dissatisfaction was the passage in April, 1810, of Macon Bill number two, — the first and more stringent bill proposed by Macon having failed to pass the Senate, — which applied the system in its mildest form. This bill threw open all trade, but offered, in case either of the belligerents should change its obnoxious policy and the other should not follow this example within three months, to revive the nonimportation act against the country that remained obdurate.

Macon Bill number two.

Madison and Florida.

This act brought Madison into collision with Napoleon. It was not the first time. The Louisiana treaty had presented an ambiguity with regard to the eastern boundary. Madison claimed the territory up to the Perdido River, the present western boundary of the state of Florida, whereas the boundary intended was the Iberville River, just north of New Orleans. The dispute was between the United States and Spain, for France had ceded all she owned, whatever it might be, but Napoleon was master of Spain, and negotiations were actually with him. Napoleon cared nothing for the bit of territory, but it was important to the United States because it contained the mouths of many rivers whose upper waters were beginning to attract settlers. Ever since 1803 Napoleon had used this situation to influence American policy, offering to secure title when the United States might be of use to him, and withdrawing when the need had passed. On the whole Madison got the best of the game; for in 1810, as the result of a revolution by some American settlers in the region, he took possession of Baton Rouge and about half of the disputed area. The United States, however, had as yet no good international title.

Up to this time, however, Napoleon had reason to think of the United States as a friendly and almost docile power, for the commercial policy of restrictions, although not adopted to please him, was actually what he wanted, as it cut off an important branch of English trade. He had, to be sure, disapproved of the nonintercourse act, as it had allowed trade with the allies of France, which it had forbidden with her. As long as there was a possibility that England and the United States might come to terms, however, he had remained quiescent, in fact friendly, fearing an alliance between the two countries. When the disavowal of the Erskine treaty had made certain a period of ill feeling between them, he actively expressed his disapproval. He first ordered all American vessels within the range of his influence to be sequestered, that is, held for official examination, on the ground that those in French ports were violating United States law, and that those in the ports of French allies should not be allowed to trade while trade with France was prohibited. On

Napoleon and nonintercourse.

March 23, 1810, the Rambouillet Decree ordered the sale of this property, amounting to $8,400,000, and consisting of 51 vessels in France, 44 in Spain, 28 in Naples, and 11 in Holland. Napoleon was in hopes that this order might cause a reëstablishment of the embargo, which he would be glad to see, and the property which he held might be used to secure concessions from the United States, and to prevent retaliation. The main purpose of his policy, the cutting off of England's trade with the United States, was still secure.

The Cadore letter.

Very different was the situation created by the Macon Bill number two, which threw the restrictive system to the winds and unsealed one of England's best markets. Napoleon promptly, but secretly, ordered the absolute confiscation of all the American property sequestered and sold, to clear up accounts for the past, and on the same day, August 5, 1810, dictated a letter which his foreign minister, Cadore, communicated to the United States. This announced that the Decrees of Berlin and Milan "are revoked, and after November 1, they will cease to have effect, . . . it being well understood that in consequence of this declaration the English are to revoke their Orders in Council and renounce the new principle of blockade which they have wished to establish," or that the United States "cause their rights to be respected by the English." "His majesty loves the Americans. Their prosperity and their commerce are within the scope of his policy."

Madison accepts the Cadore letter.

Madison received this letter with delight, and requested England to revoke her Orders. The Marquis of Wellesley, who had now succeeded Canning in the management of English foreign affairs, replied that Cadore's letter made the repeal conditional on the action of England, and that the Decrees were actually being enforced. Napoleon did not hasten to explain the ambiguity. In fact he had no intention of abandoning his continental system, but proposed, even if England withdrew her Orders, to secure his ends by internal regulations. Madison, however, was not aware of this intention, and as England still refused to recall her Orders, he issued a proclamation under the authority of Macon Bill number two, reviving nonintercourse with that country on February 2, 1811. Congress sustained him by an act of March 2, but word soon reached America that Napoleon still seized all vessels violating the Decrees, and during the spring the balance hung between peace and war.   Monroe, who had become Secretary of State, was in favor of breaking negotiations with France; Madison still clung to his belief in Napoleon. The latter, at the critical moment, released the American vessels he held. The administration decided in his favor ; a new minister, Joel Barlow, the poet, was sent to France, and Napoleon had the satisfaction of closing the American market to England once more. It was already beginning to be evident that he might look to the United States for still more active assistance.

The situation was changing in the United States. A new generation was coming to the front, composed of young men born during or after the Revolution, whose boyhood had been filled with tales of that war. They felt a greater confidence in the future of the country, a more unreasoning patriotism than the older men who had been so long at the helm, and their pride was stung by the bickering, ineffectual neutrality which we had for twenty years been practicing. One group of such young leaders came from South Carolina. That state was now ready to play a leading part in the national life. A long struggle between the planters of the coast and the frontier farmer element descending from the mountains, had been brought to a close in 1808 by a constitutional arrangement between the sections, by which each controlled one house of the legislature. The spread of the plantation system resulting from the expanding cultivation of cotton was soon to make the state a political unit. The South Carolina leaders, some sprung from the cultivated English and Huguenot stock about Charleston, some from the sturdy Scotch-Irish

A new generation.

element of the piedmont, were freed from state contests, and prepared to turn their united attention to national affairs. In the new Congress William Lowndes and John C. Calhoun appeared for the first time, while Langdon Cheves had been a member for but a part of the previous session. These were all for war, but, except for their inherited antipathy to England, were impartial as between France and England. Calhoun would fight both.

The influence of the frontier.
The direction in which this energy would turn was determined by the young men of another section. The frontier had been expanding with great rapidity. Population had stretched along both banks of the Ohio and parts of the Mississippi, the Tennessee, and the Cumberland. This advance had not been with regular, closed front, as Washington had advised, but along the lines of most attraction or least resistance. The government under the Republicans had rapidly extended the purchase of Indian lands, with the general idea of obtaining the possession of river banks rather than of steady progressive occupation. In 1804 the minimum amount of public land sold, was reduced to one hundred and sixty acres, the minimum price remaining at two dollars an acre, and the method being that none was sold by private sale until after it was offered at public auction. New land offices were opened at convenient points in the West, and, under the credit system established in 1800, the settler could buy land that was on the market for eighty dollars down, eighty more at the end of two years, and similar payments at the end of the third and fourth years. This did not satisfy the restless frontiersmen, who pressed on, seeking the most attractive spots or impelled by a desire for change, regardless of government regulations. They settled in land not yet placed on sale, or even in regions not yet purchased from the Indians, and asked that, when these locations were actually surveyed, the settler be given the right to purchase at the minimum price by private sale before the public auction took place. At first

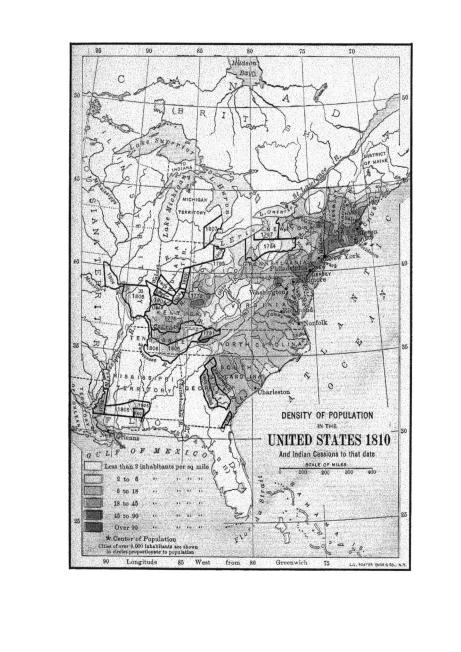

DENSITY OF POPULATION
IN THE
UNITED STATES 1810
And Indian Cessions to that date

SCALE OF MILES
0   100   200   300   400

Less than 2 inhabitants per sq mile
2 to 6   "   "   "   "
6 to 18   "   "   "   "
18 to 45   "   "   "   "
45 to 90   "   "   "   "
Over 90   "   "   "   "

★ Center of Population
Cities of over 8,000 inhabitants are shown
in circles proportionate to population

L.L. POATES ENGR'G CO., N.Y.

the government endeavored to drive out such unauthorized squatters, but government authority was not sufficiently strong to keep them out of the wilderness. As western influence grew in politics the demand for legal recognition of the right of the squatter to preëmption in the purchase of his holding became more insistent. In several special cases it was granted, and this encouraged others to settle where they wished, in the hope that they would subsequently be granted rights. The result was that the frontier was irregular and far flung. Great and powerful Indian tribes interposed between the settlements of eastern Georgia and those of Louisiana, on the one hand, and of Tennessee, on the other. Back of the thread of river farms in Indiana and Illinois were other tribes still unbroken. Hence the people of Georgia, Tennessee, Kentucky, Ohio, Louisiana, and even Vermont may be said to have been living under frontier conditions; one fifth of the whole population of the United States and represented, after the admission of Louisiana as a state in April, 1812, by 12 senators out of 36; and, under the census of 1810, by 35 out of 182 representatives.

This section was even more powerful from its unanimity than from its size. Every new purchase of land aroused greater hostility among the Indians. Two great Indians, brothers, — Tecumseh, the statesman, and Olliwochica, the prophet, — were organizing the tribes to resist further encroachments; and they were universally believed to receive support from the British in Canada. The crisis came when the Indians denied the legality of the last great purchase along the Wabash. Hostilities broke out, and on November 5, 1811, William Henry Harrison, governor of Indiana Territory, won the important victory of Tippecanoe. An Indian war was thus begun, and the frontiersmen believed that they must fight the British, at any rate, secretly. They thought that it would be better to do it openly, and that the conquest of Canada was possible and was the soundest solution of the

Indian war in the West.

Indian question. Representatives of such ideas were Felix
Grundy and John Sevier of Tennessee, and R. M. Johnson
and Henry Clay of Kentucky.

These young leaders, known as the "War Hawks," controlled the Congress that came together in the fall of 1811.
Clay was elected Speaker, and he gave the important committee chairmanships to men of like views. A war program
was rushed through Congress. Republican repugnance to a
navy was still, indeed, strong enough to thwart Cheves and
Lowndes in their endeavors to prepare for ocean warfare,
but land forces were abundantly provided for. The regular
army was to be increased by 25,000 men, the President was
authorized to employ 50,000 volunteers, new regulations for
the militia were adopted, and half a million was appropriated
for coast defense. Madison, though looking upon war rather
with apprehension than with enthusiasm, followed the new
leaders and put their policy into effect. Already he had withdrawn our minister, William Pinkney, from England, as a
result of the misunderstanding over the Cadore letter. The
English government, now somewhat alarmed at the prospect of war, sent over A. J. Foster, who at length arranged the
Chesapeake affair and some minor matters. Public opinion,
however, was not appeased, and Madison inflamed the hostility toward England by making public the papers of a
British spy, John Henry, who had been sent in 1809 to report
on public sentiment in New England. These papers, which
Madison had secured in a somewhat romantic manner, contained no startling disclosures, but they evinced an unfriendly
and suspicious attitude on the part of England. On April 1,
1812, Madison recommended an embargo of sixty days, which
was considered as preparatory to war. On June 1 he sent in a
long message reviewing our negotiations with England, and
suggesting that Congress consider the question of war. On
June 18 Congress passed the crucial measure, and the war
was begun. On June 23, before news of the war reached

England, the ministry, after a hard struggle in Parliament, had yielded to the accumulated complaints of English manufacturers who were impoverished and laborers who were starving because of the cutting off of American trade, and withdrew its Orders. The war party in the United States, however, was really more influenced by ill feeling caused by twenty years of rude treatment, and by the Indian question, than by a desire to win commercial privileges. The impressment question, moreover, remained unsettled, and so this action of England did not affect their determination to persist in the war.

This war policy was not adopted without opposition. John Randolph and a few other Republicans joined with the Federalists, led by Josiah Quincy, in fighting it, step by step, through Congress. Even now that war had been declared, it was still hoped by these leaders that the election in the fall would reverse the decision. The Republicans in congressional caucus renominated Madison, and selected Elbridge Gerry for the vice presidency. Monroe, now Secretary of State, supported the administration. George Clinton was dead, but his more talented nephew, DeWitt Clinton, decided to run as a northern and peace candidate. He was nominated by the Republican members of the New York legislature, and his nomination was indorsed by a convention of Federalists which met at New York. The election was fought out strictly on the war issue, and the result showed the important position, as arbiter between the sections, which the frontier had come to occupy. The old thirteen coast states gave 90 electoral votes to Madison and 89 to Clinton; the five new western states gave their 38 votes solidly for war. Of the coast states, New England gave its 43 votes for peace; the 59 votes south of the Potomac were for war; the Middle States divided 31 for war and 46 for peace. Madison's majority was unexpectedly narrow; the change of the single state of Pennsylvania situated in the closely divided region would have elected Clinton.

The election of 1812.

The international situation.

The War of 1812 was no more a single-handed conflict between the United States and England than was the Revolution. In 1776 the conflict began in America and spread to Europe; in 1812 the United States was at length drawn into the great struggle from which all her elder statesmen had been for nineteen years endeavoring to keep her free. It is noticeable that the one great country whose interests were very similar to our own, Russia, had just taken the other side in the conflict. We felt most keenly the violation of neutral rights by England; Russia, the exactions of Napoleon's continental system. At the very time that Russia accepted war with France for the express purpose of protecting her growing commerce with the United States, the latter went to war with England, and the weight of the neutral powers was thus balanced. Russia allied herself with England, but we did not correspondingly join Napoleon. We had suffered almost equally from both parties; since the beginning of hostilities in Europe, according to a report made to Congress July 6, 1812, Great Britain had made 917 seizures, of which more than half had been returned as illegal; France 558, of which about one quarter had been similarly returned. In spite of traditional sympathy, even Madison shared in the feeling of Calhoun that the logical thing, however impractical, was to make war upon both. The administration, therefore, refrained from an alliance with France, but French success meant the success of the United States, and the war press followed with exultation the invasion of Russia, and with growing affright Napoleon's desperate struggle of 1813 and 1814.

Conditions in the United States.

The United States was ill prepared for war. During the long period of Jefferson's economy the means of defense had been cut down to the slenderest. The great reduction of the debt might have been expected to improve credit, but this was offset by the hostility of the merchant class, which possessed the greater part of the ready money, and by the disappearance of the United States Bank, which would have managed the necessary loans. There was, moreover, a great reduction in the revenue. Nearly all sources of income had been discarded except the tariff, and during the war the blockade of the coast by the overwhelming navy of Great Britain rendered the income from that source small and precarious. Trade did not indeed cease. The English needed American foodstuffs for their armies in Spain, and by special license Baltimore merchants drove a thriving trade thither; sending in 1813, $15,500,000 worth, chiefly flour, to the peninsula. The English, too, did not extend their blockade to the New England coast until April 25, 1814, and Boston merchants supplied, at least to some extent, the English at Halifax; but between December 10, 1813, and April 4, 1814, this trade was partly interrupted by a domestic embargo. The import trade, upon which alone duties could be collected, was still more interrupted, being confined almost entirely to New England ports. As the duties were doubled, the collections at Boston actually increased until that port was blockaded, but were not sufficient to offset their almost entire cessation elsewhere. In 1813, Congress imposed for the second time a direct tax, and revived the Federalist expedient of an excise. All these resources together produced only a little over $10,000,000 a year; and to meet the excess expense of about $20,000,000 a year Gallatin resorted to treasury notes and permanent loans. These loans amounted during the war to $98,000,000, and the government found great difficulty in marketing them; they brought in much less than their face value and paid high interest, the first seven and one half per cent. The government, moreover, was not a strong one on the administrative side. Gallatin was not popular and left the country in 1813 as peace commissioner. His office was filled, after an interval, by Alexander Dallas, also of Pennsylvania, and a strong man, though not the equal of Gallatin. In the other departments Monroe was the only really able official, and he cannot be considered as first class. Madison, himself, was not a vigorous chief executive, and inefficiency permeated the administration.

Naval duels. The American navy at the opening of the war — aside from Jefferson's gunboats, one hundred and seventy in number, intended only for coast defense and of very little use even for that purpose — consisted of frigates and sloops built during the Federalist régime. All together there were about twenty vessels, and not one able to oppose an English line-of-battle ship. Eleven British ships of the line and about ninety other vessels were on American stations at the outbreak of hostilities. The administration proposed to keep the American vessels in harbor for coast defense, but Rogers with a small squadron put forth to sea without waiting for orders, and the remonstrances of naval officers backed by the early successes of the navy succeeded in bringing about a change of plan. The American commanders' object was to cruise on well-known British trade routes and destroy commerce. While they were forced to flee when they encountered a ship of the line, they were anxious to meet British frigates singly, for the American naval department had hit upon the clever device of building frigates somewhat superior to those of corresponding rank in the British navy. On August 19, 1812, the *Constitution*, Captain Hull, encountered the *Guerrière*. After a sharp fight the *Guerrière* struck and soon after sank. This was the first of a series of naval duels: the *Wasp* fought the *Frolic*; the *United States*, the *Macedonian*; the *Constitution*, the *Java*; the *Chesapeake*, the *Shannon*; and in all of these contests except the last the American vessel won. These encounters attracted an attention far beyond their intrinsic importance. The English had looked upon themselves as invincible upon the sea against almost any odds. Brougham had said in Parliament: "The assembled navies of America could not lay siege to an English sloop of war." The fact that in nearly all these

cases the American vessels were slightly superior in size
and weight of metal, was less important than the fact that
they showed in each encounter superior speed and maneuver-
ing qualities and better marksmanship. The American crews
were better treated, and proved to be more efficient.

In America these successes aroused much enthusiasm,
Congress became much more liberal towards the navy, and
several battleships were laid down. These were not, however, finished before the war ended; the existing vessels were
picked off one after another by the British, or blockaded in
port, and by 1814 the navy was almost driven from the sea.
Five hundred and twenty-six privateers from time to time
assisted the navy in the work of commerce destroying, taking
over thirteen hundred prizes, but most of these too were
finally captured or blockaded. The naval record of the War
of 1812 was brilliant, considering American resources. In
captures, the two countries were about equal; the Americans claimed all together about 1750, the British navy captured 1683, and British privateers a small number. The
effect upon the ocean, however, was totally different in the
case of the two countries. Although English insurance rates
rose decidedly, and the commercial interests became, to
some degree, hostile to the war, English commerce was not
demoralized, while that of the United States was, by the
end of the war, arrested. Moreover, none of the English
military operations on the seacoast were impeded. Great
Britain remained mistress of the ocean. Naval warfare on
the Lakes, however, told a different story.

The war party had put its hopes chiefly on the land war, The first year
hoping to coerce England by the conquest of Canada. It was of the war on
land.
thought by many that the Canadians would welcome the
American armies as liberators from a hated yoke. This view
overlooked the fact that the seat of war, upper Canada or
Ontario, had been settled very largely by American Loyalists,
whose devotion to the Crown was strengthened by their

bitterness toward those who had driven them from their homes and deprived them of their estates. The incompetence of many of the generals first selected, and the difficulty of mobilizing armies composed chiefly of militia, added to the difficulties, but perhaps still more important was the wild nature of the ·country, rendering an extensive campaign of conquest almost impossible. The first invasion, directed from Detroit by General Hull, recoiled upon American soil. Hull and his army were captured, and the peninsula of Michigan fell under British control, while British expeditions penetrated the wilderness of Wisconsin to the Mississippi, and occupied Fort Dearborn on the site of what is now Chicago. Meanwhile, the fighting on the Niagara frontier was indecisive, — in effect an American defeat, as the Americans had taken the initiative. An advance northward along the line of Lake Champlain also proved abortive.

The navy of the Lakes came to the assistance of the army. On September 10, 1813, Oliver Hazard Perry, having constructed a fleet, largely out of green timber, defeated the English and won control of Lake Erie. With his assistance, *The overthrow of the Indians.* William Henry Harrison invaded Canada, and on October 5 defeated the English in the battle of the Thames. This battle was particularly pleasing to the frontiersmen, for Tecumseh was killed and the confederation of northwestern Indians broken up. The same fall saw the last uprising of the Creek Indians. They had been roused by the eloquence of Tecumseh, who had visited them in 1811, and, knowing of the English war, on August 30, 1813, surprised and massacred about four hundred whites gathered in Fort Mimms on the Alabama. Tennessee was promptly aroused, and General Andrew Jackson, with an army of frontiersmen, descended upon the Indians and on March 27, 1814, at the Great Horseshoe Bend, administered a severe and lasting defeat.

English projects in 1814. In spite of these successes the year 1814 opened inauspiciously. Napoleon abdicated April 11, and England could direct her entire energies to the American war. A vigorous campaign was planned; an expedition on Burgoyne's old route down Lake Champlain, a harrying of the coast, particularly of the Chesapeake, by mixed naval and military forces, with attacks on Washington and Baltimore, and, most important of all, a great expedition against New Orleans.

The coast expedition had a fair share of success during the summer. It made several descents on New England, and in August temporarily occupied Washington and burned the Capitol. In September, however, it received a severe check on its attack on Baltimore, where Fort McHenry successfully resisted the fleet, making a defense which inspired Francis Scott Key to write *The Star Spangled Banner*, which immediately became the most popular of the national anthems. The Champlain project was thwarted by a naval battle near Plattsburg, New York, where, on September 11, Commodore Macdonough defeated an English flotilla, and maintained control of the lake, thus making an advance by the English army impracticable. The greatest and the most ominous of the undertakings, that against New Orleans, was still impending during the fall. The fate of the Mississippi valley seemed again uncertain. The Louisiana region contained only about 150,000 inhabitants; it was isolated from the rest of the United States; the loyalty of its Creole population to the United States had never been proved and was strongly suspected. In the hands of a foreign power, it would become a menace to the Union, as it had been before the purchase. Timothy Pickering wrote that he did not expect any western members to attend the opening of Congress. Just at this time domestic affairs reached a crisis more acute than any since 1798; if, indeed, they were then as full of peril.

The administration, following Jefferson's plans, had hoped to rely to a very great extent on the militia for its military operations. This reliance proved delusive, for the state

Depression in 1814.

Domestic disaffection.

authorities made many difficulties about the appointment of militia officers, and about the employment of the militia in Canada or even outside the state to which it belonged. While General Van Rensselaer and his troops were fighting against superior numbers on the Canada side of the Niagara River, New York militia, eyewitnesses of the conflict, refused to cross to their assistance. This attitude was most marked in New England, where opposition to the war was very strong. The general dissatisfaction which had been felt for twelve years at New England's constantly decreasing influence, naturally culminated when she was drawn into a war against England, which country she believed to be defending the cause of just and sound government. George Cabot had predicted, in 1804, that in case of "a war with Great Britain, manifestly provoked by our rulers, . . . separation will then be unavoidable, when our loyalty to the Union is generally perceived to be the instrument of debasement and impoverishment." The Federalists secured control of all the New England state governments, and on October 17, 1814, Massachusetts called a convention to meet at Hartford to discuss the situation.

The Hartford Convention.

Twenty-three delegates met at Hartford on December 15, 1814. George Cabot presided but, either from constitutional dislike of action, or because his wisdom grew with the importance of the event and he realized that the majority still favored the Union, he took a fairly conservative stand. In secret session the convention formulated its demands: that the power of Congress to make war, to make new states, and to lay embargoes or restrict commerce be limited by constitutional amendment; that amendments be adopted providing that the President serve only one term, and that successive Presidents should not come from the same state; and that the representation of the southern states based on slave population be abolished. The states were also advised to demand a portion of the national taxes raised within their limits to be used for purposes of local defense; and, while awaiting the answer to these *ultimata,* to make certain antidemocratic changes in their laws, and to protect their citizens from the draft for military service which the administration was at that very time, though unsuccessfully, urging Congress to order. If the national government should not grant these demands within six months, it was recommended that another convention be held. While it is very doubtful whether a majority in any New England state would have supported an actual proposition to secede, even if these demands had been refused, the state of the Union seemed very dubious when the Massachusetts and Connecticut commissioners appointed to present the conclusions of the convention approached Washington in the middle of January, 1815.

Two events occurred before they reached there, however, that rendered their mission so obviously useless that they returned home without presenting their demands. The first of these was the defeat of the New Orleans expedition by General Jackson, in a battle on January 8, which aroused to enthusiasm the patriotic pride of the Americans. Frontiersmen from Tennessee and Kentucky had descended to the assistance of the local levies, and had defeated a superior force of the enemy, consisting of picked troops who had served with Wellington, and who were supported by a large fleet. The battle enheartened those who were discouraged, and renewed the war spirit. Both the spirit and the battle, however, were unnecessary, for, before the battle had been fought, peace had been signed, although news of it did not reach America until later.

Negotiations had been begun almost as soon as hostilities. Russia, desirous of concentrating all England's strength against France, and friendly to the United States, had offered mediation. This offer was accepted by the United States in the spring of 1813. Napoleon's fortunes were waning rapidly, and it was to be feared that the whole weight of England's

Battle of New Orleans.

Peace negotiations.

power might be directed against us. John Quincy Adams,
Gallatin, and James A. Bayard, a Federalist senator from Delaware, were appointed commissioners. England refused the
mediation, but the commissioners remained abroad, and
in 1814 direct negotiations were begun. Henry Clay and
Jonathan Russell were added to the commission, and Ghent
was arranged as the place of meeting with the English commissioners. The latter were instructed to demand a "recti-
fication" of the boundary line, the establishment of an independent buffer Indian state between the Ohio and the Lakes,
and other concessions. The American commissioners refused to treat on this basis. The Duke of Wellington told
the British government that the military situation did not
justify such demands and would not while the Americans
had control of the Lakes. The English industrial and commercial classes were eager for peace and a renewal of trade, and
brought such pressure to bear upon the government that it
receded, first from one point, and then from another, until
at length a treaty was agreed to on Christmas eve, 1814,
upon the basis of the *status quo ante bellum*, or a return to
the conditions before the war. As we had gone to war for
the redress of grievances this was, strictly speaking, a defeat,
but the change of circumstances resulting from the defeat of
Napoleon made it seem a distinct victory. It was not a
return to the condition before the war, because with the cessation of war in Europe, the violation of our neutral rights
actually ceased; moreover, the Indians of the southwest and
northwest, although they still remained on their lands, had
been decisively defeated and ceased to be a factor in war or
diplomacy. The news of the treaty, coming in close conjunction with Jackson's great victory, turned the country
from depression to rejoicing; the commissioners of Massachusetts and Connecticut returned without even proceeding
to Washington, and all fear of disunion vanished with the
announcement of the peace.

BIBLIOGRAPHICAL NOTES

For war speeches: Colton, C., *The Life, etc., of Henry Clay*, I, Sources. 159–185; and Calhoun, J. C., *Works*, II, 1–13. For peace speeches: see Harding, S. B., *Select Orations*, 175–190 (John Randolph); and Quincy, E., *Josiah Quincy*, 281–300. These speeches are also to be found in the *Annals of Congress*. For the peace negotiations: Adams, J. Q., *Memoirs*, III, 1–144, perhaps the best opportunity for the general student to become acquainted with this diary, owing to the concentration of interest. Ames, H. V., *State Documents*, 54–88, and Macdonald, W., *Select Documents*, No. 32, give material on the Hartford Convention.

Babcock, K. C., *The Rise of American Nationality*, is particu- Historical larly good on the western aspects of the war movement. Into accounts. the more intricate complications of the diplomatic web the author has not found it expedient to lead the students in a general course. McMaster, *United States*, III, 529–540, and Schouler, *United States*, vol. II, ch. VIII, sec. 1, give most students more than Henry Adams. On the Hartford Convention, H. C. Lodge's *George Cabot*, chs. X–XIII, throws more light than anything else. Hildreth, R., *United States*, VI, 464–477, 544–554, is useful where available. On the war itself, Mahan, A. T., *Sea Power in its Relation to the War of 1812*, especially chs. V, IX, XI, and XVII, makes good and valuable reading. His chapter XVIII is also the most comprehensible account of the peace negotiations. Schouler, *United States*, II, 417–491, has a lively account of the war.

CHAPTER IX

THE PERIOD OF TRANSITION — NEW SOCIAL, ECONOMIC, AND POLITICAL CONDITIONS

The period of transition. THE close of the War of 1812 marks the beginning of a new epoch in the history of the United States. From 1760 to 1815 two great problems, our relations with Europe and the organization of government, absorbed the energies of the nation. The tendencies of national development and the characteristics and interests of the several sections remained fairly constant. Now, new problems, new tendencies, and changing characteristics are discernible. For about fifteen years, however, representatives of the passing generation remained in partial control, and we have a period of transition. During this transitional period the old conflict between Federalists and Republicans quieted down, the party in power utilized what was more permanent in the policies of both, and the period is called the "Era of Good Feeling." At the same time new sections were working out their principles, new leaders were endeavoring to find natural bonds of union and points of difference, and politically it might be called with equal truth the "Era of Factional Conflict." Party politics almost ceased, but personal, sectional, and economic differences were more pronounced than ever before.

The disappearance of the Federalists. The Federalists never recovered from the ill repute brought upon them by the Hartford Convention and the rumors circulated as to its secret purposes. They continued to be a factor in some states and to send to Congress a minority distinguished by such men as Rufus King and Daniel

Webster, but their influence was merely as a makeweight between factions of their opponents. The democratic spirit of Jefferson had definitely triumphed over the aristocratic leanings of the Essex Junto.

On the other hand the war had caused the administration to depart still farther from the path of strict construction from which Jefferson himself had begun to stray. The new war leaders were inspired by a love of the Union, and favored an active policy which required liberal national powers. Therefore Congress adopted more and more, in spite of occasional protests and checks, the Hamiltonian policy of broad construction. It is not altogether fantastic to say that Hamiltonian policies, carried out in the Jeffersonian spirit, formed the political code of the new period. *Acceptance of broad construction.*

With these favoring conditions, the Supreme Court, under the leadership of John Marshall, began a series of great decisions which crystallized this constitutional theory and gave it permanence. In 1803 the Court, in the case of *Marbury* v. *Madison*, declared that a law of Congress, when repugnant to the Constitution, was void. In 1810, in the case of *Fletcher* v. *Peck*, it decided that the national Constitution forbade a state to violate a contract made with a private person. In 1819, in the famous case of *Dartmouth College* v. *Woodward*, the Court accepted the argument of Daniel Webster, the counsel for the college, that a charter of a private corporation is a contract within the meaning of the Constitution and cannot be impaired by state law. In the case of the *United States* v. *Judge Peters*, in 1809, the Court asserted the supremacy of the national courts over the state authorities. In the case of *Martin* v. *Hunter's Lessee*, in 1816, the Supreme Court accepted an appeal from the decision of a Virginia court, on the ground that the interpretation of the national Constitution was involved; and in 1821, in the case of *Cohens* v. *Virginia*, it was decided that a case might, if the interpretation of the national Con- *Activity of the Supreme Court.*

stitution were involved, be transferred from the state to the national courts, even before the former had given a decision. These last two rulings brought an immense amount of business to the national courts, and therefore increased their prestige. The strict constructionists of Virginia were seriously alarmed. Official protests were made, and John Taylor, in vigorous pamphlets, defended the state courts, but no successful method of checking the activity of the national court was devised. In the cases of *McCulloch* v. *Maryland*, 1819, and *Osborn et al.* v. *The Bank of the United States*, 1824, the doctrine of "implied powers" was broadly affirmed, Marshall using much the same line of argument that Hamilton had employed in 1791 when the question of the first United States Bank came up. Of very great and increasing importance is the case of *Gibbons* v. *Ogden*, decided in 1824, which held that the monopoly of steam navigation in the waters of the state, which the New York legislature had given Fulton and his patron Livingston, was unconstitutional and void because it conflicted with the power given by the Constitution to Congress to regulate interstate commerce. This decision at once threw open all the navigable waters of the country to competition, and it became the starting point for the interpretation of this clause, upon which so much of the subsequent legislation of Congress has rested.

The Court, under Marshall, was careful to guard what it held to be the rights of the states, as in the case of *Ogden* v. *Saunders*, 1827, in which it upheld the right of New York to pass a bankruptcy act, if fairly drawn and administered, and thus give a debtor a discharge from his debts. Marshall, indeed, held that the states were as strictly sovereign within the range of their powers as was the United States government. Yet the general trend of his decisions was in the direction of nationalization and extension of the functions of the general government.

Marshall's influence.

No series of judicial decisions ever exerted so much

political influence as these. Framed largely by one mind and upon a consistent theory, they formed a starting point from which the Supreme Court has developed the great structure of constitutional law as it stands to-day. Judge Marshall, moreover, wrote unhampered by the necessity of constant reference to preceding cases which renders judicial decisions at present so technical and difficult of understanding for the average man. His style was simple and convincing, his personality venerable and sympathetic, and, far from merely reflecting the trend of thought, he was a decided factor among the many that were leading the nation to think nationally.

A less attractive manifestation of the nationalistic feeling is noticed by travelers writing of the United States after 1815, who speak of a certain blatant patriotism, not mentioned by those before the war. The typical American was boastful of himself, of everything connected with him, and particularly of his country. This patriotism was in part a real sentiment of devotion to the country and pride aroused by the war. It was in part, also, the result of provincialism. No other generation of Americans has ever been so isolated from the European world as that which flourished between 1815 and 1845. The close of the Napoleonic wars brought a period of comparative international quiet, and the United States was allowed to disassociate itself from the course of European politics in which it had been involved from the beginning. Foreign affairs ceased to be a leading subject of party division, and became to a very large extent an administrative question. *Provincialism.*

This provincialism was intensified by the condition of the United States trade. The European peace not only put an end to the difficulties of neutral trade, it put an end to the trade itself. It was now possible for the French to carry their cargoes in their own vessels. The business of importing goods into the United States to reëxport them to *Decline of trade.*

other countries continued to decline, slowly in amount, rapidly in comparison with our total trade.   In carrying foreign goods from one foreign port to another, our vessels encountered many restrictions intended to protect the merchant marines of the various countries involved, and the carrying trade diminished.   The direct trade between the United States and foreign countries grew during the first part of this period at a much smaller rate than the wealth of the country.   The consequence was that even the commercial bonds with the outside world were considerably weakened.   The United States was as much isolated as it is possible for a nation to be under the conditions of modern civilization.

Decline of New England commerce.

This diminished importance of trade particularly affected New England, which had always profited largely by handling the goods of other sections and countries.   Some merchants fought against the new tendencies.   With the renewal of peace they expected trade to revive, and in the interests of trade they called for a reduction of the doubled war duties, for stricter navigation acts, and for treaties providing for reciprocal privileges to level the barriers being raised against them in Europe.   In Congress their demands were pressed by Daniel Webster, who had succeeded Josiah Quincy as the representative of solid New England business interests.

The really ample protection that was obtained from the navigation acts, combined with the natural advantages which New England possessed in building wooden ships, caused a revival of the shipbuilding and shipowning industry, especially after 1830.   These vessels, however, were chiefly employed in exporting cotton and western products, and New York, Baltimore, and other ports in contact with those regions profited by the reviving trade more than did New England.   Relatively her commerce entered upon a slow decline, and many of the old seaports, as Portsmouth, Newburyport, Salem, and ᴺ wport, passed from the bustle of life into a dignified old dec:.

New England no longer spoke with a single voice. The embargo, the nonintercourse, and finally the war had acted as a heavy protective tariff, at times prohibitive, in favor of American manufacturers. Many New England merchants had turned their capital from shipping into manufacture. They found that New England possessed an almost unexploited source of wealth in the abundant and perpetual water power furnished by its swift rivers. The population was naturally adapted to manufacturing, for the spinning wheel was to be found in every farmhouse, and the bulk of the population had for over a hundred years been clothed mainly with the products of domestic industry. With capital, water power, and skilled labor, the factory system, which had been developing in England, was rapidly and successfully transplanted to New England; and about the river falls and rapids arose new towns, as Lowell, Pawtucket, Central Falls, Valley Falls, and many others. To the English inventions, brought over to America by such men as Samuel Slater, were added those of American inventors, as the wool card of Whittimore and the power loom of Lowell. By 1812 there were within 30 miles of Providence 53 mills with 48,000 spindles. In 1815, 500,000 spindles and 76,000 persons were employed in the manufacture of cotton, chiefly in New England, and the annual output of woolens was estimated to be worth $19,000,000.

These newly rising New England factory centers did not reproduce the unfortunate conditions which accompanied the industrial revolution in England. The factories were, until after the Civil War, widely scattered through many towns, and the employees came, to a large extent, from the country adjacent. They were mostly self-respecting farmers' daughters, who looked upon the experience as temporary, many hoping to gain money for education, or at least to escape the narrow horizon of farm life. As one of their number subsequently wrote: "Just such girls as now knock at the

doors of the Harvard Annex and the various women's colleges, then knocked at the doors of the Lowell cotton mills.'
In some of the towns, particularly in Lowell, the mill owners took especial care to guard and regulate the life of these working girls.

Neither did the replacement of domestic industry by the factory system lead to the social disorders found in England. It was, of course, a less important movement, for home labor had not been so highly developed as in that country. It was, moreover, gradual, and during many years some of the manufacturing processes were performed in connection with farm labor. As manufacturing became more and more concentrated, and spinning and other auxiliary occupations disappeared, many of the smaller and less fertile farms did indeed become unprofitable, but it was so easy for the farmer to move westward that instead of distress at home we find an increasing stream of westward emigration.

The growth of manufacturing was reflected on the outskirts of New England, in western Massachusetts, Vermont, New Hampshire, and Maine, by the increase of sheep raising

to supply the necessary raw wool. In 1810 there were reported in New England 638,326 sheep; in 1840, 3,617,305. This replacement of crop growing by sheep raising meant enlargement of farms, and the employment of fewer laborers in proportion to the area. Here again a movement which had caused untold distress in England during the fifteenth and seventeenth centuries was accomplished in America so quietly as to be almost unobserved, owing to the ease with which those crowded out found homes in the West.

The new factories produced so much more than had the old domestic processes that markets for the disposal of the product were needed beyond the borders of New England. During the embargo and the war such a market was found in the South and West, but the difficulties of the trade were immense, owing to the lack of means of transportation. As early as 1790 many turnpike companies had been organized, and the roads were steadily improved. Soon after there followed many canal schemes, largely devised by the merchants to bring in the country products to some port from which they could be shipped in coasting vessels. With such purpose, connection was made between the Merrimac and Boston, between Worcester and Providence, and the Connecticut and the Merrimac were made navigable for long distances. After the war, the problem of the western trade became more and more important. This problem was more difficult. It was necessary to drive the roads and canals over the mountains. Portland and Portsmouth discussed and began elaborate undertakings to cross the Green Mountains and utilize Lake Champlain; Boston considered the possibility of piercing the Berkshires and linking itself with Albany. These undertakings were too extensive for the private purses of the merchants, and it would be futile to build canals in New England unless there were connections farther west. Many, therefore, began to look upon them as national undertakings, and to believe it to be the duty of the national government to build them. Foremost in this movement was John Quincy Adams, son of President John Adams. Having served as a Federalist senator, in 1808 he broke with the Federalists, and was now high in the councils of the Republican party.

As the means of transportation improved, not only did the products of New England find their way westward, but western foodstuffs came east and entered into competition with those of the New England farms. Against this competition the farmer could find no protection, as interstate trade was free by the Constitution. Many sold or deserted their farms and used the roads which had ruined them to journey to new opportunities in the West. *Other reasons for emigration.*

The manufacturers had to meet in the southern and *New England policies.*

western markets the competition of the English. From this competition, however, they believed that their still "infant industries" could and should be protected by the national government; and accordingly they petitioned for a high tariff so arranged as to offset the advantages which the English still possessed because of a low cost of production. In making this request they came into direct conflict with the declining commercial interests, which were opposed to all limitations put on foreign trade. This conflict lasted from 1815 to about 1830, and resulted in the triumph of the party of protection. By 1828 Webster had become an acknowledged champion of the movement; manufacture, rather than commerce or agriculture, was understood to be the great New England interest, and protection and internal improvements its policies.

Protection in the Middle States.

The Middle States — New York, New Jersey, Pennsylvania, and Maryland — were at the beginning of this period more solidly in favor of protection than was New England. Pennsylvania had been the first state in which manufactures became important, and made a strong demand for protection of industry, in this case chiefly of iron instead of textiles as in New England. There were more than three times as many persons engaged in agriculture as in manufactures in these states, but the agricultural element also favored protection. Peace in Europe had turned thousands of Europeans from soldiers into farmers, and the demand for American foodstuffs almost ceased. Under these circumstances the American farmers were much impressed by the argument that it was advantageous for them to encourage manufactures in order to build up a home market for their products. Such a home market would not only consume their surplus food, but also make profitable the raising of raw materials, such as wool. The development of grazing was particularly noticeable in western New York, which in 1840 had over 5,000,000 sheep, and, as in New England, re-

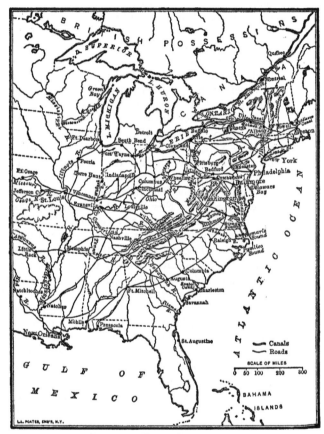

ROADS AND TRUNK CANALS IN 1825

It will be observed how closely this road map resembles a present-day railroad map. Both followed natural geographic routes. At this period the greater proportion of bulky articles still went by water.

sulted in the crowding out of many individuals and families, who swelled the westward flowing stream.

The contest for western trade. The Middle States were all interested in the improvement of transportation. The growing trade of the West, the manufactured goods which it imported, whether from England or from New England, and the agricultural products with which it paid for them, might be made to pass through their territory if the mountain barrier could be pierced. This great prize of the western trade was the object of vigorous rivalry between the ports of Baltimore, Philadelphia, and New York. The last mentioned was the first to undertake a radical solution of this truly gigantic task, the other two being better served by roads which brought in a dribbling trade from the Ohio valley and deadened greater enterprises. Here, as in New England, such an undertaking was too great for individuals, and corporate organization was not sufficiently developed in America to attempt it; but unlike the New England schemes, this project fell within the limits of a single state. DeWitt Clinton urged that New York state could do nothing so greatly to its advantage as to construct a canal up the Mohawk valley to connect with Lake Erie. He overcame the opposition of those who doubted the feasibility of the plan and of those sections of the state which it would not directly benefit. The project was definitely accepted in 1817, and in 1825 the canal was completed. The canal cut freight rates in some cases to a thirtieth of what they had been, and yet paid for itself in nine years. It was to the Lake region what the Mississippi was to its valley, and soon canals connecting the Lakes with the Ohio drew much of the trade of that region to New York. The ties binding the Northwest to the South weakened, while those attaching it to the East grew stronger with every passing year.

Pennsylvania was stirred by this success into activity, and in 1824 appointed a canal commission; but the working out of the plan involved much greater physical difficulties and more violent local jealousies. Although a route consisting of canals, supplemented by an inclined plane over the highest ridge, was completed some ten years later, connecting Pittsburgh and the Susquehanna, Philadelphia did not regain its lost ground until the railroad era. Baltimore was still more active, and had hopes of national assistance, for any national transportation route would be apt to follow the Potomac, through the western part of Virginia, to the Ohio. In 1823, a canal convention was held at Washington to promote such a design. Ultimately, however, Baltimore capitalists became fearful that such a scheme would benefit Washington too exclusively, and as early as 1827 they planned the Baltimore and Ohio Railroad, which was intended to, and for a time did, give Baltimore a very large share of the Ohio valley trade. The hopes of Washington rested entirely upon Congress; and those of Richmond, — based on the routes by way of the Potomac, the James, and the Kanawha, — although they antedated all the others and did not cease to be of moment in state politics until the Civil War, continued unfulfilled.

Internal improvements and the tariff were, therefore, the leading political issues in the Middle States, and while a decided majority favored the tariff, the transportation schemes tended to develop state rivalries and factions within the states based on special and local interests. *Policies of the Middle States.*

The great problem of transportation and the great prize of the western trade were not without interest to the Southern States. Charleston and Savannah were almost as near Cincinnati and Louisville as were Philadelphia and Baltimore, but the mountain ranges between were recognized by the most daring engineers as impossible for canals, and no serious efforts at competition were made until the development of railroads. Such projects as were seriously devised and executed were of a local nature to bring the country *The South and western trade.*

produce to some seaport, as were the canals about Boston and Providence. Charleston in particular was served by a mesh of canals making most of the Carolina rivers tributary to her harbor.

Increase of the cotton crop.

The attention of the South was increasingly absorbed by the development of cotton culture. The invention of Eli Whitney's cotton gin in 1792 made cotton growing profitable. Cotton rapidly displaced indigo in the tidewater region of South Carolina and Georgia, and arrested the development of rice growing. It was soon found that the short staple cotton, which could be grown on the uplands, was almost as valuable as the long staple of the coast, and the farmers of the piedmont region abandoned in large measure the culture of cereals for the new crop. In 1800 the total product was about 35,000,000 pounds, of which 17,790,000 were exported, worth, at New York prices, about $9,000,000. In 1820 the product was 160,000,000 pounds, of which 127,860,000 pounds, worth, at Liverpool prices, $27,000,000, were exported.

Revival of slave labor.

The culture of cotton was peculiarly well adapted to the employment of slave labor. Its simple requirements, not involving the use of expensive machinery, gave systematic employment for three quarters of the year. Hence there was no call for the diversification of industry for which slave labor is usually inadequate. The low cotton plants, moreover, allowed the overseer to superintend a large gang of workers in a manner impossible, for instance, in a corn field late in the year. The price of slaves, which had dropped very low when the mountains checked the western spread of tobacco growing, now rose. In 1808 the international slave trade had been forbidden, in spite of some opposition. This limitation of the supply of slaves, at the same time that the demand was increasing, made this rise unusually sharp. The average value of a good field hand about the time of the introduction of cotton culture was $200; in 1815, $250;

in 1836, $600. This rise benefited Virginia and Maryland, where slave property had become somewhat of a drug on the market. Now, some of the surplus was sold to the cotton states. The improvement in slave values checked the rise of antislavery feeling. This had never been strong in South Carolina and Georgia, and now even in North Carolina, Virginia, and Maryland there developed the feeling that though slavery was evil, it was necessary. The spread of slaveholding into the upland region diminished the friction between those districts and the coast, and tended to produce a solidarity of interest, especially in South Carolina, where the agreement of 1808 marked the close of sectional conflicts between the coast and the piedmont, and gave the state a political unity that very much contributed to its political weight.

As in the case of tobacco, the spread of cotton culture went hand in hand with the spread of the plantation system. The increase in production meant a progressive decline in price, and the cultivators felt the constant desire to increase their landholdings and the number of their slaves, in order to maintain their incomes. The successful planters came to hold constantly larger investments, and the unsuccessful, to sell out and depart for other regions. As plantations spread into the uplands, many of the non-slaveholding farmers of those districts, some galled by their inferior social and economic position, and some, such as the Quakers of North Carolina, by their dislike of slavery, moved to the northwest, across the Ohio. Consequently the advance of the cotton plantation pushed before it into the West a considerable proportion of the white population. *Spread of the plantation system.*

The absorption of the population in one industry led to a growing dependence of the Cotton South upon the rest of the world. While the bulk of its foodstuffs was always produced at home, it came to depend for a larger and larger proportion of them upon the states to the northwest. In the *Economic dependence of the South.*

latter part of the twenties a million dollars' worth of live stock, chiefly sheep, cattle, and hogs, came annually through the Cumberland and Saluda gaps into South Carolina, and with the building of railroads came corn and also wheat. At the same time the factory system failed to develop and the population relied for cloth and tools and luxuries upon England, France, and New England.

Protection in the South. In 1816 the great political leaders of the cotton belt, Lowndes and Calhoun, were strongly in favor of a protective tariff. They felt the nationalistic impulse of the war and wished to make the United States self-sufficing; they were not yet convinced that the South might not share in the development of manufactures. The South had been on a par with the rest of the country in the production of cloth by household spinning and weaving. North Carolina in 1810 produced more than all New England. Southern dealers did not yet realize that factory-made cloth would drive domestic manufacturers from the market, or that the factory system would not develop in the South. Moreover, the "home market" argument appealed to them. England levied an import duty on cotton, which New England could not do. Again, a large portion of the cotton goods imported into the United States was made of cotton grown in India. To keep out such goods and build up American manufactures would mean a larger and steadier market.

Fall in the price of cotton. This opinion changed decisively and with great rapidity as the result of changing circumstances. The increasing production of cotton brought down the price. The average price of "middling uplands," the standard American cotton, in Liverpool fell from 36.50 cents a pound in 1816, to 23 cents in 1820; in 1821, it was 16.46, in 1822, 13.90, and only once again before the Civil War did it reach as high as 20 cents. Indian cotton was driven out of competition, and the cotton belt assumed at once a commanding position as holding a world monopoly. At the same time, the processes of manufacture were cheapened, and, with the lower cost, the demand for cotton goods and, therefore, for raw cotton continually expanded. It became no longer an object to the southern planter to secure a home market ; it was as profitable to sell to Europe as to New England. A United States duty on raw cotton could not enhance its price here, as the competition was among American producers. Nor did the protective tariff on cotton cloth cause manufacturing to develop in the cotton district. On the contrary, the factory-made cloths of England and the North drove the spinning wheel from farm and plantation. At the same time, the planter did not obtain the full benefit of the cheapening processes of manufacture, because of the tariff, which enabled the American manufacturers to keep up prices in spite of the declining cost of production. McDuffie of South Carolina, the leading exponent of the anti-tariff sentiment, said of the bill proposed in 1824 : "Whatever may be its effect upon the domestic manufactures, I speak advisedly when I say, it will operate as a tax upon the people, to the extent of at least four million of dollars, and whether the proceeds of this tax shall go into the national treasury, or into the pockets of individuals, the thing about which there can be no doubt is, that the tax will be paid by the people."

The very decrease in the price of cotton, which gave the South its undisputed monopoly, made its opposition to the tariff more bitter. Part of this decrease was due to a lower cost of production resulting from better agricultural methods, better means of internal transportation, lower freight rates across the ocean, resulting from the increasing competition of English vessels, and declining cost of manufactured foods. Much of the decrease of price, however, was taken from the profits of the planter. That this was so all could feel, but how it happened few could satisfactorily explain. There could be no doubt that it was a serious blow to the rising prosperity of South Carolina and the settled

Cotton and the tariff.

portion of Georgia. Some planters could keep up their net incomes by increasing their plantations, but it was impossible greatly to increase the area of cotton cultivation within the state, and the total income of the state was therefore diminished. Moreover, the soil was beginning to be exhausted in the oldest regions; for under the crude methods employed, twenty-five years of continuous cotton crops left it almost worthless. This depression in the prosperity of the South was attributed in very large measure to the tariff, and through that, to those sections of the country which upheld it. McDuffie said in 1828: "Individuals are always open to impressions of generosity. But classes of the community, and sections of country, when united and stimulated by the hope of gain, being destitute, like corporations, of individual responsibility, are, like them, destitute of hearts and souls to feel for the wrongs and sufferings they inflict upon others."

Spread of cotton culture.

The most potent cause of the lower price of cotton, however, was the opening up of new cotton areas in other states — Alabama, Tennessee, and Mississippi; and the more the depression was felt in the older region, the more rapidly the expansion went on. While one stream of population was flowing out to the free states of the northwest to win small farms by manual labor, another, composed largely of men with capital in money and slaves, was directed southward and westward in the hope of opening new plantations under more favorable conditions. It was significant of the difference in the character of these two streams that in 1818 land offered for sale by the government in Alabama for agricultural purposes sold, in some cases, for as much as $107 per acre, while the average price in Missouri, where most of the purchasers were of the individual pioneer type, was a little over $2, the highest being $10. Between 1824 and 1841 the average annual cotton production of the South Atlantic States increased only from 433,000 bales to 529,000, while that of the

Gulf States grew from 253,000 to 1,030,000. While this spread of the cotton area led to the economic distress of the coast by continually lowering the price of cotton, it added to the political weight of the "Cotton" or "Lower" South. Ultimately the cotton interests gained control in all the seaboard and Gulf states from South Carolina to Mexico, and all became conscious of a common interest and united for a single purpose.

The process by which this political unity was obtained was a very gradual one. The young planter, flush with the rich crops of a new section, saw matters with a very different eye from one in South Carolina struggling to keep up appearances. Moreover, while cotton stretched out over the best land and that most accessible to transportation,—over the "Black Belt,"—the poorer and more remote regions of the South were occupied by the small farms of non-slaveholding whites. The gradual processes by which the plantation system spread over the lower South, and by which all classes became united in the support of slavery and what came to be known as "Southern Rights," are the leading features of southern history from the War of 1812 to that of 1860, and are illustrated particularly by the career of Calhoun, who came to be the national spokesman of the section. *The "Cotton South."*

Somewhat distinct from the rest was the newly admitted state of Louisiana. New Orleans was in large measure the port of the Mississippi valley, and a larger proportion of the population of the state was engaged in commerce than in any other state of the Union. Every improvement in the navigation of the river or its tributaries increased trade, every improvement in means of transit across the mountains might diminish it. Moreover, Louisiana's leading native product was sugar, and as it was impossible to produce enough to supply the United States, the tariff might be arranged to raise the price and increase the incomes of the producers. Thus Louisiana was vitally interested in *Sugar culture.*

the two problems of internal improvements and the tariff, and was on the tariff question divided from the Cotton South. Both sections, however, employed the plantation system, and in the end this proved a bond stronger than that binding Louisiana to the North.

Spread of the frontier.

Most conservative of all the sections was the Appalachian Mountain region, the old frontier of the Confederation; but beyond the mountains there was growing up a new frontier, the center of the bustling activity of the period. Into it were flowing streams of population from all the other sections, the predominating tone being given by the people from the old frontier. Around the southern end of the mountains, and down the long valleys from Virginia and thence through the passes into Georgia, Alabama, and Tennessee, came picturesque caravans of planters with their slaves, in search of new fields. Northward through Cumberland Gap and down the Kanawha valley and over the Cumberland Road, when it was completed, poured a constant stream of emigrants, seeking better opportunities, and freedom from the galling competition of slave-owning capitalists. The roads of Pennsylvania were, at seasons, literally thick with emigrants from the eastern states. After 1825 the Erie Canal began to be the great avenue for New Englanders and emigrants from central New York, directing them into the Lake region, which until then, for lack of means of access, had lagged behind the Ohio valley. The peopling of the Mississippi valley and the Lake region in this transition period was one of the greatest movements of population the world has ever seen. Five territories there — Indiana, Illinois, Missouri, Mississippi, and Alabama — quickly became so populous that they were admitted as states between 1816 and 1821. In 1810 the frontier districts contained about 1,200,000 inhabitants; in 1830, 4,200,000. The great bulk of this population consisted of men and women, in the prime of life, who had themselves moved into their new homes.

The major problem of this region was transportation.
Much had already been done. The acquisition of Louisiana
had cleared the mouth of the Mississippi, and in 1807 Fulton
produced the first practicable steamboat. These two events
worked together. The rapid current of the Mississippi had
made it almost useless as an inlet for merchandise, although
goods could be easily enough floated down on rafts, which
were afterwards broken up and sold for lumber. With the
aid of steam, boats could go up as well as down. In 1811
there was launched at Pittsburgh the first of the river fleet
of steamers, the *New Orleans*, with a ship-shaped hull and
side wheels. Soon a new type was evolved, more suited to
the western waters: a raft-like hull, drawing very little water,
on which was raised a superstructure of one, two, three, or
four decks or stories, and with a great driving wheel at the
stern. Such vessels could cross shallows and run rapids,
and they multiplied marvelously. In 1820 there were 60 in
the Mississippi basin; in 1830, as many as 230. This natural
navigation, however, by no means answered the needs of the
West. Every farmer could appreciate the advantage of
direct connection over the mountains with the eastern markets, and the limits of navigation could be greatly extended
by a few judiciously planned improvements such as canals
about rapids or cutting off detours, and the building of supplementary roads.

The attempts at solving the problems of internal improvement in the valley were all affected by the absence of
capital. Few of the settlers brought much with them, and
in the few years of settlement little had accumulated. There
was, therefore, a large party in favor of securing national
assistance for the accomplishment of these undertakings.
Others, opposed to the interference of a governing body so
far away and not under their control, favored some scheme for
increasing the resources of the several states, such as the
grant of unsold land within their borders. Still another

proposition was for the states to provide capital by generous
emissions of paper money. As the states were forbidden by
the Constitution to issue bills of credit, this end was obtained
by the creation of banks, some owned in part by the state governments, some entirely private, and all having practically
unrestricted power of issue. The extinction of the National
Bank in 1811 withdrew a regulative influence, and between
1811 and 1816 the number of banks in the country trebled,
and their issues of bank notes grew from $45,000,000 to
$100,000,000. The majority of these banks were poorly
managed, particularly in the West. In 1814 all those outside of Massachusetts suspended specie payment, and the
value of the paper currency varied widely. In 1813 and 1814
forty banks of issue had been chartered in Kentucky; other
states were equally lavish, and loose supervision, combined
with the lack of necessary business experience, brought widespread ruin.

On the subject of the tariff also the frontier was divided.
Owing to the great expense of transportation, a small amount
of manufacturing had sprung up in Kentucky early in the
century, and this gave a temporary support to the protective
movement. Although this development was checked when
the importation of such products from Europe and the eastern states, where more abundant capital and denser population made manufacturing thrive more naturally, became practicable, the protective sentiment was fostered by the fact that
a tariff might help the farmer indirectly by the building up
of a home market, and, in the case of certain raw materials,
directly by protective duties. Kentucky planters became interested in the production of hemp, and farmers north of the
Ohio in that of sheep and hides. Their interests conflicted
somewhat with those of the eastern manufacturers, who wished
these raw materials to be as cheap as possible; but here were
the elements of a bargain, such as has marked almost all
tariff bills. The tariff could be so framed as to be of advan-

State banks
of issue.

The " Ameri-
can system."

tage to both western farmer and eastern manufacturer. Moreover, a high tariff, as conceived at that time, meant increased
revenue, and hence was favored by those who wished the
national government to aid in internal improvements. These
two ideas were combined by one of the two great representatives of the frontier, Henry Clay, with that of having the
national government distribute among the states the proceeds of the sales of public lands, and the combination was
labeled the "American system." In general, apart from the
particular interests which varied from locality to locality,
the people of the frontier divided on these subjects according
to fundamental political principles. Those who believed in
exerting the powers of the government to aid the individual
favored the American system; those who preferred to be let
alone opposed it; but in 1815 this division was by no means
clearly marked.

In all sections there was growth, activity, and change. Actual
For the first time travelers were impressed with the nervous democracy.
energy of Americans. The "quick lunch" was at once a
symptom of the new spirit and a cause of the sallow, un-
healthy complexion which was equally a subject of comment.
A new impulse had taken hold of the nation; it had awakened
to a realization of the tremendous economic possibilities
which lay before it. Other nations have had similar out-
bursts of activity when vistas of progress have been opened
before them; but it is safe to say that never before has a
whole nation been so thrilled, because never before has so
great a prospect been offered so freely to every individual
citizen. The possibility that any boy might aspire to become president or to make a fortune was undoubtedly a great
stimulating motive that spurred the entire population to unprecedented exertions. The advanced doctrines of the Revolution were just coming to be true in actual life; and,
unquestioned, unqualified by the limitations of experience,
they were the real inspiration of the people.

Democracy in politics.

This democratic spirit naturally extended to politics. In the old states constitutions were altered, particularly in Connecticut in 1818, and in New York and Massachusetts in 1821, in the direction of universal suffrage and popular election of all officers. In Pennsylvania and Ohio the term of judges was limited. In the new states, the constitutions were framed on even more popular lines. Where no changes were made, as in Rhode Island, there was popular dissatisfaction. The growth of democratic feeling is also indicated by the change in the method of choosing presidential electors. In 1824 six states continued to leave their appointment to the legislature; in 1828, there were only two; in 1832 and thereafter, South Carolina stood alone.

Party organization.

In New England and the other eastern states the more democratic elements were bound somewhat closely together in party organization. In each state there were well-recognized leaders or groups of leaders, such as the Albany Regency which gained control of New York during the twenties. These leaders generally arose to power by the clever manipulation of politics in their particular localities, and were in touch with local leaders in every township or county, whom they held by the gift of public offices. The spoils system was now fully recognized in New York and Pennsylvania, and by this type of politician in New England and elsewhere. The local leaders often gained their power by combining all elements dissatisfied with the existing authorities, and when once in power they sought to retain it rather by organization and avoidance of issues upon which people were divided than by the active advocacy of a positive program. At this period few men could rise to the position of state "boss" unless personally honest and possessing some of the qualities of statesmanship; but many of their lieutenants, particularly those controlling the cities, were without principle and were in politics simply for what they could get out of it. Throughout this period these leaders were continuously endeavoring to get control of the national government that they might divide the national spoils. As the progress of democratic sentiment is illustrated by the choice of presidential electors by popular vote instead of by the legislature, the development of party organization is to a slight degree shown by the spread of the general ticket at the expense of the district system of election. Party leaders felt keenly the difference in the political weight of a state that was sure to cast its entire electoral vote in one scale or the other, as compared with one which habitually divided it, as did Maryland. When the change of a few hundred popular votes might mean the gain or loss of many electoral votes, every inducement would be offered to influence those who held the balance. In 1824 five states used the district system; in 1828, four; in 1832, only Maryland; in 1836, none.

In the plantation area, both the old tobacco region and the new cotton belt, the structure of society and political methods were very little affected by the new growth of democracy. The governing class readily admitted to itself all who won economic success, and the laws were democratic in appearance, but the actual practice was aristocratic. Such democracy as existed in these states was in those districts into which the plantation system did not extend. Nevertheless, a democratic sentiment is indicated by the fact that the constitutions of the newer states in the South gave representation in the legislatures according to white population, which favored the poorer sections; whereas the older states counted some proportion of slaves, thus increasing the power of the planters who owned them. *Plantation democracy.*

In the Mississippi valley political democracy was the natural result of a real equality. It took its form largely from the habits acquired in the old mountain frontier. It was a democracy without organization, depending on personal leadership. It was an equality without specialization. The man most successful as an Indian fighter was expected to *Frontier democracy.*

make the best judge or the best congressman. While a leader
was trustworthy and represented the interests of his followers
he could count on their support. If he were victorious, he
was expected to punish his enemies by turning them out of
office, and to reward his friends with the vacated·positions.
On simple political questions the people were intelligent
and independent, well trained through the necessity of self-
government in their own communities. They were unwilling
to accept the authority of experts even on such matters as
diplomacy and finance, and were suspicious of what they
could not see and understand. Administrative red tape,
such as had been evolved at Washington, seemed to them but
a veil to hide peculation and fraud. They chafed under a
government managed decorously by middle-aged gentlemen
from Virginia and New England.

State rights
versus strict
construction.
This frontier democracy cared little for the fine-spun
constitutional controversies which had divided parties in the
past. Its members revered the Constitution as the emblem of
the Union which had done and was to do much for them;
they appealed to it when Congress seemed likely to interfere
with their own freedom of action or that of their state; but
the majority of them would readily brush it aside if it stood
in the way of any measure they wished the government to
undertake. They were generally in favor of state rights,
but they were not strict constructionists.

Religious de-
velopment.
Unlike the Revolutionary generation, that which was now
arising was religious and emotional. Religion took on the
prevailing democratic spirit. In Massachusetts the Unita-
rian element ceased to lay stress on the negation of points of
doctrine, and, under the leadership of Buckminster and Channing, began to lay emphasis on the positive side of their belief, the nobility of man. In 1820 the Unitarians definitely
separated themselves from the Congregationalists, and their
societies spread rapidly through and beyond New England.
In the theology of Emerson the democratic spirit reached

its supreme point. He put into the mouth of Jesus the words: "I am divine. Through me God acts; through me, speaks. Would you see God, see me: or, see thee, when thou also thinkest as I now think!" The spread of Unitarianism in this region was checked only by the work of men like Horace Bushnell of Connecticut, who harmonized the Calvinistic theology with the new spirit of democracy. Still more rapid was the growth of the Methodists, Baptists, Universalists, Disciples of Christ, and similar denominations whose systems were equally democratic and whose methods were more emotional. In the West, this spirit showed itself rather by methods of work than by theological adjustment. The itinerant preacher, in his house-to-house rounds, found more fruitful ground for his religious teaching because his visits made one of the few breaks in the monotony of the isolated frontier life. The revivalist sought to stir his hearers, not only to spiritual emotion, but to physical manifestations of it in shouts and lamentations and even to such outward and visible signs of a changed life as "treeing the devil" with the ever ready firearm. The camp meeting, with its prolonged picnic features, combined needed social relaxation with the odor of sanctity. The sects that succeeded were those that adapted themselves to the needs of a people religious at heart, but unable to grasp theological distinctions, and unwilling to be bound by what seemed to them the cold conventions of ordered religious observances.

The religious spirit was also deeply humanitarian, and, now and again, took form in crusades for the betterment of mankind, for the heathen, the insane, the drunkard, the negro, women, children, the ignorant, and the poor. Naturally such a period found expression in literature. In the excitement just preceding the War of 1812, William Cullen Bryant and Washington Irving began to write. In 1815 the *North American Review* was founded. In the transitional period, Emerson, Hawthorne, Holmes, Poe, Whitman, and

Humanitarianism and literature.

many others of the greatest American writers and thinkers passed their boyhood, to attain man's estate and take up their life work during the thirties.

BIBLIOGRAPHICAL NOTES

Sources.   For a general course the opinions of Judge Marshall afford satisfactory constitutional assignments, disregarding the opinions of other judges. See *Constitutional Decisions* (ed. by J. P. Cotton, Jr.) or the following references: *Chisholm* v. *Georgia* (1793): 2 *Dallas*, 419. *Marbury* v. *Madison* (1803): 1 *Cranch*, 137; Thayer, J. B., *Cases*, 107–114. *United States* v. *Judge Peters* (1809): 5 *Cranch*, 115; Marshall, *Writings*, 119–125. *Fletcher* v. *Peck* (1810): 6 *Cranch*, 87; Thayer, *Cases*, 114–123. *Gibbons* v. *Ogden* (1824): 9 *Wheaton*, 184. *Martin* v. *Hunter's Lessee* (1816): 1 *Wheaton*, 304; Marshall, *Writings*, 525–555. *Dartmouth College* v. *Woodward* (1819): 4 *Wheaton*, 518; Marshall, *Writings*, 188–210. *McCulloch* v. *Maryland* (1819): 4 *Wheaton*, 316; Marshall, *Writings*, 160–187. *Cohens* v. *Virginia* (1821): 6 *Wheaton*, 264; Marshall, *Writings*, 221–261. *Osborn et al.* v. *The Bank of the United States* (1824): 9 *Wheaton*, 738; Marshall, *Writings*, 315–342. Travelers' impressions of the United States are perhaps more valuable for this period than any other. *Early Western Travels*, edited by R. G. Thwaites, contains a mine of supplementary reading. Paulding, J. K., *Letters from the South*, and Tudor, W., *Letters from the Eastern States*, are among the best on those sections. Callender, G. S., *Economic History*, 359–373 (Transportation), and 487–561 (Tariff), contains usable selections. The *Works* of H. Clay, V, 461–480, and D. Webster, III, 94–149, contain important speeches on the tariff. Where the *Annals of Congress* are available, the debates of the 14th Congress are suitable, especially 1 sess., 684–688 (Speech of John Randolph on the tariff). See also Taussig, F. W., *State Papers and Speeches on the Tariff*, 252–385.

Historical accounts. General conditions.   Adams, H., *Administrations of Jefferson and Madison*, IX, 175–242. Schouler, J., *United States*, II, 505–516. Turner, F. J., *Rise of the New West*, 10–67.

Constitutional questions.   Babcock, *American Nationality*, 290–309. Cooley, Judge T. M., and others, *Constitutional History of the United States as seen in the Development of American Law.* Farrand, *The First Hay-burn Case* (*Am. Hist. Review*, XIII, 281–285). Thayer, J. B., *Marshall.* Story, J., *Commentaries*, secs. 1033–1044; 1259–1281; 1374–1397; 1685–1688. Turner, F. J., *New West*, 299–306.

Bretz, J. P., *Postal Extension into the West* (Am. Hist. Assoc., Transporta-*Report*, 1909, 143). Hulbert, A. B., *Historic Highways of America* tion. (especially, *Cumberland Road, Great American Canals, Portage Paths, Waterways of Westward Expansion*). McMaster, *United States*, IV, 381–429. Monette, J. W., *Progress of Navigation* (Miss. Hist. Soc., *Publications*, VII, 479). Richardson, *Messages*, II, 142–183 (veto message of Monroe). Turner, *New West*, 96–111.

Boggess, A. C., *Settlement of Illinois.* Brigham, A. P., *Geographic* Migration. *Influences*, ch. V. Callender, G. S., *Economic History*, 313–320, 597–610. Faust, A. B., *German Element*, I, chs. XIII, XIV. Hinsdale, B. A., *Old Northwest*, 295–328, 368–392. Matthews, L. H., *Expansion of New England*, 178–224.

Stanwood, E., *American Tariff Controversies*, I, 111–157. The tariff. Stevens, W. P., *Foreign Trade of the United States*, 1820–1840 (*Journal of Pol. Econ.*, VIII, 348–452). Turner, *New West*, 224–245.

Commons, J. C., *Documentary History of American Industrial* Cotton. *Society*, II (U. B. Phillips), 165–299. Hammond, M. B., *The Cotton Industry* (Am. Econ. Assoc., *Publications*, new series, no. 1).

Fish, C. R., *Civil Service*, 79–104. Murdock, J. S., *First Na-* Politics. *tional Nominating Convention* (*Am. Hist. Review*, II, 680–682). Walton, J. S., *Nominating Conventions in Pennsylvania* (*Am. Hist. Review*, II, 262–278).

CHAPTER X

POLITICS DURING THE PERIOD OF TRANSITION, 1815 TO 1829

The Fourteenth Congress.

THE Fourteenth Congress, which met in December, 1815, was one of the most talented ever elected. Only about the year 1850, when as at this time the leaders of a passing generation served side by side with those rising into power, has there been another such aggregation of talent. As the elections in most states had been held in the dark days of the fall of 1814, a large number of Federalists had been chosen; they numbered 65 out of 182 in the House and 14 out of 36 in the Senate. With Jeremiah Mason, Rufus King, and Robert Goodloe Harper in the Senate, and Webster and Pickering in the House, they could match their representation in any Congress for ability. Among the Republicans were Macon, Randolph, and William Pinkney of the older generation; and, of the younger generation, Calhoun, Lowndes, R. M. Johnson, McLean of Ohio, and Henry Clay, the Speaker. The youthful element were in control, and they went blithely to work to heal the wounds of the war, and to solve the newly arising problems.

The currency.

The most pressing question was that of the currency. Specie was extremely rare; in Boston only New England bank notes were at par; those of New York were at fourteen per cent discount; those of Baltimore and Philadelphia, at sixteen per cent, and those of the western banks at a still lower rate. These rates varied from time to time and from place to place; notes valuable at home declined as they were taken away, for their value depended

156

on personal knowledge of the banks and their directors. The government found itself embarrassed even more seriously than were the private interests, for it collected money in one place that must be spent at another, and these inequalities caused it the utmost inconvenience. The Secretary of the Treasury, Dallas, had recommended in 1814 a new national bank, and it was even then evident that a majority could be secured in its favor, in spite of Republican repugnance to a measure so distinctly Hamiltonian.

Its establishment, however, was delayed by a difference of opinion as to its form. Calhoun wished a distinctly government bank, chartered in the District of Columbia, and so free from any question as to its constitutionality. Webster wished a bank entirely private in ownership and management. Dallas's plan, as he finally presented it, was for a bank modeled very closely on that of Hamilton. In such form it passed the Fourteenth Congress. The capital was to be $35,000,000, one fifth in cash, the remainder payable in United States securities. One fifth was to be subscribed by the United States, which was to have the appointment of five of the twenty-five directors. It was hoped to have the shares widely held, and therefore their par value was fixed at $100 instead of $400 as in the case of the first National Bank. The Bank was to establish branches in the several states under certain conditions, was to receive government deposits unless the Secretary of the Treasury could show Congress satisfactory reasons why this should not be done, and was to transfer government money from place to place without charge. It could issue notes, convertible into specie, to the full amount of its capital. The charter was to run until March 3, 1836, and the corporation was to pay a bonus of $1,500,000 to the government. Webster secured the passage of a joint resolution requiring that, after February 20, 1817, all government dues be collected in gold and silver, "the legal currency of the United States, or in treasury notes,

The second Bank of the United States.

notes of the Bank of the United States," or "in notes of banks payable and paid on demand" in specie.

These measures and other favoring circumstances relieved the government, which on February 1, 1817, resumed the payment of its obligations in specie. Business, however, did not at once recover. The National Bank was at first badly managed, recklessly extending credit until, in 1819, it was on the verge of ruin. Langdon Cheves was then made president, and by dint of rigid economy and contraction of loans saved it, after a stormy period, during which the whole country was racked by a financial crisis. Its safety, however, was gained at the expense of unpopularity, due to the belief that Cheves sacrificed private interests to the Bank and so precipitated the crisis of 1819. Maryland, Ohio, and other states attempted to subject its branches to heavy taxes, and were prevented only by the decisions of the Supreme Court declaring such action unconstitutional. This exemption, giving the Bank's branches a decided advantage over the state banks, added to the local opposition to this great national financial institution.

Opposition to Bank.

In the meantime Congress was considering the question of the revenue. The doubled war duties would soon expire, and the manufacturers petitioned Congress to save them from the overwhelming competition of English goods that they expected when this took place. Madison recommended a limited and temporary protection, and Dallas proposed a definite scheme. In spite of opposition from the Federalists representing the commercial interests, and of numbers of the old-school Republicans headed by Randolph, the bill passed much as Dallas proposed it. Upon products of certain well-established industries, such as carriages, hats, firearms, shoes, and paper, the duty was made practically prohibitive, on the ground that domestic competition would keep prices down, and the market could thus be preserved for Americans without distressing the consumer. On cottons, woolens, and iron,

The tariff of 1816.

of which we should be obliged to import some proportion, the
duty was placed high enough to enable the domestic manufacturers to compete easily.   As the American mills produced
most extensively the cheaper grades of cottons, the system of
minimum valuation was adopted.   That is, all cotton cloth
costing less than 25 cents a yard was valued and taxed as if it
cost that price.   As the price of cotton cloth rapidly declined,
this afforded the New England mills an unexpected amount of
protection.   In the case of iron a specific rate of $1.50 per
hundredweight was levied on rolled iron, and corresponding
amounts on other grades, thus again giving the manufacturers the advantage of any diminished cost of production.
Upon goods not successfully produced in this country, it
was proposed to levy such duties as the revenue demanded.
In general in the tariff of 1816, these latter revenue duties
ranged much lower than those levied for protection.   Numerous local battles were fought on particular duties, as between
the rum distillers of New England, who wanted molasses to
be free, and the sugar growers of Louisiana, who wanted it
protected.   Louisiana won, the duty being placed at five
cents per gallon.   The tariff of 1816 was the first framed by
Congress on distinctly protective lines, and it was afterwards
contended by Calhoun that even this tariff was but a temporary expedient and did not commit its supporters to the
policy of protection.

The tariff of 1816 seemed at first successful both as a
protective and as a revenue measure.   The debt was reduced,
and the direct taxes and the excise were repealed in 1816
and 1817, respectively.   The crisis of 1819, however, changed
this situation.   The revenue fell, the majority were unwilling
to restore the direct taxes and the excise, and the result was
a demand for an increased tariff.   This demand came still
more loudly from those who felt the economic pinch of hard
times and looked to a tariff for relief from their personal ills.
The movement spread and became organized.   Hezekiah

The crisis of 1819.

Niles, who published at Baltimore the powerful weekly, *Niles' Register*, pushed the issue in every number; societies were organized, conventions held for the promotion of American industry, and petitions urged Congress to act.   In 1820 a vigorous effort was made for the adoption of a new bill with a higher range of duties.   This bill passed the House, but was defeated by a very close vote in the Senate.   The cotton-growing interests had become thoroughly hostile to protection in the four years between 1816 and 1820, and voted solidly against it.   On the other hand, New England was still divided.   Thirty-eight New England members voted for the bill, fifteen against it, and thirteen were absent.   The movement needed to become still more popular in the North and West to overcome the united opposition of the South.

Internal improvements.   The Fourteenth Congress applied to other matters the same bold, nationalistic policy which it adopted in the case of the tariff and the currency.   An enlarged navy was provided for, pensions were increased, and public buildings ordered.   Particularly noticeable was the policy with regard to internal improvements.   Three hundred and fifty thousand dollars was voted for the completion of the Cumberland Road to Wheeling, and at its second session the bonus from the National Bank, and the dividends on its stock, were assigned as a fund for general internal improvements.   The changed attitude of Congress is well illustrated by a letter written by Gallatin in May, 1816: "The war has been productive of evil and of good, but I think the good preponderates.   Independent of the loss of lives and of the property of individuals, the war has laid the foundation of permanent taxes and military establishments, which the Republicans had deemed unfavorable to the happiness and free institutions of the country.   But under our former system we were becoming too selfish, too much attached exclusively to the acquisition of wealth; above all, too much confined in our political feelings to local and state objects.   The war has renewed and reinstated the national feelings and character which the Revolution had given, and which were daily lessening. The people have now more general objects of attachment, with which their pride and political opinions are connected. They are more Americans: they feel and act more as a nation; and I hope that the permanency of the Union is thereby better secured."

Congress, however, had advanced along this path more rapidly than the country, and was destined to receive two important checks. Madison, representing the old Republican spirit, on the last day of his term vetoed the "Bonus Bill" for internal improvements, on constitutional grounds. The second check came from the people. Congress had voted to raise the pay of its members from $6 a day to $1500 a year. Against this the democratic sentiment of the country revolted, the press was filled with denunciations, very many members were defeated for reëlection, and so popular a man as Henry Clay barely escaped defeat. The new Congress was somewhat more democratic than its predecessor. It reduced the pay of its members, and it failed to pass a national bankruptcy bill strongly desired by the older moneyed sections, but it still inclined to take a broad nationalistic position on questions of general policy. Congress checked.

The absorption of the Federalist policies by the Republicans resulted in the absorption of most of the Federalist voters; and Republican success in the presidential election of 1816 was a foregone conclusion. Interest, therefore, centered in the nominations. The administration candidate was James Monroe, Secretary of State. Opposition was made to him on the ground that it was dangerous and unfair to perpetuate the Virginia dynasty. New York, always eager to obtain the presidency, presented Governor Tompkins, a man of little national reputation, and a hopeless candidate. The most formidable opposition candidate was William H. Crawford of Georgia, now Secretary of War, soon afterwards The election of 1816.

Secretary of the Treasury, and the particular friend of Gallatin. A caucus attended by 119 of the 141 Republican members of Congress, nominated Monroe by a small majority for the presidency and Tompkins for the vice presidency. This action was acquiesced in, though not without a murmur as to the dangerous character of such a caucus. The Federalists simply nominated electors, leaving them free to vote for whomever they desired. They carried only Massachusetts, Connecticut, and Delaware; and Monroe received 183 electoral votes to 34 for Rufus King, upon whom the Federalist electors united.

Monroe's administration.

James Monroe seems to have resembled Washington in character, being less remarkable for particular talents than for his general balance and sanity. He certainly impressed contemporaries who knew him intimately more favorably than he does modern students of his career. As a diplomat, in spite of an obvious liking for the occupation, he was a most dismal failure, but as an administrator, as governor of Virginia, and as Secretary of War in 1814 and 1815, during which years he continued to serve as Secretary of State also, he was decidedly successful. In fact his may be said to have been the only civic reputation enhanced by the war. As President he fully lived up to what was expected of him, and came to be venerated by the people. He surrounded himself with a cabinet of unusual ability. John Quincy Adams brought to the state department an experience unparalleled in our history, and an ability fully equal to his experience. With an outlook more cosmopolitan than that of most of the leaders of his generation, he was one of the firmest in his assertion of American rights, and retained the unbending conscience and strict moral code of New England. He was painfully eager to succeed Monroe, and he constantly suspected the motives and methods of his opponents. Crawford continued at the treasury and was regarded as the leading candidate for the

succession. The probability of his success gave him a large
body of supporters in Congress, and he contended tenaciously
for full control of the patronage of his department, to aid in
the accomplishment of his ambition. John C. Calhoun, Secretary of War, had also, in the latter part of the administration, presidential aspirations and seems, for a time, to have
been Monroe's favorite candidate. The Attorney-General,
William Wirt, was an able, conscientious public servant, who
might have acceptably filled the presidency, but was not
now a candidate. With men of such capacity and political
position, the cabinet overshadowed both the President and
Congress, and exercised a greater power than ever before or
since. Yet Henry Clay, Speaker of the House, and representative of the growing West, had his own ambitions, and
harassed the administration by a dashing opposition.

The great crisis of Monroe's first administration came, *Balance of
the sections.*
as Jefferson said, "like a fire bell in the night," and yet it
had for a long time been preparing. The great slavery
compromises of the Constitution had thus far served to
keep that question in the background. Nevertheless, there
were occasional controversies, and general dissatisfaction
with the institution was slowly growing. In 1808 the slave
trade was closed by act of Congress, and in 1820 it
was declared to be piracy. Sentiment was not, however,
strong enough to secure its absolute repression. Still the
South felt that now it had secured all its share of benefit
from that particular compromise, while the commercial states
continued to enjoy the advantages of the navigation acts.
In the North there was a growing feeling that the slave population should not be represented at all in the national legislature, while the South felt keenly the fact that it was being
outdistanced by the North. In 1790 the states south of the
Mason and Dixon line had a total population of 1,925,000
to 1,968,000 north of it, which gave them 48 representatives
to 57 in the House; the new census of 1820 would show

4,372,000 to 5,144,000 inhabitants, which according to the
Federal ratio would give 89 representatives to 123.   Much
of this change was due to the migration of southern whites
to the Northwest.   While the slavery interest was thus losing in the House, accident and agreement had managed to
keep the two sections equal in the Senate.   Five of the
original thirteen states had by 1789 adopted the policy of
emancipation, either immediate or gradual.   Vermont, free
since 1777, was admitted in 1791; New York and New Jersey
in 1799 and 1804, respectively, changed from slavery to emancipation, and Ohio in 1803 was admitted as a free state, making nine in all by 1804.   Kentucky and Tennessee, admitted
in 1792 and 1796, made good the loss of New York and New
Jersey to the list of slave states, and Louisiana, in 1812,
brought their number up to nine.   Thereafter the balance
was preserved by admitting Indiana, free, in 1816, Mississippi,
slave, in 1817, Illinois, free, in 1818, and Alabama, slave, in
1819.

Attitude to-
ward slavery.

Interest in the question of slavery from the ethical
standpoint seemed to have declined.   After the abolition of
the slave trade in 1808 the antislavery societies, which had
at one time been quite numerous in both North and South,
and had since 1793 held an annual convention, ceased to be
active; and they were succeeded in 1816 by the Colonization
Society, many of whose members were more interested in
freeing the South from the incubus of the free negro than in
freeing the slaves.   This society began a settlement called
Liberia, on the coast of Africa, as a refuge for transported
blacks, but its efforts are said to have relieved the country
in nineteen years of the natural increase of only nine and a half
days.   While the moral issue slumbered, an important economic question was arising.   The renewed interest of the
South in slave labor, and the rapid expansion westward of the
plantation system, made southern statesmen anxious to save
as much as possible of the national domain for slavery.

New laws were fortifying this institution at home, and capitalists of southern birth were endeavoring to overthrow the prohibition in Indiana and Illinois. On the other hand the moneyless pioneer, whether from a free or a slave state, was anxious not to encounter the competition of the plantation and the social obloquy of working at labor shared by negro slaves. This struggle between the systems of free and slave labor approached a climax when the frontier of population touched territory the status of which with respect to slavery had not been determined.

In December, 1818, Missouri petitioned to be allowed to form a state constitution. An enabling bill was introduced into the House, and on February 13, 1819, Mr. Tallmadge of New York moved to amend it in such a way as to prohibit the further introduction of slaves into Missouri and to provide that the children of slaves already there, born after the admission of the state, become free at the age of twenty-five. Thus amended the bill passed the House, but Tallmadge's amendments were struck out in the Senate. The House insisted on its amendments by a vote of 78 to 76, and consequently there was no action during that session of Congress. The dispute, once started, blazed throughout the country. Cobb of Georgia told Tallmadge: "You have kindled a fire which the waters of the oceans cannot put out, and seas of blood can only extinguish." The fact that it was the Senate only that prevented the passage of the amendments aroused the South to the necessity of preserving its political balance and the equality in the number of states. The North was stirred to defend the interests of its settlers, and to prevent any increase in the slave representation. The long dominance of the South in national politics strengthened the popular feeling in the North, and it became evident that, in spite of the absence of agitation, antislavery feeling was developing. *The Missouri question.*

The debate in Congress brought out little argument in favor of slavery except as a necessary evil. The argument of *The Missouri debate.*

Clay that the diffusion of slavery would weaken and ameliorate it was a popular one.   The main contention of the opponents of restriction was that Congress had no right to
bind a state.   This doctrine, most effectively set forth in the
next session by William Pinkney of Maryland, appealed
strongly to the state rights' advocates of the South and West.
It was no new or theoretical argument.   From 1805 to 1824
the central point of Illinois and Indiana politics was the
question whether they should remain bound by the prohibi-
tions of the Northwest Ordinance.   Ultimately the majority
decided that they did not want slavery.   If they had decided
differently, it is difficult to see how slavery there would have
been prevented, although the national courts might have
been able to do it.   The leading spokesman of the restriction-
ists was Rufus King of New York, who presented many instances of such conditions applied by Congress to states, in
particular those which had been applied to the Northwest
Territory, and a number contained in the Louisiana Purchase
treaty.   The popular discussion was fully as keen as that in
Congress.   Legislatures petitioned Congress on the one side
and the other.   John Quincy Adams and Calhoun conversed
on the possibility of a separation of the sections.   Adams
believed that the North would forcibly prevent such action
if attempted by the South.

The Missouri Compromise.   When Congress came together again, in December, 1819,
the situation was complicated by the request of Maine for
admission.   If Congress did not consent before March 4,
1820, the permission of Massachusetts for such a division of
her territory would be withdrawn and the opportunity to
form an additional free state would be lost.   Under this pressure, a compromise was brought about.   Maine was to be
admitted as a free state, and Missouri as a slave state, and
in the remainder of the Louisiana territory north of 36° 30'
(the southern boundary line of Missouri) slavery was to be
prohibited forever.   In the House, the vote for this latter

clause was 134 to 42, of whom 37 were from the South.
On the admission of Missouri as a slave state, the South
was solid for it, the Northwest solid against; from New England seven voted for it and from the Middle States eight,
three purposely absented themselves, and it passed. The
compromise thus effected Randolph characterized as a dirty
bargain of eighteen northern "dough-faces," an epithet
which clung for years to northerners voting for proslavery
measures. Monroe, after much consultation, signed the bill,
probably understanding that "forever" meant until the territory was created into states, thus supporting Pinkney in
the view that Congress could not bind a state.

The Missouri question broke out afresh at the next session,   Second Mis-
for Missouri had adopted and asked approval for a constitu-   souri Com-
                                                              promise.
tion forbidding free colored persons to settle in the state, thus
abridging, it was claimed, the rights of citizens of other states.
Debate again raged. It was argued that Missouri was violating the Constitution, and on the other hand that Missouri was
already a sovereign state and could not be disciplined. In
this crisis, Henry Clay succeeded in bringing about a compromise, admitting Missouri on condition that the obnoxious
clause should never be construed to abridge the rights to
which any citizen is entitled under the Federal Constitution; a vague and imperfect agreement, which nevertheless served its purpose. Good feeling was in large measure
restored, and the struggle over slavery was postponed for
many years.

In the interval between the two Missouri compromises   Election of
Monroe was quietly reëlected. Only one electoral vote was   1820.
cast against him, although the Federalists elected a fair
number of congressmen and might have cast some electoral
votes had they decided to do so. Most of the northern
representatives favoring the compromise were defeated, but
the subsidence of the slavery issue deprived this fact of
much of its significance.

Spanish-
American
Revolution.

The second administration of Monroe saw the settlement of a question that had long been troubling the government. During the Napoleonic wars the American colonies
of Spain had been relieved from her active control, revolutionary movements had been started, and trade relations had
sprung up which the inhabitants were loath to relinquish.
These relations were for the most part with England, and
the amount of trade was so great that Napoleon, when at
Elba, stated that it was the opening of this new outlet for
English commerce that had prevented the success of his
continental system. From 1810 on, Buenos Aires maintained a practical independence, although it was not declared
until 1816. Her great leader, General San Martin, in 1817
crossed the Andes, and in 1818 won the independence of
Chile. In 1821 he drove the Spaniards out of Peru. In
1817 a successful revolution was begun in Venezuela under
the inspiration of Simon Bolivar, who had succeeded to
the position and plans of Miranda after the latter's death in
1812. Victorious at home, he pushed the Spaniards from
what is now Colombia and Ecuador, finally defeating their
last South American forces, in 1824, on the plateaus of
Upper Peru, which was renamed Bolivia. Somewhat similar and simultaneous movements freed Mexico and Central
America from Spain, and Brazil from Portugal.

Duties of
neutrals.

These movements excited intense interest in the United
States. The breaking down of the Spanish colonial empire
seemed to open broad avenues to American commerce, and
the democratic sentiment of the country thrilled with sympathy for a movement so like our own struggle with England.
While there was substantial agreement that Spain could not
recover her American possessions and that no other country
should be allowed to take them, there was divergence as to
method. Henry Clay represented the enthusiastic public
sentiment, particularly of the West, and urged immediate
action. The administration saw a position so complex and

difficult that it dared move but slowly, and secured in 1817 the passage of a neutrality law more strict than that of 1794, to prevent Americans from compromising the government by equipping vessels or expeditions in United States ports to assist the revolutionists.

John Quincy Adams was particularly anxious to preserve the fairest appearance of neutrality in order that no excuse might be given for European intervention, and that his negotiations for the purchase of Florida might proceed smoothly. At the same time he pressed to the utmost all advantages against Spain, to hasten the latter negotiation. In 1812 Mobile had been seized as a part of the Louisiana Purchase, and was still held. In 1817 Florida was invaded by American troops to suppress a nest of pirates, posing as South American patriots, at Amelia Island, and in 1818 a more formidable invasion was made to the westward to punish certain Indians who had been raiding the southern part of Georgia. General Jackson, who commanded this expedition, conceiving that he had received tacit instructions from Monroe to seize Florida, took possession of all the western portion of that province. This latter action was disavowed by the United States, but it so forcibly illustrated the helplessness of the Spanish authorities, and Adams so firmly insisted that we would not stand annoyances arising from her weak government, that Spain finally consented to sell what she could not hold. In 1819 a treaty was made which, in addition to ceding Florida, defined a line of demarcation between the United States and Mexico, which Spain still held. This line ran irregularly from the mouth of the Sabine River to the parallel of 42° north latitude, and along that parallel to the Pacific. This line was unsatisfactory to some, particularly to Clay and to Adams himself, because it left what is now Texas, to which we had a somewhat shadowy claim as part of the Louisiana Purchase, in the possession of Spain ; it was, however, an important step in terri-

The Florida treaty.

torial expansion, because it gave the first international recognition to our claim to extend to the Pacific. The treaty
was not ratified until February, 1821. This matter settled,
in March, 1822, recognition was given to certain of the new
Spanish-American republics, though neutrality was still maintained between them and Spain.

The Holy
Alliance.

In the meantime this American difficulty was attracting
the attention of Europe. The leading continental powers,
Russia, Austria, Prussia, and France, were united in the Holy
Alliance, for the purpose of maintaining peace and monar-
chical government. Rebellion after rebellion was put down in
Europe, and American statesmen had well-grounded fears
that the establishment of peace there would be followed by
intervention in America. The crisis came in 1823, when
France, as agent of the Alliance suppressed a republican revolution in Spain, and order seemed to be established throughout the territories of the Holy Alliance and dependent states
except the American colonies of Spain. Fortunately England was as unwilling as the United States to see the new
republics restored to their former condition or given to a foreign power. There was much sympathy in England for
liberal government, many English took part as volunteers
in the struggle for South American independence, and the
English merchants did not wish to surrender the markets
they had found in the newly opened ports. Canning, the
English minister of foreign affairs, suggested that as their
interests were alike, the United States and England join in
protesting against the threatened intervention by the allied
European powers. President Monroe and others considered
the situation so critical that this offer by Canning ought to
be accepted. Adams, however, succeeded in convincing
them that England, because of her interests, would oppose
the movement whether her offer was accepted or not, and
that we should avoid such an entangling alliance. He believed that the United States was the leading American

power, and should not admit England to equal coöperation.

In December, 1823, this policy was announced to the The Monroe Doctrine. world in the President's annual message. It was stated that Europe had a set of primary interests with which the United States would not interfere; that, in return, it was expected that Europe would not interfere with the primary interests and particularly the governmental system of the American continents. "With the existing colonies or dependencies of any European power, we have not interfered, and shall not interfere. But with the governments who have declared their independence, and maintained it, and whose independence we have, on great consideration, and on just principles, acknowledged, we could not view any interposition for the purpose of oppressing them, or controlling, in any other manner, their destiny, by any European power, in any other light than as the manifestation of an unfriendly disposition towards the United States. . . ." Special intimation was given, because of the encroachments of Russia on the northwest coast, that the era of colonization was over, there being no longer any unclaimed land on the two American continents.

The success of the Monroe Doctrine was immediate and lasting. It had been for many years before the American Revolution the desire of the people of the American colonies to break away from all European interference. The Revolution had only partly accomplished this separation, the close of the Napoleonic wars made it actual, and the Monroe Doctrine applied the principle to both American continents and, by preventing European powers from obtaining a foothold, reduced the danger of future complications. In Europe the plan of intervention was abandoned, Spain ultimately acknowledged the independence of her American colonies, and Russia in 1824 consented to a satisfactory boundary on the northwest coast. Since 1823 no European country has at-

tempted to establish new colonies in America, and there
has been only one dangerous attempt by a European power
to overthrow the government of an American republic.

Rivalry of England and the United States.

The immunity of Spanish America from European attack
was at this time due more to the British fleet than to Monroe's
message; but the political wisdom of Adams in refusing to co-
operate with England was at once shown. The designs of
England in America were less obnoxious than those of the
other European countries, but her power was greater. England was, after all, the great rival of the United States, and the
ideas of the two countries were essentially divergent. Canning highly resented the claim that no European power should
interfere in America and the attitude of leadership assumed
by the United States in thus laying down the law for the
American continents. There at once arose a contest between
Adams and Canning, which continued after Adams ceased
to be Secretary of State and became President, for the
actual primacy in Spanish America. Adams urged upon
the new governments the advantages of the Monroe Doctrine;
he negotiated for commercial treaties, and in 1825 accepted
an invitation to send delegates to attend a Pan-American
Congress to be held at Panama. Canning claimed that
Spanish America owed its independence chiefly to English
aid and the protection of the English navy. He was able to
offer better terms and so secured more commercial treaties.
Moreover, in an open market American manufacturers could
not compete with the English. The result was that England
obtained the main commercial advantages and was brought
into more intimate relationship with Spanish America than
was the United States. While the Monroe Doctrine, supported by the growing power of the United States, limited the
range of England's activity by causing her to refrain from a
policy of territorial acquisition, the rivalry of the two nations
was constant throughout the nineteenth century, and England
was the dominant power in the Caribbean Sea almost to 1900.

In domestic policies, the direction still seemed to be toward a broad use of national power. Congress voted to make the Cumberland Road a turnpike supported by tolls, but this was prevented by a veto of Monroe in 1822 based on constitutional grounds. Nevertheless he favored an amendment to make such action possible. Congress took up the problem of harbor improvements, and in 1824 passed a bill providing for a general survey, looking toward a comprehensive system. In 1824 a new tariff was passed, more decidedly protectionist in character than that of 1816.

Nationalistic legislation.

The most important legislation was with regard to public lands. The existing system, as reorganized in 1800 and in 1804, provided that land be put up at auction and sold at or above the minimum price of $2 an acre. Land not sold at auction might be bought at private sale for $2. In either case at least one hundred and sixty acres had to be purchased, and a limited credit was given for three quarters of the purchase price. This system encouraged speculation; men put all their money into the first cash payment, buying as large an area as possible, and trusted to the future for the rest. Many became insolvent, and their distress was redoubled by the crisis of 1819. It was estimated that in 1820 half the heads of families in the Northwest owed the government for land. Gerson Flagg wrote from Edwardsville, Illinois, December 10, 1820: "The price of land has fallen more than half — a bad time for speculators — there are many here who paid out all the money they had in first installments on land and depended on selling it before the other payments became due. And as the price of land is now reduced nobody will buy it at the former price. It will of course revert to the United States unless Congress does something for their relief." Various measures were taken in 1820 and 1821 to relieve this situation. The minimum price of land was reduced to $1.25; the minimum amount to be sold was reduced to eighty acres, and the credit system was

The land question.

abolished. Those holding land unpaid for were allowed to pay at this new rate, and to turn over to the government a portion of their land as payment, keeping such amount as their payments already made would cover. These changes relieved the acute distress. By the end of the next administration the public land system was on a businesslike basis. There was a demand that the system be still further changed, that the idea of making a revenue be abandoned, and the land opened on easier terms to the actual settler, but while this proposition was continually agitated, the policy was not adopted.

The campaign of 1824. Crawford.

As the election of 1824 approached, the contest for the succession became more bitter. The friends of Crawford, believing him to have the strongest support in Congress, called a caucus, as had been the custom. It was held, and recommended Crawford to the people for the presidency and Gallatin for the vice presidency. The friends of the other candidates refused to attend the caucus, denounced it as a corrupting and undemocratic method of selecting a candidate, and made it one of the issues of the campaign. It was said to be but an evasion of the wise provision of the Constitution forbidding congressmen to be presidential electors. It made the President dependent on Congress. This attack injured Crawford, particularly in Pennsylvania, a state which he had hoped to win by the selection of Gallatin as running mate. The legislative caucus had long been a local issue there, and was growing increasingly unpopular. Crawford received less than one tenth of the vote of that state. Crawford's campaign was further hampered by his physical breakdown resulting from a stroke of paralysis. His political strength lay in Virginia, where he was considered the soundest exponent of the old Republican principles, to support which, against the attacks of Marshall, many of the best minds of that state were now rallying. In Georgia, where he lived, he represented a similar interest, and he was supported in New

York by Martin Van Buren and other politicians. He received 41 electoral votes.

John Quincy Adams was put in nomination by the legis- John Quincy
latures of Massachusetts and other states, but it was claimed Adams.
that actually his nomination involved a more dangerous
precedent than that of Crawford. Madison had been Secretary of State under Jefferson, Monroe under Madison, now
Adams was serving under Monroe. Practically, it was
argued, the President chose his own successor. Adams was
in favor of a broad nationalistic policy at home, and his conduct of foreign affairs had been admirable, but his strength
lay in the fact that he was the only northern candidate. He
received 84 electoral votes, including all those of New England, 26 out of 36 in New York, and 7 others scattered through
Delaware, Maryland, Illinois, and Louisiana.

The policies which Adams represented in the North, Clay Clay and
represented in the West. He had expected to receive the Jackson.
full support of his section now clamorous for recognition.
This hope was defeated by the sudden appearance of a new
candidate, — Andrew Jackson, the victor of New Orleans.
The conflict between these rivals began in 1819, when Clay
endeavored to have Congress censure Jackson for his conduct
in Florida. Jackson betook himself to Washington to defend
his reputation. He gathered friends by his simplicity, his
dignified bearing, and his sterling common sense. He defeated the attack of Clay, and through his friendships laid the
foundation for a political machine. Carefully advised by a
group of able friends, he grew in strength. Clay attacked him
as a military chieftain, a new Alexander or Cæsar, threaten-
ing the liberties of the republic; but his quiet demeanor in his
public progresses reassured the people. His appeal was not
so much on particular policies as on the general ground of
democracy and opposition to the bureaucratic tendencies
of the established administration. Many felt that a change
was needed, a man of the people, fresh from among

them, untainted by long residence at Washington and abroad.

Clay and Jackson divided the electoral votes of the West, 33 to 29. Elsewhere, however, Clay received only 4, while Jackson proved to be the only candidate with national support. He divided the seaboard South with Crawford, receiving 33 votes to the latter's 36, and the Middle States with Adams, 37 to 26. In all he received 99 votes, New England being the only section not to contribute to the number.

Election in the House.

Calhoun was elected Vice President by a very large majority, but no candidate received a clear majority for the presidency. The election was thus thrown into the House of Representatives, which had to choose between the three receiving the highest numbers of electoral votes, — Jackson, Adams, and Crawford. In this election, according to the Constitution, each state cast one vote, decided by a majority vote of its representatives. Clay, excluded from the competition, became to a certain extent king maker, for the candidate he favored would be apt to receive the vote of the Clay states. His preferences and vote were naturally for Adams, whose general views were the same as his own, rather than for Crawford, supposed to be a strict constructionist, or for Jackson, whom he had so violently opposed. The vote was taken on February 9, and Adams was the choice of thirteen states, Jackson of seven, and Crawford of four. Adams was therefore declared elected.

"Bargain and corruption."

Before the election in the House took place, a Washington newspaper published a letter, the authorship of which a Mr. George Kramer, a member of Congress from Pennsylvania, afterward acknowledged, to the effect that Clay was negotiating to sell his support for the position of Secretary of State. On February 14 it was announced that Adams had decided to offer this position to Clay. This was at once hailed by their enemies as proof of the charge. The administration was attacked as founded on bargain and corruption. John Randolph, referring to the personal habits of the two men, — the strictness of Adams's and the somewhat loose life of Clay, — characterized it as a combination of Blifil and Black George, the Puritan and the Blackleg. He spoke of Clay as "this being so brilliant and so corrupt that like a rotten mackerel in the moonlight shined and stunk." Clay fought a duel with Randolph, and produced evidence, convincing to the historian, of his purity of motive in supporting Adams. Nevertheless the charge was, widely believed, and seemed to confirm in the public mind, particularly in the cruder portions of the country, the vague suspicions long entertained of public immorality at Washington.

Another charge of much greater significance was made *Popular sovereignty.* against the administration. It was urged that the election of Adams was a violation of the will of the people. Kramer wrote: "The nation having delivered Jackson into the hands of Congress backed by a large majority of their votes, there was in my mind no doubt that Congress would respond to the will of the nation by electing the individual they had declared to be their choice." The election was perfectly constitutional; there was in fact no ground for saying that Jackson was the choice of the majority. No candidate received a majority of either electoral or popular votes, and it was impossible to say how the people would have voted had the issue been a simple one between Adams and Jackson. Senator Benton of Missouri, one of the Jackson leaders, wrote to Scott, the Missouri representative: "The vote which you intend thus to give is not your own. It belongs to the people of the state of Missouri." In Missouri the vote had been, 1401 for Clay, 987 for Jackson, and 311 for Adams. With Clay no longer a candidate and now supporting Adams, it was certainly difficult to say how the people of Missouri wished their representative to vote. Benton claimed that the vote should be for Jackson ; Scott voted for Adams. Difficult as it was to tell who "the people" were and what they wished, this assertion that the government did not rest on their will very much weakened the administration. It made a direct appeal to the growing democratic spirit of the time.

Party con-
flict.

The inauguration, therefore, found two parties existing in place of the four factions of the previous November. The administration, combining in its support the followers of its two leaders, embarked upon an active progressive nationalistic policy. It found itself confronted by an opposition, ably led, composed of most of those who had favored Crawford and Calhoun as well as Jackson. This opposition endeavored to avoid committing itself on subjects of national policy, and contented itself with attacking the administration as corrupt, and with upholding the rights of the people: a program which could unite all elements of opposition without exciting discord.

Adams and
the civil
service.

Adams wished to ignore these political divisions and continue the "era of good feeling." In spite of the fact that many of those in office were his violent opponents, he would make no removals. In fact, he proceeded upon a still broader basis than Monroe, for he gave, in pursuance of an anteëlection promise, recognition to the Federalists, by naming Rufus King minister to England. Probably no administration before or after has been so nonpartisan. Adams lost more support than he won by this policy. He was not the man to love his enemies, even though he kept them in office, and they loved him no better; the good fellowship of rewarding one's friends was more popular than the correct virtue of impartiality.

Internal im-
provements.

The public policy which most interested Adams was that of internal improvements, and great impetus was given to this movement in 1825 by the completion and immediate success of the Erie Canal. During this administration more than twice as much was given for roads and harbors as in the whole previous history of the country. The total amount, however, was only something over two millions, and with the progress of surveys, it was becoming evident that this was but a drop in the bucket compared with the great sums needed for the development of transportation, and with the sums actually spent by states and companies in the wealthy coast region. Government aid was still rather a promise for the future than an accomplishment, and less popular support was gained than Adams anticipated.

In his own peculiar field of foreign affairs, also, Adams was unfortunate. When invited to send delegates to a Congress of American Republics called to meet at Panama, Adams and Clay gladly accepted. They foresaw a great future of continental coöperation, and hoped to secure the leadership for the United States. The plan, however, was made the subject of violent attack. Southern orators breathed on the smoldering coals of slavery feeling, by pointing out that the black republics of Haiti and Santo Domingo would also attend. The administration won its point, and Congress provided for delegates, but the delay made them late at the Congress, nothing was accomplished, and this advertised failure overshadowed the quieter routine successes of the period. *Foreign affairs.*

Meantime there was forced upon the government a question on which Adams was totally out of sympathy with a majority of his countrymen. Since the War of 1812 the government had been rapidly pushing its purchases of Indian land. Indian title had been extinguished in Ohio and almost completely in Indiana, Illinois, the lower peninsula of Michigan, Louisiana, and Arkansas. The Indians, however, still retained possession of rich tracts in Georgia, Alabama, and Mississippi, which were strongly desired by the westward-moving cotton planters. The treaty of Indian Springs in 1825 ceded a large portion of this land held by the Creeks in Georgia and Alabama. Intimations were brought to Adams *The Georgia Indians.*

that this treaty had been secured without the due consent of the Creek nation. He ordered an investigation, and decided that the treaty had been illegally negotiated. The matter was a complicated one. By a treaty of 1791 the United States had guaranteed to the Creeks the boundary agreed upon in that treaty. By Gallatin's agreement with Georgia in 1802 the United States had promised to remove the Indians as soon as possible. In the dilemma created by these conflicting promises, Adams decided to regard the treaty of Indian Springs as void, and ordered negotiations to be reopened. This seemed to the people of the frontier misplaced conscientiousness. Georgia was particularly incensed, deeming it part of her sovereign rights to control the Indians within her borders, and resenting any interference by the national government beyond the strict letter of the Constitution. Governor Troup proceeded to act according to the treaty of Indian Springs; the President notified him that he would cause the authority of the national government to be respected. Troup replied: "You are sufficiently explicit as to the means by which you propose to carry your resolution into effect. Thus the military character of the menace is established, and I am at liberty to give it the defiance which it merits."

This controversy was particularly unfortunate for Adams because it placed him in the doubly obnoxious position of supporting the Indians and of opposing state rights. The frontier, essentially devoted to the Union, and careless of strict construction though it was, nevertheless opposed the central government when it appeared as a monitor instead of a beneficent purveyor of roads and canals. This Georgia question served to weld together the frontier and the old Jeffersonian democracy. The fact that Adams ultimately succeeded in extinguishing the claim of the Creeks to territory in Georgia did not offset in the public mind his punctiliousness as to the methods employed.

The tariff question bid fair to be as disturbing for the oppo- The tariff
sition as Georgia was for the administration. Whereas Adams question.
and Clay and the districts supporting them were avowedly
in favor of a protective tariff, the Jackson leaders were confronted with the fact that their allies in Pennsylvania and
some other states wanted protection, while South Carolina
and Georgia were becoming every day more violently opposed to it. The protectionist sentiment was persistent, and
in 1827 a convention was held at Harrisburg to recommend
new legislation to Congress. At the next session it was
necessary to take up the subject.

Under these circumstances certain Jackson leaders de- The tariff of
vised a clever scheme by which to secure credit for pro- 1828.
tectionist sentiment without passing a bill, and to divide
their opponents. A bill was reported from a committee
controlled by Jackson men, which provided for high duties
on the iron of Pennsylvania and the raw products of the
West, but which gave inadequate protection to the textile manufacturers of New England. This might cause dissension between the two classes of protectionists, and it was
expected that the bill would be defeated by the combination
of New Englanders opposed to its details, and southerners
opposed to protection altogether. Thus legislation would
be prevented, the Jackson leaders would secure credit for
introducing a bill satisfactory to those regions in which their
strength lay, and the burden of the defeat would lie at the
door of Adams's home section, New England. This plan was
upset; for enough New England members, headed by
Webster, voted for the bill to carry it. This act, passed in
1828, framed with the intention of being defeated, based
upon no scientific principle, and relating, as John Randolph
said, "to manufactures of no sort or kind but the manufacture of a President of these United States," quite properly
acquired the title of the "Tariff of Abominations." Politically the tariff question had become so involved and compli-

cated that the attitude of the Jackson party on the subject was an enigma, which, after all, was one of the objects at which its leaders aimed.

The civil service. While they stood thus uncommitted on the subject of the tariff, the Jackson leaders endeavored to strengthen themselves by attacking the administration. In 1826 Benton brought in a report on the patronage. He was unable to show that corruption existed, but he magnified the size and influence of the civil service, and pointed out the danger to the republic if it should fall into the hands of unscrupulous politicians. To those who believed that the administration was founded on bargain and corruption, this seemed an added reason for overthrowing it and giving the control to Jackson, the true representative of the people. This attack was the more effective because of the unpopularity of the civil service. Owing to the failure to remove officials, many officeholders were old, while appointments were made, on the whole, from the more aristocratic classes. The red tape of administration generally seems unnecessary to those on the outside, and to the frontiersman it seemed devised but to cover up the theft of public money. The demand for "Reform" became one of the most effective of the issues made by the opposition.

Campaign of 1828. The campaign of 1828, therefore, was fought rather on the issue of who should run the government than what that government should do. The administration had not succeeded in defining any issue with its opponents on public policy, and it was not able to defend itself successfully against the charges and innuendoes continually directed against it.

Election of 1828. The electorate was thoroughly aroused by the busy four years' campaign, and several times as many votes were cast as in any previous election. The election resulted in the choice of Jackson, who received 647,276 popular votes to 508,064 for Adams, and 178 electoral votes to 83.

BIBLIOGRAPHICAL NOTES

For general politics, Adams, J. Q., *Memoirs*, and Benton, T. H., Sources. *Thirty Years' View*, are satisfactory. For the tariff the references given at the close of the last chapter continue sufficient. For internal improvements, Calhoun, J. C., *Works*, II, 186–196; and Richardson, *Messages*, II, 144–183 (Views of James Monroe, May 4, 1822). For the Missouri question: Adams, J. Q., *Memoirs*, V and VI. Jefferson, T., *Writings* (edited by H. A. Washington), VII. King, C. R., *Life, Correspondence, and Speeches of R. King*, VI, 690–803. For the Monroe Doctrine: *American History Leaflets*, no. 4. Hill, M., *Liberty Documents*, ch. XX.

In addition to the references on special subjects given at the Historical close of the last chapter, the following may be used: Basset, J. S., accounts. *Jackson*, vol. I. Holst, H. von, *United States*, I, 421–458. Hunt, politics. C. H., *Livingston*, ch. XIV. Lodge, H. C., *Webster*, 129–171. Parton, J., *Jackson*, III, 94–120. Phillips, U. B., *Georgia and State Rights* (Am. Hist. Assoc., *Report*, 1901, II), ch. II. Quincy, J., *Adams*, chs. VI, VII. Roosevelt, T., *Benton*, ch. III. Schurz, C., *Clay*, ch. X. Sumner, G. W., *Jackson*, chs. IV, V. Taussig, F. W., *Tariff History*, 68–108.

Moore, J. B., *American Diplomacy*, ch. VI. Turner, F. J., Monroe *New West*, 119–124. Gilman, D. C., *Monroe*, appendix, contains Doctrine. a bibliography.

Catterall, R. C. H., *Second Bank of the United States*, 1–21. Banking and Dewey, D. R., *State Banking before the Civil War* (Senate Doc., no. currency. 581, 61st Cong., 2d sess. Publication of the United States Monetary Commission).

Burgess, *Middle Period*, 61–108. Hammond, *The Cotton Industry*, chs. I, II, and III. Harris, *Slavery in Illinois*, 6–16, 27–50. Missouri Compromise. Hinsdale, B. A., *Old Northwest*, 345–367. Holst, H. von, *United States*, I, 324–381. McMaster, *United States*, III, 514–529. Schafer, W. A., *Sectionalism and Representation in South Carolina* (Am. Hist. Assoc., *Report*, 1900, I), 184–400. Turner, *New West*, 149–172.

CHAPTER XI

FRONTIER POLICIES

THE inauguration of Andrew Jackson, on March 4, 1829, brings to a close the period of transition beginning in 1815. The new tendencies, struggling during this period for expression, became established. The change from the second Adams to Jackson was much more important than that from the first Adams to Jefferson. The election of Jefferson had caused a temporary halt in the centralization of the government. The Jeffersonian democracy wished government to do as little as possible, because it was afraid of being oppressed. In practice the Jeffersonian Democrats were almost as aristocratic as the Federalists had been; control was still in the hands of a class. The Jacksonian democracy, on the other hand, had a robust belief in its power; it was unafraid; it wished the government to be active. The Jackson victory, moreover, meant the actual transfer of power to the majority. The people at large were brought into more direct contact with the government, by the extension of political organization, by the growth of the press and by the appointment of men of all classes to office. So complete was this transfer of power, that politics in the North became unfashionable, and for a period of fifty years men of wealth and refinement, to a large extent, kept out of political life. It was not only that the Jackson party triumphed, but in this fundamental point of appealing directly to the plain people their opponents were obliged to copy them. The basis of political power in the United States was permanently broadened.

This change was dramatically represented by the charac-

Jacksonian democracy.

The inauguration.

184

ANDREW JACKSON

ter of the inaugural exercises. In the place of the trimly
dressed gentlemen of the old rêgime, who gravely bore their
part in the imposing ceremony of the inauguration, and the
crowds of female relatives who came to visit Washington and
attend the dignified social functions of the season, came
thousands of unselected Democrats, editors from the frontier, ward heelers from New York, and Pennsylvania farmers.
The chief social function was a vast reception at the White
House, which ended in a drunken revelry. Justice Story
wrote: " King Mob seemed triumphant." The breakdown
of social barriers illustrated the leveling of those of politics.

While it was clear to most intelligent on-lookers that Composition
the victory of Jackson meant a closer relationship between of Jackson's party.
government and people, it was not clear what form this
relationship would take, or what public policies would be
adopted by the new administration; for the victory had been
won by a combination of elements differing widely in their
view of what was meant by democracy and what policy
was advantageous for the government.

First was the democracy of the frontier, represented by The frontier.
Jackson himself, self-reliant, based on actual equality among
the people. Politically, it was kept together by personal
leadership. It expected from the new government a renova-
tion of the civil service, a solution of the land problem, the
elimination of the Indian, relief from currency troubles. On
the tariff and internal improvements it was divided. This
frontier element was the most powerful. Influential in deciding issues between the other sections since 1812, it was
from now on for fifteen years the dominant section, but·it
could not rule alone. The ten frontier states, including
Georgia, which can at this time be considered as frontier,
cast, in 1828, 74 electoral votes to 187 cast by the rest of
the country; the census of 1830 would make the proportion
96 to 190. Jackson received the total electoral vote of this
section and almost two thirds of the popular vote.

Virginian democracy.

Allied with the frontier was the Jeffersonian democracy of Virginia, North Carolina, and Maryland; democratic in theory rather than in practice, controlled by an upper class of intelligent planters, sensitive on constitutional questions, opposed to centralization, and hoping for a reversal of the active policy pursued by the Adams administration. The planters, however, favored a government decorously conducted by gentlemen, and they looked at currency questions from the point of view of men with large vested interests. This section contributed 44 electoral votes to Jackson and only 6 to Adams.

The Cotton South.

The eleven votes of South Carolina, which was as yet the only state thoroughly controlled by the cotton interest, were given to Jackson with the firm conviction that he was, or could be made, an advocate of tariff reduction if not an opponent of protection altogether. South Carolina furnished the Vice President, Calhoun, and it was expected that after a single term, Jackson would retire and leave him the succession. In character the democracy of South Carolina resembled more that of Virginia than that of the frontier, the control being in the hands of a capitalistic upper class. It differed from that of Virginia in that the industry upon which it was based was steadily growing, encroaching constantly upon the frontier region, as cotton plantations were established in western states.

Northern democracy.

With the votes received from the West and South, Jackson would have just failed of election ; his great victory was due to the democracy of the North. The northern democracy differed from that of the other sections in that it was a democracy opposed to an aristocracy. It consisted in the main of the poorer and less fortunate classes who lived in the same communities with the richer and more powerful. It had, therefore, somewhat of the bitterness of European democracies, and it felt the need of close organization for self-protection. The minor leaders of this section were of a lower character than those elsewhere, and the most important figure, Martin Van Buren, governor of New York, was regarded very generally as a man whose talents were confined to the successful manipulation of the party machinery. This northern faction of the party was strongly interested in maintaining the tariff. It cast 49 electoral votes for Jackson, only one of which came from New England.

The organization of the administration gave little clew as to which would be the ruling faction, but it did serve to emphasize the fact that the character of the government had completely changed. None of the new cabinet officers were men of previous experience in national administration. Martin Van Buren was made Secretary of State; of the remaining members, three were more or less closely allied to Calhoun, two were personal friends of Jackson. Virginia, for the first time in the history of the country, was without a representative at the council table of the cabinet. The influence of Calhoun was strengthened by the patronage given the *Telegraph*, a Washington paper, which was edited by his friend Duff Green, and which became the official organ of the administration. It was soon evident, however, that the personnel of the cabinet meant comparatively little, for Jackson gave no more weight to the advice of his constitutional advisers than to that of outsiders. He gradually drew about him a group of personal friends whose advice he often took, and whose pens he often employed to make up for his own want of literary skill. Most important of these were Amos Kendall of Kentucky, Isaac Hill of New Hampshire, Major Lewis of Tennessee, and F. P. Blair of Missouri, who occupied inferior positions, but who were dubbed, because of their influence, the "Kitchen Cabinet." The administration.

The attention of the administration was first given to the civil service. In fact it was forced to act by the crowd which had flocked to Washington, not only to witness the triumph of the people, but also to divide the spoils. After a campaign Removals.

waged largely on the plea that the government was corrupt,
it was natural that the first result of victory should be to
remove from office those supposed to be unfaithful. Moreover, the frontier believed in the capacity of any man
for any kind of work, a belief based on the frontier necessity
for one man to do many things. It distrusted experts. As
Jackson said in one of his messages: "The duties of all
public offices are, or at least admit of being made, so plain and
simple that men of intelligence may readily qualify themselves for their performance; and I cannot but believe that
more is lost by the long continuance of men in office than is
generally to be gained by their experience." It was held
that the offices should be manned by friends of the administration, and, at least in theory, that even these friends
should "rotate" every so often. Office was regarded rather
as a sinecure than as a duty. Although these doctrines were
popular, the adoption of a general policy of removal created great popular excitement. For thirty years an appointment in the civil service had meant almost certainly
a life position, and officeholders were not prepared to fall
back on other occupations. The population of Washington
depended almost wholly upon public employment. Moreover, the Jackson administration did not make removals
slowly and for special reasons. as did Jefferson, but upon the
broad grounds that public offices should not be held long by
any one person, and that it was right to punish one's enemies.

Appoint-
ments.

More important was the difference in the character of
the men who got places "out of the general scramble for
plunder," as Samuel Swartwout describes the struggle for
appointments. The decisive qualification for office was
service to the party. The motto of the administration was,
"To the victors belong the spoils." Nor was it past service
only that was considered, but also the possibility of future
usefulness. A great many appointments were given to editors who had spread broadcast the charges of corruption

against the previous administration. Few newspapers paid at that time, and many had been maintained with a view to reward when the victory came. These editors planned to combine their new official duties with their editorial labors. Very soon there developed also the policy of assessing the officeholders for the purpose of paying party expenses. Thus the spoils system was fully established.

Closely connected with the establishment of the spoils system was the development of party organization. Such organization was expensive, and the civil service was thus made to bear this expense. In New York and Pennsylvania this process was already complete in 1829; now it spread rapidly. After 1831 national conventions were held for the selection of presidential candidates, and these became the centers of party organization. They soon began to provide for a permanent national committee which became the executive of the party. The convention system having been adopted for national purposes, it rapidly spread into those states where it had not previously been established. The old custom of individual nominations and of legislative caucuses gradually disappeared, and the convention system became, in the course of time, practically universal. *Party organization and the spoils system.*

These innovations were not brought about without opposition. The spoils system was popular on the frontier and with the northern democracy; it was unpopular with the southern democracy. In fact the Atlantic coast states of the South were generally exempted from political proscription until after the Civil War. The spoils system was bitterly attacked by the opponents of the administration. They claimed that it would lead to maladministration, and that it gave the President too great power by making all officers dependent upon him for their livelihood. The convention system was perhaps even more disliked, particularly in the South, on the ground that it gave the majority a tyrannical power in dictating party policy. Calhoun and many other *Opposition.*

southern leaders never gave up the fight for local party
independence.   In fact the formation of efficient national
party organizations was a long step in the consolidation of
the government, against which the South was always contending.

Significance
of the new
system.

In spite of opposition, both the spoils system and party
organization became definitely fixed upon the country.
When the opposition came into power in 1841, they pursued
the Jacksonian policy with regard to the civil service, and
they found themselves forced to adopt also the convention
system.   Circumstances compelled them to resort to national conventions in 1831 and 1832, and gradually the
practice was taken up by one state after another.   The
change of attitude is illustrated by the experience of a
young Illinois lawyer and Whig politician, Abraham Lincoln.
In 1840 he wrote a pamphlet denouncing the Democrats
because of the convention system; in 1843 he vigorously
defended it on the ground that its conveniences offset its
evils.   In fact these were necessary features of the Democratic
victory.   The people desired to control the ordinary everyday course of the government; to do this organization was
necessary, and to support this organization the spoils system
was the simplest method.   As party organization became
highly developed it was often used to thwart the will of the
people, and often the national conventions agreed to compromises acceptable to the people of no one section of the
country; but in a crude way it brought government nearer
the people, and by harmonizing sectional differences strengthened the government.   It was fifty years before these rough-
and-ready methods of democratic government were outgrown.

Indian
policy.

As a frontiersman and an Indian fighter, it was natural
that Jackson should take a vigorous attitude on the Indian
question.   In his first annual message he attacked Jefferson's policy of civilizing them and "reclaiming them from a
wandering life."   This policy seemed to be succeeding too

well in Georgia, where the Cherokees had become sedentary, had adopted a tribal constitution, and had claimed immunity from the jurisdiction of the state. Georgia and Alabama had passed laws for the government of their Indian territories, and the Indians had appealed to the President for protection. He informed them that they must recognize state authority, and he recommended that Congress set apart an' Indian territory beyond the Mississippi, and gather there all the tribes then living to the east of it.

In carrying out this policy Jackson encountered the same opponent who had prevented the complete triumph of Jefferson thirty years before, — John Marshall. The Indians appealed their cause to the Supreme Court, which, in the cases of the *Cherokee Nation* v. *Georgia*, 1831, *Worcester* v. *Georgia*, 1832, and *Graves* v. *Georgia*, 1834, decided that the Cherokees constituted a "domestic dependent nation"; that the laws of Georgia were void within their territory, and that treaties between them and the United States were valid. As there existed a treaty guaranteeing their territory, the United States seemed bound to defend them. President Jackson, however, ignored these decisions. He would not admit that the Supreme Court could dictate the policy of the executive. "John Marshall has made his decision," he is reported to have said ; "now let him enforce it." *Jackson and Marshall.*

Throughout the administration the constructive portion of Jackson's Indian policy was consistently carried out, with skill and success. In 1834 an Indian territory was roughly defined. Already in 1830 arrangements had been made for the removal of the Choctaws from Mississippi. In 1836 the great majority of the Creeks and Cherokees were at length removed from Georgia and Alabama. The same policy cleared northern Illinois and Wisconsin of the Winnebago and Sac and Fox tribes, though not until after a short period of hostilities in 1832, known as the Black Hawk War. *Indian removals.*

As a result of these removals the population of Illinois bounded, in the decade, from 157,445 to 476,183; that of Alabama from 309,527 to 590,756; that of Mississippi from 136,621 to 375,651. Only the Seminoles in the swamps of Florida successfully resisted removal. The power of the Indians east of the great river had been broken by Jackson and Harrison in the victories of 1814; the credit for actually clearing the territory belonged to Jackson, and in performing this task he did one of the things which the frontier had elected him to do.

Opposition to internal improvements. On the subject of internal improvements Jackson's course was less clearly marked out. While Adams and Clay had relied upon this policy for popularity, the Jackson leaders had not committed themselves against it, and the frontier was divided. Every one saw the overwhelming need of improving transportation; differences existed as to whether it was the proper function of the national government to carry on such works. Jackson discussed the matter in his first annual message, and on May 30, 1830, decidedly revealed his policy by vetoing the "Maysville Road Bill." Unlike Madison and Monroe, he based his veto on the inexpediency as well as the unconstitutionality of such appropriations. This was an act of political courage, for the road proposed was intended to benefit that portion of Kentucky in which Jackson's support lay. Kentucky did not go Democratic again until 1856. A struggle now ensued between a majority in Congress and the President. Congress passed several appropriations for such purposes by including them in general appropriation bills which the President dared not veto; items thus passed being known as "riders." Jackson killed several bills that might have been passed over his veto by a two-thirds majority, by "pocket vetoes." If the President does not desire a bill passed by Congress to become a law, he must return it within ten days, otherwise it becomes effective without his signature, "unless the Congress by their adjournment prevent its return." The great majority of bills are passed in the last few days of the session, and a number of these Jackson simply "pocketed," neither signing nor vetoing them, and as Congress adjourned before the ten days expired, they simply lapsed. Within his party, Jackson won a decisive victory on this subject. Opposition to national grants for local purposes became one of the cardinal principles of the Democrats. On national legislation his attitude was influential for the time being; in 1838 the Cumberland Road was turned over to the states in which it lay, and no important new projects were undertaken; but many years later appropriations for rivers and harbors, and land grants to railroads, revived the practice.

Jackson's policy on this subject was not entirely negative. He realized the need of the frontier for capital with which to construct roads and canals, and proposed that, in case the national government had a surplus revenue, this money be divided among the states according to their representation in the electoral college. That is, he advocated leaving the work of improvement to the states, but supplying them with money. It seemed probable that there would soon be a surplus available, for the revenue far exceeded expenditures, and the public debt was being rapidly paid off. Jackson could look forward to action while still President, and he advised the adoption of a constitutional amendment to remove all doubt as to the legality of such action. In this he showed himself more in favor of practical state rights than Jefferson, who, in 1806, under similar circumstances, recommended an amendment giving the national government power to undertake such work. Jackson subsequently changed his mind, but his plan was in part carried out. *Distribution of the surplus.*

Closely connected with the question of internal improvements was another question deeply interesting to the frontier: that of the public land. By the time Jackson became *Public lands.*

President the business difficulties resulting from the credit system and the crisis of 1819 had been almost settled and the passage of some additional relief acts completed the work. A large question of policy remained. The demand of the settlers for a reduction in price, if not the sale of land at the actual cost of survey, was growing continually stronger. Benton, Jackson's great western champion, advocated it, and in 1832 Jackson himself said: "It seems to me to be our true policy that the public lands shall cease as soon as practicable to be a source of revenue." This policy was exceedingly distasteful to the older states, which, even as things were already, saw too many of their strong young men enticed away by the desire to become landowners. Particularly the manufacturing states feared the depletion of the ranks of their workers and felt the very present necessity, in order to keep the laboring population at home, of paying wages so high as to make competition with England increasingly difficult. On December 29, 1829, Senator Foote of Connecticut introduced a resolution that the committee on public lands inquire into the expediency of restricting sales at the minimum price to land already surveyed. This resolution became the excuse for one of the greatest debates that Congress ever heard, to which it will be necessary to recur in another connection, but it was not passed. On the other hand, the price of land was not reduced. Something, however, was done for the home seeker by the passage of a number of preëmption laws, which gave actual settlers the right to preëmpt or occupy land before it was put upon the market, and buy it at private sale at the minimum price before the public auction was held. These laws were passed for one year only, and applied only to those who had already taken such holdings. They were renewed almost every year. Finally, in 1841, a permanent general law was passed. The "squatter," instead of being driven from the public land, — a plan the government had tried in the eighteenth century,

— became the recognized forerunner of civilization, with a prior claim to the land he selected. More might have been accomplished had the land question not been closely involved with the general question of revenue and the tariff, and later with that of slavery.

As land was still to be sold at a profit the question arose as to what should be done with the revenue derived from it. Benton had the rather fantastic idea that it could best be employed in constructing fortifications which would forever render the United States secure against attack. Jackson proposed that the United States turn the lands within each state over to that state. His idea was that the states could use the proceeds of their lands for the purposes of internal improvement. Opposition to this plan was overwhelming. Either the states would sell cheaply and thus draw population more quickly from the East, or the first settlers would receive for their own purposes large sums from land secured by national effort, and which the landless states felt should be administered for the general benefit. The opposition, however, could not let matters rest without action. If the proceeds of land sales, after the payment of the debt, simply went to swell the general revenue, a large surplus would result. With a surplus revenue, the demand for a lower tariff would become compelling. Henry Clay, therefore, in 1833 presented a plan whereby the lands were to be administered by the national government, ten per cent of the proceeds of sale in each state was to be given to that state, the remainder was to be divided among all the states. This would dispose of the revenue; give special recognition to the state in which the land lay, recognize also the common claim of all the states, and furnish all states with a fund for internal improvements. The bill passed Congress, but Jackson "pocketed" it, and the question remained open. At length in 1836 a bill was passed which disposed of the whole surplus revenue, and which avoided any appearance of unconsti

Land revenue.

tutionality by providing that the money be loaned to the states instead of given to them. The special grant to the state in which the lands lay was also omitted. In this form Jackson accepted the measure, although somewhat unwillingly, and the question of land revenue was thus temporarily settled.

BIBLIOGRAPHICAL NOTES

Sources.   On the composition of the Jackson party: Adams, J. Q., *Memoirs*, VI, 5–104. Benton, T. H., *Thirty Years' View*. Chevalier, M., *Society, etc., in the United States*. [Cooper, J. F.], *Notions of the Americans*. Kendall, A., *Autobiography*. Quincy, J., *Figures of the Past*. Tocqueville, Alexis de, *Democracy in America* (translated by Bowen), 1–72. Mrs. Trollope, *Domestic Manners of the Americans*. Jackson's messages in Richardson's *Messages and Papers*, vol. I, 265, and vol. II, 308, are useful.

Historical accounts.   The best general accounts are: Macdonald, W., *Jacksonian Democracy;* and McMaster, J. B., *United States*, vol. V. Of biographies, those of *Jackson*, by W. G. Sumner and J. S. Bassett; of *T. H. Benton*, by W. M. Meigs and by T. Roosevelt; and of *M. Van Buren*, by E. M. Shepard, are useful. Woodburn, J. A., *Political Parties*, ch. IV.

Party organization.   Fish, C. R., *Civil Service and the Patronage*, chs. III, IV, V, VI. Macy, J., *Political Parties*, ch. IV. Ostrogorski, M., *Democracy and the Organization of Political Parties*, II, 1–75; also published in one volume. Parton, *Jackson*, III, 164–255.

Indian questions.   Phillips, U. B., *Georgia and State Rights* (Am. Hist. Assoc., *Report*, 1901, vol. II), ch. III.

Land and internal improvements.   Hart, A. B., *Practical Essays*, IX, X. Johnson, E. R., *River and Harbor Bills* (Am. Acad. of Polit. and Soc. Sci., *Annals*, II), 782 ff. Mason, *Veto Power*, secs. 83–94. Schouler, *United States*, ch. XIV, sec. II. Shosuke Sato, *Land Question* (*Johns Hopkins Historical Studies*, IV), nos. 7–9. Sioussat, S. L., *Tennessee Politics* (*Am. Hist. Review*, vol. 14, 50–69). Wellington, R. G., *Political and Sectional Influence of the Public Lands*.

CHAPTER XII

JACKSON AND SOUTH CAROLINA

WHILE the problems of the frontier were thus receiving Demands of South Carolina. attention and the voice of the northern politician was growing powerful, another section of the Jackson party demanded attention. No state had such high ambitions, none was so united in its desires, as South Carolina. The boon that it expected as a result of Jackson's triumph was the reduction, radical and prompt, of the tariff. All the distress caused by exhaustion of the soil, and the decline in the price of cotton due to the opening of new cotton areas, was attributed to the high tariff. Seldom has an entire population been so united in its understanding of an economic question, and it was equally insistent on relief.

It was the general belief in South Carolina that a pro- Constitutionality of a protective tariff. tective tariff was unconstitutional. The Constitution gives Congress power "to lay and collect Taxes, Duties, Imposts, and Excises to pay the Debts and provide for the common Defense and general Welfare of the United States; but all Duties, Imposts, and Excises shall be uniform throughout the United States." It was argued that there was no power to lay duties to protect domestic industry, and that such duties, so far from being uniform and providing for the general welfare, were ruining the cotton planter and enriching the cotton manufacturer. McDuffie also argued that an import duty on goods necessary in the production of cotton, by making it more costly, amounted to an export duty on cotton, and the Constitution specifically forbids export duties. Whether these arguments were or were not valid, they at any rate secured no relief from the courts. No tariff bill except that of 1789 contained any formal expression of its object, and it was impossible to prove that any particular duty was levied only for the purpose of protection. The constitutional argument was equally without effect in Congress. McDuffie claimed that the cotton interests were practically unrepresented, because they had a minority representation; subject as they were to the tyrannical rule of the majority, it would be as well to withdraw their representatives from Washington altogether.

Talk of secession.   The tariff of 1824 had caused men to formulate these views; the tariff of 1828 intensified their belief in them. Some leaders began to "calculate the value of the Union." Incendiary toasts were drunk at public dinners; a congress of the states opposed to the tariff was proposed; some suggested state laws to tax or prevent the importation of "tariffied" articles. Secession was discussed. "Fear nothing," said a correspondent in the *Charleston Courier;* "foreign nations will protect us. We have commerce and products to tempt them, and they have men and ships to defend us. Congress can do nothing but blockade us, and this may soon be obviated."

Calhoun's position.   To this situation it behooved Calhoun, the political leader of South Carolina, to set his mind. A cotton planter among cotton planters, he naturally sympathized with their views. At the same time he was deeply devoted to the Union. He had entered Congress as one of the enthusiastic young leaders who brought about the War of 1812; he had been active in the Fourteenth Congress, taking part in its discussion on the nationalistic side; for sixteen years he had been in Washington as congressman, cabinet officer, and vice president. In 1829 his prospects for a national career seemed high; he was strong in the cabinet, and had friends and supporters all over the North and West; he was the logical candidate for the succession. He therefore devoted all the powers of his great mind to make possible the prosperity of his section and the preservation of the Union.

The metaphysical bent of his Scotch ancestry was plainly apparent in his views. As he studied the situation in the light of past history he became convinced that all governments tend to become tyrannical. The problem is to create a government having sufficient power to be efficient, and yet so limited as to be unable to oppress any portion of the governed. The right to vote is not sufficient, for the tyranny of the majority is far worse than that of a single man. The only remedy is to allow each body of citizens of a particular section or special interest to vote separately, and require, to make a law valid, a "concurrent majority" in every section and interest. In this way all legislation for the general welfare could be passed, but nothing offensive to any section; the minority would be absolutely protected. "The concurrent majority . . . tends to unite the most opposite and conflicting interests, and to blend the whole in one common attachment to the country." "Instead of factions, strife, and struggle for party ascendency, there would be patriotism, nationality, harmony, and a struggle only for supremacy in promoting the common good of the whole." This view of the true structure of government Calhoun set forth later in an essay entitled: *A Disquisition on Government;* and it formed the basis of his political thought throughout the last twenty years of his life.

The doctrine of "concurrent majorities."

Applying these views to the United States, he argued that the government had been founded by thirteen independent states. These states had united and formed a compact or bargain, the terms of which were set forth in the Constitution. They had not surrendered their independence, they had not divided the sovereignty; because, according to his belief, sovereignty is indivisible, they had merely assigned certain specified functions to the central government. The national government must confine itself to the powers

The doctrine of nullification.

specified. If it exercised other powers, it was acting without authority. In such case a decision of the national Supreme Court could not be considered final, for it was a part of the national government. Back of the Court stood the states. In case of a "deliberate, palpable, and dangerous exercise of other powers not granted by the said compact," each state was at liberty to "nullify" the law. Thus the government would be prevented from oppressing any one state, and the principle of the concurrent majority would be maintained.

Calhoun's purpose.

This doctrine of nullification recalled the Virginia and Kentucky Resolutions of Madison and Jefferson, in the assertion of the right of a state to declare an act unconstitutional. Calhoun, however, went so far beyond them in drawing conclusions as to what action should be taken by the state, that Madison indignantly refused to be held responsible. According to this new view, if a state legislature were fully convinced that the Constitution was being violated and Congress refused to change its action, then a convention should be called, representing the people of the state as a whole, for the express purpose of discussing the question. The sovereign people acting thus in their collective capacity could declare such law null and void within the limits of the state. Thus the state would be relieved of oppression without resorting to the violent remedy of secession. This was undoubtedly the purpose of Calhoun. While he believed in secession as a right, he was, until just before the close of his life, opposed to it in practice. He was not even a strict constructionist in the sense that John Randolph was, for he was willing to see the range of national activity widen, so long as it was in accordance with the will of a concurrent majority and thus oppressed no one section or interest.

Webster-Hayne debate.

In 1828 Calhoun prepared an elaborate account of his views for the use of the South Carolina legislature, which adopted and published it under the title of the *South Carolina*

Exposition. In 1830, in the debate on the Foote resolution with regard to public lands, Robert Y. Hayne, a senator from South Carolina, speaking under the eye of Calhoun, the Vice President, elaborately explained and defended these views, and sought to win for them the support of the West by recalling the long alliance between that section and the South. Daniel Webster responded, and there followed the most famous debate in American legislative history. Webster asserted that the Union was older than the states. He maintained that the Convention of 1787 effectually framed, not a compact, but a government, which was sovereign within the range of powers specified in the Constitution; that the United States Supreme Court was the only proper arbiter as to the extent of these powers. He attacked Hayne's idea as bad history, bad law, and as utterly impracticable. Webster's speech was far more than a constitutional argument. It was a defense of the Union against the spirit of sectionism. It was filled with praise of the Union and what it had done and was to do for the country. It appealed to all to sink their differences in the struggle for the common good, and not only did it thrill the audience which he held spellbound in the Senate chamber, but its glowing periods carried conviction and enthusiasm to tens of thousands throughout the country. Oratorically the triumph rested with Webster, but in most respects it was a drawn battle. Historically neither view was wholly sound. There can be little doubt that the framers of the Constitution intended, as John Marshall's decisions indicated, to divide the sovereignty. There was nothing in the political thinking of the eighteenth century to cause that to be considered impossible. Here Webster clung nearer to the past than Hayne, for he recognized that the states were sovereign as well as the Union, while the latter utterly denied any sovereignty to Union. Probably, however, as his opponents asserted, Webster's views tended, if carried to their logical conclusion, to exalt the Union almost as much as Hayne's

exalted the states.   Webster carried with him the greater part
of the country.   The northeastern states, profiting as they
did by the western and southern markets for their products,
and by the navigation and tariff acts, were becoming every
year more devoted to the Union.   Hayne spoke to the growing cotton interest, whose feeling for the Union was so rudely
shaken by the oppression of the tariff, that many were coming
to believe that independence and an alliance with England
might best promote its prosperity.   The impression which the
two senators made on the West, to which they were both appealing, was a divided one.   The northern hostility to a liberal land
policy was the very cause of the debate, and its opposition to
expansion had not been forgotten.   The West, moreover, was
thoroughly in favor of local self-government, or state rights.
On the other hand, it had been strongly unionist in sentiment
ever since the Louisiana Purchase, and could not afford to lose
the navigation of the Mississippi, the markets for its products in the South and in the East, and national protection
for its sugar, hemp, and wool.   Moreover, in the West, Webster's argument that the Union was older than the states was
literally true, and the new states there lacked the historic
traditions that endeared the older states to their inhabitants.

Jackson and
Calhoun.

Upon the West, as represented by Jackson, Calhoun relied to obtain a reduction of the tariff ; if that failed, he hoped
that Jackson's state rights principles would cause him to tolerate peaceful nullification.   Calhoun and Jackson, however,
did not get on well together, and Van Buren steadily under-
mined Calhoun's influence.   Van Buren had the advantage
of being more congenial socially and more willing to be an
instrument, for it was becoming evident that Jackson was
to be the real head of his administration and desired assist-
ants rather than mentors.   The first breach came on April 13,
1830, when Jackson was invited to a banquet given by certain southern congressmen on Jefferson's birthday.   After
much state sovereignty oratory, he was asked to give a toast,

and proposed: "Our Federal Union, it must be preserved," a phrase which rallied the Union sentiment of the country even more than Webster's oratory. Just after this, a powerful weapon fell into the hands of Calhoun's foes. William H. Crawford wrote a letter in which he asserted that in 1818, when both he and Calhoun had been members of the cabinet, the latter had been in favor of censuring Jackson for his action in Florida. This letter, produced at the proper time, made Jackson intensely angry. He could not realize that Calhoun might be his friend and still have proposed such action, and he wrote, demanding an explanation. Calhoun made every effort to present the matter in the most favorable light, but no impression was made on Jackson, who on May 30, 1831, broke off all communication with the Vice President.

The break between Calhoun and the President was followed **The new cabinet.** by a reformation of the cabinet. All but one of Jackson's own supporters resigned to accept other positions, and Calhoun's friends were forced to retire. The new cabinet was much more representative of the party than was the old. The Secretary of State, Edward Livingston, was a very able man and a great friend of Jackson's. Lewis Cass, Secretary of War, and Levi Woodbury, Secretary of the Navy, were democratic leaders in the Northwest and in New England, respectively; Louis McLane of Delaware, Secretary of the Treasury, and Roger B. Taney of Maryland, the Attorney-General, continued to be prominent for many years. At the same time, the patronage of the administration was withdrawn from Calhoun's organ, the *Telegraph*, and was given to a new paper, the *Globe*, founded by Blair and Rives in the interests of Jackson. The summer of 1831 saw, therefore, the total reorganization of the administration, and the complete cutting off of one powerful faction of the Jackson party.

Meantime, Congress was giving as little consideration **Tariff legislation, 1830–1832.** to the economic views of the cotton planters as Jackson was to Calhoun's constitutional theories. In his first message Jackson had commented on the fact that the approaching payment of the debt made it necessary to plan for a reduction of the tariff, and that "the duties on those articles which cannot come in competition with our own productions are the first which should engage the attention of Congress." This distinctly protectionist idea was actually carried out by a reduction of duties on tea and coffee. The next Congress took up the matter more seriously. Clay, who was now in the Senate, moved a resolution to the effect "that the existing duties upon articles imported from foreign countries, and not coming in competition with similar articles made or produced in the United States, ought to be forthwith abolished. . . ." This represented the protectionist ideal of a reduction of the revenue without a reduction of protection. Hayne proposed "that the existing duties upon articles imported from foreign countries should be so reduced that the amount of the public revenue shall be sufficient to defray the expenses of the government according to their present scale after the payment of the public debt; and that, allowing a reasonable time for a gradual reduction of the present high duties on the articles coming into competition with similar articles made or produced in the United States, the duties be ultimately equalized so that the duty on no article shall, as compared with the value of that article, vary materially from the general average." The bill, as finally passed, was largely the work of John Quincy Adams, who was now a member of the House and chairman of the committee on manufactures. It was largely in accordance with Clay's resolution. The chief "abominations" of the tariff of 1828 were done away with, but reduction was accomplished mainly by putting noncompetitive articles on the free list. The protectionists claimed that by redressing the worst grievances this new tariff of 1832 would render the protective system more popular than ever, and mean its permanent adoption.

The time had now come when, if ever, South Carolina Nullification applied. should try the efficiency of its newly forged weapon of nullification. At this critical moment there was a sharp division within the state, and the party of action won by a vote of only 23,000 to 17,000. The decision made, the legislature called a convention, and the convention on November 24, 1832, declared the tariff act null and void after February 1, 1833. No appeals were to be allowed to United States courts, and if force were used, the state would be driven to the more extreme remedy of secession. On December 18 South Carolina suggested a convention of states to discuss the questions involved. If the South Carolina leaders expected that Jackson's respect for the rights of the states would paralyze the action of the central government, they were speedily undeceived. On December 10 he issued a proclamation drawn up by the new secretary of state, Edward Livingston, which denied in emphatic language and with cogent arguments both the right of nullification and that of secession, and was as strongly nationalistic as Webster's reply to Hayne. His determination to preserve the Union and enforce the laws was expressed firmly in the proclamation, with the accompaniment of profanity in private conversation, and in action by giving General Scott the necessary orders to collect the revenues in Charleston harbor.

South Carolina expected support from other states, particularly those in which the cotton interest was important. Unpopularity of nullification. Calhoun firmly believed that if he could but rally these states to a unity of action, they could dominate the country. Here he and his supporters met a decided disappointment. Although some states expressed opposition to the tariff, and Georgia and Alabama proposed conventions, — the one, of the southern states, and the other, of all the states, — no state supported the constitutional position of South Carolina, and several officially condemned nullification, and expressed their confidence in the general government. The Gulf States, with their fresh fields, did not feel the pinch of the tariff as did South Carolina. Moreover, the national government was at this very moment performing the inestimable service of driving out the Indians and opening wide new areas to cultivation. Men could not seriously fear the consolidating tendencies of an administration which was standing between them and the Supreme Court. South Carolina was thus left to stand alone.

Compromise of 1833. While the state did not secure any support for its constitutional views, it did cause a reconsideration of the tariff. Jackson led the way by advising a change: "In effecting this adjustment, it is due, in justice to the interests of the different states, and even to the preservation of the Union itself, that the protection afforded by existing laws to any branches of the national industry should not exceed what may be necessary to counteract the regulations of foreign nations and to secure a supply of those articles of manufacture essential to the national independence and safety in time of war." Calhoun resigned from the vice presidency in order to be on the floor of the Senate during this vital discussion, and South Carolina suspended the date of nullification to give Congress a fair chance to repent, and to repeal the bill it had just passed.

Compromise tariff act. The debate in Congress showed a decided weakening in the protectionist forces. This was partly due to natural causes, and partly to a general dislike to force to a crisis the issue presented by South Carolina. The matter dragged, however, and it seemed quite possible that Congress would adjourn without action. In the middle of February, urged by the seriousness of the situation, Clay conferred with Calhoun, and with his approval introduced a bill. With the leader of the protectionists and the leader of the opposition united in its support this bill was rapidly passed through Congress and became a law March 2, 1833. It was essentially the act of 1832 with a slight increase in the duty on woolens. In all cases where the duty exceeded twenty per cent, however, one tenth of this excess was to be removed every two years until 1840; on January 1, 1842, one half of the remaining excess was to be taken off, and on July 1, the other half. The result would be, on July 1, 1842, a uniform horizontal tariff of twenty per cent as Hayne proposed in his resolution.

While Congress thus offered an olive branch with one hand, it at the same time condemned nullification by passing, on March 1, a force bill giving the President powers adequate for dealing with the situation. In South Carolina the convention came together again and, declaring itself satisfied with the new tariff, withdrew its nullifying resolution, March 15, 1833. On March 18 it nullified the force bill, a proceeding quite harmless, as the President now had no occasion for acting under it. The force act.

As regards protection, the tariff of 1833 was distinctly a compromise. Clay claimed that he had really proved himself the savior of protection, for the new Congress, elected in the fall of 1832, would have reduced the tariff very considerably; now, bound by the compromise measure, the tariff would remain fairly protective until 1842, and then a new bill could be drawn up. Calhoun claimed that by adopting the compromise measure Congress had bound itself to the view that protection was justifiable only as a temporary measure; that the time for its abandonment was fixed in the bill, and that in the future the tariff would be levied on the horizontal basis. The question of the right of nullification also remained technically open. Calhoun claimed that it had proved entirely successful; that by it South Carolina had obtained redress that it could have found in no other way. The general impression in the country at large was decidedly different. The repudiation of the doctrine by all the states that expressed themselves on the subject, and particularly the emphatic tone of the President's proclama- Effect of the compromise.

tion, backed up as it was by acts, and supported by the passage of the force bill, 32 to 1 in the Senate and 110 to 40 in the House, impressed upon all the fact that the Union could and would enforce its laws.   As a matter of fact nullification was not again tried.   Politically the nullification controversy cleared the situation in many ways, particularly by showing the difference between the state rights views of Jackson, who believed in leaving much public business to the control of the states, but who, nevertheless, looked upon the Union as permanent; and the position of those who by state rights meant that the Union had no sovereign powers.   The unqualified Union doctrine, set forth in Jackson's proclamation, alarmed many who disapproved of South Carolina's action, but were fearful of a consolidated general government.   Many conservative southern thinkers began to act independently of the Democratic party, which its leaders had made so emphatically the party of the Union. The crisis caused by the tariff system was thus passed, but not without a decided shock to the nation, and permanent political results.

BIBLIOGRAPHICAL NOTES

Sources.

American History Leaflets, no. 30. Calhoun, J. C., *Works*, I, 1-107 (Disquisition on Government) ; IV, 164-212 (Speech on the Tariff) ; VI, 1-208 (Papers on Nullification). *Congressional Debates*, 20th Cong., 1 sess., 2382-2406 (Speech of McDuffie on the tariff, perhaps the best exposition of South Carolina's views) ; 21st Cong., 1 sess., 43-92 (Speeches of Webster and Hayne, which are also to be found in Macdonald, W., *Select Documents*, nos. 47-49, 53, 55, and 56; and many other places). For Jackson's Proclamation, see Richardson, *Messages*, II, 640-666. For documents see H. V. Ames, *State Documents*.

Historical accounts.

In addition to the general accounts mentioned at the close of the last chapter: Holst, von, *Calhoun*, ch. IV. Houston, D. F., *Nullification in South Carolina*. Lodge, H. C., *Webster*, chs. VI,

VII. McLaughlin, A. C., *Lewis Cass*, 139–149. Schafer, W. A., *Sectionalism and Representation in South Carolina* (Am. Hist. Assoc., *Report*, 1900, vol. I), 384–400. Stanwood, E., *American Tariff Controversies*, chs. VIII, IX. Sumner, W. G., *A. Jackson*, ch. VII, ch. VIII, sec. 7. Taussig, F. W., *Tariff History*, 74–112. Turner, F. J., *New West*, 314–333.

CHAPTER XIII

JACKSON AND THE BANK

WHILE Jackson and his party emerged from the nullification struggle distinctly pledged to support the Union, they were not committed either for or against a protective tariff. In fact the compromise took the tariff out of politics for ten years, and political issues had to be sought elsewhere. The main issue had already been formulated before the tariff compromise had been arranged. Few persons in the older states imagined in 1828 that the existence of the National Bank would by 1832 become the leading question of party division, but it was a question that the frontier was determined to press, and with the will the frontier had the power.

A frontier community is always in search of capital, for opportunities to expend it are innumerable and accumulation has not yet begun. It was to answer this demand that Adams and Clay proposed to have the national government undertake internal improvements, and that Jackson wished to give to the western states the public land. These plans had little practical result until the distribution bill of 1836, and western states and individuals were supplying themselves as they could by borrowing. Throughout the frontier the bulk of the inhabitants were debtors, and the most enterprising owed the largest sums; there was a general community of interest, and a tendency to look at all questions from the debtor rather than the creditor point of view. This showed itself particularly with regard to the currency. There was a demand for an abundant supply of money; there was less interest in its stability. The people wanted to get money easily to pay their debts; they did not feel keenly the necessity of paying in money worth one hundred cents on the dollar. The states were forbidden by the Constitution to emit bills of credit, and thus the financial expedients resorted to differed from those of the Shays's Rebellion period, though the situation was in many respects similar. It was discovered that the states could charter banks, and that these banks could emit bills of credit and thus partly satisfy the demand. As creditors refused to accept such bills at their face value, it was thought desirable to make them legal tender, and thus compel their acceptance somewhat as Rhode Island had done in 1786. Kentucky took such action, whereupon the state supreme court declared the act void on the ground that it violated the United States Constitution, which prohibits a state from making "anything but gold and silver Coin a Tender in Payment of Debts." This decision was at once attacked by the "Relief" party, and in 1825, by a vote of 38,000 to 22,000, a legislature was elected pledged to erect a new supreme court. The next year saw a reaction, and the matter was not forced, but the strength of the demand for an easy currency was made evident. The supporters of state banks, which were thus refused the indorsement which their states were anxious to give them, were naturally opposed to the United States Bank, whose notes were freely accepted by creditors both public and private. They believed that if this giant, privileged corporation, were once removed, they would be able to furnish a currency satisfactory to creditor and debtor alike. They disliked the strict and inflexible rules by which its branches regulated their relations with the state banks, thus keeping business up to a standard which public opinion believed too high. The frontier wished to set its own business standards.

To those who opposed the National Bank as a competitor of the state banks were added those who feared it as a great

The Bank and monopoly.

corporation and representative of the money power. At first
it had been as liberal in making loans and in encouraging
speculation as the better state banks; it extended its credit
so far, in fact, that it was on the verge of bankruptcy. At
this time Langdon Cheves had become president and adopted
a rigorous conservative policy which brought the Bank out
of its difficulties and enabled it to weather the crisis of 1819;
but the Bank was saved at the expense of foreclosures that
ruined hundreds of those who owed it money, and brought
into its hands immense amounts of general property. Benton said: "I know towns, yea cities, where this bank already
appears as an engrossing proprietor." "All the flourishing
cities of the West are mortgaged to this money power. They
may be devoured by it at any moment. They are in the
jaws of the monster! A lump of butter in the mouth of a
dog! One gulp, one swallow, and all is gone."

Objections to banks in general. Jackson, Benton, and others of the western leaders had
still another ground of opposition. They had seen the evil
effects of the overissues of paper money during the War of
1812 and of the contraction by the National Bank in 1819.
They became doubtful of the value of banks at all, and suspicious of all money except hard cash. Jackson in 1829
wrote to Nicholas Biddle, the new president of the United
States Bank: "I do not dislike your bank any more than all
banks, but ever since I read the history of the South Sea
Bubble I have been afraid of banks." They feared also
the influence of banks in politics, and with some reason.
Up to this time all banks were chartered by special act of a
state legislature or of Congress, and no legislature would
think of granting a charter to a bank whose board of directors
belonged to the party in opposition to the legislative majority.
Banks were often as closely connected with some party or
faction as were the newspapers, using their credit to further
the schemes of their partisans. Jefferson had written to
Gallatin that it would be advisable to make all banks Re-

publican by sharing the national deposits among them. It was, therefore, not unnatural to suspect the greatest of all banks of being concerned in politics.

The constitutional question seemed to have been settled by the decisions of John Marshall, but, as has been seen in the case of the Indians, Jackson did not consider the judgments of the Supreme Court binding on the executive. In the letter to Biddle just referred to, Jackson states his constitutional doubts and inclinations. His preferences were for a bank belonging entirely to the government and with its home in the District of Columbia. He disliked the mingling of public and private business as he did of state and national functions. He wished all government affairs to be so simple that the humblest citizen could understand them; all complexities were obnoxious to his temperament and to the men whom he represented. *The Bank and the government.*

Even before Jackson's election, hostility to the Bank was a political asset. In 1827 one Illinois politician wrote to another with respect to a third: "The Bank is suing everybody — several thousand dollars are now in judgment, and there is not money to meet the emergency. Many appeals are taken, and McLean is the defendant's lawyer in all the bank cases. He takes none for the Bank, nor ever has." "Such are the distresses of the people and his usefulness to them as a lawyer that it is difficult to say whether he can be excluded from the legislature." This opposition had found its way into national politics, and bills had been introduced into Congress for the sale of the government bank stock and for reducing the amount of government deposits held by the Bank. *Opening of the question.*

This agitation over the bank question was almost entirely confined to the frontier; in the older sections of the country the Bank was looked upon as a sound institution, doing its work well, and as a satisfactory financial agent of the government. There was, therefore, general surprise in the East

when Jackson referred to the matter in his first annual message, but there would have been disappointment in the West
if he had not done so. He called attention to the fact that
the charter expired in 1836, and that the question of a recharter would come up. "In order to avoid the evils resulting
from precipitancy in a measure involving such important
principles and such deep pecuniary interests, I feel that I
cannot, in justice to the parties interested, too soon present
it to a deliberate consideration of the legislature and the
people. Both the constitutionality and the expediency of
the law creating this bank are well questioned by a large
portion of our fellow-citizens; and it must be admitted by
all that it has failed in the great end of establishing a uniform
and sound currency."

This message was a great disappointment to Biddle,
who was on good terms with many of the Jackson leaders,
particularly with Major Lewis of the "kitchen cabinet," and
who had tried to conciliate Jackson by placing many of his
supporters on the directorates of the branch banks. It
placed him in an embarrassing position, for he could not tell
whether to cling to Jackson and rely on overcoming his opposition by allowing a few changes in the new charter, or
to fight him and help select a new President who would genuinely support the Bank. The alternative of doing nothing
and simply awaiting events was impossible for Biddle, who
was temperamentally a man of action. His dilemma continued even after the break between Jackson and South
Carolina, for McDuffie was the leader of the Bank interest
in the House, while the new Secretary of the Treasury, Mc-
Lane, was also friendly to the Bank.

The crisis came in the session of 1831–1832. Jackson
referred to the subject in his message and left it to the judgment of "an enlightened people." If nothing were done,
and Jackson were reëlected, the Bank would be entirely at his
mercy. If an appeal were to be taken to the people, the issue

must be framed in this session of Congress for presentation in the fall elections. Many of the leaders of the opposition urged Biddle to force the issue, and some insinuated that he must take sides if he expected their support. On January 9, 1832, he applied for a recharter. Certain modifications were made in the law with the hope of making it, even now, acceptable to Jackson. Before the bill was passed an investigation was ordered, which proved satisfactory to the Bank's friends, and the bill was passed in the Senate, 28 to 20, and in the House 109 to 79.

It now rested with Jackson to sign the bill or take issue with a decided majority in Congress. It required no small political courage, on the eve of a presidential election, to take a position on a question on which his own party was divided, and which he might easily avoid by accepting the vote in Congress as the decision of the "enlightened people," to whose judgment he had left the question in December. He, however, accepted the issue squarely, vetoing the bill in a message which was intended to be the leading political document in the next campaign. He was not satisfied with the modifications made in the charter. He contended that the charter created a monopoly: "The powers, privileges, and favors bestowed upon it in the original charter, by increasing the value of the stock above its par value, operated as a gratuity of many millions to the stockholders." The recharter would raise the value twenty to thirty per cent more and be practically an additional gratuity of at least $7,000,000. The whole monopoly he estimated to be worth $17,000,000, and it was being sold for an annual payment of $200,000 for fifteen years, or $3,000,000 in all. In other respects he found that the charter created distinction between the "high and the low, the rich and the poor." He pointed out that the bank stock was held almost entirely in the East, the South, and in Europe, while nearly half its profits were derived from its western business; thus making its divi-

The new charter vetoed.

dends a tax upon western industry. He threw doubt on its constitutionality, and hinted at the dangerous political influence it might wield. The message skillfully combined arguments against a national bank in general with those against this bank in particular, and appealed to American prejudice against foreigners, western prejudice against the East, the distrust of the poor for the rich, and the hatred of democracy for privilege.

The Anti-masons. Attention was now concentrated on the approaching election. The first nomination was made by a new party formed upon a special issue. In 1826 a certain William Morgan, who had printed a book purporting to reveal the secrets of Freemasonry, disappeared, and the rumor grew that he had been abducted by the Masons. The Masonic order was powerful at this time, not only in America, but in other countries, and the Masons belonged generally to the wealthier classes of society. It was claimed that they used their influence in juries and in legislatures to advance the interests of their fellows. Suspicion spread like wildfire through the rural districts of New York, Pennsylvania, and New England. All secret societies were attacked, and men so sane and experienced as John Quincy Adams and Edward Everett spent days in discussing whether the Phi Beta Kappa should reveal its secrets to the world. This movement was taken hold of by a number of very able young political leaders, such as Thurlow Weed and William Seward in New York, and Thaddeus Stevens in Pennsylvania. They made it bulk large in local politics, and with a view to improving their position at home, they caused to be held, in 1830, the first genuine national party convention in American history, and in September, 1831, they met again at Baltimore, and selected William Wirt as candidate for the presidency.

The National Republicans. In naming a candidate so early, the Antimasons had hoped to combine all the opposition to Jackson, but in this they were unsuccessful. The great bulk of the opposition wished to vote for Henry Clay. He was a natural leader of men; he could not move about the country on private business without an accompaniment of public dinners and an atmosphere of triumph, and in the session of Congress just finished he had led the opposition in the Senate. His name was formally presented by a National Republican convention at Baltimore in December, 1831, and also by a national assembly of young men at Washington in May, 1832, which adopted the first national party platform.

After the break with Calhoun, it was inevitable that Jackson should be the Democratic candidate. To be sure, he had declared himself opposed to the reëlection of a President, but he believed it should be prevented by constitutional amendment; while the people allowed it, he had no scruples in accepting it. The Democratic convention was held in Baltimore in May, 1832. The only question was with regard to the vice presidency. Jackson desired Van Buren, but there was strong opposition to him, on the ground that he was a time-serving politician. It was largely with the idea of strengthening Van Buren that a national convention was held at all. As a result of skillful manipulation, Van Buren was chosen, though probably in opposition to the wish of the majority of the Democrats of the country. The Democrats of Pennsylvania voted in the election for a candidate of their own. *The Democrats.*

In the campaign which followed these nominations, the main issues were the existence of the National Bank, and the defense of the administration. The National Republicans placed first in their program the protective system, but that could not be made an issue because so many of the Democrats were protectionists also, and Jackson had just signed the tariff of 1832, which was reasonably satisfactory to that element. On internal improvements the situation was clearer, and the result of the election seems to show that Jackson *The campaign of 1832.*

lost some few votes because of his opposition to expending national money for such purposes. The attitude of the administration toward the civil service was much discussed but exerted little influence.

The election.   The result of the election was surprising in showing that in spite of the new issues before the country, and of the active record of the administration, the people voted almost precisely as they had four years before. Jackson gained about 40,000 votes; Clay and Wirt, together, about 20,000 as compared with Adams in 1828. The changes in the electoral vote were greater, but are easily accounted for. Clay naturally gained Kentucky, where his popularity as a favorite son was enhanced by his advocacy of internal improvements. Jackson gained Maine and New Hampshire rather because the Democrats in those states were brought to the polls by better organization than because they were more numerous than before. He gained in New York because that state now chose its electors upon a general ticket rather than by districts as it had in 1828, when its vote was divided 20 to 16. New Jersey had voted for Adams and now voted for Jackson, but this was brought about by the change of only a few hundred votes. The only significant change was in South Carolina. Actual nullification did not take place until the election was over, but the break between Calhoun and Jackson, and the passage of the tariff of 1832, had effectually alienated that state, which cast its vote for John Floyd of Virginia. In spite of this opening breach Jackson held all the rest of the Cotton South. Gratitude for his Indian policy and confidence in the state rights views of a man who ignored John Marshall, and who had not yet issued the proclamation in reply to nullification, caused Georgia, Alabama, and Mississippi to vote for Jackson as before. In fact the election showed that the people still regarded it as fundamentally important to have at Washington a true representative of their ideas, and that they regarded Jackson as such a representative.

BIBLIOGRAPHICAL NOTES

Callender, *Economic History*, 564–592. Richardson, *Messages*, Sources.
II, 576–591. Macdonald, *Select Documents*, nos. 46, 50–52, 57–68.

In addition to those given at the close of ch. XI: Catterall, Historical
R. C. H., *Second Bank of the United States*, 186–314. Dewey, accounts.
D. R., *State Banking before the Civil War*, and *First and Second
Banks of the United States.* Sumner, E. G., *Jackson*, ch. VI,
sec. 9. McCarthy, C., *The Antimasonic Party* (Am. Hist. Assoc.,
Report, 1902, I, pp. 371–464).

CHAPTER XIV

The war on the Bank.

ALTHOUGH Jackson's reëlection was primarily a personal triumph, he interpreted it as a popular indorsement of all his views; from that time he considered himself as the true representative of the people and distrusted all their other representatives. His first duty was to deal with nullification, and his strong and successful handling of that question has been already described. With the settlement of that crisis in March, 1833, he resumed with vigor the fight with the money power as personified in "Nick" Biddle, president of the Bank. It was not to be supposed that so powerful an institution would give up the fight for its life as a result of the election. It still had four years in which to effect its salvation. Jackson genuinely feared that it would use in its defense the immense resources at its disposal, and he had little confidence in the ability of Congress to resist its arguments. The report of 1832 brought out the fact that the question of its loans to members of Congress had been dropped, because so many members had been its debtors. How far such loans might influence their public action was a question which probably not even the members involved could have answered, but the practice was obviously dangerous. Moreover, the willingness of the Bank to spend money in its own behalf was indicated by its distribution of literature for use in the campaign of 1832. It was also true that the Bank had indulged from time to time in business methods of doubtful wisdom. These, however, were not on a scale really to endanger its solvency, and while the administration cited them to strengthen its case and prove that government deposits were unsafe, the real motive for its subsequent policy seems to have been the political one.

In this situation Jackson and his advisers were not content to remain quietly on the defensive. It was decided to take the initiative and attack the Bank by removing the government deposits. As business was handled, a balance of between eight and nine million always remained in the Bank. This large sum, upon which the Bank had no interest to pay, constituted a most valuable resource. These deposits were in the charge of the Secretary of the Treasury, who was, in regard to them, so far independent of the President that he was required by law to report to the House of Representatives. The first necessary step was to secure a Secretary of the Treasury favorable to the plan of removal. McLane was transferred to the state department, and William J. Duane appointed to succeed him at the treasury. On September 18, 1833, Jackson read to the cabinet a paper stating his intentions and assuming entire responsibility for their execution. Duane, however, refused to act in accordance with Jackson's desire, or to resign, and was, therefore, removed September 23. He was succeeded by Roger B. Taney, the Attorney-General, who was an ardent supporter of the plan, and at once carried it into execution. Government expenses were paid from the deposits already in the Bank, but no more government money was deposited there. A financial panic followed, which the supporters of the Bank attributed to the removal, and the administration to the manner in which the Bank contracted its business.

Removal of the deposits.

When the new Congress came together, the bank question at once became the leading topic of discussion. The House sustained Taney's action by a vote of 118 to 103. The Senate, however, had a strong antiadministration majority, and, powerless to take active measures, adopted resolutions condemning the removal and accusing the President of having violated the

Censure of the Senate.

Constitution. This vote of censure, Jackson considered to be an unwarranted attack on the people's representative. He replied by a "Protest," in which he defended his action. He pointed out that the censure was a judicial act, and that the Senate had no right judicially to condemn the President unless he were impeached by the House of Representatives; he asserted the independence of the executive, and deprecated the growing power of the Senate, whose members held their offices for a long term, were not elected by the people, and were not directly responsible to them. To his mind the structure of the government was simple: the legislature made laws, the courts decided cases, the President executed the Constitution and the laws; each was independent of the others and should leave the others entirely alone. Of the three branches of government he had come to think that the executive stood closest to the people, and should, therefore, enjoy a certain precedence.

The "expunging resolution." The Senate refused to place the "Protest" upon its minutes, while Benton, the Jackson leader in that body, endeavored to have the "Censure" stricken from its records. This purely personal aftermath of the bank struggle became one of the leading issues in politics for the next two years. At length on January 16, 1837, the administration having secured a majority in the Senate, Benton succeeded in passing his "expunging resolution" by a vote of 24 to 16 — at a time when Jackson was suffering from the removal of a bullet fired at him by Benton's brother in one of the shooting affrays of their youth.

End of the second Bank of the United States. Though its national charter expired in 1836 and its connection with the national government was at an end, the United States Bank secured a local charter in Pennsylvania, and strove to maintain its leading financial position. Its new charter, however, cost much money; its business methods grew more unsound; and finally, in 1841, it failed, and Jackson's victory was complete.

With the withdrawal of the deposits from the Bank of the United States, it was necessary for the government to devise some other method of handling public moneys. It was not attempted to do the government business on a smaller margin of deposits; in fact the public debt was fully paid, January 1, 1835, and from that time the deposits grew constantly greater. On January 1, 1836, they amounted to $25,000,000 ; on June 1, of the same year, to $41,500,000. These deposits were divided among certain banks selected by the Secretary of the Treasury. In making this division the attempt was to distribute the money equally throughout the country rather than concentrate it in the financial centers; population rather than business necessity was considered. In deciding among the banks of any locality, the considerations were very largely political; in fact in many places adherents of Jackson were encouraged to found banks for the express purpose of receiving such deposits. The administration had it in mind to use its influence as a check upon these banks, but its attempts in this direction were ineffective; and the overthrow of the National Bank meant really the turning over of the great question of banking and currency to the states. The different sections of the country were so far apart in their ideas on these subjects that a national policy could not be other than unpopular.

State control meant practically no control throughout the frontier region. The banks receiving government deposits looked upon them as a permanent loan without interest, and increased their business accordingly. They enlarged their issues of currency far beyond the limits of safety, and loaned it on easy terms.

At length the frontier business community had obtained what it had long desired, easy credit; any merchant could secure money on almost any security. Men undertook enterprises far beyond their resources or the demands of the community. Particularly speculation in land was carried to an extreme. Town sites were purchased; elaborate plats were prepared, showing streets and public buildings, where in fact the muskrat was the only inhabitant; swampy creeks were magnified into streams which would furnish water power for factories yet unthought of; and steamboats were pictured as sailing through channels which a hunter's canoe could not have navigated. Seven such cities were projected within ten miles of Madison, Wisconsin, and town lots sold before there was a single hut in any one of them. The average annual sales of public lands for the ten years before 1835 amounted to $2,363,004; for the ten years after 1836, to $3,534,171; these figures would seem to represent the normal amount of land needed by the increasing population. In 1835 the sales amounted to $11,990,515.75, and in 1836 to $24,877,179.86. Such purchases were almost purely speculative; they discounted the advance in land values for many years to come.

Distribution of the surplus.

The immediate effect of these land sales was to increase the income of the government to an unprecedented amount; in 1834 it was $21,800,000, in 1836 it was $50,800,000. This increase of revenue coming just after the payment of the public debt, and at a time when the compromise of 1833 prevented a reduction of the tariff, caused both parties to unite in the passage of the bill for the distribution of the surplus, already noted. It was expected that this surplus available for distribution would amount to $40,000,000, and in the three quarters of a year during which the act was in force, $28,000,-000 was actually given over to the states. This distribution of the surplus stimulated in many ways the era of speculation begun by the distribution of deposits and overthrow of the Bank. The states counted upon the surplus as permanent, and some, hoping to increase their share, founded state banks, for which the money they received served as capital, and which issued more paper currency, thereby increasing the plethora of money, the ease of securing credit, and the temptation to speculate. The states themselves set the example, for while some of them used their new resources as a school fund, the greater number planned internal improvements on such a scale that their share of the surplus would hardly pay the annual interest charge. Ohio, Indiana, and Illinois began an elaborate system of canals, and the country seemed at length destined to be provided with transportation facilities at public expense.

While land speculation in the West was the controlling factor in the situation, the fever spread everywhere and to everything. All kinds of new undertakings were entered upon, real estate rose to figures which in some places it did not touch again for over sixty years, fortunes were made, and extravagance of living increased with every year. The *nouveaux riches*, with their European silks, wines, and carriages, began to set the tone of society, and the dignified aristocracy of the colonial type began to lose its control of the world of fashion, as it had, in 1829, of politics. European imports increased, and, paper money supplying domestic needs, great quantities of gold and silver were shipped out of the country. Extravagance.

The country was rapidly increasing in real wealth, population was pushing westward and creating land values with unprecedented rapidity; but the people were attempting to realize on them more rapidly than they were created by means of credit currency. The danger of the situation was very generally recognized, but there were differences as to the remedy. Few statesmen venture to put a check upon prosperity. Jackson, however, saw a simple remedy for the evil, and he applied it with the same courage he had previously shown. In 1835 and 1836 Benton tried to have Congress adopt a bullionist policy, and vote to accept nothing but gold and silver in payment for public lands. This policy he pressed with such characteristic energy that he acquired the nickname of "Old Bullion." Congress, however, refused to accept the principle, and finally, on July 11, 1836, The Specie Circular.

Jackson took action on his own authority. His experience with paper money had made him, like Benton, suspicious of it; he was anxious to get rid of it altogether, at least in the transaction of government business. Consequently he issued what is known as the "Specie Circular," ordering that only gold and silver be received for the public land. Congress, by a majority of 41 to 5 in the Senate and 143 to 59 in the House, voted to reverse this policy, but a pocket veto maintained it.

Before the tide of prosperity had begun to ebb, the election of 1836 approached, and Jackson looked once more for vindication of his policy; not in his own reëlection, but in that of his chosen successor Van Buren. In every direction

Diplomacy. he had been victorious. Even in diplomacy, the particular field of his rival John Quincy Adams, he had won victories of moment. Diplomatic questions were not so vital to the national existence as they had been before 1815. It was only now and then that some episode attracted the public attention. The first of these was the question of the trade with the British West Indies. Under Adams that trade had been brought to an end by the unwillingness of either the United States or England to make necessary concessions. Van Buren, in 1829, notified the British government that a new administration had come into power, which would negotiate on a new basis. Thus to refer to politics in a diplomatic dispatch was unusual, and gave his opponents in the Senate an excuse for rejecting his nomination as minister to England in 1831. Yet, improper though his method may have been, it was successful. England reopened negotiation, a compromise was agreed upon, and this valuable trade was reëstablished. The policy of mutual concession which marked the settlement of this dispute was characteristic of the commercial policy of the Jackson administration throughout, and that of Van Buren which succeeded. Treaties were made with some of the South American powers, on

terms more liberal than those offered by Adams. In 1831 a
reciprocity treaty was made with France which benefited Reciprocity.
the cotton trade. Moreover, throughout this period the
greatest international publicist that America has produced,
Henry Wheaton, was working for reciprocity of customs dues
and legal regulations with the countries of the Baltic. The
taxes on emigration levied by the German states were
abolished, and a number of treaties of commercial reciprocity
were made, culminating in that with the Zollverein in 1844,
which was rejected by the Whigs. Treaties with Siam and
Muscat for the first time put the country into direct relations with the nations of the East. While an extensive trade
had been carried on with China and India, the only previous
treaty protection had been that afforded for a time by the
Jay treaty with England.

A more sensational incident resulted from the purpose Indemnities.
of the government to collect, from various foreign nations,
damages for injuries sustained by our merchants during
the Napoleonic wars. In 1831 a very satisfactory treaty
was framed with France, but difficulty soon arose, as the
French Assembly was unwilling to pay the obligations the
French government had assumed. Jackson referred to the
matter in his regular message to Congress in language that
the French press regarded as insulting, and a demand for
war rang through France. The French Assembly finally
voted to pay the money if a proper explanation or apology
was made for the language contained in the President's
message, while the American government stated that a presidential message was a purely domestic document which
could not form a proper subject of diplomatic negotiations.
Ministers were withdrawn from the respective capitals, and
the situation became extremely acute. This question during
1835 attracted the attention of the country. Jackson insisted on the payment of the indemnity, and was supported
by the House of Representatives under the lead of John

Quincy Adams, now chairman of the committee on foreign affairs. In the Senate Clay brought in a more conciliatory report and prevented any action hostile to France. Before Congress met again France had yielded, accepting, as sufficient explanation of the President's language, a later message of Jackson, in which he stated that he had never intended to threaten her. The success of the United States in this episode was felt to strengthen its position abroad. At home the credit for the solution was claimed alike by the friends of Adams, Clay, and Jackson, but the majority of the people, as in the case of nullification, gave it to Jackson. While this was the most important of the treaties securing damages, several others were made, and practically all American claims against foreign countries were liquidated.

Texas.   The most important question of diplomacy, and the one which might be expected chiefly to interest the administration, was that concerning Texas. The treaty of 1819, by which our western boundary was fixed at the Sabine River, was not regarded as final by many persons in the United States. No sooner had Adams become President than he began to negotiate for the purchase of the territory beyond, if possible as far as the Rio Grande. He pointed out to the Mexican government that this region, in which there were only a few thousand Mexicans, was rapidly being occupied by settlers from the United States, alien to the Mexicans in language and customs and apt to prove a disturbing factor. The Mexicans refused to sell, and adopted active but ineffectual measures to prevent the Americanization of Texas. Under Jackson the negotiation was reopened and might have succeeded had he not absolutely refused to bribe the Mexican authorities. In the meantime the prophecy of Adams came true more quickly perhaps than he had expected. Americans, adventurous frontiersmen and cotton planters with their slaves, were pouring into this district where rich land could be bought for twelve and a half cents per acre, while in the United States the minimum price was $1.25. Although they took the oath of fidelity to the Mexican government, the majority were unwilling to allow its interference, and at the first indication that its authority would be exercised, resisted. In 1832 there was a revolt, and in 1835 a revolution which established the Republic of Texas and a government entirely American. The next year Santa Anna, the Mexican president, swept through the country with fire and sword, driving before him the Americans under General Sam Houston, a friend of Jackson. Throughout the United States the war fever took hold of the people, and thousands made their way to Texas, attracted by sympathy and by the unparalleled liberality of the land offers made by the new republic to those who would come to its assistance. The aid thus afforded Texas by American citizens gave Mexico a just ground for complaint, but the administration was not seriously at fault, as the neutrality laws were somewhat ambiguous and the overwhelming pro-Texan sentiment would have rendered a strict interpretation of neutrality impossible unless supported by force. *Question of neutrality.*

The government was more directly involved by its order to General Gaines, in case of certain possible Indian hostilities, to cross the Sabine and occupy Nacogdoches, a position of great strategic importance in Mexican territory. It was believed by many that this movement was really intended to assist the Texans, and the Mexican minister at Washington withdrew in consequence of it. In fact, however, Gaines did not cross the Sabine, although encamped near its banks, until after Houston, by his victory over Santa Anna at San Jacinto on April 21, 1836, had practically assured Texan independence without his assistance.

The Texan question now began to assume a certain political importance in the United States. Jackson's opponents accused the administration of being responsible for the revolution, and of intending to annex Texas to the United *Question of annexation*

States. The first point to be decided was whether the new republic should be recognized. Jackson left this to the discretion of Congress, but advised postponement. The Senate voted recognition, and money was appropriated for the establishment of diplomatic relations. The day before he retired, March 3, 1837, Jackson nominated a *chargé d'affaires* to Texas. Recognition was thus granted, but on annexation the administration would not commit itself. Its policy, however, was said to be foreshadowed by a message which Jackson sent to Congress in February, 1837. In this he called attention to the extensive claims of American citizens against Mexico and asked authority to use the navy to assist in collecting them. It was suspected that it was his intention to press these claims and thereby force Mexico to recognize the independence of Texas or to sell it to the United States. In either case annexation would result. Whether this motive predominated or whether the message marked merely a continuation of the policy to collect American claims against all nations, the evidence at present available will not determine, for the carrying out of the policy was left over to the Van Buren administration.

Democratic Convention of 1836.

Preparations for the presidential election had begun unusually early. The Democratic convention was held in May, 1836, at Baltimore, the favorite meeting place for conventions at this period. That city could be most easily reached from north, south, and west, and the political complexion of Maryland was extremely doubtful, so that it was advisable to arouse there the enthusiasm excited by these great national gatherings. Van Buren was nominated for the presidency rather as the choice of Jackson than of the party; and Colonel Richard M. Johnson, the amiable reputed slayer of Tecumseh, was selected for the vice presidency. No platform was adopted, but the party principles were well enough understood. In fact the campaign that followed was more clearly a contest of issues than any since 1800.

In 1828 and 1832 Jackson and Democracy had overshadowed any particular issue. In 1836, with a candidate lacking in magnetism and distinctly unpopular in many parts of the country, the attitude of the party toward particular public questions was of more moment, and thanks to Jackson's decisive action that policy was explicit on nearly every point. The Democratic party stood for leaving all questions possible to the states and therefore against internal improvements and a national bank; it stood nevertheless for the preservation of the Union at any cost and for the active use of the national power to extend commercial relations and to protect American property; the tariff was not an issue. On finance the administration stood for hard money, though the bulk of the party were as yet in favor of paper. *The Democratic platform.*

The opposition did not call a national convention, partly because that system of party government was still opposed by many of Jackson's opponents, and partly because the elements objecting to Van Buren were not ready to coöperate among themselves. The great bulk of the opposition consisted of men who in 1828 and 1832 had supported Adams and Clay, respectively, and who were generally known as National Republicans. They now had the advantage of personality in appealing to the frontier, as their candidate was William Henry Harrison, victor at Tippecanoe and at the Thames and author of the land law of 1800. In 1828 Jackson had carried all the ten frontier states, receiving 240,000 to 130,000 popular votes. In 1832 the states divided nine to one and the vote stood 225,000 to 145,000. In 1836 there were twelve frontier states, Arkansas having been admitted in 1836 and Michigan being in the process of admission. Five of these voted for the opposition, and Van Buren received only 285,000 votes to 300,000. In pleasing the frontier the National Republicans somewhat displeased the East, and in Massachusetts Daniel Webster ran instead of Harrison and received the vote of that state. In Pennsylvania and *Harrison and Webster.*

some other states the Antimasons joined with the National Republicans, giving them a strength in the rural districts they had never had before. All together Harrison and Webster received in the northern states a popular vote decidedly larger than that cast in 1832 for Clay and Wirt, gaining, as compared with them, New Jersey, Ohio, Indiana, and part of Maryland, and losing only Rhode Island and Connecticut.

Southern Whigs.

The opposition to Van Buren was not confined to the supporters of Harrison and Webster. In nine of the eleven states south of the Potomac, the opposition candidate was Judge White of Tennessee. In these states, in 1832, Clay had received 20,000 votes; Judge White received 145,000, carrying Georgia and Tennessee. This represented a new falling away from the Democratic party. This element consisted of men who, first one and then another, had ceased, between 1832 and 1836, to support Jackson. Some had left because they considered that his proclamation on nullification contained sentiments inimical to the rights of the states. Among these was John Tyler and a large faction of the pure Jeffersonian democracy. Others of the same element abandoned Jackson after the removal of the deposits and other acts of executive power, claiming that the President was preparing the way for a despotism by the executive. Many of the wealthier planters were alarmed at the financial aspects of the attack on the Bank, and were equally opposed to the bullionist policy of Benton. They desired a credit currency on a sound basis. Many, while uneasy at these things, had supported Jackson, confident in his personal honesty of purpose, but they left the party now that Van Buren took his place. In general these southern adherents of Judge White belonged to the more conservative and wealthier classes; they regarded themselves as the custodians of the pure traditions of the past, and they breathed with relief when they shook themselves free from the party contaminated by the spoils system and political organization.

Still a third element of opposition were the nullifiers of South Carolina, who rejected Van Buren and would not accept Judge White, and so again threw away the vote of the state, this time on Willie P. Mangum of North Carolina.

South Carolina.

That Van Buren was successful, although by the narrow margin of 25,000 in the popular vote and 46 in the electoral college,[1] was a strong testimonial to the popularity of Democratic doctrines, and a final gratification to Jackson, who could now retire with the consciousness of having completely triumphed over his enemies. Nor had his successes been due to a temporizing or passive policy. He had boldly grappled with the real problems before the country; he had applied to each such remedy as to his simple practical mind seemed likely to be efficacious, and had worked for its application, often against the advice of his closest friends and in the face of the overwhelming opposition of the people's representatives in Congress; and in every case, even to his personal vindication by the expunging resolution, his judgment had finally been indorsed by the people. He retired triumphant, leaving in his place a man of his own choice, who gave, as his highest qualification for the office, the fact that he was the representative of Jackson's policies, and whose retention of Jackson's cabinet was an earnest of his intentions.

Results.

BIBLIOGRAPHICAL NOTES

The references given at the close of the last three chapters continue to be of use. In addition, the following historical accounts are of value: Foster, J. W., *A Century of American Diplomacy*, 272-280. Roosevelt, T., *Benton*, ch. VII. Shepard, E. M., *Van Buren*, ch. VII.

[1] One state, Virginia, which voted for Van Buren for President, refused to vote for Johnson for Vice President. As a result, no one received a majority of the electoral votes for Vice President, and Johnson was elected to this office by the Senate.

CHAPTER XV

THE VAN BUREN ADMINISTRATION

The crisis of 1837. SCARCELY had Jackson withdrawn to the "Hermitage," his country home in Tennessee, and left the government in the hands of his lieutenants, when prosperity, which had been at high-water mark throughout his administration, ebbed like the tide in the Bay of Fundy. From one end of the country to the other disaster spread: prices dropped, demand for commodities declined, banks closed their doors, and mills shut down. The crisis of 1819 had not been so acute, nor was that of 1873 so extensive. A great amount of specie had, before the year 1837, been driven from the country by the abundance of paper money. With the first halt in prosperity the banks were forced to suspend specie payment, and thereupon the value of their paper money fell. The majority of the business men of the country were engaged in undertakings far beyond their resources; with the disturbance of credit they went into bankruptcy, or were hopelessly involved where bankruptcy was not an authorized procedure. Everywhere was financial ruin, and this was often accompanied by actual personal distress, particularly in the manufacturing regions. Petitions poured in, asking the administration to come to the relief of the country; riots seemed to threaten the maintenance of order, and Van Buren so far yielded to the popular unrest as to call an extra session of Congress for September.

Proposed remedies. When Congress met, the leaders of the opposition naturally united in laying the blame for the crisis upon the shoulders of the Democratic party. Clay believed that the failure to

234

recharter the United States Bank, the disturbance caused by the removal of the deposits, and the Specie Circular had been responsible; that the remedy should be the immediate re-establishment of the Bank. Van Buren found the cause of the crisis, not in the policy of the national government, but in that of the states. He pointed out that banking capital had been allowed to increase between 1834 and 1836 from $200,000,000 to $251,000,000, bank notes in circulation from $95,000,000 to $140,000,000, and loans and discounts from $324,000,000 to $457,000,000, and that states, banks, and merchants were heavily indebted to Europe; that this unusual and unsound distention of credit had but brought its natural result. Calhoun so strongly espoused this view that he broke with the opposition, with whom he had been co-operating since the compromise of 1833, and gave fairly consistent support to the administration. He looked upon the Specie Circular as a wise measure, because it pricked the bubble of inflation and brought land speculation down to the basis of real values. There is little doubt now that the crisis of 1837 was a natural economic reaction from the fever of speculation that preceded. The Specie Circular may have hastened the disaster, by exhibiting the deficiency of real capital, but it could not have been long delayed, as a similar crisis was taking place in Europe; if the American government had not made its call for gold and thereby revealed the barrenness of the banks, the European bankers would soon have done so. If a well-established national bank had been in existence, to exercise a wise regulative influence, it might have rendered the crisis less severe, but it is difficult to see how the establishment of a bank in 1837 could have much relieved the situation.

The administration policy was dictated by a portion of the party, and was based upon Van Buren's analysis of the causes of the crisis. The carnival of paper money had added many adherents to the bullionist element, represented by

Administration policy

Benton and Jackson.   This faction was particularly strengthened by a local movement in New York.   Here a portion of
the party had revolted against the dominant Albany Regency, claiming that this clique was becoming as much of an
aristocracy as that of the Federalists before them; that it
was time for a new distribution of the spoils.   This revolt-
ing faction, from an episode of their campaign, acquired the
name of "Loco-Focos."   Just before the election of 1836
they were reunited with the party.   Their most important
political belief was the fallibility of all credit currency and the
unique efficacy of hard money—gold and silver.   In their
fusion with the party they carried this idea with them, and
the President became the advocate of this their leading principle.   It was not, therefore, without justice that the name
Loco-Focos came to be applied to the whole Democratic
party, although it was so used by their opponents chiefly
to recall certain socialistic ideas of the faction, which tended
to discredit it in the eyes of the conservative.

Subtreasury
plan.

With this backing, Van Buren boldly supported the
Specie Circular, and in fact extended it to receipts for the
postal service.   He recommended that Congress adopt, as
a permanent policy, the requirement that all receipts of the
government be in gold and silver.   The newer portion of his
scheme related to the care and disbursement of this money
when once collected.   He pointed out that two methods
had been employed by the government in the past: one,
the use of a national bank from 1791 to 1811 and from 1816
to 1836; the other, the use of state banks.   Both of these
plans, he thought, had proved unsatisfactory.   He recommended, therefore, that the government take care of its own
money by the establishment of branches of the treasury in
cities where the major portion of its business was conducted.
The receiving officers would be responsible until they placed
it in these subtreasuries, and payments would be made out
of the money thus collected and stored.   By the administra-

tion this plan was called the "Independent Treasury"; by the opposition the "Divorce Bill," because its object was to divorce public and private business. John Quincy Adams wrote: "A Divorce of Bank and State! Why, a divorce of Trade and Shipping would be as wise to carry on the business of a merchant. A Divorce of Army and Fire-Arms, in the face of an invading enemy, a divorce of Law and a Bench of Judges to carry into execution the Statutes of the Land, would be as reasonable!"

Every step in the policy of the administration was con- *Legislation.* tested in debates which seemed to bring to a head the accumulated bitterness of the decade. Even the obviously prudent proposal that the fourth installment of the surplus which had not yet been paid to the states be withheld, now that the government was confronted with an actual deficit, was opposed by Clay and a majority of his supporters. Nevertheless, it was passed. The Independent Treasury Bill was defeated by a combination of the regular opposition and a number of Democrats calling themselves "Conservatives." The succeeding Congress contained a still narrower Democratic majority, but it was better united, and with the powerful assistance of Calhoun the Subtreasury Bill was at length passed in 1840, with the addition that after June 30, 1843, nothing but gold and silver should be received or paid out by the United States. National business was separated from private business, and national politics from all questions of the currency, as completely as it was within the power of the government to do it.

This complete withdrawal of the national government *The states* left the states even more independent in their regulation of *and banking.* banking than they were while the state banks held the national deposits, and were, therefore, held to some form of national supervision. To this entire freedom from national control was added the sanction of the Supreme Court. In 1835 Judge Marshall had died. He was succeeded by Roger B.

Taney, who was to hold the chief justiceship until 1864. The Court was now in sympathy with the dominant Democratic attitude, as five of the seven judges were of Jackson's appointment. In 1837, in the case of *Briscoe* v. *The Bank of Kentucky*, the court confirmed the power of the state to establish banks endowed with the power to issue paper currency, though the Constitution forbade the states themselves to "emit bills of credit." Though they could not declare such currency legal tender, practically a period of complete state independence in financial matters followed, lasting until the Civil War.

Panic of 1841.

This freedom the states in the different sections proceeded to use in accordance with their several views. In some of those of the frontier it was felt that the remedy for their financial distress lay in more banks and more currency. Mississippi chartered in 1838 a new $15,000,000 bank. Its capital was subscribed in real estate mortgages, and as it was not easy to raise money on these directly, the state gave its security and agreed to raise the necessary specie. This general scheme, though with varying details, was very generally employed in the newer states, and it recalls the land-bank projects of the seventeenth century in England, and of the eighteenth in Massachusetts; it marked a primitive stage of financial development. The hard times proved to be more lasting than these frontier financiers anticipated. Although many banks which had not definitely failed resumed specie payments in 1838, the next year saw them suspend again, and many of them gave up the struggle between February, 1841, and April, 1842, when eighty-one banks, with $98,500,000 capital, became insolvent. Exhausted and discouraged by

Repudiation of state debts.

five years of suffering, Mississippi in 1842 repudiated the debt incurred in behalf of the bank of 1838. Easy is the way that leadeth to destruction, and in 1848 the state's obligations in behalf of the older Planters Bank were also denied. In 1840 the territory of Florida began its descent of the same road, and in 1842 Michigan repudiated, in part, certain bonds issued in behalf of internal improvements. In each of these cases the state set forth certain technicalities to justify its action; but, protected by their sovereign character as states (for Florida became a state in 1845) and by the Eleventh Amendment of the Constitution, they all steadily refused to allow a judicial review of their action.

While most states manfully stood by their obligations, *Loss of credit in Europe.* though it meant deferred projects of public works and heavy taxes, and though strong parties in the repudiating states struggled for many years to secure a reversal of their decision, American finance in general was discredited in Europe, and for many years the stream of European capital seeking investment in America, which had been an important factor in the prosperity of the thirties, was diminished. George Ticknor, a Federalist, a conservative, and a capitalist, wrote in 1843: "What Prince Metternich once said to me, in reproach of our democratic institutions, is entirely true: we must first suffer from an evil before we can apply the remedy; we have no preventive legislation on such subjects," but he went on to point out that a remedy thus applied is all the more apt to be effective. After the hard lesson of the period *Banking reform.* between 1837 and 1842, the excesses of frontier banking became more and more restricted, and while opinions still varied from opposition to all banks to a belief that any kind of bank could solve all economic difficulties, public sentiment grew continually more sound. Between 1842 and 1860 the increase in banking capital and currency issues was more moderate, and the amount of actual business done grew to have a safer proportion to the two. The panic of 1841, moreover, had a marked political effect. Before this time the states had been able to borrow at better terms than individuals and companies. There was, therefore, a constant effort to secure state credit for all kinds of enterprises. With this blow to state credit, the tendency to link public credit and private initiative was checked. The era of the private corporation was at hand. That this change took place just when railroad construction was beginning, was of profound significance in determining the character of our economic institutions.

Free banking and reserves. While the frontier was learning its lesson, the older states were devising permanent safeguards against a recurrence of banking evils. Massachusetts for a long time had had a sound system of banking, but it was in New York, which was rapidly becoming the leading state financially, that successful legislation was first evolved. In 1829 a safety fund had been established by law. Every bank chartered was required to pay into the state treasury a certain percentage of its capital, which was to be used to pay the liabilities of any that might fail. This fund proved too small and did not prevent disasters in 1837. In 1839 a better system was adopted. Every bank was required to deposit securities with the state, equal in value to the bank notes that it issued. This furnished a bank-note currency which was safe against all ordinary business disasters. Another equally important part of the plan was the provision that bank charters be not granted as heretofore specially by the legislature, but that any group of persons, producing the requisite amount of capital, and willing to accede to the other requirements of the state law, could demand a charter. This "free banking" system tended to take banking out of politics and place it on a purely business basis. Banking ceased to be a monopoly, and the law of supply and demand would in the end regulate the amount of capital invested and the amount of currency issued. Time proved the efficacy of these provisions, but only eleven states copied them before the Civil War.

The civil service. It was a discouraging task to administer the government during the lean years from 1837 to 1841. Receipts from land sales dropped like magic; the customs revenues not only fell, but were vacillating. In the first year of the administration

they amounted to only $11,000,000; the next year, with
the temporary revival of business, they almost doubled, only
to fall again the year after. In order to meet the expenses
of government it was necessary to run in debt to the amount
of $34,000,000, for which treasury notes were issued.
Every year saw a deficit. Still more discouraging was the
utter demoralization of the civil service. Nearly all the
government land officers had used public funds in their possession for the purposes of speculation. When the panic
came, the value of their holdings fell, and they found themselves unable to pay. It was estimated in 1837 that sixty-
four out of sixty-seven land officers were defaulters. Few
of these men were intentional rogues; they fully expected
to pay back the money that they used, and the financial sense
of their frontier communities did not condemn their action,
but pitied their misfortunes. Treasury agents stated that it
would be impossible to find a different class of men to appoint
to office, and in many cases advised their retention. Probably this lenient policy reduced the government losses to
a minimum, but fully $750,000 was never recovered, and the
opposition naturally attacked a policy which seemed to pal-
liate the offense of using public funds in private speculation.

Still more serious was the condition of the customs serv- **Corruption.**
ice. The collectorship of the customs in New York city
was one of the most important political positions in the country, for the number of subordinates and the assessments that
they paid made the collector almost dictator in the city
caucuses. This position had been held under Jackson by
Samuel Swartwout, who had been appointed almost purely
because of personal friendship and in opposition to the wishes
of Van Buren. The latter naturally failed to reappoint
him, and upon his leaving office, an examination of his
accounts showed a defalcation of about $1,250,000. This
would not have seriously reflected on Van Buren's administration, but he appointed as Swartwout's successor, Jesse

Hoyt, whose conduct of the office was also marked by amazing irregularities. Here in New York the losses were more clearly attributable, than in the land office, to the careless supervision of the government and to the demoralization introduced by the spoils system. The main interest was centered on politics, and maladministration followed as a natural result. These New York defalcations were clearly not the result of misguided ignorance; they were thefts pure and simple.

The
Seminoles.

In still other ways Van Buren reaped the chaff of policies from which Jackson had threshed the wheat. The Indian removals were now complete excepting the Seminoles of Florida. These Indians, taking refuge in the swamps of the Everglades, resisted all the attempts of the government to execute the treaty for the sale of their lands which they now repented of having made. They harassed the settlers with raids and outrages, until the latter persuaded General Jesup to seize the Indian leader Osceola treacherously, by inviting him to a conference under a flag of truce. This act failed to close the war, which dragged on until 1842, involved the expenditure of $40,000,000, and exposed the administration to bitter attack, particularly in the North. It was alleged that the Seminole land was not needed for settlement, and that the real object of the war was the recovery of negro slaves who had taken refuge with the Indians.

Van Buren
and Texas.

In diplomacy, also, Van Buren was unlucky. Upon him fell the responsibility of determining the policy with reference to the new republic of Texas, whose recognition as an independent nation was Jackson's last official act. The first Texas official representatives brought a request for annexation, which was also desired by a great number of people in the United States. By this time, however, the question had become so much involved with that of slavery that a discussion of the question seemed likely to plunge the country into an agitation as distracting as that over the admission of

Missouri. Van Buren prevented such a crisis by refusing to treat for annexation, thereby angering a powerful element of his southern supporters. His efforts to show his party associates in the South that he would, on the other hand, allow no tampering with slavery, proved more irritating to the antislavery element in the North than reassuring to the slavery advocates of the South, and hence he was distrusted by both sections.

Even more attention was attracted by the situation on the northern frontier. During 1837 and 1838 there were a few ill-concerted attempts at revolution in Canada. There was widespread sympathy for this movement all along the northern frontier, from Wisconsin to Maine. Thousands of Americans joined "Hunters' Lodges," for the purpose of assisting the insurgents, with the immediate motives of adventure and of securing the land grants freely offered by the insurgent leaders, and with some distant thought of annexation. Van Buren firmly maintained the neutrality of the United States. General Scott was sent to the border, and a new neutrality act was passed in 1838. The failure of the scheme was laid upon the President, and thousands of votes, especially of the Irish along the northern frontier, were alienated from the Democrats. William Lyon Mackenzie, one of the Canadian leaders, a few years later attacked Van Buren and his political associates in a series of books which successfully blackened their reputations, not only among politicians, but also among historians, for many years to come. *The Canadian insurrection.*

Seldom have so many causes of unpopularity descended upon the head of a President of the United States. Whatever may be the judgment of financial experts upon the system of divorce between the government and business, it was at any rate open to popular attack as unfeeling. Van Buren was likened to a ship's captain who, in case of shipwreck, should put himself, the crew, and the ship's papers safely in the *Van Buren's unpopularity.*

best boat, and leave the passengers to shift for themselves. The government offered no relief to a stricken community. The entire responsibility for the breakdown of the civil service was thrown upon the spoils system, and Van Buren was held to be its author. His diplomacy, though safe and sane, failed to satisfy the ambitions of either North or South, and withal his gentle, affable demeanor failed to inspire love or respect among the masses.

His renomi-
nation.

In spite of these hampering circumstances, there was no opposition to Van Buren's renomination by the Democratic party. All the leaders of the party were committed to his policies, the organization was in his hands, and he was much more popular among those who knew him than with the masses. It was, in fact, for some time doubtful whether it would be necessary to hold a convention, but one finally met at Baltimore in May, 1840. The chief interest in the action of this body was the platform. The reunion of the Calhoun nullifiers with the party was marked by the fact that this was entirely negative; denying the power of Congress to carry on a general system of internal improvements, to assume state debts, to adopt a protective tariff, to charter a bank or "to interfere with or control the domestic institutions of the several states." Economy, strict construction, Jeffersonian principles, and the "separation of the moneys of the government from banking institutions " were commended.

The Whig
party.

The unpopularity of the Van Buren administration gave his opponents unusual opportunities for success, if only harmony could be secured. During the administration the different elements of the opposition had been drawing more closely together. As early as 1834 the opposition had begun to use a new party name, "Whig," which did not revive any recent political memories, but called to mind only the Revolutionary struggle during which it was applied to the patriotic party. John Quincy Adams wrote: "There are no two that hold any great political principle in common. Most

of them call themselves Whigs, only for the sake of calling
their adversaries Tories." Apart from opposition to the
party in power, their strongest bonds consisted in the magnetism of their great leaders, Clay and Webster, and in the fact
that they represented to some degree a banding together of
those having vested interests thought to be imperiled by the
radical doctrines of the Jackson Democracy. As Adams said
in the letter quoted above: "Clay, as you know, rose upon the
broadest shoulders of democracy. But his European expedition tinged both his principles and his deportment with
aristocracy — perhaps to the improvement of his character,
but to the loss of his standing with the Democracy." The
one political bond of union among all the Whigs was a demand
for good government, and a confidence that their leaders
were best calculated to give the country a clean administration. Their divergence upon all other questions, and the
personal independence both of leaders and followers, made
any close organization impossible, and, perhaps partly through
jealousy, they always condemned the organization of the
Democrats as destructive of personal freedom. The unity
of the Whigs was more social than political.

Under these circumstances it was very important to
select a candidate who would arouse no antagonisms. Clay
was very anxious to secure the nomination and considered it
but a just return for his long years of political service. Practical politicians, however, felt that he had too long a record to
defend, and that his position on public questions was too well
known; his withdrawal from the Masonic order failed to conciliate the powerful Antimasonic leaders, Stevens and Weed.
The Whig national convention — for the leaders had determined again to employ that useful method of securing unity
of action — met at Harrisburg, in December, 1839. A plurality
favored Clay, but the NewYork delegation had been won from
him by that astute political manager, Thurlow Weed, and cast
its vote for General Scott. General Harrison stood between

Nomination
of Harrison.

them in strength, and after a number of ballots New York voted for him, and he was chosen. As Harrison sympathized with the Antimasons and had been the National Republican candidate in 1836, John Tyler of Virginia was nominated for the vice presidency to give representation to the element that had, in 1836, voted for Judge White. The convention adopted no platform, nor could its policy be guessed from its candidates. Harrison's record did not indicate any decided political preferences, and any inferences that might be surmised from his running in 1836 as National Republican were offset by the record of Tyler, who was a genuine Jeffersonian Democrat. It was a neutral tinted ticket, properly representing a coalition party.

Campaign of 1840.

As if to disguise their lack of unity the Whigs inaugurated a campaign of enthusiasm. For the first time the methods of the circus were employed for political purposes. Campaign songs were sung, uniformed processions paraded the streets, giant mass meetings were held, drawing in the country population for miles around. Bizarre bets were made, and dignified gentlemen indulged in buffoonery for the delight of the masses. Harrison was popularized as "Tippecanoe," or "Old Tip," and he was represented as wearing a coonskin cap and drinking hard cider, as opposed to Van Buren, who was accused of having English servants and using gold spoons. The log cabin was exalted into a symbol of liberty, and no procession was complete without one. Logic and political argument were thrown to the winds, and the Whig party, the party of gentlemen, abandoned itself to a frenzy of popular merrymaking. Unusual as such methods appeared, they were based upon sound judgment. Life in America in the middle of the nineteenth century was far from jolly. Particularly in the newer portions of the country the hard struggle with the wilderness left little energy for the pursuit of pleasure, and to an unusual degree it was a solitary struggle, often waged far from any settlement or even neighboring habitation. There was little leisure in such circumstances for the development of the fine art of amusement. The tragedy of the lonely emigrant wife, far from her home associations, with her nearest neighbors miles away and brought together but a few times a year by "bees" for barn raising or corn husking, was long drawn out and drab and bitter. The men fared somewhat better. They met oftener and entertained each other by rough practical jokes and those bragging tales which are so peculiarly characteristic of American humor. Institutions which nearly touched the people naturally adapted themselves to these conditions. The churches, with their camp meetings and revivals, their devil treeing and violent conversions, afforded an opportunity for the outburst of the pent-up emotions of the discouraged father or the homesick wife. The colporteurs and itinerant preachers were welcome for their society as well as for their religious consolation. Political life, with the barbecues, the stump speeches, and the processions with gay uniforms and the banners flying, satisfied their innate human longing for display, and their love for the cruder manifestations of humor. The political orator took the place, for many, of all solid reading; the public meeting, of the theater; for a great number the mere fact of being in a crowd was sufficient reward for a twenty-mile ride over a stumpy road. The Whigs, by making politics amusing, made them popular: in 1836 the popular vote was about 1,500,000; in 1840, it was over 2,400,000. That the Whigs adopted these methods because of their unwillingness to discuss issues, is to a large extent true, but one can scarcely regret that they gave the people a few weeks of relaxation.

Naturally the Whigs gained the larger part of this increased vote, though Van Buren also gained in every state except in Kentucky. Harrison received about 540,000 more votes than he, Webster, and White had received in 1836; and Van Buren, about 365,000 more than he had then received. The Whig *The election.*

gains were distributed over all the country, but they were greatest in Maine and New Hampshire, which were disturbed over the boundary disputes, and in the regions where the ideas of Jefferson retained the largest number of adherents. The Democrats carried only 7 states and 60 electoral votes, to 19 states and 234 electoral votes given to Harrison; the Whigs obtained a majority of 37 in the House and 7 in the Senate.

BIBLIOGRAPHICAL NOTES

Sources.   For economic questions, Callender, G. W., *Economic History*, 578–584 is useful. For politics: Clay's *Private Correspondence*, ch. XI. Sargent, N., *Public Men and Events*, II, chs. V and VI. Wise, H. A., *Seven Decades of the Union*. Where none of these are available, Tyler, L. G., *Lives and Times of the Tylers*, chs. 19 and 20, gives many letters and an intimate though decidedly partisan view.

Historical accounts. Financial questions.   Bourne, E. G., *The Distribution of the Surplus*. Dewey, D. R., *Financial History*, ch. X; and his, *State Banking*. Kinley, D., *The Independent Treasury*. Ormsby, E. McK., *The Whig Party*, ch. XXV. Schurz, C., *Clay*, II, ch. XIX. Scott, W. A., *Repudiation of State Debts*. Shepard, E. M., *Van Buren*, chs. VIII, IX. Sumner, W. G., *American Currency*, 131–161.

Politics, etc.   Fiske, J., *Essays Historical and Literary*, I, VII, VIII. Garrison, G. P., *Westward Extension*, 43–67. McCarthy, C., *The Antimasonic Party* (Am. Hist. Assoc., *Report*, 1902, I, 367–575). Schurz, *Clay*, II, ch. XX.

CHAPTER XVI

HARRISON AND TYLER

THE events which turned the exuberance of the Whig victory into bitterness and recrimination seemed to the leaders of the party surprising, disappointing, and accidental, but to one looking back at them after a lapse of time, they seem natural and in part inevitable. It is comparatively easy to build up a party of opposition out of divergent elements; there is strong cohesive power in hatred and distrust, and active administrations like those of Jackson and Van Buren naturally create a host of enemies willing to sink their differences in order to obtain a victory over the common foe. It is a very different thing to hold such a party together when it comes to power and is confronted with the question of how to make use of its victory. It has already been shown how the Jackson party of 1828 disintegrated as the positive program of the administration developed. It could hardly be expected that the Whigs could reap any definite fruits of their success without alienating some of those who aided to elect Harrison. It remained to be seen whether, out of the loosely bound Whig party of 1840, the leaders could save, as Jackson had done, enough support to carry through a constructive program.

Harrison formed a strong cabinet, with Webster as Secretary of State, and with four friends of Clay, the South being represented by three members and the North by three. Clay refused a position, but made it evident that he looked upon himself as the leader of the party. So eager was he to begin work that he persuaded the President to summon an extra session of Congress to meet May 31, 1841. At once

249

signs of trouble began to appear. The first dispute arose
from the distribution of the patronage. The point of greatest
unity among the Whigs had been their attack upon the spoils
system. They had condemned the practice of indiscriminate
removal, they had attempted to establish the principle that
the Senate should share the removal power, and they had
denounced the Democratic policy of making appointments for
political reasons. When they came to power, however, they
made almost as many removals as Jackson had done. The
practice of removal once begun, it was found to require unusual self-restraint to bring it to an end. If the civil service
under Van Buren was as corrupt as the Whig orators had
declared, it was, indeed, necessary to make extensive changes
of personnel. Moreover, there was as great pressure for appointment in 1841 as in 1829; in fact, the crowd of applicants
was greater, and if, as Adams writes, more orderly, it was at
any rate as persistent. The greater leaders of the party
were disgusted at this appetite for office and tried to keep
their hands clean of it; but the lesser leaders were as active
as the Jacksonian patronage mongers, and soon it was evident
that now, as twelve years before, political considerations were
to have the greatest weight in determining appointments.

Death of Harrison.
It was impossible to keep entirely clear of this turmoil, and
within ten days after the inauguration Clay and Harrison had
quarreled over the appointment to the New York customs
collectorship. How this personal disagreement would have
affected the carrying out of Clay's legislative plans, can never
be known. Before the Congress met, office hunting had had
a still more serious result. The tireless importunities of the
crowds which infested the White House broke down the constitution of the President, and were in part the cause of his
death on April 4, 1841, just one month after taking office.

John Tyler.
The death of Harrison brought for the first time to the
presidency a man chosen as Vice President. Gouverneur
Morris and other Federalists had in 1801 opposed the adop-

tion of the Twelfth Amendment on the ground that a man
elected expressly to that somewhat ambiguous position would
nearly always be of the second rank. They preferred the
older method, by which each elector voted for two persons for
President, and the person receiving the second largest number
of votes became Vice President, believing that in this way the
latter officer would always be a man of presidential caliber.
While their method of preserving the dignity of the office
might not have been effective, the danger that they foresaw
was a real one. In the present instance still another element
of danger was present; the vice presidency had been used to
conciliate a minority faction, and now that the President was
dead, the representative of this minority fell heir to all the
executive power. So much alarm was felt among the Whig
leaders that there was some disposition to treat Tyler as "acting President," somewhat shorn of the extreme prerogatives
of office; but his decided and proper insistence that he be
credited with the full range of executive power, prevented this
attempt to stay the natural result of their improvidence.

The alarm of those Whig leaders who wished to revive
an active nationalistic policy was certainly justified. Tyler
was strongly committed by thirty years of public life to the
strictest school of constitutional construction, nor was he
likely to modify his views. His leading personal characteristic was an extreme vanity which had been fostered by the
established position of his family, the precocious development of his talent, and a rare beauty and grace of manner
which had made the path of life easy for him. The pride of
his political life was his unwavering consistency, which had
led him back and forth from one party to another as each
seemed to him to depart from the clear injunctions of the
Constitution. That every such change of party had been
followed by political advancement seemed to him but the
proper reward of virtue, and the historian must record that
these changes of party allegiance were made with all sincerity

Tyler's char-
acter and
career.

of purpose. He had none of those occasional doubts as to the
fallibility of his own opinions which are apt to come to the
humble-minded ; he had none of that respect for the opinions
of others which is developed by the difficulties of life. He was
a pure man, with high and laudable ambitions, but he lacked
the comprehensive sympathy and understanding of a statesman ; he was a man of talent, and a gentleman, but not a
great man.

Clay's pro-
gram.

Tyler kept in office the cabinet of Harrison and he met
the special session of Congress with a message that was somewhat ambiguous and somewhat conciliatory. The message,
however, received little attention, for Clay at once took the
lead and introduced a resolution outlining the business of the
session. The chief measures he proposed were: first, the re-
establishment of the pre-Jacksonian fiscal system, by the
formation of a new bank and the repeal of the Independent
Treasury Act; secondly, the reëstablishment of the American
system, by the passage of a tariff act and a bill for the distribution of the proceeds of land sales among the states. There
were other suggestions of minor importance, and the party
which had come into power without a platform, found before
it one of the heaviest programs of work ever suggested for
immediate accomplishment.

The restoration of the finances was first taken up. The
deficit, which Van Buren had met by the temporary expedient of treasury notes, was now provided for by a loan of
$12,000,000, though the objection to a permanent national
debt was still so strong that the term of the loan was too short
to make capitalists eager to buy the bonds. More important
was the repeal of the Independent Treasury Act, which was
speedily rushed through and signed by the President. The
Whigs had now to provide a substitute for the system they
had overthrown. In doing so they wished to furnish a means

The cur-
rency.

not only for doing the business of the government, but for
regulating the currency. They wished to put an end to the

divorce between the government and the business world. Tyler, after discussing the subject in his message, concluded:."To you, then, who have come more directly from the body of our common constituents, I submit the entire question, as best qualified to give a full exposition of their wishes. I shall be ready to concur with you in the adoption of such system as you may propose, reserving to myself the ultimate power of rejecting any measure which may, in my view of it, conflict with the Constitution or otherwise jeopardize the prosperity of the country — a power which I could not part with even if I would, but which I will not believe any act of yours will call into requisition."

Congress could suggest no method other than the establishment of a bank. Knowing Tyler's constitutional objection to such an institution, the Whig leaders took the greatest care to meet his views so far as they were known. The plan provided for a "Fiscal Bank," located in the District of Columbia, over which the power of Congress was complete. The crucial question was with regard to the power to establish branches in the states. Clay wished the bank to have .power to establish them, but Congress attempted to compromise by implying the permanent assent of the state unless the legislature, at its first session after the passage of the bill, protested against such action. The bill passed in this form, and Tyler vetoed it on August 16, 1841. Negotiations were at once begun between Congress and the administration, and a bill was drawn up by Ewing, the Secretary of the Treasury, and Webster, which it was understood that Tyler would sign. This provided for a "Fiscal Corporation" instead of a bank and deprived it of the power of discount and of local exchange, but it was allowed to operate throughout the country. On September 9 Tyler vetoed this bill, bringing the utmost discouragement to the Whig leaders, and overwhelming anger to the rank and file of the party, which had

The bank vetoes.

been given reason to believe that Tyler had promised to accept it.

Break between Tyler and the Whigs.

The second veto was the signal for a party crisis. The entire cabinet resigned with the exception of Webster, and Clay so bitterly assailed the President as to make reconciliation impossible. Tyler was accused of breaking his word in regard to the second bank bill, and of being a traitor to his party. Clay as emphatically declared that the people in the election of 1840 had decided for the bank, as Jackson had asserted their opposition to it in 1832. One session of Congress had sufficed to rend the party in twain. Tyler did not at once despair of carrying the bulk of it with him, making himself its leader, and being its candidate in 1844. He had a coterie of personal friends, called in derision because of their number the "corporal's guard," but of an ability that somewhat atoned for their lack of votes. Foremost among them was Henry A. Wise, who was to succeed him as the representative of the purest Virginian political tradition. Another prominent figure was Caleb Cushing, who represented a long line of individualists that had dominated the thought of Salem, Massachusetts, from the earliest colonial times, and had continually opposed the aggressive strong government element of Boston and other portions of that commonwealth. The fact that Webster was willing to retain his place was a great encouragement to Tyler, who warmly rejoiced when he heard of it, and said, "Give me your hand on that, and now I will say to you that Henry Clay is a doomed man from this hour."

Whig legislation.

Tyler's hopes proved delusive, for Clay's magnetic and vigorous leadership kept together a sufficient portion of the party to give him still a majority in Congress. As this majority was far less than two thirds, however, measures could not be passed over a veto, and only such parts of his program could be carried as Tyler was willing to accept. Increased appropriations were made for the navy, and a national bankruptcy bill, always demanded by the business interests, was passed, though it remained on the statute books only two years. The preëmption system, which had been maintained since 1830 by annual acts, was made permanent. The American system was adopted, but only in fragmentary fashion. The first portion attempted was a bill for the distribution of the proceeds of land sales. It was urged that the funds thus given would enable the states to meet the interest on their debts and might prevent the threatened repudiation. An object still more prominent in Clay's mind was that, by thus reducing the income of the national government, there would be stronger inducement for raising the duties on imports at the next session, when the compromise of 1833 would work itself out. So clearly was this political purpose appreciated that the opposition succeeded in appending an amendment to the effect that the distribution should not be made if at any time the duties should exceed twenty per cent.

When Congress met for the next session, the finances of The tariff. the government were in a rather serious condition. The country had not yet recovered its prosperity, and the impending reductions of the tariff on January 1 and June 30, 1842, threatened a serious deficit. The situation was, therefore, favorable for a reëstablishment of the protective system. Even Tyler stated in his message that, while that compromise was sacred and its spirit should control all tariff legislation, " the government may be justified in so discriminating by reference to other considerations of domestic policy connected with our manufactures." The situation was made still more easy by the willingness of a large number of Democrats from Pennsylvania and New York to vote for protection. Under these circumstances the protectionist leaders would have had an easy task had it not been for the determination of Clay to join the issue of distribution with the tariff. A bill was introduced which raised duties, gave pref-

erence to freights brought in American vessels, and provided
for the repeal of the restrictive amendment to the land distribution bill.   Gilmer, of the corporal's guard, said of this:
"The restriction in the distribution act of 1841 was designed
to guard against increasing the burdens of taxation to fill a
vacuum which might be occasioned by distribution.   The
legislation of 1842 is designed to create a vacuum that it
may be filled by increased taxation."   The Whig majority
held firm, and passed first a provisional, and then a permanent, bill, only to have both vetoed by the President.   The
House of Representatives, following the precedent of the
Senate in 1833, censured the President, who like Jackson
responded with a "Protest."   Impeachment was threatened,
but the President was not to be coerced; and the Whigs were
forced to abandon distribution or take the responsibility of
adjourning without providing the government with sufficient
revenue.   Clay was in favor of holding out, forcing the President to veto again, and taking the issue to the people, but the
majority decided otherwise, and the bill without its distribution feature was at length passed.   Even this fragment of
the Whig program was carried only with the assistance of
twenty Democrats, for thirty-five Whigs voted against it,
about twenty of these because they wished to hold out for
distribution and the rest because they disapproved of a protective tariff.   The Whigs soon found cause to congratulate
themselves on their yielding in this case.   Almost coincident
'with the passage of the tariff act came the long-hoped-for
revival of prosperity, and, whether it were the result of this
legislation or from natural causes, it could at any rate be
used by their orators as an argument of their wisdom.

Relations
with
England.

While Congress and the President were thus at odds,
Webster was quietly at work adjusting our difficulties with
England. In 1841 Peel became Prime Minister, and he evinced
a strong desire for a complete settlement of all outstanding
difficulties between the two countries.   To accomplish this

he sent, as special minister to the United States, Lord Ashburton, a man always friendly to America and having close relations with Webster. The negotiations, thus pleasantly begun, involved many questions, some of long standing and some of peculiar delicacy.

Two problems arose out of the Canadian insurrection. The first was that of the *Caroline*, an American vessel used by the insurgents, which the English had seized while at dock on the American shore of the Niagara River, and sent blazing into the current and over the falls. In the excitement an American citizen was killed. This matter was closed by an interchange of notes, which proved mutually satisfactory and which were calculated to make such episodes unlikely in the future. The second case arose as an aftermath of the *Caroline* affair. A certain Alexander McLeod, coming from Canada to New York, in 1840, boasted of having killed the American whose life was then lost. McLeod was promptly arrested and put on trial for murder before the proper state court. McLeod asserted that he had acted upon instructions from his superior officer, and was not personally responsible. The British government upheld this view and demanded his release. Webster admitted the principle advanced, but could not secure the release of McLeod from the state court, over which the national government had no control. The matter was serious, and for a time even Webster feared war. The United States Attorney-General was sent to watch the case, and finally McLeod was acquitted on an *alibi*. In 1842 Webster secured the passage of an act by Congress which authorized the transfer of such cases in the future to the national courts. The lack of power on the part of the national government over state courts has subsequently given trouble in our relations with foreign countries, but no other case of quite so delicate a character as this has arisen.

The Caroline and McLeod.

Several matters were settled by the Webster-Ashburton

Webster–Ashburton treaty.

Slave trade.   treaty, which was concluded in 1842. One question of
growing annoyance concerned the slave trade. This had
been a very profitable branch of English commerce until
Parliament abolished it, after which England was especially
eager that other nations should not profit by her self-abne-
gation. By 1840 it had been legally abolished by nearly all
civilized nations, but all were not equally eager or able
actually to suppress it. With many countries England had
made arrangements that her navy be allowed to enforce their
laws. Foremost among the nations not bound by such an
agreement was the United States, and many slavers hoisted
the American flag and defied the English men-of-war. The
English claimed that under such circumstances they had the
right to "visit" the vessel to ascertain whether it was properly flying the American flag. The American statesmen,
remembering the inconveniences caused by England's extension of this right of visit into a right to search before the
War of 1812, utterly refused to consider it as existing in
time of peace, and demanded that under all circumstances
the American flag be respected. General Cass, at this time
minister to France, on his own initiative persuaded that
country and other European powers to refrain from indorsing a proposed convention granting England the powers she
sought.

Slave trade   The United States would not allow the right of visit,
compromise.   and England would not explicitly give it up. Thereupon, at
the suggestion of Tyler, Webster and Ashburton compromised
the matter by providing that a joint squadron patrol the
African coast, thus providing for the suppression of the trade,
which was what England particularly wished, and making
"visits" of foreign war vessels unnecessary, which was what
the United States desired to avoid. Cass at once attacked
this compromise because it did not contain an express renunciation, on the part of Great Britain, of the "right of
visit." Webster declared that there was a tacit renunciation,

and there ensued a pamphlet war between them. Events proved that Cass was right, and sixteen years later, when he was himself Secretary of State, he obtained the concession which he thought Webster should have secured in 1842.

Still more important were the questions regarding the boundary. That on the northeast had been in dispute since 1783. In 1838 armed conflicts, dignified in the press by the title "Aroostook War," took place in Maine. That state and Congress both appropriated money to place the frontier in a state of defense. Peace was temporarily restored by a *modus vivendi* arranged by the indefatigable General Scott, but the situation remained acute. Webster and Ashburton took up this question in a friendly spirit, and by mutual concessions succeeded in agreeing upon the line from the Atlantic Ocean to the Rocky Mountains, which has remained until the present day. *Boundary questions.*

Much as was determined, many problems remained. Oregon was left undivided under the joint occupancy agreement arranged in 1818 and renewed in 1828. Also unsettled was the case of the *Creole*. This was a vessel engaged in the domestic slave trade between Virginia and New Orleans. The slaves rose, killed a portion of the crew, and brought the vessel into the British port of Nassau in the West Indies. There some of the negroes were hanged for murder, and the remainder released upon the ground that they became free on touching free soil. The American government claimed that the vessel and all the negroes should have been turned over to it, and demanded apology and compensation. Lord Ashburton defended the British action. The case caused much agitation in the United States because of its connection with slavery. It was not arranged until 1853, when an arbitration was agreed upon, and damages awarded to the American owners. More important, the general rivalry between England and the United States for predominance on the American continents remained. Like most compromises which are *Questions unsettled. Oregon and the Creole.*

arranged on the basis of mutual accommodation rather than
of principle, the Webster-Ashburton treaty was unpopular
in both countries. In America the failure to settle the
Creole case and to obtain a renunciation of the claim of
visitation were unpopular in the South. In Maine the partition of the disputed territory in the northeast was so much
disliked that it took that state forever out of the Whig ranks
and, perhaps, cost Webster the presidential nomination in
1852. Still, the main object was secured, for fairly amicable
relations were restored between England and the United
States, and, possibly, a war was averted.

**Election of
1842.**

With the adoption of the tariff bill and the conclusion of
the Webster-Ashburton treaty, the last fruits of the Whig
victory were garnered. The elections of 1842 went overwhelmingly against them, and while they retained a precarious
control of the Senate, the Democrats obtained a majority of
sixty in the House. With the two branches of the legislature
of opposing political allegiance, and with the President and
Senate hostile, there resulted a legislative and executive
deadlock, and political attention was directed toward the

**The Whig
party in 1844.**

next campaign. The Whig party had come out of the struggle
with Tyler, diminished in numbers, but with some gain in
homogeneity and much in unity of spirit. Even Webster, after
completing his diplomatic task, and when both he and Tyler
found that his remaining in the cabinet had not been of
political advantage to either, resigned and resumed his old allegiance. The party leaders had had enough of figureheads
and compromise candidates. They fully determined to nominate Clay, who had bade an affecting farewell to the Senate
in 1842 and retired to his seat at Ashland to await the call
of the people. The Whig program would be a demand for
the indorsement of what it had done and for opportunity to
adopt those measures which had failed.

**Van Buren's
following.**

The Democratic party seemed to be still in the hands of
the old leaders. It was their belief that Van Buren must be

renominated to vindicate the party. Jackson was in favor
of him and he was indorsed by the *Globe* and by a series of
state conventions, and a majority of the delegates to the national convention were pledged to his support. A Van
Buren platform was as easily formed as one for Clay, and the
people of the country would have the opportunity to vote intel-
ligently on issues which had long been defined and discussed.

Besides these regular candidates there were two other   Calhoun's
important aspirants. Calhoun, now once more within the   candidacy
Democratic party, planned to secure the nomination he had
expected in 1832. He left the Senate in 1843, his works and
a biographical sketch were published, and he was a declared
candidate. The main issues upon which he opposed Van
Buren and to which he wished to commit the Democratic
party, were free trade and reform. He "laid down the broad
proposition, that imports and exports are reciprocal, and
mutually limit one another; that we cannot export in the
long run more than we import, and *vice versa* — a proposition,
which," he wrote, "I think has never been fully realized."
On this point he would have the support of all southern and
many other Democrats, but it was a question which the northern politicians wished to avoid. Calhoun feared also that
Van Buren's election would lead again to administrative
demoralization. He wrote: "There is much, very much to
do, to reform the administrative departments. It will prove
to be a difficult task, requiring vast labor, great firmness,
and no little sagacity. I feel assured, the expenditures may
be reduced millions, without impairing the efficiency of the
government, but the work will require the hearty coöperation
of the executive and legislative departments of the government, the former taking the lead; and even then, it will
require years to effect it. Congress can do little of itself.
It must be the great work of the next administration; and
unless it is thoroughly done, all will be lost. If I can be of
any future service to the country it will be in carrying through

this great reform. . . . My congressional task, in short, is done. . . . It rests with the people to say, whether I shall be selected to finish the work, which has been carried forward to where it now is." He was opposed to party organization and the tyranny exerted by state conventions, and favored the choice of delegates to the national convention by districts. In a word, he wished to run as Democratic candidate on a platform which was chiefly made up of southern demands; his weakness lay in his lack of an issue distinctly appealing to the frontier and northern democracies.

Tyler's plans.   The fourth candidate was the President. His hope of securing the Whig nomination had vanished, but he had other plans. With his natural suavity of manner he found it easy to keep on agreeable terms with the Democratic leaders in Congress, and he had some thought that he might be the choice of that party. In the meantime he actively employed the patronage in rewarding and enheartening his own personal following, and was determined to run independently if rejected by both parties. He too, like Calhoun, needed a fresh issue, and he was planning to associate with his name the question of Texan annexation, which had proved distasteful to those in control of both party organizations.

In order to understand the circumstances that shaped the fortunes of these rivals, and determined the campaign of 1844, it is necessary to review the situation of the country at large, and note the development of certain new factors that, while playing small part in politics before 1843, were to dominate them for the next twenty years.

BIBLIOGRAPHICAL NOTES

Sources.   The *Papers* of J. C. Calhoun (letters to and from him), published in Am. Hist. Assoc., *Report*, 1899, vol. II, are especially illuminating for this period. The sources mentioned at the close of the last chapter, also, continue to be of use. See also National Monetary Commission, *Laws Concerning Money*.

Dewey, D. R., *Financial History*, §§ 102, 103. Garrison, Historical accounts. *Westward Extension*, 43–84. Lodge, H. C., *Webster*, ch. VIII. Schurz, *Clay*, chs. XXII, XXIII. Stanwood, E., *Tariff Controversies*, II, ch. XI. Tyler, L. G., *Letters and Lives of the Tylers*, II, chs. I–VI. Von Holst, H., *Constitutional History*, II, chs. V, VI.

Moore, J. B., *Arbitrations*, I, chs. I–VI; *International Law* Diplomatic. *Digest*, II, 24–29. Reeves, J. S., *American Diplomacy under Tyler and Polk*. Webster, D., *Works*, V, 116–135; VI, 247–269.

CHAPTER XVII

NEW ECONOMIC AND SOCIAL CONDITIONS, 1830 TO 1860

THE period of the thirties, forties, and fifties was one of unusually stimulating activity affecting the whole life of the people. Many of the new tendencies and developments which first attract attention soon after the War of 1812 now attain full stature and become dominating forces, and many new factors appear which were destined to vie with them in significance. The changes of this period were not perhaps of so deep and underlying importance as those between 1815 and 1830, but they were more widespread and some of them more striking.

Canals.
Most significant of the economic changes was the improvement in the means of transportation. Washington had seen the importance of that problem to the future of the country and had grappled with it, but hardly anything had been done before his death except the building of not very good toll roads and bridges. The invention of the steamboat had suddenly opened up the immense stretches of navigable water in the interior, and made it possible to live and do business on almost every river bank. Then came the lock canal, clearing away many of the obstacles which rapids and falls offered to the steamboat, and, by connecting the heads of rivers, joining one river basin to another. Many seaports by such constructions brought to their wharves the products of all the surrounding country, and the Erie Canal and the Pennsylvania Canal and inclined planes afforded cheap means of connection between the East and the West. In Ohio, Indiana, and Illinois, canals connected rivers flowing into the Lakes with branches of the Ohio, and plans were made to

utilize the portage between the Fox and the Wisconsin. The twenties and the thirties were preëminently the period of the canal. Already, however, another method had been devised which was to supersede water transit, for a time at least.

The railroad was introduced in 1825, and after a few years Railroads. the steam engine came to be used in connection with it. Railroad construction was cheaper than that of canals, railroads could be built over many routes where canals were impossible, and at first the abundance of firewood and later the use of coal made the cost of operation seem small. At first they were built largely to carry passengers, and to supplement canals. Very few miles were built before 1830 ; but by 1840, 2302 miles were in operation between important centers of population, and extending from Wilmington in North Carolina, with small break, to New York. From 1840 to 1850, 5043 miles were built, supplementing those of the previous decade and stretching over several distances inconvenient for canal construction, as from Detroit to New Buffalo on Lake Michigan, from Sandusky to Cincinnati, and from Chattanooga to Charleston and Savannah. Up to this time little had been accomplished in the West, where the Mississippi on the one hand and the Lakes with the Erie Canal on the other afforded such easy access. Moreover, the experiences of the thirties had made the holders of capital more cautious, and they preferred local enterprises. Even in the East, where there was the most surplus capital, several of the states were obliged to lend their credit in aid of such enterprises. During the fifties the situation changed. It had been proved that the railroads paid, which canals had rarely done ; capital was at the same time more abundant and more accessible to the promoters of new projects; the spirit of speculation revived. Private corporations were formed on a larger scale than Corporations. before, and investors became willing to venture their money farther away from home.

In the West railroads were desired to build up the country. Regions untouched by navigable waterways had been left unsettled, though surrounded by occupied territory.   If railroads could be built through them, settlement would follow, but such enterprises could not be expected to pay for some years, and private capital needed special inducements to undertake the work.   Under these circumstances Congress reinaugurated the system of national aid, but indirectly. Land grants were made to several states in order that they in turn might give them to companies engaging to Land grants.   construct roads.   The system was to grant alternate sections of land to the railroad, and the government was expected to reimburse itself by the enhanced value of the land remaining.   The first grant was to the Illinois Central, and it was largely owing to this policy that in the fifties 21,424 miles were built, and that the West, which was almost bare of railroads at the beginning, was by 1860 crisscrossed with them, from Oshkosh and La Crosse on the north, down the whole east side of the Mississippi, with short lines in Iowa and Missouri.

Strategic problem of communication.   This network of roads built in the ten years before the Civil War had a far-reaching importance.   There was a southern system which, connecting with the southern rivers, answered fairly well the needs of that agricultural region, but connected with the northern system only at Washington and Bowling Green, Kentucky.   This system served the Gulf States and Tennessee and Arkansas for both export and import.   Many products of the upper Mississippi, the Ohio, and the Missouri still sought an outlet downstream, and New Orleans was still an important port for the middle region; but a constantly increasing amount was sent from these valleys over the Erie Railroad to New York, over the Pennsylvania to Philadelphia, and over the Baltimore and Ohio to Baltimore. Sectionalism in the West.   The Lake region was entirely tributary to New York, using the Erie Canal and the Erie and the New York Central railroads.

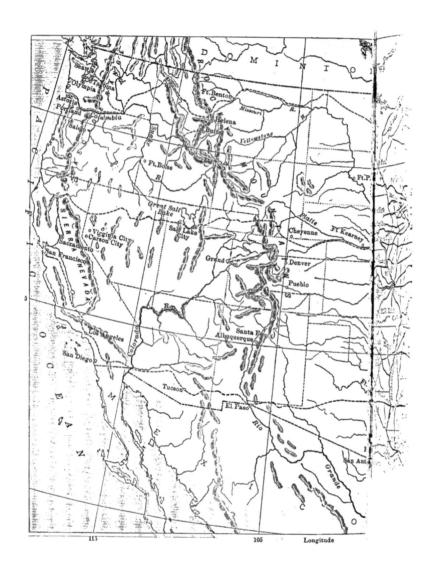

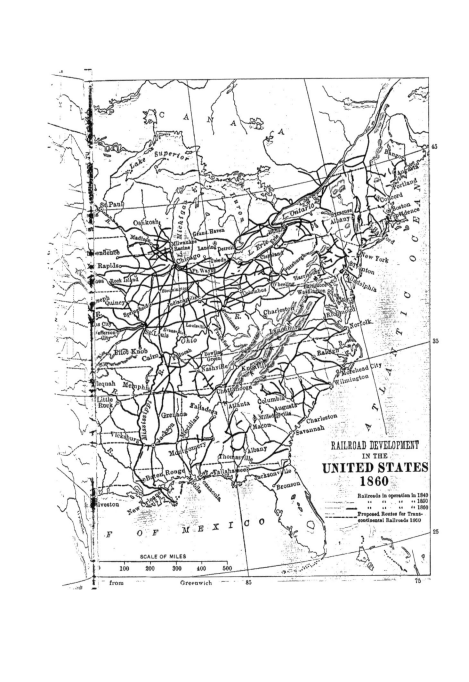

RAILROAD DEVELOPMENT
IN THE
UNITED STATES
1860

Railroads in operation in 1840
     "   "   " 1850
     "   "   " 1860
Proposed Routes for Transcontinental Railroads 1860

SCALE OF MILES
100   200   300   400   500

from   Greenwich   85   75

The great factor of communication was dividing the West, which had been so much of a unit in 1830, into three sections : the Lake region, affiliated with the Northeast; the southern belt, looking to New Orleans and other southern seaports; and the Ohio and Missouri valleys, the battle-ground of water and rail transportation, of northern and southern influences. The division of the country at the time of the Civil War was to show that by that time iron had become stronger than water.

Another dividing element in the West was agriculture. Throughout the South cotton culture was coming to be everywhere the dominant industry. Along the rich river bottoms of the Tennessee it was replacing the more diversified farming of the frontier period; it spread down the banks of the Mississippi from the Ohio to the coast, and up the valleys of its western branches. Cotton culture carried with it slavery and the plantation system. Everywhere the tendency was toward larger estates, greater investments of capital, and the crowding out of the small proprietor, as had been the case in Virginia and South Carolina, although in no other state even in 1860 had the process developed so far as it had in South Carolina by 1830. Everywhere other products were raised, but everywhere the cotton planters were coming to be the ruling class. *Spread of the plantation system.*

In the Northwest the emergence from frontier conditions was characterized by more general diffusion of wealth and improvement of agricultural methods. The successful farmer put a smaller portion of his profits into the cost of living than in the South, for social exactions were not so high. There was a widespread increase of comfort, but fewer mansions and liveried equipages. The portion of his profits which was devoted to business was spent for labor-saving machinery instead of for slaves. In 1833 the McCormick reaper was invented, after 1840 its use increased rapidly, and by 1860 twenty thousand were manufactured yearly. To a small extent the use of fertilizers was begun, and in general, through *Agriculture in the Northwest.*

the thousands of small farms in this region, there was a gradual change from the rough-and-ready methods of the frontiersman to the steady industry of the established farmer. Many settlers proved incapable of making this change, and, selling out their farms, went westward and northward again to blaze out homes in the wilderness. They generally sold to newcomers with a little capital, who hoped to make their profits by hard work and greater skill, and not, as was so often the case in the South, to a neighboring proprietor who expected to increase his income by using more land and more slaves. The system of small farms, cultivated by their owners, continued to be characteristic of the whole region north of the Ohio.

The forces which had made for the unity of the Mississippi valley—the frontier stage of development, and the use of the great river—grew continually less important; the forces of separation — the differences in climate, in soil, in products, and in economic and social characteristics — grew constantly more significant. At the same time the northern stream of population flowing into the Lake region from the Northeast brought ideas and customs differing from those of the southern settlers who occupied the lower Mississippi, and the two streams mingled and strove in the valley of the Ohio. The struggle between these opposing forces is one of the great features of the history of this period.

Growth of European trade. While a new sectionalism was being developed within the country, similar forces were beginning to break down the isolation of the United States, and bring it more in touch with the rest of the world. The rapid development of manufactures in the twenties and thirties had outrun in some respects the agricultural development. The home market argument, so potent in influencing the farmers to vote for a protective tariff at that time, seemed justified by its results; the country consumed almost all its food products, and in 1837 wheat was actually imported into New York. The improvement in agricultural methods, and the vast areas of land newly opened in the forties and fifties, changed the situation, and there was again a surplus to dispose of as there had been at the beginning of the century. Fortunately for our trade, in England the course of events was different, the farmers were unable to feed the industrial population, and in 1846 the " corn laws " (laws laying an import duty on grain) were abolished and a free market opened to American products. The two best years for purposes of trade comparison are 1836 and 1856, each immediately preceding a financial crisis and representing the culmination of a period of prosperity. In 1836 the United States exported $2,561,330 worth of animal food, in 1856, $17,665,922 worth; exports of vegetable food products increased from $7,431,119 to $59,390,906. Cotton, however, continued to be the leading single export, increasing from $71,284,925 to $128,382,351. The total value of exports of every kind rose from $128,663,040 to $326,964,908. Imports did not increase proportionately, barely keeping pace with the growth of population, rising only from $189,980,055 to $314,639,942. The greater portion of this increase was in articles like tea, coffee, sugar, and other things which could not be produced in sufficient quantity at home. The manufacturers of the country were supplying the domestic market better than before. The increased commerce with Europe resulted from the disproportionate increase in American agricultural products and the simultaneous demand for them abroad, and the balance of trade thus created in favor of the United States brought in much of the capital used in the building of railroads and other improvements.

This increased commerce demanded increased means of ocean transportation, and the improvements were as great as those in communication by land. The building of sailing vessels reached a level of efficiency, both for speed and for safety, decidedly above that of the past. The Baltimore

Ocean transportation.

clippers were famous and have not been surpassed. Their arrivals and departures could be announced with an amazing accuracy. Of greater importance was the application of steam to ocean transportation. Although attempts to cross the ocean in ships propelled wholly by steam had been made as early as 1819, they were not followed up at once, and it was for a long time believed that no ship could carry enough fuel to take it from continent to continent. By 1839, however, the problem was well solved, and in that year the Cunard Company undertook a regular service which has never since been discontinued. Improvements were rapid, and the duration of the passage was cut down from the eighteen to twenty-five days of the sailing packet, and from the fifteen days of the earliest steamers, to ten days in 1840 and a little over nine days by the middle of the fifties.

The American merchant marine.

Of the business of ocean carrying, the United States obtained a very large share. With the abundance of timber and the long experience of colonial times, the American shipwrights were able to produce vessels at low cost; and, protected as they were by our navigation acts, American shipowners were able to pay better wages than those of other countries and yet charge no higher freights. In order to stimulate American owners to compete in the fast mail service, the government in 1845 began the policy of subsidizing American vessels by giving them favorable mail contracts. This policy reached its height during the fifties, when the rivalry between the American Collins line and the English Cunarders attracted world-wide attention; but with the failure of the Collins line through marine disasters, the whole subsidy policy waned in popularity. Still every decade saw a great increase in the tonnage of American vessels engaged in ocean traffic. In 1830 it was little over 500,000; in 1840 it was 750,000; in 1850, about 1,500,000; in 1860, nearly 2,500,000. The coastwise trade was also growing, and the commerce of the Great Lakes was increasing almost beyond computation,

so that by 1860 the total American merchant marine was
greater even than that of Great Britain. It represented a
very great investment of capital, and great fortunes, such as
that of Commodore Vanderbilt, had grown out of its progress. The anxious rivalry of Great Britain was indicated
by the abundant subsidies with which she supplied the
Cunard line.

This vast fleet was employed not only in the interchange Immigration.
of commodities, but also in the importation of swarms of immigrants seeking new homes in America. Most of the movements of population which have been noted so far as taking
place after the Revolution were movements of American
stock. The outflow from the mountains into the piedmont
regions of the East and the plains of the West, the gradual
flooding of the Mississippi basin, and the constant rippling
westward of wave after wave of population, started by first
one and then another economic or social cause, had nearly
all merely changed the habitation of the fairly homogeneous
people which inhabited the country at the time of the Revolution and of their descendants. Before 1820 foreign immigration rarely reached 10,000 a year, and this small number was
chiefly of English origin and quickly assimilated with the
native population. From that time on there was an increase which continued quite steadily until the middle of
the fifties. The circumstances that caused this growth were
threefold. First was the prosperity of the United States,
as is shown by the fact that immigration grew most rapidly
in the years of greatest business activity, and declined for a
year or two after the panics of 1837 and 1857. The second
was the improvement in ocean transportation, without which
many would not have faced the journey, and it would have
been utterly impossible to bring over the vast numbers seeking passage in the early fifties. Finally, the conditions of
various countries of Europe from time to time incited emigration and determined the character of the new population.

The coming of the Irish.

The first important stream of non-English immigration was from Ireland. There had always been settlers from that island, but to a large extent they had come from the north and were of Scotch stock. During this period, however, overpopulation, famine, and constant political discontent sent over hundreds of thousands of the Celtic Irish from the southern and central portions of the island. Beginning to come in good numbers during the twenties, they increased during the thirties, in the next decade 781,000 came, and in the next, 914,000.

Activities of the Irish.

These Irish were mostly of the peasant class and accustomed to agriculture, but they seldom had money left after their arrival and were unable to go west or to buy the high-priced farms near at hand. They engaged at first in rough, unskilled labor on the canals, railroads, and other large undertakings of the period. When such a piece of work was completed, the discharged workmen often settled down in one of the towns near by, and drifted into the mills. As they were accustomed to a lower standard of living than the natives, they were willing to work at smaller wages; and gradually their competition, first in one locality and then in another, drove the native-born out of such occupations. The jealousy and hard feeling engendered by this economic rivalry was increased by religious differences. These Irish were practically all Catholics and extremely devout. It was not long before Catholic churches began to rise throughout southern New England and the Middle States, and convents and parochial schools competed with the public educational establishments which were coming to be looked upon as the basis of true democracy. The distrust with which the rigid Protestant spirit of the body of the population looked upon the growth of Catholic institutions was heightened by the part the Irish played in politics. They proved themselves adepts in political management and party organization. Living, as they did at first, together in separate quarters clustered about their churches, and having similar interests, they tended to cast their weight on one side, rather than to divide between the parties. In the large ports where they disembarked and where great numbers of the poorest remained, they soon became an important factor in politics. Politicians bid for their votes by favoring appropriations to aid their charitable and educational establishments, and the Irish Catholics came to be regarded by many as a menace to the republic.

In many places this feeling took shape in riots. In 1834 an Ursuline convent in the outskirts of Boston was sacked on the rumor that girls were confined against their will. In New York and Philadelphia riots were frequent, with the fault now on one side, now on the other. Prejudice, however, was not confined to the rioting classes, and many sought to ward off the danger by political measures. Neither of the great parties was anxious to take up the issue, because the Irish had votes, and because the majority of the population really took pride in seeing foreigners flock to our shores. It happened, therefore, that from time to time special third parties were formed to secure remedial legislation. Such factions were active in Philadelphia and New York in 1835 and 1844; in 1847 the Nativist party cast 80,000 votes in the latter state; and suddenly, in 1852, a temporary lull in national politics gave an opportunity for the issue to rise into general notice. As the principal basis of appeal of the American, or as it was popularly called Know-Nothing, party, it was thoroughly discussed between 1852 and 1856, and the nation decided to keep its doors open to the world. *Anti-foreign feeling.*

A second stream of immigration came from Germany. It is significant that the first subsidy granted by the United States was to a line running between New York and Bremen. German immigration had begun in the seventeenth century, and at the time of the Revolution Germans formed a decided *The coming of the Germans.*

factor in the population of Pennsylvania, Virginia, and New York. The stream declined, however, and did not become very important again until 1830, when the unsuccessful political revolutions of that year sent many of the disappointed to America. They were joined during the next few years by greater numbers who could not easily adjust themselves to the changes caused by the industrial revolution which was then sweeping over Germany. The fair reports that these sent back encouraged others, and finally the defeat of the revolutionary efforts of 1848 induced many brilliant young leaders and the more devoted of their followers to come to the United States, some as to a temporary refuge, and some with the idea of working out their political ideas upon more congenial soil. It was even hoped by many of them that Wisconsin might become a German state. By 1860 the German-born population of the United States amounted to over a million and a quarter.

Activities of the Germans.   These Germans generally possessed a little money, and the greater portion of them passed through the coast states and sought the agricultural opportunities beyond the mountains. Some became pioneers, and others bought farms from owners who had become restless at the approach of civilization and wished to try their fortunes upon the new frontier. With the expanding European market, there was a demand for all the breadstuffs that could be produced, and hence the economic rivalry encountered by the Irish in the East was not found. Among the Germans some were Catholic and some Protestant, they scattered about the country instead of living together in close settlements, and their leaders took an active part in setting up and supporting the public schools. The majority of them did not take so keen an interest in politics as did the Irish, but their leaders, particularly those who came after 1848, were inclined to do so, and through their German newspapers exerted a great influence. Coming into the northwestern states, where the population was very

evenly divided between settlers of southern and of northern
origin, the Germans were to some degree a balancing element in the population. They sympathized with the southern portion in their strong belief in individual freedom, opposing the strict sabbath and prohibition legislation which
was being urged by the New York and New England people,
and consequently becoming, at first, nearly all .Democratic
in politics. At the same time they took the nationalistic
view of the Constitution, for they had been endeavoring in
Germany to unify the nation and put an end to the sovereignty of the numerous independent German principalities.
On the whole, they were also strongly opposed to slavery.
Although the foreign element had become, by 1852, an
important factor in politics, the feeling between the native
and foreign population was not so tense west of the mountains
as in the East.

This immigration naturally had the effect of causing
the population to increase with unusual rapidity. In 1820
it was 9,638,453; by 1830 it was 12,866,020, having increased
33.5 per cent; in the next decade it increased 32.7 per cent,
to ·17,069,453 ; in the next 35.9 per cent, to 23,191,876 ; and
between 1850 and 1860, 35.6 per cent, to 31,443,321.
Throughout the country, population was shifting. In the
northeastern states tens of 'thousands were moving westward and were replaced by immigrants. The growth of the
country population halted, and began, in New England, actually to decline. This loss was offset by the gain in cities
and manufacturing towns. The urban population was growing almost twice as fast as the population of the country at
large. The slaveholding states were dropping steadily behind. Comparatively few foreign immigrants cared to settle
there, owing to an inherent dislike of slavery and of the negro,
the lack of manufacturing development, and the unfortunate position of the small farmers in competition with the
large plantation owners. The drain of population from the

Shifting of the native stock.

Slow growth of the South.

slave states into the free states of the West also continued. In 1820 the population of the slave area was 4,485,818, or over 46 per cent of that of the whole country, of which number 1,558,000 were slaves. During the next twenty years, the period of the opening of the cotton belt, the South lost the least relatively, having, in 1840, 7,334,431, or 43 per cent of the whole, the number of slaves being 2,487,000. Between 1840 and 1860, the period of most active immigration, the lead of the North increased rapidly. In the latter year the slave states contained 12,315,373 inhabitants, only 39 per cent of the total population, and of these 3,954,000 were slaves. To put it in another way, the white population of the South decreased relatively from about 30 per cent of the total population of the United States in 1820, to about 26 per cent in 1860.

Growth of the Far West.

The continuance of the movement westward is indicated by the fact that during every decade the states in the Mississippi valley increased at a rate about three times as great as those of the coast. During the twenties and thirties the greater portion of this western increase was in the area roughly broken to civilization before 1820. After the admission of Missouri in 1821 it was fifteen years before another state was ready for admission, and then Arkansas and Michigan were admitted in 1836 and 1837 respectively, indicating the steady push of population from neighboring settled territory. There was beginning, however, a new period of more adventurous pioneering, spurred on by deep-lying motives of religion, and love of excitement and of gain, which was to extend the population of the United States suddenly to the Pacific, and which resulted in the occupation of the Far West.

Texas.

The first of these movements into territory lying remote and not naturally next in order of occupation, was that which has already been mentioned into Texas. Here the exceptional motives needed to draw a population so far away were the cheapness of the land and the love of fighting, — motives which during this whole period were sufficient to rally hundreds to the banner of any leader, however preposterous his plans. Beginning in 1820, this movement had, by 1840, resulted in the establishment of a republic whose independence was acknowledged everywhere except by Mexico, and whose population was fifty or sixty thousand. The situation of Texas was regarded as very important strategically. If its ports should fall to the possession of the United States, that country would control the Gulf of Mexico; if a great foreign naval power should hold them, the mouth of the Mississippi would be threatened. The diplomats of England and some of those of the United States were alert to this situation, and courted the favor of the new republic. The South was anxious to annex it, because most of its population was of southern origin and its institutions and interests were practically identical with those of the southern states.

Far away to the northward was another position of great Oregon. significance to the future development of the United States. The valley of the Columbia River was the key to the whole far northwestern section, and it afforded a western outlet for the most natural transcontinental route to the Pacific, that of the Missouri River. The United States had certain claims to this region, founded on the discovery of the Columbia River by Captain Gray in 1792, its exploration by Lewis and Clark, and the cession by Spain in 1819. These rights, however, had never been definitely acknowledged by England, and the status of the country had been left doubtful by the joint occupation agreements of 1818 and 1828, which allowed the subjects of both powers to use freely the territory west of the Rocky Mountains between the parallels of 42° and 54° 40'. In the meantime the great English Hudson's Bay Company enjoyed almost solitary possession of this great domain, and its factor, McLaughlin, was the actual ruler. About 1835 a missionary interest began to be aroused in behalf of the Indians of this region, especially among the Methodists,

Congregationalists, and Presbyterians. They sent a number of families into the field, and their efforts to raise money for the work resulted in a general diffusion of interest in the Oregon territory. The missionaries encountered an active rivalry from the French Catholic priests who came from Canada and acknowledged English authority. The rivalry of the Protestant and Catholic missions developed into one of American and English, and the former appealed to the United States government to assert its claims, occupy the territory, and encourage settlement by giving stable land titles. Their cause found many champions in Congress, particularly Senator Linn of Missouri, who was familiar with the situation through the reports of the fur traders of the Missouri. Congress often discussed the matter between 1837 and 1843, and thousands of government documents carried accounts of the fertility of the soil throughout the country. The result of this religious and political agitation was that in 1842, when a government Indian agent went overland to Oregon, he was joined by a hundred and fifty settlers, and the next spring, from Arkansas, Illinois, and other states there came groups of settlers with their wagons displaying signs "For Oregon." Over a thousand pioneers passed over the mountains in 1843, and actual settlement was begun.

Great Salt Lake valley.   The vast interior valley of the Great Salt Lake also owed its opening to religious impulse. Joseph Smith, a magnetic, visionary young man of a family which had followed a usual course of New England migration from Connecticut to Vermont and thence to New York, about 1830 proclaimed himself the prophet of a new faith, and published the *Book of Mormon* as an exposition of his beliefs. An important phase of this new religion was its insistence on the communal life. There was at this time a widespread interest in communism, both in America and in Europe. Religious sects like the American Shakers and the German Rappists founded such settlements, the most notable being that at New Harmony on the Wabash under the direction of Robert Dale Owen. Associations to apply the doctrines of the French philosopher Fourier attempted experiments all the way from Massachusetts to Wisconsin and Iowa. Of all these efforts that of the Mormons alone proved to have the elements of permanence and growth. Converts were numerous from among Smith's rural neighbors in central New York and also among the foreign immigrants. The Mormons were unpopular in the districts in which they settled. Persecution drove them from New York to Ohio, from Ohio to Missouri, and then to Illinois. Here they prospered for a time, but opposition to them was increased when Smith and other leaders adopted the practice of polygamy. After the death of Smith at the hands of a mob in 1844, they despaired of living a peaceful life amid a population of alien religion, and decided, under their new leader, Brigham Young, to seek peace in the wilderness. In 1847 a host of men, women, and children, with wagons and cattle, started westward across the plains, and undertook a pilgrimage which demanded all their faith. They halted near the Great Salt Lake, in a territory which at that time belonged to Mexico, but which seemed so remote from all settlement and government that they hoped to work out their whole religious and social polity without interference for years to come. Through the fifties their missionaries practically acted as immigration agents in drawing converts from the East and from Europe.

The most attractive of all the portions of the Far West, California. but the least accessible from the Atlantic coast, was California, and there Spanish settlement, moving north from Mexico, had done much to establish a civilization and a language alien to that of the United States. Still the hold of Mexico was regarded as but feeble. The infant republic of Texas aspired to annex it, and, with ports on both oceans, to control the transcontinental trade. In the United States there was great fear that England might secure it, in exchange for the heavy debts due to her by Mexico. Webster considered the harbor of San Francisco twenty times as valuable as the whole Texan territory. Actual settlement lagged, owing to distance and the difficulty of transportation; but many of the American whaling vessels which frequented the Pacific stopped at the California ports for supplies; a few Americans settled in the country to trade with them; and some of those who came overland to Oregon continued down the coast in search of a more genial climate. All together by 1845 several hundred Americans were residing in California, and there was a general disposition to regard it as a future field for American settlement.

BIBLIOGRAPHICAL NOTES

Historical accounts. Transportation and Commerce.   Adams, C. F., *Origin and Problems of Railroads*, 36–79. Bishop, J. L., *American Manufactures*, II, 342–424. Coman, K., *Industrial History of the United States*, ch. VII. Homans, I. S., Jr., *Foreign Commerce of the United States* (1857). Mayer, E., *Origin of the Pacific Railroads* (*Publications* of Minn. Hist. Soc., vol. VI). Rhodes, J. F., *United States*, III, ch. I. Semple, E. C., *American History and its Geographic Conditions*, 246–273, 337–390. Smith, T. C., *Parties and Slavery*, 1–109. Spears, J. R., *American Merchant Marine*, chs. IX, XI–XV.

Immigration.   Bromwell, W. J., *History of Immigration* (with statistics). Byrne, S., *Irish Emigration to the United States*. Faust, *The German Element in the United States*, chs. 15, 16. Sartorius, A., Baron von Walter-hausen, *Die Zukunft des Deutschthums in der Vereinigten Staaten von Amerika*. Smith, R. M., *Emigration and Immigration*, chs. III–VIII.

Know-Nothingism.   Lee, J. H., *The Origin and Progress of the American Party*. Schmeckebier, L. F., *History of the Know-Nothing Party in Maryland* (*Johns Hopkins Historical Studies*, XVII, nos. 4, 5). Seisca, L. D., *Political Nativism in the State of New York* (*Columbia Univ. Studies in Hist.*, vol. XIII, no. 2). Stickney, C., *Know-Nothingism in Rhode Island* (Brown University Historical Seminary, *Papers*).

Occupation of the West.   Bancroft, H. H., *Oregon*. Coman, K., *Economic Beginnings of the Far West*. Garrison, *Westward Extension*, 3–43. Linn, W. A., *Story of the Mormons*. Royce, J., *California*, ch. III.

CHAPTER XVIII

INTELLECTUAL AND MORAL RENAISSANCE

THE intellectual activity of the period 1830 to 1860 was as Intellectual activity. Newspapers. remarkable as the economic, and was inseparably interwoven with it. The development of a real and widespread democracy demanded an adaptation of the newspaper to the new circumstances, but without the progress of transportation facilities this would have been almost impossible. Every improvement in communication meant the more rapid and more complete diffusion of news, and finally the invention of the electric telegraph, first used in 1844, enabled the voters, from one end of the country to the other, to read the same news at the same time and to vote with an approximately equal knowledge of each public question. The greater ease in transmitting news decreased the importance of the Washington newspapers, for the metropolitan dailies began to keep correspondents in the capital, with whom they could communicate constantly. In 1857 New York had so far succeeded to the position of news center, that the practice of having an officially recognized government organ at Washington was brought to an end. The new city papers were more independent than the Washington presses had been, which were dependent on government printing for their profits. The *New York Sun* led the way in endeavoring to support itself by selling its copies cheaply, amusing its readers, and so increasing its circulation. The *Herald*, under the editorship of the astute James Gordon Bennett, quickly adopted the new practice, and the *Tribune*, edited by Horace Greeley, and many others followed. In the place of the old advertising sheet with a few antiquated letters and verbose

editorials written by an editor looking for some petty office as
a reward of his party faithfulness, came a paper with news
columns most prominent, often with sensational headings and
"faked" stories, and with a page of short, crisp editorials
written by men whose business and social prestige was too
great to allow them to accept ordinary government appointments. Unlike the editors of to-day, most of those at this
period owned their papers and were therefore their own masters, and they exerted a greater personal influence than either
their predecessors or their successors.

Movement of
thought.
The press was an instrument necessary to the existence
of democracy at the time, like the party organization and the
spoils system. Other intellectual movements were in progress which were to do much to determine the direction
in which the ruling democracy should move. American
thinkers and writers were in intellectual communion with the
wisest and best in Europe, and were making contributions
of their own to literature and science and art. America
began to count in the world of thought. The newspapers
were but one of the agencies by which this intellectual activity was diffused among the people.

Foreign in-
fluences.
Before the Revolution, American architecture had followed the English, and the finest buildings were of the
Georgian style. There followed a period when French influence combined with a democratic reverence for the republics of the past to give a classical tone to American taste,
and a Greek portico was considered a necessity for a patriotic
dwelling or public building. To the people of this new generation, with their minds stimulated by the more subtle philosophy of the Germans and with Goethe as an inspiration, the
beauties of Italy particularly appealed. The steamship made
European travel for the first time a customary pleasure, and
while the fashionable began to seek Paris during the later
fifties, it was Rome that drew the more influential. Here the
sculptors Crawford and Story worked, Hawthorne drew in-

spiration for his *Marble Faun,* and Margaret Fuller lived and married. The American architecture of the period bears the stamp of Italian influence, and American life was enriched by a transfusion of Italian beauty. As in art, so in literature, with eyes newly opened to the beauties of the world, the thinkers of the time joyed in the delightful task of putting their thoughts into attractive and appropriate form, no longer satisfied with the mechanical outline and pedantic diction of their ancestors.

This awakening had been felt first in the Middle States about the beginning of the century. The writings of Charles Brockden Brown, James Fenimore Cooper, and Washington Irving combined English traditions with a racy and daring Americanism. In the period under review New York and Philadelphia were the leading centers of publication in the country, and *Harper's Magazine,* of the former city, brought together contributors from all over the United States and England, and enjoyed a national circulation. In 1855 Walt Whitman brought out his *Leaves of Grass,* which marked a sharp severance from European influence and did much to increase the self-confidence of American writers. *Middle States.*

In the South the University of Virginia, founded under the direction of Jefferson and opened in 1825, more nearly approached the European idea of such an institution than any other in America. Some of the professors were brought over from Europe, its students came from all parts of the South, and it did much to stimulate and unify the thought of the whole region. One of its students was Edgar Allan Poe, whose lyric verse and short stories were more widely read on the continent of Europe than the work of any other American. At the same time Audubon was receiving universal recognition for his scientific studies of bird life. Charleston and Richmond were literary centers and the *Literary Messenger* of the latter city enjoyed a substantial reputation. The bulk of the intellectual activity *The South.*

of the South, however, was devoted to political questions, and found expression in the work of her orators and political pamphleteers.

The New England renaissance. The changes in intellectual and moral concepts most significant in their bearing on the history of the period were those taking place among the New England population, which by this time stretched far to the westward, and was particularly strong in central New York and northeastern Ohio. The bonds which during the colonial period and afterward had confined the virile minds of the people within the strict limits of orthodoxy, were broken, and freedom of thought was established. So great and genuine was the emancipation that there was a short period of chaos, such as always comes when barriers are removed, and all kinds of fantastic theories of salvation, of habits of life, and of manners of dress were indulged in. With the idea that mental and manual labor should be used conjointly, Brook Farm was founded; and there numbers of the most brilliant figures in the history of the generation lived for a few years, vainly endeavoring to practice communism, but actually giving one another the stimulus of coeducation under ideal conditions. It was the era of Transcendentalism, of the New England renaissance, when long-haired men and short-haired women lived in an atmosphere of idealism and of youth.

The New England conscience. With all their new-found joy of living and daring acceptance of new ideas, they could not free themselves from those deep-lying characteristics which had been bred of two centuries of New England life. Most of the leaders in the new movements came of ministerial stock, many counted seven generations of ministers in direct male line, and the ministerial instinct remained. They might believe things different from what their fathers had, they might change their beliefs from time to time, but everything that they did believe they supported with all the dogmatic exclusiveness of the veriest Puritans. If they accepted a belief in vegetarianism, they thereupon denounced the consumption of meat by any one at any time as not only injurious but sinful, and set about vigorously to convert all men to their doctrine. Every new fad became with them a religion, demanding, not silent passive devotion, but active proselyting energy. Few were content, like Hawthorne, to practice literature for its own sake; the majority regarded their skill in writing or in art only as an instrument useful in bringing others to their ideas.

The predominant note in all their creeds was the equality of all men, and their capacity for infinite improvement. The Puritan conception of the unworthiness of man in the sight of God had gradually yielded to the democratic conditions of American life and the religious attacks of the Unitarians, until all denominations began to point out that at least man was God's noblest work; many of the radicals accepted Emerson's position that man has something of the divine within him, and consequently the possibility of making himself at one with God. The very complete attainment of political equality left comparatively little to be accomplished in that direction, and the New England crusaders turned their chief attention to obtaining economic and social equality. This period was marked throughout the European world by great movements for social regeneration, and the local developments in America and the general activity of European thought interacted to spur one another on. *The doctrine of universal brotherhood and equality.*

One of the fundamental social movements of the period was the establishment of free public education under state control. The progress of education, particularly elementary education, had not kept pace with the general development of the country. It was not only inadequate, because the community had not become fully awake to the responsibility of the whole people for the education of all children, but it was undemocratic, because even in schools where the education of the poor was provided for, the well-to-do paid fees, and their children looked upon the others as paupers. *Free public education.*

From about 1820 these conditions excited attention and controversy. It was a subject which had to be fought out separately in every state. In New York, De Witt Clinton urged the legislature to action as early as 1826, and the "Lancastrian System" was established, which was not in itself successful, but afforded a basis upon which, during the thirties, a successful scheme was founded. In Pennsylvania, the young Vermont lawyer and Antimasonic leader, Thaddeus Stevens, secured in 1834 the passage of a bill, not entirely satisfactory, but still marking progress. During the debate he made a brilliant speech in which he defended the taxing of those without children for the education of the children of others: "Inasmuch as it perpetuates the government and insures the due administration of the laws under which they live, and by which their lives and property are protected." The most notable figure in the whole movement was that of Horace Mann, who in 1837 became first secretary of the Massachusetts State Board of Education. His reports discussed the fundamental principles of education as a science, a profession, and a bulwark of the state. By 1860 the principle of free public education had been accepted by nearly all the northern states and by Kentucky and Missouri. After some additional conflict, the courts decided that taxes might be levied for higher as well as elementary education, and high schools became general. In 1839 the first normal school in the United States was opened at Lexington, Massachusetts, under the direction of Horace Mann, and teaching became a recognized profession. Universities had been regarded as proper beneficiaries of the public from the founding of the colonies, and now national land grants enabled the newer states to establish them without delay. The framework of the present educational system was laid, though many problems were as yet unsolved, and the actual accomplishment by no means equaled the projects of the various states as they appeared on paper.

One of the characteristics of the American system was the entire separation between religion and education. In New York this led to some controversy, and Governor Seward declared in favor of state aid to religious schools; but public sentiment was overwhelmingly opposed to this. The Catholics and some other religious bodies in certain states, therefore, opposed the free school movement, for they preferred to send their children to parochial schools, and objected to being taxed in addition for the education of others. This opposition, however, was overcome, though not without lending some bitterness, as has been seen, to the anti-foreign movement. In the South the middle class of skilled laborers and small farmers was unimportant, and so the demand for free public schools was less insistent. Public education lagged behind that of the North, though academies and colleges, chiefly private, flourished. *Religious opposition.*

Behind this legislation was a great popular movement and widespread interest in education of every kind. Those who were too old or in other ways unable to attend schools sought other opportunities; and in many towns lyceums were formed whose members clubbed together and hired lecturers. The ablest men of the time accepted such engagements, partly because literary work paid less than at present and lecture fees were welcome, and partly through the desire to propagate their views. Edward Everett, during the fifties, delivered everywhere his great oration on *Washington and the Union*, collecting money with which to purchase Mount Vernon as a national memorial, and endeavoring to strengthen the spirit of union. Wendell Phillips spoke on slavery whenever he was allowed. At no other time in history have the great men of a country come into such close personal contact with a widely dispersed people, and the lecture platform became one of the instruments employed in agitating reforms of every kind. *Popular educational movements.*

Another great social movement of the period was that

to check the evils caused by intoxicating drinks. During
the colonial period indulgence in such beverages was almost

The temperance movement. universal. Some attempts were made to discourage drunkenness and to encourage the use of lighter intoxicants in the
place of spirits, but they were not widespread or effective.
In 1826 a new agitation was begun, and within a year over a
thousand temperance societies had been formed. With the
new facilities for communication afforded by the improvements in transportation, state organizations were effected,
and in 1835 a National Temperance Convention was held.
The movement began with scientific studies of the effects
of intemperance, but their appeal was to a limited constituency only, and soon more emotional methods were employed.
The radical element gained control, and in 1836 it was resolved that the proper basis for effective work was the preaching of total abstinence. Wave after wave of enthusiasm
swept over the country. The "Washington movement,"
originating in Baltimore, and calling upon those convinced
to take the pledge of total abstinence, was perhaps the most
effective; and John B. Gough, a reformed drunkard, was perhaps the most effective spokesman, though Father Matthew,
the great Catholic temperance advocate, rivaled him in
influence. The lead in all these movements was taken by
men, and at first women were even excluded from the conventions. Gradually, however, women workers forced their
way to the front, as they did in all the social agitations of
the time.

Prohibition laws. During the forties the movement became so strong
that its leaders were no longer content with making a personal appeal, but sought legislative support. Neal Dow
was the chief advocate of this method, and in 1851 he secured the passage of a law in his own state of Maine, prohibiting the manufacture or sale of all alcoholic beverages,
except for medicinal use. This was speedily followed by
similar legislation in the other New England states except

Rhode Island, and in Iowa. Attempts were made to pass such laws in other states, and they probably would have been successful throughout the Northwest, had it not been for the incoming of the Germans with their almost universal habit of drinking the less harmful intoxicants, and their opposition to laws restraining the liberty of the individual. The latter reason naturally operated strongly in the South, with its Jeffersonian principles, and the prohibition movement made no material progress there.

The results brought about by thirty years of effort are hardly to be calculated. Wine and spirits were banished from the tables of probably a majority of the people in the northern states, and hundreds of thousands of men became total abstainers. In villages where drunkenness had been a common joke, it became a rare occurrence. It is probable that in our country at the beginning of the Civil War a larger number of persons refrained from the use of alcohol, than in any other country in the temperate zone up to that period. *Results of the movement.*

Movements, to ameliorate the conditions of the sick, of the blind, of the insane, of children, and of dumb animals, for women's rights and a hundred other purposes, vied for the public attention. Massachusetts led the way in protective legislation for children in factories. Some of the movements were by outsiders for the benefit of the helpless. Some, like the temperance movement, combined the philanthropy of the merciful with the strivings of those personally affected. In the case of labor, self-help was most prominent. The period of the thirties saw the formation of labor unions and the beginnings of labor journalism, and of the effort of labor to secure favorable legislation by its political influence. In the midst of this general interest in the uplift of mankind the most helpless class of all, that of the southern negro slaves, was not overlooked, and the effort to improve their condition was destined to secure the *Labor legislation.*

greatest share of popular interest and to have the deepest influence on politics.

World move-
ment against
slavery. Like many of the other reforms of the period, that for the abolition of slavery was not confined to the United States. Slavery was in fact a system of labor which at one time had been almost universal. Gradually the European world had outgrown it, and during the seventeenth century the growth of humanitarian ideas and philanthropic conceptions of the rights of man, emphasized by the American and French Revolutions, created a distaste for the institution and a desire to rid the world of it. The most obnoxious single feature was the slave trade, and England in 1807 and the United States in 1808 put a legislative prohibition upon it, after which England, having thus forsworn one of the most profitable branches of her commerce, used constantly all her great international influence to extinguish it throughout the world.

The prohibition of slavery itself was easily accomplished in those regions where such legislation was but a recognition of its actual disappearance as a vital factor in the life of the community, but it was a different matter where it meant serious interference with vested property interests, or the freeing of an alien race. In England itself and in Massachusetts, a judicial decision was sufficient without legislation; but fifty years of agitation were necessary to secure, in 1832, the abolition by the British Parliament of slavery in the West Indies, and $100,000,000 was voted as a compensation to the slave owners. After this the movement went on apace, and by 1849 slavery had been abolished in their colonies by the most important European nations. In the United States, the situation was still more difficult, because not only were there regions where slavery seemed the very basis of society and the slaves were of a despised race, but also these regions consisted of coequal states, instead of colonies, and controlled half of the Senate, which gave them a veto on legislation.

Within the southern states themselves there had been

an active antislavery sentiment from the time of the Revo- Antislavery movement in the South. lution, bred of the philanthropic feeling for the rights of all men and of the fact that slavery became unprofitable with the exhaustion of the tobacco lands. This sentiment received an almost solid political support from the mountain counties of the northern tier of southern states, and from the Quakers, who constituted a powerful element in North Carolina. In almost every state convention the subject came up, and Kentucky in 1799, and Virginia in 1830, came within a few votes of adopting a system of gradual emancipation. By the latter date, however, these fifty years of effort had accomplished no more than the freeing of large numbers of individual slaves by the personal action of their masters, and the colonizing of a few in Liberia. The unsatisfactory condition of the free negroes made an argument in favor of the continuance of slavery hard for its opponents to refute, and the rise in the value of slaves after 1830, as a result of the opening up of the cotton lands of the Gulf States, seemed to render any prompt action unlikely.

In this situation there arose a man concerning whose William Lloyd Garrison. place in history students will probably forever continue divided. To some he will appear the chief figure in the crusade which brought freedom to the slave and freed the country from a disgraceful institution, albeit through the throes of civil war; to others as the leader of a movement entirely unnecessary and without which slavery would have vanished in good time without war and in a manner better fitted to adapt the slave to his new condition. How much personal responsibility, however, whether for good or for evil, can be placed upon William Lloyd Garrison, is a question involving the most fundamental concepts of historic development and of philosophy. In this age of humanitarian reform the slave was sure to attract attention; with the growth of national feeling the people of the North were bound to feel a sense of responsibility for the existence of slavery any-

where in the land; and the resulting agitation was necessarily
marked by the fierce religious heat and the emotional methods
which characterized the generation. Personally Garrison was
an ideal type of the reformer, the enthusiast whose mind
sees only the object to be accomplished and none of the
surrounding circumstances which cause the statesman to hesi-
tate, delay, and sometimes refuse to act. He had the enormous forceful nose of moral leaders like Savonarola, Cromwell, and Pobêdonostsev, with the wide-cut mouth of the
orator; but he lacked the strong executive chin of Cromwell,
and his eyes had a kindlier gleam than any of the others.
He held but one conception of slavery; it was a sin and must
be at once eradicated. He brushed aside all talk of gradual
emancipation; it should be immediate. He would have no
compensated emancipation; that would be like paying a
thief for returning stolen property. He would not discuss
colonization; for the negro, having been brought to the land
against his will, should have absolute freedom to stay or to go
as he chose. He would have no truce with the supporters of
slavery: "I will be harsh as truth, as uncompromising as
justice." So keen was his sensitiveness, that he felt dis-
graced that he and his state were part of a nation permitting
slavery, and in 1860 rejoiced at secession, as it relieved the
free states from this iniquitous bond. The Union he described as "a covenant with death" and the Constitution
as "an agreement with hell."

Beginnings
of the aboli-
tion move-
ment.

With such a creed, Garrison took up his task in 1829
by joining with Benjamin Lundy, a veteran Quaker emanci-
pationist, in the publication of the *Genius of Universal
Emancipation*. The gentle tolerant persuasiveness of Lundy
and the aggressive and dogmatic zeal of Garrison, well illustrate the Philadelphia Quaker spirit of personal reform
and the New England determination to reform the world.
In 1831 Garrison independently brought out the *Liberator*.
Supporters began to rally around him; in 1831 the first of

the new abolitionist societies was formed, in 1832 the New England society, and in 1833 the national society. The object of these societies was abolition; their method was to bring the matter home to the mind of the public, for they believed that if the facts were known there would be universal demand for their solution of the problem. In addition to publications like the *Liberator*, which continued to be the chief organ of the movement, orators were sent about to address whoever would listen to them, and the public were successfully kept interested. Still another method was to encourage the escape of as many slaves as possible, in order that they might personally enjoy freedom, and that slaves might become a precarious form of property. To accomplish this object publications were circulated in the South, well illustrated, that they might appeal to the illiterate negroes, and gradually a system of refuges, called the "Underground Railroad," was developed, extending by many routes from the Mason-Dixon line to points on the Canadian frontier and making it easy for a slave, once escaping from the South, to reach safety and freedom within English territory.

This work among the negroes caused universal alarm throughout the South, over which the fear of slave insurrection hung like a pall. In 1831 there occurred in Virginia Nat Turner's Rebellion, the most serious movement that ever took place among the negroes themselves; and for this Garrison was held primarily responsible. Almost the entire white population became determined to put an end to the movement. The postmaster of Charleston refused to deliver abolition literature in 1835, and was in effect sustained by Amos Kendall, the Postmaster-General, and by President Jackson, though not by Congress. South Carolina imprisoned negro sailors on northern vessels, and when Massachusetts sent Judge Hoar to protest, forced him to leave the state. Alabama and Virginia each had a con- *Defense of slavery in the South.*

troversy with New York over the extradition of a writer of
articles which were incendiary according to the laws of those
states, but whom Governor Seward refused to deliver up.
On the whole, by law and by occasional violence, the activity
of the abolitionists in the South was effectually checked.
In fact a species of popular censorship grew up, the existing
local movements in favor of ultimate gradual emancipation
died away, and free discussion of the subject was almost
universally tabooed. The old defense of slavery, that it
was a necessary evil, was superseded by the belief that it
constituted the ideal relationship between the two races, that
it was sanctioned and blessed by the Bible, and that the
condition of the slaves was actually superior to that of the
factory population of the North and of England. Calhoun
wrote in 1845: "I look back with pleasure to the progress
which sound principles have made within the last ten years,
in respect to the relation between the two races. All, with
a very few exceptions, defended it on the ground of the
necessary evil, to be got rid of as soon as possible. South
Carolina was not much sounder twenty years ago, than Kentucky is now." The proslavery movement of the South
came to be based as firmly on moral and emotional arguments
as that against it in the North.

Northern opposition to abolition.   In the North, also, the abolitionists met with opposition. Mobs attacked their orators in Boston and other
places, their schools and halls were burned in Connecticut
and Philadelphia, and in 1837 Elijah P. Lovejoy, editor of
an abolitionist paper in Illinois, was murdered. In the Ohio
River states, moreover, the immigration of free negroes
was forbidden, and "black laws," based upon the inequality
of the negro, were passed. Here, however, persecution rather
added to the strength of the abolitionists than stayed their
efforts. Many became interested who were not so extreme
as were the original leaders. Garrison held: "The ballot
box is not an antislavery, but a proslavery, argument so long

as it is surrounded by the United States Constitution, which
forbids all approach to it except on condition that the voter
shall surrender fugitive slaves — suppress negro insurrec-
tions — sustain a piratical representation in Congress, and
regard manstealers as equally eligible with the truest friends
of freedom and equality to any or all the offices under the
United States government." Many abolitionists, however,
believed that political agitation should not be neglected.
In 1837 the national society divided on this question. The
political wing, under the presidency of James K. Birney,
formed the Liberty party, and presented the issue to the
electorate. While they desired immediate abolition, they
were willing to fight for even small gains. Their first object was to secure abolition in the District of Columbia,
to commit the national government against slavery, and to
employ every power granted by the Constitution to dis-
solve the institution. While these powers were limited, they
were sufficient to have crippled slavery. Especially dangerous to it was the fact that Congress could regulate interstate commerce. In 1840 Birney ran for President, and
received a few over seven thousand votes.

The strength of the movement is by no means to be es-   The right of
timated by this vote. There was a widespread sympathy   petition.
with the abolitionists, though their methods were held to be
unwise. This latent sentiment was shown by the manner
in which their cause came to be identified with that of free
speech. They very early began to petition Congress to exert
its powers, wherever it could, against slavery. These petitions greatly exasperated the southern leaders, who saw in
this way abolitionist literature published at government
expense. In 1836 the House voted that such petitions be
tabled without printing, and the Senate that they be received, but that nothing else be done with them. In 1840
the House adopted what was known as the "twenty-first
rule"; that they be not received or entertained. Such action

was looked upon as an infringement of the right of petition;
it excited very general opposition in the North; the signa-
tures on abolitionist petitions increased ten times, rising to
300,000 in 1838, and John Quincy Adams began a spirited
fight for their reception, which kept the slavery question
before Congress at every session, until at length, in 1844,
the House repealed its rule. The question of slavery had
thus been given unlimited publicity, and on this one point,
at least, the antislavery leaders had commanded the political
support of the North.

Attempt to
unite the
South.
This entrance of the question of slavery into politics
alarmed the southern leaders to the utmost, particularly
Calhoun, the most far-sighted among them. Gradually
he formulated a policy of defense. Politically his object
was to unite the entire South, so that, regardless of minor
differences and party allegiance, it should stand as a unit on
the subject. In 1840 he wrote: "I concur in the opinion
that we ought to take the highest ground on the subject
of African slavery, as it exists among us; and have from the
first acted accordingly; but we must not break with, or
throw off those who are not yet prepared to come up to our
standard, especially on the exterior limits of the slaveholding states." Believing, as he did, that material interest
would always be stronger than any other, and that the South
in this case was more strongly interested in retaining slavery
than the North in overthrowing it, he counted on a division
in the North through which a solid South could control the
government. He recognized, however, that such an alliance
was not sufficient, and was more strongly impressed than
ever before with the necessity of providing for the expansion
of slavery in order that the balance in the Senate at least
might be preserved. That body continued to prove, as it
had in 1820 and 1833, the bulwark against legislation which
the South opposed. The House was hopelessly northern,
not only because the South was dropping behind in popu-

lation, but because of the only partial representation of the slave population. While it seemed a hardship to the North that slaves should be represented at all, in the South it was esteemed unfair that they should not all count, for it was believed that the northern factory hands were as incompetent as they, and were driven to the ballot box by the mill owners, who thus controlled Congress and passed protective tariffs.

If the northern alliance and the balance in the Senate failed, the last resort of the South was to the Constitution. Little was said of nullification; if not a universally recognized failure, it was at least inapplicable to the newly arising problems. Calhoun continued to emphasize state rights, *Defense of slavery as national.* and to insist that the states be left entirely alone to control the domestic institutions, but he took much higher ground than this. The national government, he held, was instituted for the protection and well-being of all the states. In particular it was the representative of the states in dealing with foreign governments. It was its duty to cherish and defend all the institutions of all the states. It had no right to pick and choose as to which it should further and which it should discourage. Any institution legal in any state was national in the sense that the national government was bound to recognize and shelter it. In pursuance of this view he called upon the government to protect the maritime interstate slave trade from the interference of the British in the case of the *Creole*, and strove to commit the government in every way to his theory. He held a position precisely the reverse of that of Birney, who wished the government to exert all its power against slavery, and he sought to rally the South to his support. Daily these views made progress. The institution of slavery seemed at stake. Calhoun counted powerful leaders in the border states among his friends, and the radical views of the Cotton South began to predominate throughout the slaveholding states.

Every year the bitterness of feeling became more in-

Sectionalism
in churches.

tense; the great sectionalism between the slaveholding and non-slaveholding states began to overshadow differences between East and West, between commercial and agricultural states. On all questions involving the status of slavery the North and South each tended to become solid. The moral aspect which the question had assumed naturally made it a difficult one for those churches which were strong in North and South alike. As antislavery sentiment grew in the North, northern members wished to place their churches on record against slavery and to forbid, at least church officers, to hold slaves. Southern members, conscious that they were not responsible for the existence of slavery, resented the inference that they were sinning in holding slaves, and adopted the rising southern belief in slavery as divinely ordained. During the forties the Baptist and Methodist churches divided, the Methodist ultimately into three branches representing northern, southern, and conservative border state opinion. The Presbyterians, in 1850, practically separated, though they retained their united organization until the Civil War. Calhoun wrote in 1834: "I cannot but think the course the Western Baptist and Methodist preachers took, in reference to the division of their churches, has done much to expel Cassius Clay [a Kentucky abolitionist] and correct publick opinion in that quarter." The national parties, being less sensitive to moral questions than the churches, still resisted the dividing influence, but their cohesion would be put to a severe test if a question should enter politics which tended to bring into conflict the material interests of the slaveholding and non-slaveholding states. Each section would feel justified in fighting to the extremity when not only its well-being, but a moral principle, was at stake.

Rioting.

It was ominous that a generation so stirred by profound emotions was also to a considerable degree lawless and given to violence. In the West the pioneer spirit pervaded society, firearms were commonly carried, and law was little

observed if it were contrary to the public wish. Settlers
went where they wished, in either United States or foreign
territory, and did much what they wished. In the South
unauthorized force did much to suppress abolitionist propaganda. In the North the "Underground Railroad" was
legally criminal, yet was conducted by the most reputable
men and women. Religious riots were common in New York
and occurred in Massachusetts. In Rhode Island, where the
old charter of 1663 still served as a constitution and was un-
amendable, dissatisfaction took the form of revolution in
1842. This movement, known as the "Dorr War," was
unsuccessful and rather amusing from a military point of
view, yet it brought about the adoption of a new and more
democratic constitution in 1843. In New York the "anti-
rent" riots, between 1840 and 1852, brought to an effectual
end the feudal features of landholding under the old Dutch
patroon grants along the Hudson. In 1853 the Erie pie men
caused almost a suspension of traffic for two months at that
important point, because the Lake Shore Railroad attempted
to lay its tracks along Pennsylvania's Lake Erie coast, to
connect its New York and Ohio lines. Philadelphia, unwilling to see a through connection established between New
York and Chicago, supported the local authorities who wished
to profit by the change of passengers and goods necessitated
by the differing gauge of the tracks. In this case Pennsylvania was forced to yield to pressure from the West, and at
length a standard gauge track was laid through Erie connecting the roads of New York with those of Ohio. The use of
force became a common method of advancing causes and of
enforcing public opinion. It was viewed with tolerance,
was often resorted to by the most respected members of the
community, and was often successful. This customary
appeal from lawful to illegal and physical methods must be
reckoned with as among the significant tendencies of the
period.

BIBLIOGRAPHICAL NOTES

Sources.   Sources for the subjects treated in this chapter, with the exception of those relating to slavery, are not really available for class use. Among the best on the abolitionist side is *Recollections of our Anti-slavery Conflict*, by S. J. May; on the slavery side, *The Pro-slavery Argument*, by W. Harper. The *Papers* of J. C. Calhoun (Am. Hist. Assoc., *Report*, 1899, vol. II) illustrate the intimate thought of the South on the subject; the *Life* of W. L. Garrison, by his sons, gives much source material illustrating the abolitionist sentiment. On labor conditions, J. R. Commons, *American Industrial Society*.

Intellectual activity and characteristics.   Hart, A. B., *Slavery and Abolition*. Levermore, C. H., *Rise of Metropolitan Journalism* (*Am. Hist. Review*, VI, 446–465). McMaster, *United States*, V, 131–155; 343–372. Sparks, E. E., *Expansion of the United States*, chs. XXVI–XXVIII. Tucker, G., *Progress of the United States*, ch. V. Wendell, B., *Literary History of America*, 233–357. White, *The Book of Daniel Drew*, 28–113. Callender, G. S., *Economic History*, ch. XIV. Ely, R. T., *Labor Movement*, 7–60. Simons, A. M., *Social Forces in American History*, ch. XVII. Wright, C. D., *Industrial Evolution*, 202–269.

Abolitionist movement.   Frothingham, O. B., *G. Smith*. Garrisons' *Garrison*. Hart, A. B., *Chase*. Holst, von, *United States*, II, 80–120. Rhodes, J. F., *United States*, I, 38–75. Siebert, W. H., *The Underground Railroad*. Smith, T. C., *The Liberty and Free-Soil Parties in the Northeast*, 1–104.

Slavery and the pro-slavery movement.   Allen, W. H., and Crozer, J. P., *African Colonization* (Philadelphia, 1863). Ambler, C. H., *Sectionalism in Virginia*, 185–202. Brown, W. G., *The Lower South in American History*, ch. I, secs. 1 and 2; ch. II. Locke, M. S., *Anti-slavery in America from the Introduction of African Slavery to the Prohibition of the Slave Trade*. Goodell, W., *The American Slave Code*. Helper, H. R., *The Impending Crisis*. Nieboer, H. J., *Slavery as an Industrial System*. Olmstead, F. L., *The Cotton Kingdom*. Rhodes, *United States*, I, ch. IV.

Slavery and the Constitution.   On the Constitution and slavery: Curtis, G. T., *Constitutional History*, II, 201–226. Lalor, J. J., *Cyclopedia*, III, 725–738.

Rhodes, J. F., *United States*, I, ch. I. Story, *Commentaries*, secs. 1915–1927.

On petition and free speech: Adams, J. Q., *Memoirs*, IX, X. Benton, T. H., *Thirty Years' View*, I, ch. XXXI; II, chs. XXXIII, XXXVI, XXXVII. Calhoun, J. C., *Works*, V, 190–208. Curtis, G. T., *James Buchanan*, I, 319–357. Holst, von, *Calhoun*, 124–150; 165–184. Seward, W. H., *J. Q. Adams*, chs. XII–XIV. Story, J., *Commentaries*, secs. 1880–1895.

On diplomacy and interstate controversies: Du Bois, E. B., *The Suppression of Slave Trade*, secs. 68–73. Holst, von, *United States*, II, 312–329. Schuyler, *American Diplomacy*, ch. V. Stephens, A. H., *War between the States*, II, colloquy XIV.

Cheyney, E. P., *Anti-rent Agitation in New York*. Cutler, J. E., *Lynch-Law*, ch. IV. King, D., *Dorr*. Murray, D., *Anti-rent Episode in the State of New York* (Am. Hist. Assoc., *Report*, I, 37–96). Mowry, A. M., *The Dorr War*. Rhodes, J. F., *United States*, III, ch. I. Smith, T. C., *Parties and Slavery*, 1–109. | Unrest.

This period is particularly rich in literature illustrative of its manners and customs. Most important are the works of Mark Twain, especially *Huckleberry Finn*, giving a picture of life along the Mississippi, and of Bret Harte, as the *Luck of Roaring Camp*, etc., on life in California and the mines. F. Parkman's *Oregon Trail* is the best account of the plains. W. A. Butler, in *Nothing to Wear;* and G. W. Curtis, in *Prue and I*, give somewhat contrasting views of New York. Of course, H. B. Stowe's *Uncle Tom's Cabin* is of vital interest from many points of view. | Illustrative literature.

CHAPTER XIX

TERRITORIAL EXPANSION AND SLAVERY

Tyler and
Texas.
THE question most likely to develop the growing sectionalism between North and South, and to rend the parties
into northern and southern factions, was that of territorial
expansion. Had it not been for the rising division over
slavery, the course of the expansion movement would have
been smooth, and Texas would have been annexed in 1837.
Many in the North believed that the whole Texan situation
had resulted from a conspiracy to add one or more slave
states to the Union. While this was not the case, many in
the South did desire annexation to strengthen slavery in the
Senate. As both parties were strong in both sections, the
party managers had endeavored to avoid the question, and
the leading candidates of both parties were still in 1844
committed against it. Here lay the opportunity of Tyler,
the irregular candidate. He thoroughly believed in annexation, and determined, from the moment he succeeded Harrison, that it should be the work of the administration.
Delayed by the presence of Webster, who took no interest
in the matter, he pressed for action as soon as Webster left
the cabinet. Under Upshur, who ultimately succeeded Webster as Secretary of State, a treaty was arranged, but just as
it was on the point of completion, a sad accident, the explosion
of a gun on a new gunboat, the *Princeton*, caused the death of
Upshur and other members of the administration. The task
of selecting a successor was a very delicate one. The treaty
had as yet been kept secret, it was sure to excite political opposition from both parties, and it was important that the new

secretary add weight to the feeble forces of the administration. In these circumstances Tyler was forced, somewhat against his will, to call Calhoun. The latter, already despairing of obtaining the Democratic nomination, accepted in the hope that he might at least bring the Texas question into politics, and defeat the candidacy of Van Buren.

Calhoun closed the treaty, and it was sent to the Senate for confirmation in the spring of 1844. It was accompanied by certain correspondence intended to give the grounds for obtaining it, and to serve as an argument for its adoption. Of all the lines of argument at his command Calhoun chose the most debatable. He produced letters to prove that England was endeavoring to abolish slavery in Texas, he argued that such action would endanger slavery within the United States, that annexation was necessary to the preservation of slavery, and was therefore the duty of the national government. He was perfectly aware that the situation was much broader than he represented it. England was endeavoring to establish her influence in Texas. The Texas cotton planters might at any time form a commercial alliance with her, and, adopting a system of free trade, put themselves in a position to produce cotton more cheaply than their rivals in the United States, hampered as the latter were by a protective tariff. At the same time they would buy their manufactured goods of Old England instead of New England, and American manufacturers would lose a growing market. It seems, in fact, to have been love of their native country, the United States, rather than interest which led the Texans to desire annexation. If the treaty were rejected, the republic might throw herself into the waiting arms of England. With all these arguments, and abundant material to support them, at his hand, Calhoun preferred to place the whole issue on the duty of the national government to defend the institution of slavery. He was more interested in establishing that general proposition than in securing immediate

Calhoun and Texas.

annexation, and he was so firmly convinced of the justice of his position that he believed he could convince a two-thirds majority of the Senate.

Public senti-
ment and
Texas.
Both parties combined to defeat a treaty which thus flauntingly brought into politics the most irritating of all questions, and which would serve politically only to reflect glory upon Tyler and Calhoun. It was rejected by a vote of thirty-five to sixteen. But in spite of the defeat of the treaty, Tyler and Calhoun both succeeded in the object dearest to their hearts. The issue of annexation had been launched into politics, and would not down. Throughout the West and South the Democrats were overwhelmingly in favor of it. Lincoln wrote: "The Locos here are in considerable trouble about Van Buren's letter on Texas, and the Virginia electors. They are growing sick of the Tariff question, and consequently are much confounded at Van Buren's cutting them off from the new Texas question. . . . They don't exactly say they won't vote for Van Buren, but they say he will not be the candidate and that they are for Texas." The difficulty in preventing Van Buren's nomination lay in Jackson's unswerving friendship for him. But just at this juncture a letter of Jackson's was published in which he called attention to the danger of English influence in Texas and expressed his desire for immediate annexation.

Nominations
in 1844.
With the influence of the "Old Hero" thus divided, the defeat of Van Buren became only a question of the means to be employed. A majority of the delegates to the national convention were pledged to vote for him, but by adopting the two-thirds rule they made his selection impossible, and, after salving their consciences by a few votes in his favor, they felt freed from their instructions and sought another candidate. The man selected was James K. Polk of Tennessee, who had been the leading candidate for the vice presidency, was a friend and protégé of Jackson, and had a dis-

creet and not too well-known record in national politics. He was the least conspicuous man who had ever been nominated for President, and is known as the first "dark horse." The uninspiring character of the candidate was atoned for by the vigorous nature of the platform. The party declared emphatically for the annexation, or, as it was phrased with reference to the claims of the United States that the territory had been included in the Louisiana Purchase, the "Reannexation" of Texas. To avoid as much as possible any feeling of sectional jealousy, a demand for the "Reoccupation of Oregon" was added, and the campaign was conducted on the plain and attractive issue of expansion. The Whigs pronounced in favor of the issues to which Clay had committed them during the struggles of the past four years, and nominated him as their candidate.

The campaign that followed was very different from that of 1840 in its seriousness and the general interest in the issues at stake. Both parties felt the strain of the increasing sectionalism. Calhoun, in spite of the Democratic declaration in favor of annexation, held aloof with the votes of South Carolina in his pocket, until by special messenger he made sure that Polk would stand for southern interests in general. But Polk had also to satisfy the northern Democrats. A large and influential faction were incensed at the defeat of Van Buren, while still more, particularly in Pennsylvania, were afraid that the victory of the southern wing would endanger the protective system. The majority of the Pennsylvanians were Democrats by inclination and inheritance, but they had also been the first, and were still the most insistent, advocates of protection. In this sitnation Polk, while assuring Calhoun of his devotion to all southern interests, wrote what is called the "Kane letter," which was at least susceptible of being interpreted as a declaration in favor of protection. Upon the basis of this letter the Democratic orators of Pennsylvania claimed credit

Campaign of 1844.

for the existing tariff and successfully called upon the voters to support "Polk and the Democratic tariff of 1842."

Slavery in politics.

While Polk kept his party together in the North and retained the southern radicals, Clay was less successful. Aware that there was a strong feeling in favor of annexation throughout the South, he wrote a number of letters qualifying his general attitude of hostility to that measure, by pointing out certain circumstances under which he might favor it. This equivocation alienated many at the North, and the Liberty party again ran James K. Birney in order to give an opportunity for those desirous of expressing unconditional opposition to annexation to do so emphatically. The result was a decided, though not overwhelming, victory for Polk. He received a popular plurality of less than 40,000, but an electoral vote of 170 to 105. It is often said that Clay lost the election by his hedging, but this is not the case. Had he not taken the position that he did, he would, indeed, have gained New York and Michigan, where the Liberty party held the balance, but he would assuredly have lost Tennessee, which he actually carried by only 123 votes, and would still have been defeated. Moreover, his position was probably honest, representing exactly his opinion. Polk's hedge on the tariff gained him little, for had he lost Pennsylvania, he would still have been elected. As it was, the Kane letter neutralized the tariff question and allowed people to vote more strictly on a single issue than is usually the case in a national election, and no doubt could remain that the country desired annexation. The election was still more significant as the first in which the slavery problem was an important factor. The fact that the Liberty party held the balance of power in two states made a decided impression on the public mind.

Annexation of Texas.

Tyler had been nominated by a convention of his friends, but, hopeless of election, he withdrew, sought to identify himself with the Democratic party, and took upon himself much credit for Polk's success. He still cherished the hope of consummating the union with Texas during his term, of passing into history as an augmentor of the republic. When Congress met in December, he called attention to the popular wish for annexation, to the danger that in case of delay England might anticipate the United States, if not by annexation at least by commercial alliance, and he suggested that in the absence of a two-thirds majority in the Senate, Texas might be annexed by joint resolution instead of by treaty. This proposition seemed startling, as the constitutional argument in support of the annexation of Louisiana, that the power to annex territory might be inferred from the treaty-making power, was thus thrown to the winds. Necessity, however, acted as a spur, and on March 1 a joint resolution was passed permitting Texas to enter the Union as a state, under certain conditions, among which was the extension of the Missouri Compromise line through her territory in case it should be subdivided into additional states. Benton and a number of others voted for it under the impression that Tyler would leave to Polk the working out of the details; but the President acted at once, and when, on March 4, Polk was inaugurated, annexation was an accomplished fact so far as the United States was concerned. Texas accepted the opportunity and the conditions, and in December, 1845, her senators and representatives took their seats.

Polk proved to be a man of iron will and remarkable fixity of purpose. Intensely religious, he had unbounded faith in the purity and wisdom of his purposes, and balked at no obstacle to accomplish them. This devotion to his own ideas made it difficult for him to act harmoniously with others, and, politically, his administration was marked to an unusual degree by factional controversy; but his program was put through. His independence was shown at once. Tyler had supposed that his support of Polk, al- *The South controls the administration.*

though tardy, would secure the retention of his friends in office, but he was disappointed. It was supposed on other grounds that Calhoun would be retained as Secretary of State, but Polk did not invite him to remain. The most striking indication that the new régime would be no tame addendum to that of Jackson, was the taking away by Congress of the government printing from Blair, Jackson's official editor, and the giving of it to Thomas Ritchie, editor of the *Richmond Enquirer*, who now came to Washington and established the *Union*. Ritchie was a representative of the Jeffersonian Democracy, but he had of late been moving in the direction of Calhoun's views, and his transfer to the capital was a sign that the Cotton South was replacing the frontier as the predominant element in the Democratic party. The new Secretary of State was James Buchanan, leader of the Pennsylvania Democracy, and the Secretary of the Treasury was Robert J. Walker of Mississippi. George Bancroft, the historian, served as Secretary of the Navy for a time, during which he obtained the establishment of the naval training school at Annapolis. The appointment of William L. Marcy, a conservative or "Hunker" of New York, as Secretary of War, further alienated the "Barnburner" wing of the party in that state, which was already displeased by the defeat of Van Buren in 1844.

The free trade movement.

The domestic policy of the Polk administration was overshadowed by its foreign policy, but in one respect it was of very great significance. There was practically no objection to the reëstablishment of the Independent Treasury, and the management of national finance was placed upon the basis which has ever since been maintained. The significant question, however, was with regard to the tariff. Polk in his first message, to the surprise of the Pennsylvanians, recommended a change; and Walker soon submitted a report intended to furnish the scheme of the new bill. This report was held to mark an important step in the progress of national financial policy. European economists, particularly Cobden and Bright in England, had for some time been preaching the doctrine of free trade. At first they had received little attention from men of affairs, but for a number of years their theories had been rapidly gaining adherents. In this same year, 1846, Sir Robert Peel, the Prime Minister of Great Britain, announced his conversion to the principle and took the first step in the new direction by securing the repeal of the corn laws. In the United States the doctrine proved really popular only at the South. Now Walker advocated the new policy, and his report was held to be second only to Peel's conversion in importance.

The bill framed by Walker's advice produced a bitter fight in Congress. In the House, but one Pennsylvania Democrat voted for it, but it passed. The Senate being evenly divided, its fate there hung upon Vice President Dallas. His position was like that of Tyler. He had been nominated to the vice presidency to reassure the protectionists of Pennsylvania. Was it his duty to vote in accordance with the manifest wish of his state and faction, or to support the policy decided upon by his party? He decided differently from Tyler and voted for the bill. As in Tyler's case, however, his decision put an end to his career. Pennsylvania was frantically angry with Dallas, with Polk, and with the party, and at the next congressional election turned against the administration. To the rest of the Democracy the new bill seemed satisfactory, especially to the Northwest, where the increase in the exports of foodstuffs, due to the repeal of the English corn laws, was connected with it in the popular mind. Actually the changes made by the tariff of 1846 were not sensational, and the tariff was still protectionist to a large degree. Still the declared intention of framing a tariff that looked in the direction of free trade, the fact that progress in that direction continued until the Civil War, and the fact that it was another triumph of the Cotton South over

The tariff of 1846.

the northern Democracy, all combined to render it an important landmark.

Oregon.

Meantime the administration was working out the policy of expansion which it had been elected to effect. The first question dealt with was that of Oregon. Buchanan first offered England a compromise which had been several times proposed — that of dividing the territory by the parallel of 49°. Upon England's rejecting this, Polk expressed his opinion that the claim of the United States to the whole territory as far north as 54° 40′ was good and should be upheld; he asked Congress for authority to give England notice that the joint occupancy would be terminated within a year, thus making a settlement imperative; and he quoted the Monroe Doctrine in support of his contention that England should not be allowed to establish a new colony on American soil. Feeling became intense and the expansionist sentiment of the country found expression in the phrase: "Fifty-four-forty or fight." In Congress, Calhoun and Webster united to prevent any hostile action, and they were aided by the new feeling of cordiality between the two countries resulting from the Walker tariff and the repeal of the corn laws. Eventually notice was given to England, but in the expressed hope that it would lead to an amicable adjustment of difficulties, and not in the form of a threat. Negotiations were resumed and in the summer of 1846 a treaty was framed, which provided for the partition of the territory by the parallel of 49°, except that England was to retain the whole of Vancouver Island. One portion, therefore, of the Democratic platform was executed, though in restricted form, and the United States for the first time obtained an absolutely undisputed hold, with fixed boundaries, upon the Pacific coast.

Ambitions of Polk.

While the Oregon question was embarrassing relations with England, the annexation of Texas had led to serious difficulty with Mexico. That country had never acknowledged the independence of Texas. She therefore protested against the absorption of territory which she still claimed, and withdrew her minister at Washington. In fact, however, the republic of Texas had successfully maintained its independence for nine years, and there was in 1845 no prospect of the reestablishment of Mexican authority. It seemed probable, therefore, that the protest would be formal only, and Webster in 1845 anticipated a peaceful settlement of the dispute. Polk, however, cherished projects which enhanced the difficulties of the situation. The boundary of Texas was in doubt. The old Mexican province of that name had been bounded on the southwest by the Nueces River; the republic of Texas actually occupied the southern bank of that stream, while the constitution of Texas laid claim to all lands north and east of the Rio Grande. Congress had, in its joint resolution, recognized the necessity of negotiation to determine the boundaries of the new state, but Polk was determined to assent to no compromise here, and to assert and obtain the uttermost limits claimed by Texas. He set before himself also the aim of adding to the United States the entire region to the west, then included under the names of California and New Mexico.

For the accomplishment of these objects he sent John Slidell as minister to Mexico, instructed to call attention to unsettled claims for damages on the part of American citizens against the Mexican government, and to suggest that a readjustment of the boundary on certain terms might afford a means of relieving Mexico of these, and of obtaining even additional sums from the United States. The Mexican government, fearing popular disapproval and a revolution if it submitted to such dictation, refused to treat of anything else until the Texan affair was definitely settled. Diplomacy was therefore at a standstill, and the situation grew continually more acute, until in May, 1846, Polk was satisfied that sufficient cause for war existed, and drew up a message recom-

War with Mexico.

mending that Congress take action. Before the message was sent in, however, another train of events culminated in a more direct cause for war. General Zachary Taylor had been ordered to occupy Texas as soon as annexation was agreed to, in order to protect it against Mexican invasion. At first he confined himself to the Nueces, but when it became obvious that Slidell might fail, he was ordered to advance through the disputed district to the Rio Grande. Here the army encamped in the fields from which the Mexican proprietors had fled, across the river from the Mexican city of Matamoras. Such a position was provocative of attack, and on April 24 a brush occurred between the troops of the two countries. The news of this affair reached Polk just before his message was sent to Congress. He thereupon revised it, and on May 11 recommended war chiefly upon the ground that Mexican troops had attacked and killed those of the United States, upon United States territory. "War exists," he said, "and notwithstanding all our efforts to avoid it, exists by the act of Mexico herself."

Campaigns of the war. While the war had been brought on by the policy of the administration, it was not expected at Washington that actual hostilities would result. It was thought that when Mexico was convinced of the seriousness of the situation, she would recede and grant all demands, even to the cession of California. The Spanish blood of the Mexicans, however, was aroused, the nation entered boldly upon the hopeless contest with the superior power of the United States, and, under the lead of Santa Anna, offered a stiff resistance. The war lasted nearly two years. The United States squadron in the Pacific at once seized the ports of California, and an overland expedition from the Missouri occupied Santa Fe and obtained control of New Mexico. The main fighting movements were two. One was directed by General Taylor, who gained brilliant victories at Palo Alto and Resaca de la Palma, advanced southwest across the Rio Grande, took Monterey,

and, defeating Santa Anna's relief expedition at Buena
Vista, held it. This fighting on the borders might have
been prolonged indefinitely without bringing a final result.
Another movement was therefore proposed, to make
use of the sea power of the United States, land an army
at Vera Cruz, the port of the city of Mexico, and advance
directly overland to the heart of the country. General
Winfield Scott was given charge of this expedition, and
conducted it to a successful conclusion. Every step was
contested; Vera Cruz offered some resistance, but fell on
March 29, 1847; the scaling of the mountain wall beyond
involved a severe struggle at Cerro Gordo; and finally,
when the central plateau was reached, there was hard
fighting at Contreras, Churubusco, and Chapultepec. At
length, however, on the fourteenth of September the city of
Mexico was captured, and the country lay at the mercy of
its conquerors.

The overthrow of effective resistance in Mexico produced   Peace with
utter governmental confusion there. Revolutions broke out,   Mexico.
some of the states of the republic threatened secession, and
Yucatan actually asserted its independence and formally
sought annexation by the United States, England, or Spain.
In the meantime the war spirit was growing stronger in portions of the United States, and the expansionists began to
clamor for the taking of the whole of Mexico, as advantageous to both countries alike. Polk, however, was not a man
to yield to popular clamor; he was satisfied with his original
demands, and accepted the treaty negotiated by Mr. Trist
at Guadalupe Hidalgo on February 2, 1848, although it
did not include "Lower," or peninsular, California. This
treaty was confirmed by the Senate in May; and thus the
war closed with a recognition by Mexico of the Texan constitutional boundary and the cession of more than 500,000
square miles of additional territory, for which the United
States agreed to pay Mexico fifteen million dollars, besides

releasing her from claims of American citizens and assuming their liquidation to an amount not exceeding three and a quarter million.

The election of 1846.

Throughout the war even more attention was devoted, in the United States, to the political problems which it involved, than to the actual hostilities. The Whigs opposed the war, and in 1846 and 1847, on that issue combined with the tariff dissatisfaction, won a majority in Congress. The South and West showed little change, but Pennsylvania, New York, and New England turned emphatically against the administration. The Whigs were themselves, however, divided into "Cotton" Whigs, who were in favor of supporting the war now that it was begun, and "Conscience" Whigs, who would declare immediate peace and confess that the United States was in the wrong. So acute was this division that Palfrey, a Whig from Massachusetts, refused to vote for Winthrop, a "Cotton" Whig from the same state, for Speaker of the House. The "Conscience" Whigs, while intelligent and active, were few, and though Palfrey's breach of party discipline alarmed the leaders, the more distracting question was as to the disposition of the new territory which it was expected that the war would bring.

At a very early stage in the war the administration asked for $2,000,000 to be used in negotiating peace. It was understood that this would be given in payment for territory, and Senator Branch, a North Carolina Whig, moved a proviso that it should be granted on condition that no territory be acquired from Mexico. This well represented the Whig opinion of the South, in fact conservative southern sentiment generally; for it was clearly foreseen that with the growing intensity of feeling, a division must occur as to the status of slavery in such new territory. The Missouri Compromise would not extend to it unless especially applied, and there were growing indications that that compromise would no longer be satisfactory to the North, and particularly to that large number who believed that the war had been brought about for the express purpose of extending slavery. These fears were realized when, in August, 1846, David Wilmot, a Pennsylvania Democrat, proposed another proviso: that in any new territory to be acquired from Mexico "neither slavery nor involuntary servitude shall ever exist." This proviso became at once the center of all political interest. It passed the House of Representatives and was barely, perhaps by accident, defeated in the Senate of the twenty-ninth Congress. It was brought up again in the subsequent Congress, where Lincoln, who was then serving his only term there, says that he voted for it, under one form or another, forty-two times. The Wilmot Proviso represented the wishes of a majority of the northern people. How strongly they would press their desires, and whether, if confronted with the danger of sacrificing the Union, they would consent to compromise, was a question for the future.

The Wilmot Proviso.

The majority of the people of the South were as yet willing to agree to an extension of the Missouri Compromise line to the Pacific, and a large minority in the North were willing to agree to such a solution. This proposition was definitely brought forward in connection with a bill to organize the Oregon territory, which needed a government now that it was completely under United States jurisdiction. It was provided that slavery be excluded from this territory, and a vigorous effort was made in the Senate to insert a clause stating that this exclusion was made because it lay north of 36° 30'. This would have been an acknowledgment that the principle of the Missouri Compromise was to apply to the new annexations, and would naturally have been followed by an admission of slavery south of that line. This attempt to commit Congress to the policy of compromise failed in the House, and the bill was passed without explanation. President Polk, however, announced formally that he approved the bill because it was in harmony with the Missouri Compro-

The Oregon bill.

mise, and thus gave the weight of the administration to that plan of settlement.

Calhoun and territorial control.

Both the Wilmot Proviso and the compromise line rested upon the view that Congress had the absolute power to control the territories as it saw fit. This view was perfectly natural, as Congress had constantly acted upon it, and in particular had excluded slavery by indorsing the Northwest Ordinance in 1789, and by adopting the Missouri Compromise in 1820. Calhoun, however, contested this primary point upon which both proposals rested. He had deeply regretted the Mexican War, because he foresaw precisely the fundamental controversies to which it gave rise. He foresaw the defeat of the South in Congress, and he sought to take the whole question from that body and find in the Constitution a bulwark for southern rights in the territories as well as in the states. He contended that the territories, being the common property of the partnership of states, must be administered for the common good of all. He held, moreover, that the restrictions of the Constitution extended to the territories, that slaves were property, that the Constitution guaranteed all property rights, and that it was therefore the right of any citizen to take slaves into any territory, and the duty of the national government to protect them there. This doctrine of "non-interference" was welcomed by the southern radicals and grew rapidly in popularity in the South.

"Squatter sovereignty."

Still another view was that taken by Cass of Michigan, a view popular in the new communities of the frontier from before the Revolution. He also denied to Congress the power to regulate slavery in the territories, but instead of finding the power in the Constitution, found it in the people. The people of the territories, he argued, were not represented in the national government; therefore, in accordance with the principles of democracy, they should not be governed by it. To the people of the territory belonged the right of admitting or of excluding slaves. This doctrine of "squatter sovereignty" was calculated to be especially agreeable to those party leaders who feared the disintegrating influence of national slavery discussion, but its period of popularity was not to come until some years later, nor was it framed as definitely by Cass as it was afterwards by Douglas. Cass grounded it on justice or natural right more than on the Constitution.

Squatter sovereignty, or "popular sovereignty" as it was later called, should not be confused, as it sometimes was during the next twelve years, with the idea that Congress did not have the power to put conditions upon a state when it entered the Union. Squatter sovereignty applied only to the territorial period. Many thinkers of all parties and of both North and South believed as Pinckney had argued in the case of Missouri in 1820, that when once a territory became a state, it entered into all the rights of all the other states, and that such rights could not be curtailed by any action of Congress previous to admission; that the states made from the Northwest Territory, for instance, could introduce slavery if so inclined, in spite of the Ordinance of 1787. A few even held the illogical conclusion that when the people of a territory organized themselves as a state, and requested admission into the Union, Congress was bound to grant their request, regardless of their institutions. This question of the rights of states, however, was only of subsidiary importance at this time, although it was occasionally and confusingly interwoven with that of the territories. *State sovereignty versus that of territories.*

In the midst of this constitutional discussion occurred the election of 1848. The preservation of party unity became a problem of the greatest difficulty, tasking the utmost skill of the politicians. The Democrats nominated Lewis Cass, a northern man who was popular in the South because of his controversy with Webster over the right of search. This nomination, however, did not mean an indorsement of his *Whig and Democratic conventions.*

doctrine of squatter sovereignty. In fact, the convention emphatically declined to make any declaration of policy with regard to slavery in the territories; thus attempting to keep North and South together by ignoring the great issue which was dividing them, and to conduct the campaign on the old line issues. The Whigs adopted the same tactics. Clay again desired the nomination, but he had declared at Lexington in 1847 that the party should disclaim all "wish or desire on our part to acquire any foreign territory whatever, for the purpose of propagating slavery, or of introducing slaves from the United States." Thurlow Weed again assumed the position of President maker, and secured the nomination of General Taylor, the favorite hero of the war, a man totally new to politics, whose views were not only unknown but undeveloped. As James Russell Lowell remarked in the *Biglow Papers*, a series of satiric political poems published at this time: —

"Another pint thet influences the minds of sober jedges
Is thet the Gin'ral hez n't gut tied hand an' foot with pledges,
He hez n't told ye wut he is, an' so there ain't no knowin'
But wut he may turn out to be the best there is agoin'."

As no platform was adopted, the voter was left to conjecture as to what Whig policy on the mooted question would be, from a knowledge that the majority of the northern Whigs were opposed to slavery in the territories, and that General Taylor owned three hundred slaves. Even on the question of the war, the dividing line between the parties was obscure, for the Democrats claimed credit for having fought it and the Whigs nominated a war hero.

The Free-Soil party.

This calm ignoring of a vital issue did not quiet popular agitation. In the North particularly dissatisfaction was keen, and a third party movement was inaugurated. The Liberty party served as a nucleus and about it gathered many, both Whigs and Democrats, who considered that the territorial question was the main issue of the time. It happened also that the New York Democracy was seriously divided between the administration "Hunkers," or "Hards," and the adherents of Van Buren, known as the "Softs" or "Barnburners." This split had become so acute, as a result of the strong party rule of Polk, that the two factions had for some time run separate state candidates, and the "Softs" had been refused full recognition by the national Democratic convention. The "Softs" had been on the antislavery side ever since Van Buren had, in 1844, declared against the annexation of Texas, and now a combination was easily effected between them and the Liberty party, at a convention held at Buffalo. Van Buren was nominated for the presidency, and the party adopted the title "Free-Soil" and an unequivocal platform: "*Whereas*, the political conventions recently assembled at Baltimore and Philadelphia, the one stifling the voice of a great constituency entitled to be heard in its deliberations, and the other abandoning its distinctive principles for mere availability, have dissolved the national party organizations heretofore existing, by nominating for the chief magistracy of the United States, under the slaveholding dictation, candidates neither of whom can be supported by the opponents of slavery extension. . . . Resolved, therefore, that we, the people here assembled, . . . do now plant ourselves upon the national platform of freedom." Thus the plans of the politicians for snuffing out public discussion of slavery failed, and the omens of party disintegration multiplied.

The election resulted in the triumph of Taylor by a large majority, but this was by no means its only interest. The new party evinced remarkable strength, Van Buren receiving nearly 300,000 votes, and except in New York the greater portion of this vote was cast by single-minded antislavery men, rather than by "Soft" Democrats. It was ominous to note that this vote was entirely sectional, being confined to the free states. In the North about 15 per cent of the total

Election of 1848.

vote was Free-Soil; and in eleven states, including all those
of the Northwest, the Free-Soilers held the balance between
the two regular parties.   In New Hampshire and in Ohio,
they secured a balance in the legislature, and the election
of two of their adherents to the Senate, John P. Hale and
Salmon P. Chase.   The Democrats gained ground in the
Northwest, partly because of the Free-Soil vote, but more
because that section was rejoicing over the expansion of the
country and the new English market for foodstuffs.   The
Whigs won New York and Pennsylvania, as a result of Democratic dissension and the tariff of 1846.   They also won in the
South the states of Georgia, Florida, and Louisiana; but
apparently only because the voters preferred a southern to a
northern President, for the congressional elections showed an
opposite tendency, thus making evident a sectional feeling
in the South as well as in the North.

Gold in California.

To President Taylor, elected as he was without any statement on the subject of slavery in the territories, was intrusted
the handling of that delicate problem from his inauguration
until the meeting of Congress in the ensuing December.   In
the meantime a speedy solution had become a practical
necessity.   In January, 1848, gold had been discovered in
California.   Up to this time that region had attracted public
attention chiefly because of the exploring expeditions under
the brilliant and popular young son-in-law of Senator Benton,
Colonel Frémont.   Its strategic position had been recognized
by statesmen who had feared that it would fall from the
weak hands of Mexico into those of Great Britain.   The
Mexican treaty relieved this fear, but it was believed that
many years would elapse before actual American settlement
would become important.   As soon as the news of gold
reached the East, however, there began the most picturesque migratory movement of the century.   The quest
for gold roused all the spirit of adventure that characterized the period, and thousands flocked to the Pacific

coast, by way of the long, lazy journey around Cape Horn, by the Isthmus of Panama, or by the dreary perilous path across the arid regions. Before two years passed, California possessed a population of about 100,000, nearly all men, and men of all sections and all nations, the majority of them turbulent and restive in disposition. For the first time an American community had come into existence whose economic life was based on mining for the precious metals. New problems had to be met, and some form of government was imperative; the question had become immediate.

The President showed himself somewhat jealous of the greater Whig leaders, and the adviser most powerful with him was William H. Seward, the new senator from New York and the *alter ego* of Thurlow Weed, the organizer of Taylor's nomination. Seward was more radically antislavery than the older party chieftains, and his influence combined with the course of events to determine the presidential policy. The main feature of Taylor's plan was to use the nine months before Congress gathered, in organizing state governments in the new territory. Congress would, therefore, be confronted by the simple question of admitting or rejecting them, and the status of slavery would be determined by their constitutions. This plan was easily carried out in the case of California. Utah applied for admission as the state of Deseret, and a like movement was well started in New Mexico, when Congress met and the responsibility was shifted to that body. The President advised that by awaiting the action of the people "all causes of uneasiness may be avoided. With a view of maintaining the harmony and tranquillity so dear to all, we should abstain from the introduction of those exciting topics of a sectional character which have hitherto produced painful apprehension in the public mind, and I repeat the solemn warning of the first and most illustrious of my predecessors against furnishing 'any ground for characterizing parties by geographical denominations.'"

Taylor's policy.

The presidential scheme was received with violent opposition. California and Utah had excluded slavery by their
constitutions, and New Mexico was expected to do so.
Moreover, the President had taken a vigorous attitude against
the slave state of Texas, which was involved in a boundary
dispute with the national government over its western limits.
The prospect of losing all the new-won territory, and of having
even Texas curtailed, aroused bitter opposition throughout
the South. Quitman of Mississippi, a war hero and a "Fire
Eater" as the southern radicals were called, said that for the
first time in the history of the country the North was in
control of the government. Agitation was everywhere
intense. Mississippi, at the suggestion of South Carolina,
called a convention of southern states to meet at Nashville,
June 1, 1850, to discuss southern rights. Many feared that
a persistence in the President's policy would bring about
disunion. Quite apart from such fears, there were other
reasons why Congress would not be inclined to accept his
solution. There is a well-grounded jealousy of its rights which
always renders Congress suspicious when legislative problems are handled by the executive. This *esprit du corps*
was felt to an unusual degree by the Congress which met in
1849, for it contained a combination of talent and reputation
equaled only by that of 1815. This time it was the Senate
which was the stronger branch, containing, of the men who had
been at the helm for the last thirty or forty years, Clay,
Webster, Calhoun, Benton, and Cass, and of the coming
leaders, Seward, Jefferson Dávis, Chase, and Douglas. Such
a body was not apt to accept as final a solution worked out by
a President comparatively young in years and totally new
to the business of politics. Still further, it was proper that
in such a case, where the different sections were contending
for so great a prize, the contest should be decided in Congress
where all sections were represented.

The task of working out a compromise which should

reconcile the various conflicting interests, and of securing Clay and
compromise. its acceptance, fell to Henry Clay. It was the most difficult political task since the adoption of the Constitution. Just that line of agreement had to be drawn which would satisfy one section without causing repugnance in the other, for it was not enough to secure the passage of an act by Congress, but it was necessary to win for it the approval of a majority in both sections. For this undertaking Clay was ideally fitted. Compromise is a work of sacrifice, the slaughter of ideals; it is the proper labor of age rather than of youth. Clay's seventy-four years had been crowded with political experience, and he knew every pathway through the maze of national affairs. He had recently become a member of the Episcopal Church, and while his religion did not displace other interests, it gave him a seriousness which had been somewhat lacking in his earlier career. The fact that he had at last given up his presidential ambition, and that after eight years' absence he had returned to the Senate for the express purpose of bringing peace to his distracted country, gave him prestige with all his colleagues, while his feeble health added a rather pathetic interest to his efforts. His intellect was as keen as ever, and through the entire winter and spring he fought for his purpose in a manner which Congress has never seen surpassed. His plan was laid before the Senate on January 29, 1850, in a series of resolutions. It included a settlement of all points in dispute. California was to be admitted with its free constitution, although this would upset the balance of the states in the Senate; the remaining territory was to be organized without the Wilmot Proviso; the Texan boundary was limited, but Texas was to receive $10,000,000 practically as a compensation. In addition to this adjustment of the territorial problem, a strict fugitive slave law was included to protect slave owners against the machinations of the abolitionists; and to soothe the antislavery sentiment of the North, the importation of slaves into the District of Columbia for purposes of sale was forbidden.

Calhoun and compromise. On March 4 Calhoun made his last appearance in public life. In a speech which he had to have read, as he was too ill to deliver it, he opposed the compromise. He had come to despair of ultimate harmony between the two sections, the balance in the Senate was about to disappear, and his only hope of the Union now lay in a constitutional amendment providing for two Presidents, one from each section, and each having a veto. **Webster and compromise.** It remained for Webster, the third member of the great senatorial triumvirate, to declare himself. Upon him its fate was felt to depend. If he opposed it, it would be doomed to failure; if he favored it, it might have a chance to succeed. Webster realized to the full the responsibility that was upon him. Living as he did in daily association with the ablest lawyers and business men of the country, and regarded by them with an almost unparalleled confidence as the one sane conservative force in public life, he acted with a deliberation and a confidence which won for him the title of "Godlike." He now tested the sentiment of the South and became convinced that secession was impending. His devotion to the Union was his strongest passion, and to preserve it he sacrificed his feelings with regard to slavery. On the seventh of March, in a great speech which was awaited with breathless interest throughout the country, he pronounced in favor of the compromise. He gave it his support fully and generously, addressing his argument to the South, as the section in greatest agitation.

Radical opposition. Webster's speech only made it possible that the compromise might pass. It was still opposed by the radicals of both sections. Jefferson Davis, who was coming to be recognized as the rising leader of the southern radicals, gave all his weight against the compromise. The chief spokesmen of the northern radicals were Chase and Seward, both of whom declared against it, the latter creating a sensation throughout the country by appealing from' the Constitution to the "higher law." It was evident that the majority in Congress were not willing to sacrifice sectional interests and their slavery or antislavery principles to preserve the Union; or, at least, that it was not possible to convince them that the Union was really in danger.

The opening of summer, however, brought changes fa- The Compro-
vorable to a settlement. On July 9, President Taylor died. mise of 1850
He was succeeded by Vice President Fillmore of New York, who was more docile in the hands of the party leaders. He made Webster his Secretary of State, and the entire influence and patronage of the administration were turned in favor of the compromise. Finally the first attempt to pass the more important measures united in the form of an "omnibus" bill was abandoned, and each part was passed separately, by the votes of the section which it favored plus those of men from the other sections who, like Webster, put the Union first. Only four senators voted for every part of the compromise, though three more would have done so had they not been unavoidably absent.

BIBLIOGRAPHICAL NOTES

The Calhoun *Papers* continue to be illuminating. For the Sources.
Polk administration, Polk's *Diary*, edited by M. M. Quaife, and published in the Chicago Historical Society, *Collections*, vols. VI–IX, is usable. The most significant speeches on the compromise are the following: Calhoun, J. C., *Works*, IV, 542–573. Chase, S. P., in *Cong. Globe*, 31st Cong., 1 sess., app. 468–480. Clay, H., *Works*, VI, 601–634. Seward, W. H., *Cong. Globe*, 31st Cong., 1 sess., 260–269. Webster, D., *Works*, V, 324. These speeches can also be found in many other places. On the tariff, report of Secretary Walker, Taussig, *State Papers and Speeches on the Tariff*, 214–251, and also to be found as his regular *Annual Report* for 1845, in the *Executive Documents* of the Twenty-ninth Congress. Historical

Burgess, J. W., *Middle Period*, ch. XV. Garrison, G. P., accounts.
Texas, chs. VIII–XXI. Garrison, *Westward Expansion*, 85–157. Texas question.

Holst, von, *Calhoun*, ch. VIII.   Tyler, *Letters and Lives of the Tylers*, II, chs. IX, X, XI.

Mexican war.   Bourne, E. G., *Essays in Historical Criticism*, 303–313. Curtis, G. T., *Buchanan*, I, ch. XXI.   Garrison, *Westward Expansion*, 188–228. Holst, von, *Calhoun*, ch. IX. Jay, W., *The Mexican War*. Reeves, J. S., *American Diplomacy under Tyler and Polk*, chs. III, XIII. Schurz, *Clay*, II, ch. XXV.   Smith, J., *Annexation of Texas*.

The territorial question.   Garrison, *Westward Expansion*, 254–285. Holst, von, *United States*, III, chs. XI, XII.   McLaughlin, A. C., *Cass*, chs. VIII, IX. Smith, T. C., *The Liberty and Free-Soil Parties in the Northwest*, chs. VIII–XI. Stephens, *War between the States*, II, colloquy XIV.

The Compromise of 1850.   Dodd, W. E., *Statesmen of the Old South*. Garrison, *Westward Expansion*, 285–333. Lodge, H. C., *Webster*, ch. IX. Rhodes, J. F., *United States*, I, chs. II, III.

Tariff and finance.   Dewey, D. R., *Financial History*. Taussig, *Tariff History*, 109–154.

Illustrative literature.   *The Biglow Papers*, by J. R. Lowell, give a vivid view of the anti-war sentiment.

CHAPTER XX

BREAKING OF THE BONDS OF UNION

THE passage of the compromise acts of 1850 did not of Attempts to popularize the compromise. itself assure good will and harmony. The authors of the compromise devoted themselves energetically for the next few years to securing its general acceptance by both North and South. Webster was in a position to accomplish the most. He went about the country, spending himself to the very limit of his strength in popular orations, lauding it as a finality. As Secretary of State he strove to emphasize the grandeur of the United States and to arouse an interest in foreign affairs that might dull the passion of domestic controversy. Writing to a friend, regarding a rather jingoistic letter he had just sent to the Austrian representative, M. Hülsemann, he said that he wished to "touch the national pride and make a man feel sheepish and look silly who should speak of disunion." Clay, physically unable to make a direct appeal to the people, drew up a pledge to be signed by members of both parties, not to support for the presidency any man "not known to be opposed to the disturbance of the settlement, and to renewal, in any form, of agitation upon the subject of slavery." Edward Everett, who succeeded Webster as Secretary of State during the last portion of Fillmore's term, wrote a ringing dispatch upon the Cuban question, calculated to appeal to North and South alike.

These efforts were not without success. The country The compromise accepted. was enjoying an extreme prosperity, the result partly of the steady advance since 1842, and partly of the flood of new capital afforded by the gold of California. The business interests

327

of the country deprecated disturbing influences. In the South, which had fared rather the better in the terms of the compromise, the majority nearly everywhere acquiesced. The Nashville convention, which had met in June, 1850, held an adjourned meeting after the measures had passed, but took no radical action. In Georgia the Whig and Democratic leaders, Stephens, Toombs, and Howell Cobb, combined successfully in favor of peace; in Mississippi, Foote, who favored the compromise, ran for governor in 1851 against Jefferson Davis, who had opposed it, and defeated him, though only by 1,009 votes. South Carolina was at least not ready to act alone, and so secession was stayed. In the North, feeling was perhaps more intense. Webster was mourned by Whittier as a fallen angel, and became anathema even to the less extreme antislavery sympathizers. The great majority, however, were satisfied to let things stand as they were, and when the election of 1852 approached, the condition of public sentiment was calmer than it had been since 1844.

Political parties in 1852.   The Whig convention adopted resolutions of a pro-southern cast, favoring the compromise. The presidential candidates were Webster and Fillmore, the nomination of either of whom would be an especial confirmation of the compromise, and General Scott, who rather represented northern opinion. Both Webster and Fillmore came very near being chosen, but at length Scott won the nomination, and the Whigs thus tried the expedient of going before the country with a candidate to please one section, and a platform to please the other. This was not an abnormal circumstance, for the platform was adopted as drawn up by the committee on resolutions, consisting of one member from each state, thus giving the South a large proportion; while the nominations were made in full convention, where the numerical weight of the North counted.

The Democrats were now reunited, harmony was their watchword, and when the contest for the nomination between four of their great leaders, Cass, Marcy, Buchanan, and Douglas, seemed likely to become too serious, they decided to nominate Franklin Pierce, an inconspicuous man, of un-doubted party loyalty, whose selection would cause no jeal-ousies. They indorsed the compromise without serious question, and thus both the great parties stood pledged to its continuance. The result of the election seemed still further to assure its finality. The Democratic party was nearly everywhere supposed to give the best assurance of internal peace, and as a consequence of this feeling, Pierce was elected by 254 electoral votes to 42 for Scott. The Free-Soil party lost decidedly, even beyond what might have been ex-pected from the return of the Van Buren Democrats to the party fold. On the other hand, the overthrow of the Whigs was ominous, for an analysis of the vote showed that they had suffered even more from those who failed to vote than from deserters. Their attempt to please both sections had displeased both instead, and actually the party failed to rise again, so that the settlement of the territorial ques-tion had been at the expense of one of the great national parties, which had constituted an important bond of union. *The election of 1852.*

In fact the calm was more superficial than real. Already by 1852 affairs had almost passed out of the hands of the generation which made the compromise. The statesmen of the middle period were rapidly disappearing ; Calhoun died before the compromise was passed, Webster and Clay before Pierce was inaugurated. Benton had the unhappier fate to outlive his popularity in Missouri, and Van Buren was defi-nitely out of politics. The new generation was practically in the saddle, and it brought to national affairs a somewhat different spirit from its predecessor. Younger and without the experience and poise which years bring, the new leaders were during the next decade less expert than their predeces-sors in handling public matters. Reared during a period of sectional controversy, they lacked that single-minded de- *The new leaders.*

votion to the Union which the experience of the War of 1812 had produced in the men young at that time. The majority of them looked upon most political questions as moral questions also. They differed from the abolitionists in being men of constructive statesmanlike ability ; they differed from the politicians of Jackson's time in holding intense convictions as to both the expediency and the morality of slavery.

Northern
antislavery
sentiment.

It was almost too much to hope that such men would accept the Compromise of 1850, in the making of which they had little share, and which many of them had opposed, as the final solution of a vital question. It was inconceivable that new questions would not arise, dividing the sections, and if they did, a settlement would be even more difficult than in 1850. It was becoming harder with every passing year to make one section understand the position of the other. It was significant that, while in the thirties the mobs in the North had attacked the abolitionists, in the fifties they attacked the United States officers engaged in returning fugitive slaves. The mob had not become abolitionist, but it had moved a long way in that direction. During the next ten years several states passed "Personal Liberty" laws interfering with the execution of the fugitive slave law, and such laws were held by southern statesmen to constitute nullification. In Wisconsin, the supreme court of the state in a series of decisions actually declared the fugitive slave law unconstitutional and denied the right of the national courts to enforce it within the state limits, while a justice of the supreme court of the same state was elected on a platform of state rights.

*Uncle Tom's
Cabin.*

The most striking illustration of the growth of widespread hostility to slavery was afforded in 1852 by the reception given *Uncle Tom's Cabin*, which at the same time did more to popularize antislavery feeling than any previous agency. That novel was so powerful a weapon in molding public opinion, that its merits are to this day a subject of conflicting assertion rather than of criticism. It did not endeavor so much to give a scientific description of the average condition of the slave as a picture of the best and the worst possibilities of his life. Its human nature, at least, was true enough to convince the great mass of the northern people, and its incidents were so well adapted to dramatic form that the play written from it reached tens of thousands who would never have read the book. When a book like *Uncle Tom's Cabin* became the fetish of one section and was excluded from the other, men of acute political foresight might well doubt the finality of any agreement on the subject of slavery, however calm the surface of practical politics might seem.

It was thus in an atmosphere clear of clouds, but surcharged with electricity, that Pierce began his administration. The impulses given by the Polk administration were still dominant in the party. The new President made Marcy his Secretary of State, Buchanan minister to England, and planned to signalize his administration by the expansion of national territory. It had in fact been contemplated for a moment by some party leaders to fight the campaign of 1852 on the issue of "Cuba and Canada." The annexation of Canada was scarcely practicable, but it might have served as makeweight in the platform. To advocate the annexation of Cuba alone would have stirred the sectional animosities which it was sought to quell. If, however, the annexation could be brought about between elections, the administration might go before the country presenting a record of a kind much appreciated by that generation in both West and South. It was thought, moreover, that the bringing in of Cuba as a slave state would quiet the disappointment of the South over California, without too seriously alarming the North. Annexation might be brought about by purchase from Spain, by revolution within Cuba assisted from the United States, or as the result of war with Spain. The first of these methods

Diplomacy as a distraction.

had been unsuccessfully tried by Buchanan in 1848. During the next six years the second was attempted. Several filibustering expeditions were organized by a Cuban, General Lopez, who received much popular sympathy in the United States. Twice a landing was effected on the island, but no general rising followed. In 1851 Lopez lost his life, and General Quitman became the leader of the movement, which, however, came to naught. In 1854 it seemed as if accident would bring about a resort to the third method, for the seizure of the *Black Warrior*, an American vessel, by the Cuban authorities, almost led to war between the United States and Spain. An apology by Spain, and the good sense of Secretary Marcy, however, prevented such a result. The administration, therefore, was forced to drop the Cuban question or to take deliberate action. Pierce decided upon the latter, and ordered Buchanan, Mason, and Soulé, the ministers to England, France, and Spain, respectively, to meet and formulate a policy. In 1854, at Ostend, a watering place in Belgium, they consequently drew up what is known as the "Ostend Manifesto." In this they contended that the United States should offer to buy Cuba. If Spain refused, the United States would be justified in taking Cuba by force, as a measure in self-defense. The dangers they feared were, first, that a slave insurrection was impending in the island, which would influence the minds of the slaves in this country; and second, that England might take Cuba by arrangement with Spain, and thus obtain a position imperiling our commerce if not our safety. This document so far overstepped the bounds of public morality as generally expressed, that Marcy recommended that it be disregarded. The administration passed without advancing Cuban annexation.

Diplomacy and transportation.   This failure confined the expansionist activity of the administration to the acquirement of a small piece of land on the southern border, which was needed for railroad purposes.

The sudden growth of California had made the problem of transcontinental transit a matter of prime importance. The route by Cape Horn was too long and dangerous. The project of a canal at some one of the narrow points in Central America, which had been bruited for over three centuries, was revived, and companies were actually formed to undertake the work. The political difficulties, however, were almost as great as the physical. The countries of Central America were unable to guarantee the safety of transit or the security of capital. In 1846 a treaty was made with Colombia by which the United States agreed to guarantee to Colombia the Isthmus of Panama, in return for a free and equal right of passage and the right to intervene to preserve the neutrality of the route across the isthmus. This treaty was in accord with the general policy pursued by the United States for the next thirty years, that such passageways, whether over land or water, should be enjoyed by all nations in common. Other nations were invited to join in the guarantee. Owing to the transportation facilities provided by Commodore Vanderbilt, the Nicaragua route became more popular than that by Panama, and a canal was projected through the rivers, lakes, and mountains of that country. England was deeply interested in Nicaragua, and in 1850 Clayton, Taylor's Secretary of State, and Bulwer, the English minister, arranged a treaty providing that neither country should acquire special interests in Central America. This treaty was extremely unpopular, and was attacked by the Democrats as an abandonment of the Monroe Doctrine. Many attempts were made to abolish it, but it remained in force until 1902.

The canal project failed, because the undertaking proved too great for the financial and engineering resources of the time. In 1856, however, a railroad was built over the Panama route. In the meantime the desirability of a transcontinental railroad which might lie wholly within the territory of the

Transcontinental railroads.

United States, was becoming more and more evident, and Congress was actively at work on the details of the undertaking. The surveys of the War Department, however, brought out the fact that the route involving the fewest engineering difficulties ran south of the United States boundary as fixed by the treaty of 1848. To obviate this difficulty a new treaty was made with Mexico in 1853, by which 54,000 square miles, known, from the minister who negotiated the treaty, as the "Gadsden Purchase," were acquired, including the desired roadway. Sectional difficulties, however, combined with financial and other complications to prevent the actual work of railway construction. The same treaty provided for the mutual use of the Isthmus of Tehuantepec by Mexico and the United States, and gave the United States the right to intervene to preserve its neutrality.

Commercial expansion. Once aroused, the interest in transportation did not stop with the routes having this special interest for the United States. The Whig administration had begun an attempt to open up the great rivers of South America to the commerce of the world, and Marcy in 1854 concluded a treaty with the Argentine Confederation affecting the Plata, and actively negotiated with Brazil and Peru concerning the Amazon. Marcy also arranged for the abolition of the tolls collected by Denmark from vessels entering the Baltic, though the treaty by which this result was accomplished was concluded under his successor. He inherited the Whig policy that led to Commodore Perry's successful treaty with Japan in 1854, which proved of unexpected significance, and himself arranged for treaties with Persia and Siam. He concluded treaties on the subject of neutral rights with Persia, Russia, and the two Sicilies, and extradition treaties with many German states and the two Sicilies. He also revived the Jacksonian policy of reciprocity, making with England in behalf of Canada an agreement which placed commerce upon a most liberal footing for the next twelve years. When these treaties are considered in the light of the growing American merchant marine, filling the Caribbean Sea and circling South America for the California trade and the whaling industry, it may be seen that they might be supposed to bear promise of a revolution in American interests, and that it was not wholly visionary to hope that the public attention might be diverted from slavery to foreign affairs.

All questions, however, tended to become sectional. Chicago and St. Louis were little pleased with the southern route for the transcontinental railroad. Each planned a road, to be built with the aid of government land grants, to bring western commerce to their markets. A necessary preliminary was the organization of a territorial government in the region to be traversed, which had been left till then to the Indians. Pioneer settlers, moreover, had for some time chafed at being held within the western boundaries of Missouri and Iowa, and joined with the commercial interests, in demanding government and land surveys in the valleys of the Kansas and the Platte. The organization of the region, however, was blocked by the South, because it lay north of 36° 30', and would be destined, by the Missouri Compromise, to increase the number of the free states. With the admission of Arkansas in 1836 and of Florida in 1845, there remained to be developed into slave states only the territory of New Mexico. To break this deadlock, Senator Atkinson of Missouri, who had succeeded Benton in the Senate, was insisting that the prohibition of slavery be repealed. The leadership in the solution of the problem, however, was undertaken by Senator Stephen A. Douglas of Illinois, long chairman of the committee on territories. In 1853 he had introduced a bill to organize a territory here, and throw the land open to settlement. In 1854 he brought in a new bill resembling the first except that it contained the provision that the question of slavery should be determined by the people of the territory. He subsequently incorporated with

Douglas and Nebraska.

his proposal the direct repeal of the Missouri Compromise. He realized that such action would be violently attacked in the North, but he hoped to offset this opposition by the appeal to the strong popular sentiment in favor of self-government. His plan of squatter sovereignty, which he renamed popular sovereignty, would, he claimed, take the whole vexing question of the status of slavery in the territories out of Congress. He probably hoped that the South would welcome the possibility of territorial gain, while the Northwest would rejoice in the new land opportunities and commercial openings. Young and vigorous, and counting on the gratitude of two such powerful sections, he undoubtedly looked to the presidency as a prompt reward.

Kansas-Nebraska debate. The discussion which this bill precipitated was the most acrimonious in which Congress had as yet engaged on the slavery question. Douglas was attacked for disturbing the peace of the country, for sacrificing territory to slavery, for proposing an impracticable political scheme. Chase was his most successful opponent, although Seward really managed the opposition, and Charles Sumner, who had entered the Senate from Massachusetts as a result of a contest in which the Free-Soilers had held the balance in the legislature, contributed the pure fire of his enthusiasm. Douglas defended himself against the charge of being an agitator on the ground that his bill but embodied the principles of the Compromise of 1850. He found the southern members somewhat doubtful of the gift he came bearing them, and found it necessary to amend his bill in order to pass it. As it finally went to vote it provided for the organization of two territories, Kansas and Nebraska, instead of one; perhaps with the idea that one might become free and one slave. On the subject of slavery it read: "It being the true intent and meaning of this act not to legislate slavery into any territory or state nor to exclude it therefrom; but to leave the people thereof perfectly free to form and regulate their domestic institutions in their own way, subject only to the Constitution of the United States."

The vote on the Kansas-Nebraska bill completely demolished party lines. In the Senate twenty-eight Democrats voted for it and five against; nine Whigs for it and seven against. The South was practically solid for it, twenty-five to two; the North was divided fourteen in favor and twelve against. In the House the contest was closer; forty-two northern Democrats out of eighty-six refused to vote for this measure, although it had the backing of the administration. The Whigs were so divided that Seward wrote to his wife: "What you have so long wished for has come around at last. The Whigs of the North are separated from the Whigs of the South, and happily, by the act of the latter, not the former." The bill was passed by an approving South, with the assistance of about one half of the northern Democracy. *Kansas-Nebraska vote.*

Even before the final passage of the Kansas-Nebraska bill, on May 22, 1854, the campaign for the control of the next Congress began. Few political contests have been more important or more bitter. In the North all parties were thoroughly demoralized. The Democrats were divided between those supporting the bill and those opposing it. The Whig party almost vanished, except in a few states like New York and Massachusetts, where it was particularly well organized. A third party had already, about 1852, entered the field, based on the growing feeling against immigrants. This feeling first found expression in the formation of secret societies. Soon these began to enter politics with the design of increasing the period necessary for naturalization, of excluding foreigners and Catholics from office, and in general of restricting the privileges of those not native-born. Banded together in secret societies, with an elaborate ritual, they at first threw their weight to whichever of the regular party candidates pleased them. Their organization enabled them to predict results with startling exactness, and their success *Kansas-Nebraska campaign in the North.* *"Know-Nothings."*

encouraged them to venture independently. Under the name of the American party, but more popularly called "Know-Nothings," they carried several state elections, and hoped to control the new Congress. The unexpected introduction of the slavery question, however, divided them, as it did the other parties. A fourth party was formed in the West particularly to meet the Kansas-Nebraska issue. At Ripon, in Wisconsin, a meeting called to express disapproval of slavery extension adopted the name Republican. This name proved popular and was taken up by a state convention in Michigan. Other states followed, and throughout this region, as well as in Maine, this newest party became the meeting place of those who believed slavery to be the leading question of politics. Although there were four parties, the issue in every northern congressional district was plain. Whether the contest was between two Democrats, or between a Democrat and a Whig, a Republican, or a Know-Nothing, — everywhere one candidate stood for Douglas's policy and one against further extension of slavery. The result was an overwhelming rebuke to Douglas and the administration which supported him. The Democrats lost 347,742 votes in the North, and their majority of eighty-four in the House was turned into a minority of seventy-five.

It was a significant and ominous fact that in the South there was a campaign as different from that in the North as if it were another country. The Whig party here also had become moribund, and the majority, leaders as well as rank and file, transferred themselves to the American party, which, as the immigration question was of little importance in the South, trusted largely for vitality to its demand for reform in administration. Some who had been Democrats joined the Americans, while some Whigs, as Alexander Stephens, refused to join the new movement, and became Democrats, and the loss and gain in the transfer from the one party to the other made the elections sufficiently exciting. The

The Republican party.

Result in the North.

Campaign in the South.

territorial question, however, attracted little attention, and there was small divergence between the Americans and Democrats on that point. Such discussion as there was, however, boded ill for the future of both parties. Whereas the Americans elected in the North were one and all opposed to the Kansas-Nebraska bill because it opened up those territories to slavery, the Americans in the South attacked it because, by allowing the squatters to exclude slavery, it violated Calhoun's principle that all the territories were constitutionally open to slavery. Whereas Douglas was defending his bill in the North on the ground that it established the Democratic principle of leaving the matter to the people on the spot, Stephens defended it in Georgia on the ground that it granted the people of the territory "all the power that Congress had over it, and no more." "The inherent sovereign right of the people to establish a government independently of Congress is not recognized in a single clause of that bill." Henry A. Wise of Virginia, one of the leading Democrats of the South, openly attacked the principle of popular sovereignty as applied to the territories, and in general it was understood to apply to the states only, and to mean that they could not properly be enjoined from allowing slavery, as had been done by the Northwest Ordinance of 1787 and the Missouri Compromise of 1820. In fact the southern and northern Democrats had totally different conceptions of what had been accomplished by the Kansas-Nebraska act. For a time the ambiguous phrase of popular sovereignty held them together, but a union dependent upon a misunderstanding was of doubtful duration. In the congressional elections of 1854 and 1855 the Democrats lost to the Americans in the South, though not so heavily as to their opponents in the North. In the last Congress there had been but twenty-four southern Whigs; in the new one there were thirty-two southern Americans and Whigs.

By the time Congress came together in December, 1855,

Speakership
contest.
some degree of order had been brought out of the political chaos of 1854. Most of the northern Americans had become to all intents and purposes Republicans, and, with some of the Anti-Kansas-Nebraska Democrats, supported Nathaniel P. Banks, the Republican candidate for the speakership. The southern Americans supported H. M. Fuller, and stood by the Calhoun doctrine of non-intervention with slavery in the territories. The regular Democrats nominated William A. Richardson, an advocate of popular sovereignty. No one of these received a majority, the vote standing 105 for Banks, 40 for Fuller, and 74 for Richardson. For two months the contest went on and 133 ballots were taken. At last it was agreed that a plurality should elect, and Banks was consequently chosen.

The struggle
for Kansas.
In the meantime the country was being given a practical illustration of the working of popular sovereignty. It was universally recognized that Nebraska would be settled from the North and would decide in favor of a free soil. Kansas, however, lay directly west of Missouri, and it was feared in the North, and hoped in the South, that its population would be proslavery. The spirit in the North was such, however, that this could not take place without a struggle, and Kansas became a bone of contention. From both sections emigrants willing to settle in the disputed territory were assisted in their desires, and were furnished with arms, to be used, of course, only in self-defense. In this work the North had great advantages. The very fact that violence might be expected in Kansas deterred the slave owners from bringing into it property which might readily be lost. Many of the northern settlers were abolitionists anxious to promote their cause, and even those who had no strong moral convictions on the subject were unwilling to throw the territory open to slave labor and to capitalistic farmers employing slaves. The North had, moreover, more money, more organizing ability, and a larger migratory population.

On March 30, 1855, while the vanguard of this free-soil army was passing into the territory, the first election occurred for the territorial legislature. The greater number of votes in this election were cast by citizens of Missouri, who rode over the border, cast their votes, and returned. Western Missouri was strongly prosouthern in sentiment, and while its inhabitants were not ready to move into Kansas in order to carry it for slavery, they organized "Blue Lodges," whose purpose was to assist their friends across the border. These votes elected a proslavery legislature, which speedily passed a code of laws encouraging that institution. Governor Reeder protested against the election frauds and was removed by President Pierce, who recognized the legislature as legally representing the people of Kansas. The Free-Soilers, whose numbers grew rapidly during the summer, would not submit to a government which they held had been fraudulently established. They ignored the territorial legislature and, meeting at Topeka, drew up a state constitution, and petitioned Congress for admission as a state, on a no-slavery basis. Thus popular sovereignty had failed in its political object of keeping slavery discussion out of Congress; and the same Congress which found such difficulty in electing its Speaker was confronted by a new phase of the territorial question.

Popular sovereignty in Kansas.

The deadlock in Congress prevented action, the request for admission under the Topeka constitution was not granted, and Kansas was left in the hands of the administration. The debate, however, furnished one incident which illustrated in a peculiarly dramatic way the growing acerbity of sectional feeling. Charles Sumner delivered an oration, published later under the title of *The Crime against Kansas*. His style of oratory was polished in the extreme, and acquired a special weight from the care and deliberation with which he was known to prepare his utterances. With this extreme care he combined the fire and straight speaking of a radical

Sumner and Brooks.

to whom any injustice was a burning sore and any proposition of compromise was as enraging as an affront to his personal honor. The form of his oratory was modeled upon that of Athens, and in spite of the delicacy and sensitiveness of his taste, he sometimes used images, drawn from ancient authors, which were scarcely considered seemly in the nineteenth century. He selected as the particular object of his attack the venerable Senator Butler of South Carolina, and heaped upon his head epithets that, as between two southerners, would inevitably have resulted in a duel. Such reparation was impossible in this case, as Sumner had the New Englander's abhorrence of that method of settling disputes, and, owing to the privileges of debate, legal redress could not be obtained. Under these provocative circumstances, Preston Brooks, Butler's nephew and a member of the House of Representatives, attacked Sumner from behind, as he was seated at his desk in the Senate, and beat him on the head with a cane into unconsciousness.

Brooks and the South. Throughout the South, Brooks was applauded as a hero; the support of all but one of the southern representatives prevented his expulsion from the House of Representatives, a two-thirds majority being required, and he was reëlected without opposition at the next election. The fact that an affair between two representatives of the most refined classes of the two sections could degenerate into such a personal encounter, and that Brooks's attack upon a defenseless man could receive the approbation of the chivalry of the South, was a sign of the chasm which began to widen between North and South.

The Republican party. Under such circumstances, but with some modification of popular excitement, the election of 1856 approached. The Republicans had already reached a degree of solidarity most unusual in a party so young. They met at Philadelphia, as Pennsylvania was regarded as being the pivotal state, and accomplished their business with a degree of harmony remarkable considering that their members were drawn from all preceding parties and included many men of great ability and marked individuality who had not previously acted with any party. Their platform was, indeed, inconsistent on the territorial question, for one clause denied "the authority of Congress, of a territorial legislature, of any individual or association of individuals, to give legal existence to slavery in any territory of the United States, while the present Constitution shall be maintained," while that which succeeded, asserted the authority of Congress. The intention, authority or no authority, to keep slavery out was, however, emphatically evident. They selected as their candidate John C. Frémont, a young army officer with a brilliant and rather romantic record ; and thus avoided creating jealousies among the greater leaders. As the Whigs predominated, the platform declared in favor of internal improvements, particularly of a railroad to the Pacific and the development of rivers and harbors. The presence of Democrats and particularly of a considerable number of German-Americans from the critical region of the Northwest, prevented them from expressing unfriendliness to foreigners. The Republicans were united, determined, and they stated precisely what they wanted, but they were obliged to face the fact that this unity of purpose was at the sacrifice of representation in the southern states. The party was purely sectional.

The American party also held its first national convention, but was less fortunate than the Republicans, in that a distinct split occurred. The majority of its northern members seceded, ultimately merging with the Republicans. This left the party in the control of the southern element, but it, nevertheless, adopted a conservative tone, refused to declare itself on the territorial question except to indorse the Compromise of 1850, and tried to divert attention to its special issue of the foreign peril. Its nominees, ex-President

American and Democratic nominations.

Fillmore for President and Andrew Jackson Donelson for Vice President, were indorsed by a Whig convention, representing but a small faction of that party. Together they bid for the support of the lovers of peace and of union. The Democrats were able to present the appearance of union. Douglas's ambiguous phrase, popular sovereignty, still served to keep together men of very different views. With two new parties in the field they did well to emphasize their party continuity by the selection of Buchanan, prominent in Democratic councils for nearly forty years, as their candidate. Buchanan, moreover, was closely identified with the policy of adopting an active foreign policy in order to distract attention from domestic troubles, and commanded the support of the best of the conservative element and of a large portion of the business interests of the country. Men like Rufus Choate, the friend of Daniel Webster, and a life-long Whig, now voted the Democratic ticket as affording the best chance for continued peace.

Election of 1856.

The result of the election was the choice of Buchanan. In the North the contest was three-cornered ; the Americans held the balance in six states, but won no electoral votes. In this section Frémont received 114 electoral votes, to 62 for Buchanan. This was not sufficient, however, to overcome Buchanan's overwhelming victory in the South, where he received the vote of every slave state except Maryland, which voted for Fillmore.

Diplomacy and the crisis of 1857.

Buchanan hoped for diplomatic success. He appointed as Secretary of State, Lewis Cass, who obtained a satisfactory arrangement with England on the right of search. Buchanan's pet project of the annexation of Cuba, however, made no progress ; an opportunity for expansion in Central America, opened by the filibustering expedition of William Walker, took such form that Buchanan himself was obliged to discountenance it; and disturbances in Mexico, which he might have turned into an occasion for intervention, culminated just too late. His aspirations for a brilliant diplomatic record, therefore, came to naught. His administration, moreover, was a period of economic distress. So prosperous was the country, so full the treasury, and so nearly paid the debt, on the eve of his inauguration, that the tariff was further reduced, by a combination of the southern and the commercial interests. No sooner was this done, however, than a financial crisis came upon the country. This was particularly a railroad crisis, caused by the great amounts of capital invested during the decade in enterprises many of which were not immediately remunerative. It was heightened by general speculation along other lines, especially in land, and by the absence of effective banking laws in many states. It was not so severe as that of 1837; it affected the South, where the banks of Louisiana held strong specie reserves, comparatively little, and the West less than the East; but for the next few years business was contracted, imports declined, and the government was forced to borrow money, sometimes finding difficulty in placing its loans.

The beginning of the administration saw still one more attempt to settle the territorial question. A case had for some time been before the courts involving the status of a certain Dred Scott, a Missouri negro who claimed his freedom because his former master, an army surgeon, had at one time taken him to reside in the free state of Illinois. This case did not necessarily involve any important point, as there was good legal precedent for the view that, though to touch free soil might make a slave free, the condition of slavery would revive on voluntary reëntrance into territory where slavery was legal. It was, however, successfully urged upon Chief Justice Taney that this case might afford the means of setting forth the opinion of the Supreme Court on the whole question of slavery in the territories; for Dred Scott's wife's freedom was also at stake, and her claim rested on residence in the Minnesota territory, which was at the time

The Dred Scott case.

free under the Missouri Compromise. The prestige of the Court was so great, it was argued, that the people of the country would unhesitatingly accept its opinion, and thus political controversy might be brought to an end. Buchanan referred in his inaugural to the forthcoming decision as something which might set men's minds at rest.

The decision.   Judge Taney himself handed down the decision of a majority of the Court. He argued that Dred Scott had no right to bring suit before the Court because he was a negro, and a negro could not be a citizen of the United States. The Declaration of Independence could not be held to declare the equality of negroes with white men, because it must be interpreted in the light of conditions existing at the time, and in 1776 there were negro slaves in every state. He further argued that the Missouri Compromise was unconstitutional, for Congress could not take away, without due process of law, slave property or any other kind of property in the common territories of the United States. Particularly should this principle hold in territory bought, like the Louisiana Purchase, with the common funds of all the states. This view, though legally differing somewhat from Calhoun's doctrine of "non-intervention," resembled it in that it opened all United States territory, not yet organized into states, to slavery. This decision made a profound impression on the public mind, but it did not settle the territorial problem. Rather it weakened the respect for the Court. It was pointed out that Justices Curtis and McLean dissented, presenting weighty arguments. The legal force of the decision was also questioned. A court can declare the law only in regard to a case before it; and many held that the general questions into which Judge Taney entered were really not involved, and that his statements on those points were in the nature of *obiter dicta*.

Bloodshed in Kansas.   In the meantime, the Kansas question was again exciting attention. Locally the situation was becoming more acute.

In 1855 the free-soil and proslavery factions had met in arms during what was known as the Wakarusa War, but hardly any blood was shed. In 1856 Lawrence, the free-soil center, was burned, and murders became frequent. In that year also John Brown began to take a part in the struggle, and he, with his family and neighbors, murdered five of the proslavery party in what is known as the Pottawatomie massacre. Buchanan professed an intention to observe a policy of fair play between the contending factions, and appointed Robert J. Walker, an able and honest man, as governor. Under him an election for the territorial legislature was held, which was fairly conducted and which resulted in the choice of a free-soil majority. Before this new legislature could meet, however, a convention, called by the first or proslavery legislature and elected under such conditions as to give it a proslavery majority, came together. This convention met in the proslavery town of Lecompton, and proceeded to frame a constitution under which Kansas should apply for admission as a state. It was afraid to submit the results of its work to popular vote, for under Governor Walker rejection would be inevitable. It was decided to declare the result final without a popular vote, but to forestall congressional criticism on this point, by allowing the people to vote as to whether they would have the constitution with or without slavery. This was less fair than it appeared, for the protection of all slave property already in the territory was provided for under all circumstances, and the only point upon which the people actually could vote was whether or not they would allow further importation. The Free-Soilers refused to vote, and consequently the constitution with slavery was reported adopted, and the admission of Kansas under it was recommended by Buchanan on February 3, 1858.

Again acrimonious discussion broke out. Jefferson Davis stated that if the North had not attacked slavery, all would

The Lecompton debate.

have been well, but the contest once begun, the South must win or slavery was doomed. Already the free states stood sixteen to fifteen. The admission of Minnesota in May, 1858, was impending. Oregon had a southern population and Democratic politics, but when admitted in 1859, chose to be free. New Mexico was not ready for statehood, and so Kansas was necessary to the South to help redress the balance. On the other hand, Douglas did not dare and did not desire to support the Lecompton constitution. He had for four years been advocating emphatically the principle that the people should decide, and he could not support a scheme which openly thwarted the popular will. He broke with the administration and exerted all his influence to defeat the plan. Douglas was defeated in the Senate, but in the House his supporters, known as the Anti-Lecompton Democrats, uniting with the Republicans, won. After long debate a compromise was at length agreed to, known as the English Bill. This admitted Kansas under the Lecompton constitution on condition that the people should vote to accept the customary land grants instead of the larger land grants that had been demanded. Should the vote be adverse, admission under a new constitution was to be deferred until the population should be as great as that of the average congressional district; and no provision was made for any land grants. The majority in Kansas, however, voted against the proposition, and thus ended the chance of the South to obtain it as a slave state.

Position of Douglas.

Douglas now became the center of all political attention. He had been regarded as the probable candidate of the Democratic party in the next election, but his opposition to the Lecompton constitution had brought him into open hostility to the administration and endangered his southern support. Such a reversal of attitude did this seem, that Horace Greeley and other Republicans pronounced him the best candidate for their party. His future was determined by a contest into which he immediately entered for reëlection as United States senator from Illinois. That state was particularly well fitted to be the battleground of contending opinions on the question at issue. The first settlement had been from the South, and the southern element had filled in the lower end of the state, which came to be known as Egypt, with its commercial center at Cairo. This element had pressed northward and, in the middle portion, occupied those districts which were covered with a growth of hardwood timber. About 1830 emigrants from New England and New York began to come in by way of the Lakes. Chicago commenced its wonderful growth, and this northern element obtained control of the northern portion of the state. In the middle regions the northerners came to predominate in the prairie country, which the southerners had failed to occupy. In general, these facts determined the politics of the state. Not that every one of southern origin took one side and every one of northern origin took the other. Abraham Lincoln, the leader of the Republicans, was born in Kentucky, and Douglas himself in Vermont. Nevertheless, throughout this period, not only in Illinois, but in Indiana and Ohio as well, a knowledge of the history of settlement is a key to the course of politics. In 1856, in eight southern counties of Illinois, Frémont received an average of less than ten votes each. It was not that there was a love for slavery as an institution in the southern counties. Illinois had distinctly refused to establish slavery even before the coming of the northerners, but there was less abhorrence of slavery, and more appreciation of Douglas's principle of popular sovereignty. It was another conflict between the southern belief in personal independence and the northern desire to regulate the life of the community.

The Illinois Republicans nominated Lincoln for senator; and a series of seven debates was arranged, two in the northern section, two in Egypt, and three in the intermediate district. Upon Lincoln rested the burden of attack, and he

vigorously undertook the task. In the first place, he wished
to show that Douglas was unfitted to serve as Republican
leader. This was brought out most emphatically by Douglas's own statement that he did not care whether slavery
was voted up or down in the territories. The Republicans
did care, and this difference in sentiment was a greater obstacle to an alliance than any number of differences on particular questions. Lincoln was still more anxious to make
Douglas an impossible candidate for southern Democrats.
To accomplish this, and to make impossible a further union of
inharmonious elements under the ambiguous phrase of popular sovereignty, it was only necessary to bring out in a solemn public manner the essential difference between Douglas's
principle of squatter sovereignty and the southern principle,
now confirmed by the Dred Scott decision, of non-intervention. He therefore asked Douglas whether, after the Dred
Scott decision, it was possible for any territory by its own action to prohibit slavery? If Douglas answered that it was
not, the whole principle of squatter sovereignty fell; if he said
that it could, it would be equivalent to saying that the Dred
Scott decision was without force. If he took the first position, he was almost sure to lose the election in Illinois; if
the second, he would lose the support of the South for the
presidency. It was not that Lincoln created this dilemma;
he merely made absolutely plain an actual condition which
had existed for four years. Douglas answered that, while
the Constitution, as interpreted by the Supreme Court,
allowed slavery throughout the territories, that institution
could not exist without friendly local legislation, and, therefore, a territorial government could, if so disposed, actually
prevent its existence.

A further purpose of Lincoln in the debate was to bring
home to the voters the fact that the Dred Scott decision
involved not an abstract legal principle, but one of immediate interest to the people of the states as well as of the

territories. In the speech at Springfield, in which he accepted The national aspects of slavery. the nomination, he pointed out that there was imminent jeopardy that slavery might be made a national institution. "'A house divided against itself cannot stand.' I believe this government cannot endure permanently half slave and half free." If the Dred Scott decision was correct in asserting that slave property in the territories was under the ægis of the Constitution, might not a subsequent decision, following the same line of argument, declare that such property must be protected wherever found, even in a free state? Lincoln accused Douglas of being involved with Pierce, Buchanan, and Taney in a conspiracy to bring about such a result. This charge could not stand investigation, but the danger to which he called attention was not imaginary. Already in New York state the Lemmon case, which involved the status of slaves accompanying persons passing through a free state, was on the way to the Supreme Court. It can scarcely be doubted that the Court would have decided as Lincoln feared. The Republicans felt it necessary to control the Court and reverse its decision. All together the most important result of the debate was the fact that it brought Lincoln to the attention of the nation.

Douglas secured the legislature and the senatorship, Election of 1858. but the Republicans cast the larger aggregate vote. The northern counties were growing more rapidly than the rest of the state, and therefore the legislative apportionment, made several years before, favored the Democrats. In the other northern states the Republicans were generally successful. When the election was complete, it was found that the next Congress would contain: in the Senate, 38 Demo- The new Congress. crats, 25 Republicans, and 2 Americans; in the House, 88 Administration Democrats, 13 Anti-Lecompton Democrats, 27 Americans, and 109 Republicans. The failure of any one party to control a majority again produced a deadlock in the election of Speaker, which lasted over two months, and which was marked by growing evidence of bad feeling. The Republican candidate was John Sherman of Ohio, but it was brought up against him that he had indorsed a book which at this time created a sensation almost equal to that of *Uncle Tom's Cabin*. This was *The Impending Crisis*, written by Hinton R. Helper of North Carolina, and containing a scathing denunciation of slavery, based not upon moral, but upon economic grounds, and upon a demand for justice, not for the negro, but for the poor white. The opposition was strong enough to defeat Sherman, and cause the election of William Pennington, a more conservative Republican.

John Brown. The speakership contest was eclipsed in importance by an episode which brought home to the East the violence of Kansas, and which illustrates the unnatural condition of northern sentiment as the Brooks incident illustrates that of the South. John Brown was a virile old man, of the most extreme reformer type. His mental outlook was so narrow that he approached monomania, and his feeling was so intense that he was not content with the usual methods of the abolitionists, but believed that he was chosen of God to act as His strong right arm. He had that living conviction which makes warriors, and the magnetism of an honest man. He was among the early free-soil settlers in Kansas, and took an active and bloody part in the local contests there. He then conceived the broader scheme of establishing himself in the mountains of the South, and creating a refuge to which slaves could fly. Gradually he would extend his operations and would render slavery impossible throughout the South. He planned to guide and govern the negroes, and lead them to a peaceful mode of life; but the possibility that his plan might be accompanied with bloodshed, while he guarded against it, did not distress him, for he believed that all slave owners were sinners. He had said in Kansas: "I have no choice. It has been decreed by Almighty God, ordained from

eternity, that I should make an example of these men."
On October 16, 1859, he seized the government arsenal at
Harpers Ferry. Attacked there by government forces, he
resisted, and was captured. He was tried at Charlestown in
Virginia, convicted of treason and murder, and hanged. The
southern states were panic-stricken at this seeming approach
of slave insurrection, which they always dreaded. Everywhere the militia was put in order and the military resources
of the states were strengthened. Radical orators held the
North responsible for the attack, and began openly to declare
that a union was unnatural where one party to it threatened
the very life of the other.

Northern sentiment, however, is most significant. While
much the greater number of northerners condemned the raid,
perhaps a majority sympathized with John Brown. Emerson referred to him as "that new saint, than whom none
purer or more brave was ever led by love of men into conflict and death, the new saint awaiting his martyrdom, and
who, if he shall suffer, will make the gallows glorious like
the cross." While only four or five men in the North had
been acquainted with his purposes, these were sane, lovable
gentlemen, and their acquiescence in a scheme which might
have deluged the South in blood, is one of the most striking
manifestations of how far from the normal the public mind
had wandered. John Brown may have been insane, but he
was not a madman blindly striking in the dark; his insanity
received its direction from the vibrant mental atmosphere
about him. Although his plans were approved by but few
in the North, the South was justified in regarding him, not
as an isolated assailant, but as a product of a sentiment, not
yet dominant, but growing every day more powerful. At the
North, also, the years 1859 and 1860 saw a growing interest
in military affairs. Military companies and regiments were
formed almost every week, military exhibitions were popular,
and the New York Zouaves went to Chicago to drill. There

Northern sentiment on John Brown.

was no purpose to use their arms against the South, but there was that unrest which so often precedes hostilities.

Break-up of the Demo-cratic party. Under such circumstances the Democratic national convention met at Charleston, to determine the momentous question whether party unity could be restored. The majority, coming almost wholly from the northern and border states, pinned their faith to Douglas, but over a third of the members, delegates from the Cotton States, could not trust him, and blocked his nomination. Finally, the most extreme southerners seceded from the convention, which adjourned to meet again at Baltimore. There Douglas was nominated, though not without some irregularity, and the following resolution was adopted: "That it is in accordance with the interpretation of the Cincinnati platform [of 1856], that, during the existence of the territorial governments, the measure of restriction, whatever it may be, imposed by the Federal Constitution on the power of the territorial legislature over the subject of domestic relations, as the same has been, or shall hereafter be finally determined by the Supreme Court of the United States, should be respected by all good citizens, and enforced with promptness and fidelity by every branch of the general government." A second secession took place at Baltimore, which resulted in the choice of J. C. Breckinridge of Kentucky, the Vice President under Buchanan, as candidate for President on a platform of which the distinguishing feature was the resolution: "That the government of a territory organized by an act of Congress is provisional and temporary; and during its existence, all citizens of the United States have an equal right to settle with their property in the territory, without their rights, either of person or of property, being destroyed or impaired by congressional legislation," and "That it is the duty of the federal government, in all its departments, to protect, when necessary, the rights of persons and property in the territories, and wherever else its constitutional authority extends."

The difference between the two platforms lay in the fact that the one stated that citizens of the territories should obey the Dred Scott decision, the other that the national government was bound to make them obey it. Breckinridge and his platform were indorsed by the Charleston seceders at a meeting held in Richmond, and were supported by Buchanan and the administration. Thus the fundamental disagreement between the southern and northern Democrats became visible, and that great party, the last important political organization which had vitally bound North and South together, was torn asunder. Neither part could claim to be the regular representative of the whole. Really Douglas was the Democratic organization candidate in the North; Breckinridge, in the South.

The Republican convention met at Chicago, its managers realizing that the Northwest must largely determine the election. Seward was the leading candidate, and was universally recognized as the most prominent Republican, but he was regarded by many as too radical to be elected. Naturally a man of conservative, temporizing disposition, he sometimes yielded to an impulsiveness, especially in speech, which caused him to be distrusted. Perhaps two of his phrases, "the higher law," and "the irrepressible conflict," defeated his nomination. They really indicated a constitutional defect which rendered him unsuited for the presidency, for, unlike Lincoln's radical statement that a "house divided against itself cannot stand," they did not represent a clear-cut belief upon which he was prepared to act, but rather a momentary flash of insight, soon clouded in his mind, as the phrases were moderated in his speech, by suggestions of shadowy expedients, and a genial glow of unconvincing optimism. When his defeat became evident, the contest was thrown open. Lincoln, as the rival of Douglas, was really the logical candidate. The shouting of the Chicago mob proved his popularity in the doubtful state

Nomination of Lincoln.

of Illinois. He was nominated on the third ballot. The most important feature of the platform, aside from the unequivocal declaration on the territorial question, was the plank favoring a protective tariff, which was, perhaps, responsible for the subsequent Republican success in Pennsylvania.

The Constitutional Union party.

The American party of 1856 became the Constitutional Union party of 1860. It chose as its candidates, John Bell of Tennessee and Edward Everett of Massachusetts. It did not attempt to define its attitude on the great issues of the day, but called upon all citizens to support its candidates, who were known to be loyal supporters of the Union and to place the preservation of the Union before all else.

The campaign of 1860.

As in every campaign since 1854, there was one conflict in the free states, and another south of the Mason-Dixon line. In the North, Lincoln ran against the field. His opponents sometimes combined as in New Jersey and New York, but in most states there were four tickets. The Republicans emphasized the slavery question, especially appealing to the labor vote. J. M. Forbes had written in December, 1856: " All other influences sink into insignificance compared with that brought to bear for two years past, and especially during the past four months, from the stump and by the tremendous machinery of the campaign press, to convince the laboring classes here of the aristocratic nature of the institution of slavery ; of the small number of slaveholders compared with the white population North and South, and of the coming issue being whether this small class (supposed to rule the South) shall own half the Senate and shall use the national arm to extend their institutions at home and abroad." In August, 1860, Carl Schurz said at St. Louis: "In the North, every laborer thinks, and is required to think. In the South the laborer is forbidden to think, lest he think too much, for thought engenders aspirations. . . . Our laboring man must be a free man, in order to be what he

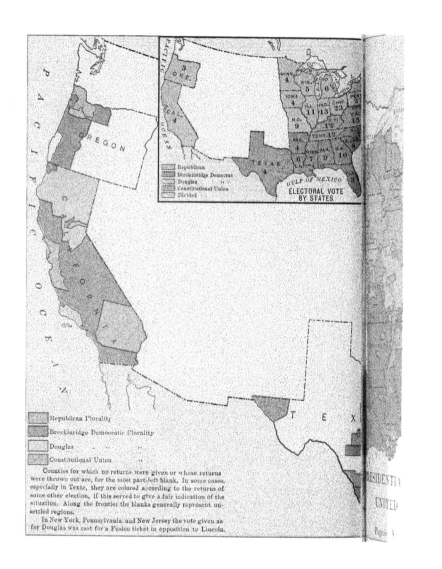

ELECTORAL VOTE
BY STATES

Republican
Breckinridge Democrat
Douglas   "
Constitutional Union
Divided

Republican Plurality

Breckinridge Democratic Plurality

Douglas   "   "

Constitutional Union   "

Counties for which no returns were given or whose returns
were thrown out are, for the most part, left blank. In some cases,
especially in Texas, they are colored according to the returns of
some other election, if this served to give a fair indication of the
situation. Along the frontier the blanks generally represent unsettled regions.

In New York, Pennsylvania, and New Jersey the vote given as
for Douglas was cast for a Fusion ticket in opposition to Lincoln.

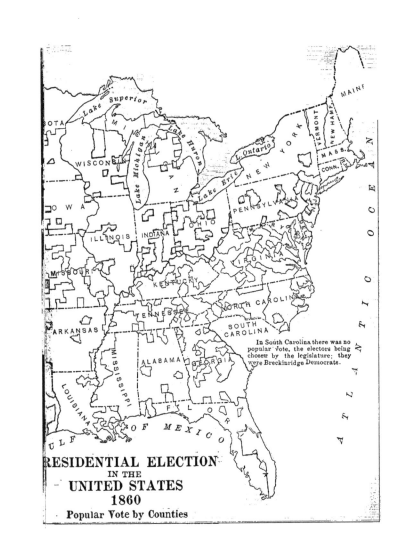

In South Carolina there was no
popular vote, the electors being
chosen by the legislature; they
were Breckinridge Democrats.

RESIDENTIAL ELECTION
IN THE
UNITED STATES
1860
Popular Vote by Counties

ought to be, an intelligent laborer. Therefore, we educate
him for liberty by our system of public instruction. . . .
Your laboring man must be a brute in order to remain what
you want him to be, a slave. . . . On your plantation fields
stands another institution, from which your system of labor
derives its inspiration; that is your schoolhouse, where
your slaves are flogged." The Bell and Breckinridge orators
in the North dwelt on the advantage of the Union and the
dangers to which it was exposed. They called upon the people
to defend the Constitution and the Supreme Court, and to
avoid the evils of a protective tariff such as the Republicans
proposed. The Douglas men appealed to Democratic
regularity, and popular rights as represented in the principle
of squatter sovereignty.

In the South, Breckinridge was opposed by Bell and
Douglas. The latter, believing that Breckinridge represented the most dangerous radicalism, canceled his engagements in the West, where he had a fighting chance of winning
votes, and made a tour of the South, where the utmost result
of his endeavors could be to turn the states from Breckinridge to Bell. The Bell orators charged the Buchanan
administration, which was supporting Breckinridge, with
corruption, and tried to rally the old Whig vote for reform.
They also accused Breckinridge of favoring secession. Breckinridge and his followers urged the South to unite in support
of its rights.

The election revealed three sections. Lincoln swept the *The election of 1860.*
North by a popular vote of 1,840,037 to 1,565,038, carried
all the electoral votes to the Mason-Dixon line, except three
in New Jersey, and was elected. Breckinridge swept the
Cotton South by a popular vote of 220,469 to 173,314,
carrying all its electoral votes. In the middle region, however, the majority favored Bell and Douglas, the representatives of conservatism and compromise. In the eight states
of the upper South they secured 506,102 popular votes to

377,002, and 48 electors to 25. They were also strong in the northern portion of the Ohio River valley. Taking the country as a whole, Lincoln and Breckinridge, the radical candidates, received 2,747,233 votes to 1,856,836 for Bell and Douglas, and 252 to 51 electors. Northern radicalism won the North, southern radicalism won the South, and the middle region was for inaction with regard to slavery.

BIBLIOGRAPHICAL NOTES

Sources.   For the Kansas-Nebraska debate — if the *Congressional Globe* is not available — *American History Leaflets*, nos. 2, 17. Johnston, A., *Representative American Orations*, II, 183–255. For conditions in Kansas, the report of the investigation committee, *U. S. Documents, House Reports*, 34th Cong., 1 sess., vol. II, no. 200, is more vivid than any secondary account. For the Dred Scott case, *American History Leaflets*, no. 23; Hill, *Liberty Documents*, ch. XXI; 19 *Howard*, 399. For conservative northern opinion, Choate, R., *Works*, II, 387–414. For Republican opinion, Lincoln, A., *His Book;* Lincoln, A., *Works*, I, 277–518. Lincoln and Douglas, *Debates*. Sanborn, F. B., *Life and Letters of John Brown.* Sumner, C., *Works*, IV, 137–256. On the election, McPherson, E., *History of the Rebellion, American Cyclopedia*, 1861, 46–420.

Historical accounts.   Brown, W. G., *Douglas.* Hart, *Chase*, ch. V. Higginson, T. W., *Phillips.* Hodder, F. H., *Genesis of the Kansas-Nebraska Act* (Wis. His. Soc., *Proceedings*, 1912). Mason, V., *Fugitive Slave Law in Wisconsin* (Wis. His. Soc., *Proceedings*, vol. 43, 117–143). McDougall, M. G., *Fugitive Slaves*, secs. 53–62; ch. V. Rhodes, *United States*, I, 424–506. Smith, T. C., *Parties and Slavery*, 121–149. Stephens, *War between the States*, II, 240–257.

Kansas situation.   Jameson, J., *Constitutional Conventions*, secs. 211–216. Rhodes, J. F., *United States*, II, chs. VII, IX. Stephens, *War between the States*, II, colloquy XVII.

Rise of the Republican party.   Bancroft, F., *Seward*, I, chs. XIX, XX. Blaine, J. G., *Twenty Years in Congress*, I, ch. VI. [James Buchanan], *Mr. Buchanan's Administration.* Curtis, *Buchanan*, II, chs. VI, VIII–XI. Hart,

Chase, ch. VI.   Rhodes, *United States*, II, ch. VII–VIII.   Smith, *Parties and Slavery*, 161–174.

Benton, T. H., *Historical and Legal Examination*.   Corwin, The Dred
E. S., *The Dred Scott Decision* (Am. Hist. Assoc., *Review*, XVII, Scott
52–69).   Grey and Lowell, *Legal Review of the Case of Dred Scott*. case.
Rhodes, *United States*, II, 242–277.   Smith, *Parties and Slavery*,
190–209.

Johnson, A., *Life of Douglas.*· Nicolay and Hay, *Life of* Lincoln-
Lincoln, vol. I.   Rhodes, *United States*, II, 384–416.   Smith, Douglas
Parties and Slavery, 209–249, 286–305. debates.

The best life of John Brown is that by C. G. Villard. John Brown.

Blaine, J. G., *Twenty Years in Congress*, chs. VIII–X.   Fite, Election of
E. D'., *Campaign of 1860*.   Nicolay and Hay, *Life of Lincoln*, II, 1860.
chs. X–XVI.   Rhodes, *United States*, II, chs. X, XI.   Stephens,
A. H., *War between the States*, II, colloquy XVIII.   Wilson, H.,
Slave Power, II, chs. XLIII, XLIV, XLVII–LV.

CHAPTER XXI

DIVISION

ALL national party organizations had broken down, three of the five great church organizations had become sectionalized, the Constitution almost alone held the country together, and the election of Lincoln was taken as a signal for its dissolution.

Secession of South Carolina.

In the state of South Carolina there was such unity of sentiment that discussion and delay were unnecessary. Governor Gist had already called together the legislature to choose presidential electors, and to provide "for the safety and protection of the state." When it met, on November 5, he recommended that if Lincoln were declared elected, a convention similar to that which in 1788 had adopted the Constitution be immediately called to consider the question of separation from the Union. November 21 was set apart as a day of prayer and preparation. On December 17, the convention met, and on December 20, it passed unanimously an "Ordinance of Secession," and adopted a "Declaration of Causes" to be published to the world. The latter set forth that the Constitution of the United States had been adopted as an experiment, that it had worked constantly to the disadvantage of the South, that the character of the government had gradually changed from a federal organization to a consolidated democracy, and that the election of a President by a purely sectional party made it unsafe for South Carolina longer to remain as a member of the Union. Commissioners were sent to Washington to arrange for a division of government property and of the national debt; and to other southern states to secure coöperation.

While this was taking place the national administration remained passive. It happened that the commander-in-chief of the army was General Winfield Scott, to whom Jackson had in 1833 given orders for the enforcement of the federal laws in South Carolina when that state nullified the tariff. He recommended that similar orders be given now. Buchanan, however, feared that to do so might cause the secession movement to spread, southern sentiment being extremely sensitive to anything that might be construed as coercion. When Congress met, on December 3, he sent in his message stating that secession was unconstitutional, was in fact revolution, and that while the South had grievances, these were not sufficient to justify revolution. To placate the doubtful in the South he stated at length his belief that the national government did not have the right to coerce a state, and he left out the view, which he held in common with Jeremiah Black, the Attorney-General, that it did have the right to enforce the national laws within a state. He therefore offered Congress no plan of action, but left the responsibility to that body.

Buchanan and secession.

Congress once more attempted to bind together the diverging sections by compromise. The most prominent leader in this movement was Senator Crittenden of Kentucky, inheritor of the Clay tradition. The plan which he worked out was considered by a Senate committee of thirteen. It included a number of measures intended to settle all points of difference, the most important being a proposed constitutional amendment, by which slavery should be prohibited north of 36° 30′ and definitely protected in government territory south of that line. This plan was rejected on December 28 by the Republican senators after consultation with Lincoln. The ground upon which Lincoln based his refusal was that if slavery should be allowed in all territory south of 36° 30′, there would follow immediately a demand for the acquisition of more such territory. Already

Attempts at compromise.

in 1860 the demand for Cuba was found in both Democratic platforms, and he believed that it would not be long before southern statesmen would again threaten to secede unless Cuba or northern Mexico were annexed. It was upon this question of future expansion, too, that the southern radicals definitely refused to compromise. Lincoln wrote: "As to fugitive slaves, District of Columbia, slave trade among the slave states, and whatever springs of necessity from the fact that the institution is amongst us, I care but little so that what is done be comely and not altogether outrageous. Nor do I care much about New Mexico, if further extension were hedged against." The Republicans on the House Committee of thirty-three, which was considering compromise, offered to organize New Mexico, containing all territory south of 36° 30' then belonging to the United States, without prohibiting slavery, but this offer was rejected.

Failure of compromise. A Peace Convention, called by Virginia and meeting at Washington with ex-President Tyler in the chair, proposed to meet this difficulty incident to territorial expansion, by a constitutional amendment to the effect that no territory be annexed unless agreed to by a concurrent majority of the senators from the free states and from the slave states. This suggestion, however, came only just before Lincoln's inauguration, and was not seriously considered. One other solution was advocated: to appeal from Congress to the people by submitting the Crittenden compromise to popular vote. This was defeated in the Senate. Compromise, therefore, failed. The actual point of difference was the question of extending slavery beyond the existing national boundaries. The divergence between the sections, however, must not be measured by that alone, but by the distance they had to stretch to come even so near together. It was not this particular difference which was the cause of the war, but rather the conflict of interests between the sections, now festered into misunderstanding and distrust as a result of thirty years of irritation over the slavery question as a whole.

In the meantime the remaining cotton states were dis- The Georgia contest. cussing secession. Except in South Carolina there was a division of opinion, not as to the constitutionality of secession, but as to its advisability. The most important contest was in Georgia. Alexander H. Stephens counseled delay. He argued that the South had received at least its share of the benefits of the Union; that in time the right would win as it had in the case of the tariff, which was now almost on the basis desired by the South; that the election of Lincoln was not sufficient cause for disunion; that the Republicans in fact professed regard for the constitutional rights of slavery, and that this would be sufficient, with some few concessions which might be obtained by a convention of southern states acting within the Union, to protect the rights of the South.

Robert Toombs was the chief advocate of secession, expressing the radical view that no confidence could be given to Republican professions, and that union with the free states was dangerous and bound to be fatal to slavery. The crucial vote stood 166 to 130; but the final vote on secession, January 19, stood 280 to 89. The whole discussion in Georgia was not so much as to whether "southern rights" should be insisted upon, or even as to what these rights were, but as to whether secession was, in the existing crisis, the best means of obtaining them. When secession was once accepted as a policy, the great majority loyally accepted the result and joined with their late opponents in making it effective. It was not the belief of the majority that war would result from secession. Prejudices long fostered painted the northerners as cowards who might bluster but would not fight. Many of the better informed believed that the northern Democrats would not tolerate the invasion of the South, and if fighting occurred it would be in the streets of northern cities. While nearly all felt a sentimental regret at the passing of the old Union, the conviction was burned deep on their minds that that Union had been of advantage to the North and of disadvantage to the South. They were stirred by much the same mixture of motives as the colonists in 1776, though there was perhaps a little less of regret and more of anger.

Secession of the Cotton South.

Contests similar to that in Georgia went on in other southern states, with similar results. Mississippi seceded on January 9, 1861, Florida on January 10, Alabama on January 11, Louisiana on January 26, and Texas on February 1. The failure of compromise had, therefore, been followed by the secession of all the Gulf States, those primarily given to the cultivation of cotton, and to which slavery and the plantation system were most vital.

The Southern Confederacy.

It was not the intention of the seceding states to remain isolated sovereignties. They planned to renew their union, under conditions more favorable to themselves, and with the old Constitution altered only so far as to make perfectly plain and evident the interpretations of it for which they had contended. Their plan was to organize a confederation which they would invite other states to join, drawing them one after the other from the old Union to the new. They believed that all the slave states would ultimately take such action, and some wished to stop at that point, with a body of states homogeneous and therefore harmonious. A greater number hoped and believed that the upper Mississippi valley would in time find it to its interest to unite with the new confederation through which its great river ran and in which it would find a market for a great portion of its products. The accession of the Northwest, it was thought, would bring the Middle States, dependent as they were on western commerce. New England was to be left beyond the pale. The first step towards reconstruction, according to this plan, was the meeting of delegates on February 4, at Montgomery, to form a southern confederation. On Febru-

ary 8 they adopted a provisional constitution, and elected
Jefferson Davis, Provisional President, and Alexander H.
Stephens, Vice President. The new government rapidly completed its organization, and the inauguration of Lincoln
found a powerful, organized Confederacy, existing within the
limits claimed by the Union.

This action had taken place without active interference *Inaction of the govern- ment.*
from the government at Washington. A cabinet crisis had
already taken place at the end of December, 1860, on the question of the defense of government property in Charleston
harbor. The southern members had resigned or been removed, and they were replaced by strong Union Democrats of the North. Jeremiah Black became Secretary of
State, Edwin Stanton, Attorney-General, and John A. Dix,
Secretary of the Treasury. The change, however, was chiefly
in tone. Measures were taken to protect government property, but they were ineffective, and the actual handling of the
situation was left to the new President.

Though few appreciated it at the time, Abraham Lincoln *Character- istics of Lincoln.*
was a man ideally fitted to cope with this greatest of all
national crises. Born in 1809, his tough and sinewy frame
and his strong, supple mind were at the point of most perfect
harmony. While his parents were extremely poor, he had in
his veins the blood of a vigorous stock drawn on the one side
from New England and on the other from Virginia. Nor was
his poverty of the kind to breed envy or sycophancy; he
was poor in a community where there were no rich. The
conditions of his life developed in him those abilities which
characterized the statesmen of the frontier, but he avoided
the consequent dangers. The lack of early education had
made Henry Clay superficial, and Jackson narrow-minded.
Lincoln, who educated himself, was always thorough; he was
never satisfied unless he understood a subject from the bottom. He was always open-minded and was still consciously
educating himself when elected President. As President-

elect, although by diligence and by genius he had become master of a style unsurpassed for clearness and effectiveness, he asked the schoolmaster at Springfield to correct the grammar of his inaugural address. This humbleness of mind extended to his political life. He never conceived himself, as Webster sometimes did, dictator of events, but as an instrument in the interplay of natural forces. When he said at Springfield, in 1858: "A house divided against itself cannot stand," he did not express a purpose, but an appreciation of a great truth, which afforded him a basis for action. He was a statesman in his adjustment of principle to policy. He formed his political principles with care, and when convinced of their ultimate truth, he never sacrificed them. He did not, however, hurry their consummation, believing that the right was sure to triumph in the end. In the belief that the Union must become all free or all slave, he worked to make it free; but when the Union itself was in danger, he concentrated all his efforts on its preservation, postponing the question of slavery until his main object should be accomplished. He had the executive faculty of acting for the better, when promptness was demanded, rather than delaying to discover the best. He was weakest as an administrator, sacrificing efficiency for political advantage. As a politician in both the large and the narrow sense, he was unrivaled. He had an unparalleled insight into the minds of men, based on a wide charity toward those who differed from him. He had the unusual capacity of regarding men as individuals and not in classes, and he appealed to the common traits of human nature, which underlie class or sectional division. He had that clearness and lucidity of mind that is sometimes called common sense, but none of the hardness which sometimes accompanies it. He was, in fact, primarily an idealist. Otherwise he would not have been, as he was, preëminently the leader of the people. His virtues of meekness, charity, and faith were the essential Christian

ABRAHAM LINCOLN

virtues, and they were understood by the nation, which was by profession and in its thought Christian. In crudeness of manner, as in the substance of his character, he was at one with a majority of the people. He understood their desires and purposes, and shaped his policies accordingly; they understood him, and gave him increasingly their confidence.

At his inauguration he set before himself the preservation of the whole Union. Caution was necessary, for, while compromise had failed, the North had not yet spoken on the question of coercion as opposed to peaceful separation. The abolitionists had welcomed separation, and Horace Greeley, General Scott, and many leading Democrats had expressed a willingness to let the southern states depart in peace. The North had not very generally believed in the genuineness of the southern threats of secession and had not in 1860 voted on the question of union or disunion. George Ticknor remarked that there had not been in years so much thinking on political subjects as in the six months following the election of Lincoln, and that until the people had made up their minds, the administration was powerless to act. It must be a decision of the whole people, for the war could not be fought by a party. *Northern sentiment.*

Each side realized the importance of forcing the other to take action, and attention was concentrated upon Charleston harbor, where the national garrison in Fort Sumter was surrounded by Confederate batteries. On April 6, Lincoln having informed himself of the situation and discussed the matter with his cabinet, caused the Confederate government to be notified that he would provision the fort. This threw upon Davis and his cabinet the responsibility of action. Toombs protested against hostile measures, saying, "You will wantonly strike a hornets' nest which extends from mountains to ocean, and legions now quiet will swarm out and sting us to death." His prophecy was unheeded, and on April 12 the Confederate forts began the bombardment. *Fort Sumter.*

Decision of
the North.

At the first news of the firing upon Sumter, the North rose almost *en masse*. Telegram after telegram assured Lincoln that there was now but one party, and that, the party of the Union. Enlistments and subscriptions of money at once began, and men who in January were in favor of peaceful separation now aided without remuneration in the war preparations. This result was inevitable. The devotion of the North to the Union had been steadily growing, and was now one of its foremost political ideals. The northern idea of liberty was that of individual liberty and right to participate in the government, and not the southern idea that each community should be allowed to follow its own devices. The northern idea of democracy was that the majority should rule, and not the southern idea that there should be as little government as possible. The Union was undoubtedly more advantageous to the North than to the South. It meant a market for northern manufacturers, employment for northern vessels. The Democratic party, which was least interested in the questions which brought on the war, was conspicuous for its Union feeling. Its appeal for many years had been that the Union was safest in its hands. Benjamin F. Butler, who had been one of Breckinridge's leading northern supporters, was one of the first to offer his services to the President. The period of hesitation was at an end, and the North was determined to preserve the Union at all hazards.

With war a fact, it was necessary for the middle region to make its decision. North Carolina, Virginia, Arkansas, and Tennessee joined with the South, as soon as Lincoln, on April 15, issued his proclamation calling for troops. The

Effects of
coercion.

majority in these states regarded secession as unjustifiable and preferred to remain in the Union. They believed, however, in the right of secession, and did not believe in the right of the national government to coerce a state. Their sympathies and interests, moreover, were southern, and when war was inevitable and choice must be made, they decided to stand by the states which they believed to be acting, even though unwisely, within their constitutional rights, rather than become the instruments of a national government which they believed to be exceeding its constitutional powers. The tide of secession spirit swept up through eastern Maryland. Mobs in Baltimore cut Washington off from railroad and telegraphic connection with the North, while the Virginians occupied Harpers Ferry and blocked it from the west. The lower Potomac was closed by Virginian batteries. By April 21 the capital was in a state of siege. In this emergency the government acted with vigor. Communication with the North was reopened through Annapolis, April 25. Soon after, troops were stationed at Relay House, cutting Baltimore off from Harpers Ferry. On May 9 communication between Washington and the North was reëstablished through Baltimore. The writ of *habeas corpus* was suspended, and, with this check on the civil law, numerous arrests were made, including members of the city government of Baltimore. In this way Maryland was kept within the Union. Probably a majority in the eastern part of the state would have preferred secession, but they were held in check by the loyal element in the western counties and by government action. The most ardent secessionists slipped away over the Potomac, and the next elections were overwhelmingly in favor of the Union. With Maryland, went Delaware, by force, but also by inclination.

For no region was the decision so difficult as for the Ohio valley. Its population was drawn most largely from the South, but slavery and the plantation system were not its major interests. It found in the South a great market for its foodstuffs and in the Mississippi its traditional outlet, but railroads and canals had long been increasingly attaching it to the North and East. Douglas did much to rally this region to the North by a series of speeches culminating

The Ohio valley.

at Chicago on May 1. He pointed out that the East also might secede, and that the West would then find itself shut off from the world. Its only safety was in the inviolability of the Union. Dying on June 3, he left as a last message to his sons: "Tell them to obey the laws and support the Constitution of the United States."

Kentucky. With small hesitation the states on the north bank rallied to the Union. Kentucky, however, took the whole summer to decide. Its trade drew it both ways. The sympathies of the rich "Blue Grass" district were southern, but those of the mountain area and the central small farming region were against slavery and the plantation economy. It adopted a policy of neutrality. Nowhere is Lincoln's skill better shown than in the differing policies he adopted for this state and for Maryland. Unable to coerce Kentucky, and confident of her ultimate decision, he respected her neutrality. At the same time he adopted many expedients to foster Union sentiment and aid the Unionists in the state. The first actual violation of neutrality came when the Confederate government sent in troops to occupy Columbus. Immediately the legislature abandoned neutrality and voted to support the old Union. At least two thirds of the population favored this course, and although about forty thousand Kentuckians enlisted in the southern armies, its national quotas were always full.

West Virginia and eastern Tennessee. State boundaries, as well as national, yielded to this supreme strain. The mountain and Ohio valley portion of Virginia, long antagonistic to the dominant eastern section, broke away, formed a government which claimed to represent the whole state, and, with the consent of this government, applied to Congress for admission as a new state. It was accepted June 19, 1863, under the title of West Virginia. Eastern Tennessee and many individuals in North Carolina desired to take similar action, but mountain ranges and railroads delivered them into the hands of the Confederacy, which held them against their will, as the national government held eastern Maryland.

In Missouri the state government was secessionist, but there was a strong Union element, largely composed of old supporters of Benton, now led by Francis P. Blair, Jr., and the Germans. With the aid of Captain Lyon, commanding the United States arsenal at St. Louis, that city was secured for the Union, and a little later, Jefferson City, the capital. A convention had been chosen in February to decide the question of secession. This convention, to the surprise of the legislature which called it, proved to be strongly Unionist. It now declared itself the supreme representative of the people, and, the state government having declared for secession and joined the Confederate forces, established a new and loyal state government. The latter received constantly the support of a majority of the population, though thousands of individuals enlisted in the southern armies. All the Pacific coast, with all the territories, remained with the national government, except that the Confederates occupied for a time parts of New Mexico, Arizona, and Indian Territory. *Division beyond the Mississippi.*

On the whole the country divided naturally. Probably the only districts held against their will were eastern Maryland, which was in the hands of the national government, and eastern Tennessee, which the Confederacy controlled. Possibly the "Blue Grass" of Kentucky would have joined the South, if it had not formed, as it were, an island surrounded by loyal districts. The people of the border states were torn with conflicting desires. In the balanced condition of their minds the motives which finally determined their choice were often trivial. It is, however, generally true that the different districts for the most part followed the sympathetic attraction of the section to which they were most akin. At the same time it is probably equally true that many portions of the border were strongly influenced by the *Basis of division.*

fact that the national government was with the North. If
the North had seceded and the South attempted coercion, the
division would have been rather different, but probably
not to the extent of fifty thousand square miles or two
millions of population.

BIBLIOGRAPHICAL NOTES

Sources.   On the secession movement in the South: *American History Leaflet*, no. 12. [Buchanan, J.], *Mr. Buchanan's Administration*, chs. VI–XI. Johnston, A., *Representative American Orations*, III, 235–274; 294–311. Lowell, J. R., *Political Essays*, 45–75. McPherson, E., *History of the Rebellion* (see reference in ch. XIX, use index for the several states). On Lincoln's policy: Lincoln, A., *Works*, II, 1–66; also his inaugurals which are found in his *Works*, in Richardson's *Messages*, and many other places.

Historical accounts. Secession and compromise.   Adams, C. F., *C. F. Adams*, chs. VII, X. Bancroft, F., *Final Efforts at Compromise* (*Political Science Quarterly*, VI, 401–423). Curtis, *Buchanan*, II, chs. XIII–XXII. Dabney, R. L., *Stonewall Jackson*, 125–196. Davis, J., *Rise and Fall of the Confederate Government*, I, 247–258. Fish, C. R., *The Decision of the Ohio Valley* (American Hist. Assoc., *Report*, 1910, 155–164). Hart, *Chase*, ch. VIII. Long, A. L., *Lee*, ch. V. Johnson, A., *Douglas*, 442–461. Mumford, B. B., *Virginia's Attitude toward Slavery*, pts. III and IV. Phillips, *Georgia and State Rights* (Am. Hist. Assoc., *Report*, 1901, vol. II), ch. VIII. Pollard, E. A., *Lost Cause*, ch. V. Rhodes, *United States*, III, chs. XIII, XIV. Stephens, A. H., *War between the States*, I, chs. XI, XII; II, 109–130. Chadwick, F. E., *Causes of the Civil War*, 151–184.

Lincoln.   Carpenter, F. B., *Six Months in the White House*. Chadwick, *Civil War*, 184–247, 278–343. Morse, J. T., *Lincoln*. Nicolay and Hay, *Life of Lincoln*, II, ch. XXIX; III, chs. XVI–XXVI. Rhodes, *United States*, III, 300–354. Schurz, C., *Lincoln*. Tarbell, I. M., *Lincoln*. The best life of Lincoln is that by Lord Charnwood, *Abraham Lincoln* (N. Y., 1916).

CHAPTER XXII

THE CIVIL WAR

THE Confederacy possessed many of the elements The Confederate government. necessary to make a nation. It occupied a homogeneous, contiguous territory, of an area amply sufficient. It would be much less vexed with the problem of sectionalism than the Union it had left, for while there were causes of differences between the northern slave-producing states, and those to the south which desired an increasing supply, there was more uniformity than is usual in a region so large. The political views and ideals of the whole people were essentially similar and there was an abundance of political experience. The permanent constitution, adopted in 1862, was modeled closely upon that of the United States. The changes were in part to define the rights of the states and of slavery, and in part changes in detail. The President was to serve six years and was not to be reëlected; members of the cabinet might be allowed seats in Congress; Congress was not to increase, unless by a two-thirds vote, appropriations called for by the various department heads, though it could reduce them; riders were prohibited, and the President was allowed to veto items in appropriation bills. The government was manned from top to bottom by men who had had years of official experience at Washington, and there can be no question that its machinery would have run smoothly, had it been launched under more favorable conditions, and that it served its purpose satisfactorily during its brief and trying career.

Economically, the homogeneity of the South was its greatest Economic dependence of the South. peril. It devoted its energies, to a degree hardly paralleled in history, to one industry, and it relied upon the outside world for its manufactures, its ships, and even to some extent for its food. The one strong point in its economic situation, was that it possessed a practical monopoly of its favorite product. It was upon the power of this monopoly that most of the southern leaders relied, and they expected "King Cotton" to impoverish the North, and compel the assistance of Europe. Theirs was the fallacy of Jefferson's embargo policy; they ignored the fact that both sides would suffer. Actually, many New England cotton spinners joined the army, while those of Europe, after some genuine distress, found cotton elsewhere. The southern monopoly of cotton was based, not upon exclusive control, but upon cheapness of production; higher prices encouraged Egypt and India to raise it. Cotton, therefore, failed under stress of war to answer the demands made upon it, and with this failure fell the whole scheme of southern diplomacy for obtaining outside aid. The Confederacy was thrown upon its own resources.

The southern armies.

These resources, while large in themselves, were small in comparison with those of the North. Of the 31,443,321 inhabitants of the whole United States in 1860, the eleven seceding states contained only 9,103,342. Of this number, 3,689,833 were slaves or free negroes, leaving 5,413,509 white persons to compare with over 22,000,000 in the North. The South drew perhaps 40,000 more fighting men from Maryland, Kentucky, and Missouri, than the North drew from West Virginia, Tennessee, and North Carolina, but the disproportion between the sections remained overwhelming. The southern population, however, furnished admirable material for war. Two types of southern soldiers are represented by Robert E. Lee and "Stonewall" Jackson. Lee was born to the best traditions of Virginia. Connected by family ties with Washington, he represented the same characteristics — administrative ability, chivalric devotion to the public good, and dignity of character. Handsome, well set up, well bred, and with a comprehensive thoughtfulness which omitted not the smallest detail of army life

From a "Thistle" Print © Detroit Publishing Co

ROBERT E. LEE

or the personal welfare and happiness of the common soldier or the soldier's widow, he was the ideal of the southern gentlemen who officered much of the army and formed much of its cavalry. "Stonewall" Jackson came of the rough and vigorous stock of the mountain and piedmont, the old frontier region. Prejudiced, and of narrow experience, he brought to the work an intense conviction of the righteousness of his cause, and inspired his troops with a fervor resembling that of Cromwell's "Ironsides." He represented the spirit that made southern infantry a marvel to military observers. The population of the South was more accustomed than that of the North to the use of firearms and of horses, and to following certain natural leaders, and consequently a military organization was more quickly effected. The disproportion in population, however, soon began to tell, and the southern Congress was forced, in April, 1862, to resort to conscription; gradually extending the ages of those called into service, diminishing the number of exemptions, and consequently reducing the standard of the troops.

Ultimately the drain of men became so great that toward the close of the war the enrollment of slaves was contemplated. Few nations of modern times have put so large a proportion of their population in the battle line. The most careful studies place the enlistments at a figure larger than the total number of men between eighteen and forty-five in 1860, which was 1,100,000, and it is estimated that the Confederacy received the equivalent of three years' service from 1,082,119 men, but this number is probably somewhat exaggerated.

The slave population counted heavily in the sum total of southern resources. The war was a revelation as to the docile, humane character of most of the American negroes. While tens of thousands fled to the northern armies marching through the country, there was no slave insurrection, and the bulk of them continued to work peaceably in the fields, Economic resources.

although in some districts nearly all the white men who usually supervised them had been drawn away. There being little market for cotton, the slaves were used partly in auxiliary service with the army, but chiefly in the cultivation of food products. Harvests were good and there was generally no lack of the necessaries of life, though tea, coffee, and such imported luxuries almost disappeared. In certain localities, however, there was much distress, for the means of transportation were overtaxed and grew steadily worse throughout the war. River and coast trade soon had to be abandoned, while the railroad system was not complete in 1860, and rapidly deteriorated, there being neither iron, skilled labor, nor capital to repair it. Toward the end of the war the railroads were practically monopolized by the government, but even then were scarcely able to supply the armies, to say nothing of the nonmilitary population.

Manufacturing.   In the matter of war material and manufactured goods, the case of the South seemed desperate. It contained but 290,000 spindles for the manufacture of cotton goods, out of 5,280,000 in the whole country, while of pig iron it produced in 1860 only 25,513 tons out of a national production of 884,474, and only 24,176 out of the 406,298 tons of rolled iron. With astonishing energy and success the southern people turned to this problem. Richmond and Atlanta became centers for the manufacture of firearms and powder. Such trade as was carried on with Europe consisted almost altogether in war materials, and was, by the close of the war, brought under government control. Probably the southern army was not seriously hampered by a lack of the munitions of war. On the other hand it was seriously handicapped by lack of shoes and clothing. The drain of men into the army prevented the development of any form of manufacturing not absolutely essential for the prosecution of the war. The noncombatant population suffered as much as the troops from deprivation of articles usually imported.

Southern finance presents a bewildering chaos of experi- Finance. ment, but its net result was to place practically all the resources of the territory at the disposal of the government. There was little floating capital and consequently little was raised by direct domestic loans, and less than fifteen millions by foreign loan. The expedient of paper money was tried in every form and to an unlimited extent, with the usual result that it depreciated, until at the end of the war it had practically no value. Taxes paid in such money naturally were of little avail, and in the last year of the war the chief resource was a tax in kind, of one tenth of various agricultural products. It was a reversion to the age of barter.

As the war went on, one power after another was con- Concentra-centrated in the central government of the Confederacy, tion. until it came to wield more absolute control than any government in United States territory had ever exercised. Lovers of state rights, like Governor Brown of Georgia, protested; in North Carolina a peace candidate for governor received twenty thousand votes. To meet more violent opposition, Congress suspended the *habeas corpus*, and political arrests were made. Necessity forced the government founded in protest against the centralization of the national government to centralize in itself powers hitherto undreamed of. In a report of April 28, 1864, the Confederate Secretary of War said: "The whole military population capable of bearing arms, from seventeen to fifty, is either marshaled to the field or organized in reserves, ready to be summoned. One third of the currency of the Confederacy has been annulled, and taxation of unprecedented amount has been exacted from all values. One tenth of the production in kind has been claimed without pay, and besides, the residue and all property has been subjected to seizure and conversion for public use at moderate rates of just compensation. The railroads, the great means of internal trade and commerce, are made primarily subservient to the necessities of government. Even the great writ of personal liberty is suspended in cases requisite to preclude evasion of military service, to repress uprisings of disaffection or disloyalty. In short, by their representatives, the people, not reluctantly but eagerly and fearful rather of shortcoming than excess, have through regular constitutional action commanded for their country and its cause the labor, property, and lives of all." It is a tribute to the political adaptability of the population, that this unwonted system was carried out so successfully as to throw almost the last ounce of weight into the contest. When the war was over the accumulated capital of two hundred and fifty years had been swept away, except that represented by the education of the people, the land, and such improvements of real estate as survived devastation.

The northern army.

In the North the military spirit was less developed than in the South. Particularly in the West, men were restive under discipline. They were, however, as willing to fight as were the southerners, and they were better educated. Their mechanical ability and inventiveness was a constant resource. The self-reliance and fearless originality of the frontier soldiery sometimes rescued armies from perilous positions into which their inexperienced generals led them. The mechanics of the East could repair and run railroads and telegraphs and build earthworks as well as fight. As the war went on discipline improved, the less effective of the volunteer generals were withdrawn from important positions, commands were given to those who proved themselves capable and to officers from the regular army, and the troops became progressively better. The northern army showed more improvement during the four years than the southern. The supply of men was always ample. Although the Federal government was forced to resort to conscription in 1863, it was because the attractions of industry were so strong. More votes were cast in the northern states in the presidential election of 1864 than in 1860. The North received the equivalent of three years' service from 1,556,678 men, and probably over 2,500,000 enlistments were made. While the South was drawing all ages into her armies, the North was able to rely upon her youth ; nearly one half the enlistments were of men under twenty-one.

Owing to the youth of the majority who entered the northern army, industry was less cramped than in the South. In fact every year saw the agricultural frontier pressed farther westward. Mining discoveries drew thousands to Nevada and Colorado. In the East manufacturing grew apace. Woolens and iron goods were produced in greater quantities than ever before. New industries, such as silk making, developed on a large scale. Throughout New England, New York, and Pennsylvania, factories arose, and the great manufacturing cities of the West, Cleveland, Cincinnati, Chicago, and St. Louis, were prosperous. Trade was not seriously disturbed. The North was to a large extent a self-sufficing community, and it remained open to the trade of the world. The loss of the southern market was made up by the increased demands for the army ; and where there was a derangement of industry, enlistment was a refuge from unemployment. Only in the Ohio valley was transportation disturbed, and there connection with the East, both directly by continuous rail route and indirectly by rail to the Lakes and thence by boat, was improved. The western armies, moreover, ate more than the South had previously taken, while the surplus products of the Lake region, from which a large part of the armies came, were demanded to supply the dearth caused by bad harvests in Europe. This occurrence of bad harvests in England and France was particularly opportune. Before the war the North imported more from Europe than it exported thereto. The balance was paid by bills of exchange given by Southerners who bought northern goods, and their bills were met in England by the southern cotton. Now that the South neither pur-

Northern industry.

chased from the North nor exported cotton to Europe, financial relations would have been strained had it not been for this sudden demand for northern wheat which afforded a credit balance in England to meet our payments due for our European imports. On the whole, while the war brought economic distress into tens of thousands of homes, the majority of the people did not feel any great distress, and the North was probably richer in 1865 than in 1860. The prices of farm products rose just about sufficiently to offset the decline in the value of money; those of manufactured goods rose somewhat more rapidly; the wages of labor, somewhat less. The farmer, therefore, was as well off as usual, the laborer less so, the manufacturer prospered.

Administration. In the matter of administration the Federal government had the advantage of retaining the capital. Aside from this, however, it was on fairly equal terms with the Confederacy. Buchanan had pursued the policy of dividing general appointments as evenly as possible between North and South, and the Confederacy was able to draw into its service a goodly proportion of the men experienced in government affairs. Of those that remained, by far the greater number were removed by Lincoln. Never before, even under Jackson, had there been so clean a sweep as in 1861. The prevailing motive in selecting their successors, moreover, was political. The spoils system was still in full vigor, and its principles for some time controlled the majority of appointments even in the volunteer military service. The cabinet was framed with the same view. It contained all Lincoln's rivals for the nomination: Seward as Secretary of State, Chase at the Treasury, Bates of Missouri as Attorney-General, Smith of Indiana for the Interior, and Cameron of Pennsylvania for War. The remaining members were Welles of Connecticut for the Navy and Montgomery Blair of Washington as Postmaster-General, making, with Lincoln, four former Whigs and four former Democrats. This meant, to be sure, that it contained able men, but it also meant that it represented differing policies, and that even apparent harmony could be maintained only by Lincoln's rare tact and patience, and then only with some loss of efficiency. Simon Cameron, the Secretary of War, proved entirely incapable and was replaced in January, 1862, by Edwin Stanton, a War Democrat.

Upon this newly manned and discordant administration fell the task of suddenly expanding the volume of government business about twenty times. This could never have been accomplished had it not been for the assistance of the state administrations, which during the first part of the war undertook the greater portion of the task of raising and equipping the troops. The "War Governors" were a group of remarkably efficient men, and they played a larger part in the national life during the war than governors had taken since the Confederation. They included such men as Andrew of Massachusetts, Curtin of Pennsylvania, Morton of Indiana, and Randall of Wisconsin. Private citizens, men and women, also contributed their services generously. The United States Sanitary Commission, a private body, took a leading part in providing for the health and comfort of the soldiers. Business talent and organizing ability were common in the North, and as the war went on they were more and more placed at the disposal of the government, so that by 1863 the administration of public business was running smoothly, and by 1864 one was scarcely conscious of the tremendous readjustment which had been made. *State and private aid.*

The financial problem of the North is of more interest than that in the South, because the situation was not so desperate and there was greater choice of means. The results, moreover, were permanent. From the beginning much was raised by taxes, and the proportion increased as the war progressed. First came an increase in the tariff. The Republicans had stood for protection, and before the war *Taxation.*

began, when the withdrawal of southern members of Congress left them a majority, passed the Morrill act. Year by year the duties were increased, until they reached a point far higher than ever before, and the tendency toward free trade which had prevailed since 1846 was reversed. A little later, the Hamiltonian device of an internal revenue tax was revived as it had been during the War of 1812, and was gradually made so comprehensive as to cover almost everything. A direct tax upon the states brought in little money, but an income tax, though slow to get into running order, was beginning in 1865 to pay heavy returns. In 1861 only about one tenth of the expenditure was met by taxes; in 1864, over one quarter.

Loans. Loans by the close of the war reached the enormous total of three billion. At first Chase borrowed on short term loans at high interest, hoping that the war would speedily end, and that he could refund at lower rates. Later, long term loans bearing lower, but still high, interest were arranged for. To float these enormous loans was extremely difficult. The most successful agent was Jay Cooke of Philadelphia, who had them hawked about the country like ordinary merchandise to attract the small investor. Before the loan system was well started, Congress resorted to paper money, making it legal tender for all debts except customs dues. By 1865 over four hundred million had been issued. This was the first national currency, except gold and silver, since the overthrow of the United States Bank. In 1863 Chase revived the idea of a national banking system, though in a new form. There was to be no central bank, but any five persons who could perform certain requirements could receive a national banking charter. They were to invest a certain minimum amount in government bonds, and could issue bank notes to the extent of ninety per cent of this security. In 1864 a prohibitive tax of ten per cent was levied on the currency of state banks, whereupon many of them sought national charters. Secretary Chase defended this notable reversion from Jacksonian policies, on the ground that it would create a market for bonds. It was, however, but one of the many extensions of national power to which the war was forcing the North as well as the South. Hamiltonian and Whig principles prevailed in the Republican party, and were slowly coming to do so in the whole North. The state banks had been hard hit in 1857, and the financial crisis of 1861, caused by the nonpayment of southern debts in 1861 and by the quick decline of southern state bonds which were used as security for much currency in the West, had thoroughly discredited them. National regulation was demanded, and the war turned a rising ground swell of nationalistic reaction into a tidal wave.

By 1865 the volume of national legal tender currency had become several times larger than that it replaced. In addition, hundreds of millions of small treasury notes had been issued, and postage stamps, national fractional paper currency, and private and municipal promises to pay, known as " shin plasters," passed from hand to hand. There was a plethora of currency, and depreciation was heavy and fluctuating. In 1861 the banks suspended specie payment, and in the spring of 1864 the premium on gold was seventy-five per cent; in one crisis in July, it reached one hundred and eighty-three per cent ; one paper dollar could purchase about thirty-five cents in gold. Speculation flourished and prices rose. The situation was particularly hard for borrowers, like the government, who were forced to create obligations, which, if paid under normal conditions, would stand for much more than had been received for them. Nevertheless the government was able to preserve order in its finances, and every year saw money spent for purposes not absolutely necessary.

Business conditions.

In the great conflict between these two sections, the South was fighting in self-defense, the purpose of the North was to reduce the South. The first essential to the subjec-

The blockade.

tion of the South was the control of the sea, because of its
economic dependence upon the outside world. If the situation had been reversed, the control of the sea, while still
important, would have been less vital, because the North
was to so great an extent self-sufficing. On April 19, 1861,
Lincoln declared the whole southern coast blockaded. The
United States navy contained forty-two vessels in commission, many not immediately available, with which to patrol
3549 miles of coast containing nearly two hundred harbors.
The Secretary of the Navy was Gideon Welles, of Connecticut, who proved to be an admirable administrator and who
was ably assisted by Gustavus Fox, the assistant secretary.
The Confederates at the outset had only a few warships
seized in southern navy yards. With practically no specially
built vessels to encounter, it was possible for the national
government speedily to fit out merchant vessels for the
blockade service, and the navy was soon increased largely
from this source. New war vessels were rapidly built, and
by the close of the war the United States had 671 vessels,
of 510,396 tons, mounting 4610 guns, and manned by 51,000
men. This number was made up of ships old and new,
propelled by sail, by steam, and by both combined, of ships
armored and unarmored, and suited for ocean, river, or coast
defense. Up to November 1, 1864, the navy captured 1379
vessels. It was not, however, primarily intended to make
captures, but to prevent trade. In order to assist the navy
in this purpose, strategic positions on the southern coast
were speedily occupied. Fort Monroe on the Chesapeake
and Fort Pickens at Pensacola were never lost by the
national government. On August 28, 1861, Hatteras Inlet
was seized; on November 7, 1861, Port Royal in South
Carolina. In February, 1862, Roanoke Island was captured;
in April, Fort Pulaski at the mouth of the Savannah River,
in May, Norfolk, Virginia, and also the great port of the
southern states, New Orleans. The chief ports remaining

in the hands of the Confederates were Wilmington, North Carolina, Charleston, Mobile, and Galveston. From these numbers of light swift vessels ran the blockade to ports in the English West Indies, and some goods were brought in through Matamoras and Brownsville on the Mexican border. Such trade, however, was very small in volume and came to be restricted almost entirely to army necessities. The capture of Wilmington, January 15, 1865, sealed the Confederacy to the outside world.

The Confederate government hoped to break the block-ade by the building of armored vessels, capable of driving away the wooden blockading fleet from the various ports. *Merrimac and Monitor.* On March 8, 1862, this ambition seemed attained when the *Virginia*, made over from the *Merrimac*, one of the United States vessels captured at Norfolk, sank and disabled several ships of the national fleet in Hampton Roads. The next day, however, the *Monitor*, an ironclad designed by John Ericsson and embodying many new and revolutionary features of naval construction, appeared and engaged the *Virginia* in a battle which, though technically drawn, actually proved decisive, as the *Virginia* did not care to renew the contest. After this the Federal naval supremacy was not seriously in question.

It was mainly, however, upon the intervention of foreign nations that the South relied to secure the opening of its *Attitude of England.* ports. Russia, Denmark, and Italy were friendly to the North, but the rest of Europe looked to England for leadership. In that country sentiment was divided. In general the conservative classes favored the South, or perhaps more exactly were pleased at the prospect of a division of the United States, because of the increased weight such a division would give to England in American questions. The Liberal party, which was in control under Lord Palmerston, contained many friends of the North, such as Bright and Forster. A large faction, however, at the beginning of the war was inclined to support the South. Such men as Gladstone saw in the attitude of the national government a tyrannical attempt to govern an unwilling community. They were opposed to slavery, but Lincoln emphatically stated that the purpose of the war was the preservation of the Union and not the abolition of slavery. The greater number of public men apparently desired delay, and the adoption of such a policy as would secure the friendship of the winning side.

Confederate policy.

The policy of the Confederate government was to force the hand of England. It was hoped that by depriving England of southern cotton, the cotton mill districts would be distressed, and would force the government to open the southern ports. It was also believed that the southern policy of a low tariff would appeal to England. In addition the Confederate government accepted those portions of the "Declaration of Paris" of 1856, which declared that a blockade to be legal must be effective, and that a neutral flag should protect the cargo even if the latter belonged to an enemy. This latter policy should be taken in connection with the building of a number of Confederate cruisers, the most important being the *Alabama* and the *Shenandoah*, in England. These vessels were not of a character to break the blockade, but were swift enough to overtake and powerful enough to capture most merchant vessels. Their activities constituted such a danger to the American merchant marine that insurance and freight rates were pushed higher and higher. The English vessels, not being liable to capture, secured the trade which American vessels had previously carried, and by the close of the war the American merchant marine had almost disappeared from the high seas. While other causes, which will be noted later, contributed to this result, the South believed that its policy was the main cause of the change, and that England should reciprocate favors by declaring the blockade ineffective, and, therefore, illegal.

In 1863 Jefferson Davis, incensed at England's failure to act, threatened to put neutral vessels with enemy's goods under the ban, but the threat was as ineffective as the bribe.

While these southern policies were not successful in forc- Northern
diplomacy. ing the hand of England, serious and delicate questions were continually arising between the Federal government and England, which might have resulted in war. Probably the volume of business between the northern ports and England was a factor for peace, especially the immense exports of American wheat which were necessary to supplement the bad harvests from which England was then suffering. The English Minister at Washington, Lord Lyons, was also a quieting influence; and still more the diplomacy of Charles Francis Adams, United States Minister at London, was of the greatest importance. Northern sentiment, however, was irascible. There was a deep-seated feeling that England should have favored the North, and small occasions became Belligerency. pregnant of war. On May 13, 1861, England proclaimed its neutrality, thus acknowledging that a state of war existed. Northern sentiment, holding that a rebellion and not a war was in progress, took exception to this action, although the Supreme Court later in the case of *Amy Warwick* decided that the President's proclamation of April 19, declaring the blockade, marked the beginning of the war. The United States government endeavored to perfect the blockade by seizing vessels on their way from Europe to Nassau, Matamoras, and other distributing points from which goods were sent through the blockade. This action was based on the Continuous
voyages. idea that such voyages were actually continuous, the mere transshipment not being sufficient to constitute a new voyage, and that most of the goods so carried were actually contraband. Such seizures were decidedly questionable in international law. The principle involved resembled that of the "Rule of 1756," against the enforcement of which by Great Britain during the Napoleonic wars, the United States had protested, but during the Civil War only vessels carrying contraband were seized. Some of the cases arising were, after the war, decided against the government by the United States Supreme Court, and others by the Arbitration Commission of 1871. During the war, however, the policy was carried out without involving foreign complications.

Trent affair.

The subject of the right of search also came up. The most important case was that of the *Trent*, an English vessel on a voyage between two neutral ports, from which Captain Wilkes, commanding the United States ship *San Jacinto*, removed James M. Mason and John Slidell, Confederate commissioners on the way to Europe. Immense popular enthusiasm over this act in the North, and intense popular indignation in England, seemed about Christmas time, 1861, to render war inevitable. It was averted by the good sense and tact of such men as Prince Albert and Lord Russell on the one side, and Charles Sumner and Adams on the other. The commissioners were surrendered. Their seizure had been in contradiction to all previous American policy, and their surrender strengthened the traditional American policy on the subject of search, although Seward did not take the full advantage of his opportunity in committing England to the earlier American policy. England's lax interpretation of her neutral duties, which allowed the building of Confederate war vessels in English ports, aroused the just indignation of the North. A crisis was reached on this sub-

Violation of neutrality.

ject in the summer of 1863, when certain fighting rams were under construction in English ship-building yards, and Lord Russell professed to be unable to find evidence that they were destined for the Confederacy in spite of general popular knowledge to that effect. Adams wrote him: "It is superfluous for me to point out to your Lordship that this means war." Just before this note was sent, the English government had actually taken steps to prevent the rams from falling into belligerent hands.

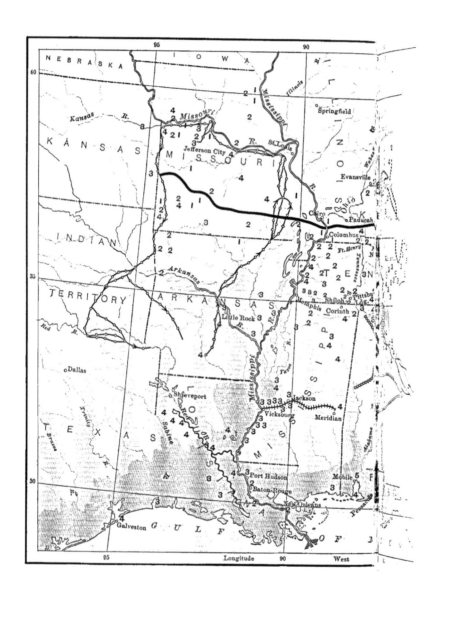

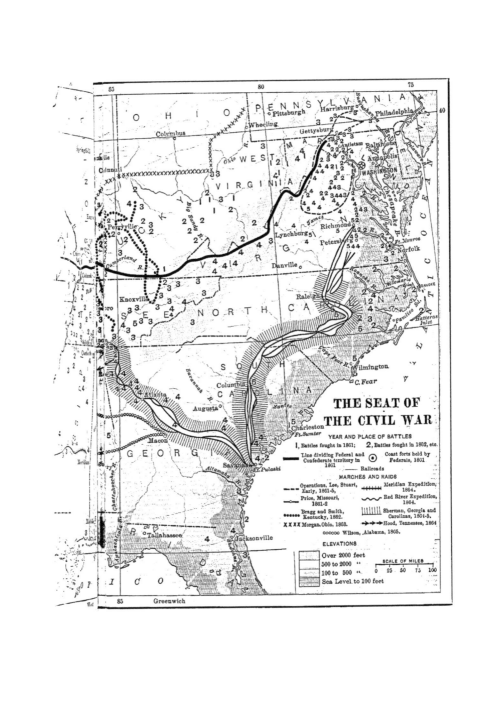

THE SEAT OF
THE CIVIL WAR

YEAR AND PLACE OF BATTLES

1, Battles fought in 1861;   2, Battles fought in 1862, etc.

⬛ Line dividing Federal and
Confederate territory in
1861

⊙ Coast forts held by
Federals, 1861

▬▬▬ Railroads

MARCHES AND RAIDS

━ ━ ━ Operations, Lee, Stuart,
Early, 1861-5,

⚬⚬⚬ Price, Missouri,
1861-2

•••••• Bragg and Smith,
Kentucky, 1862.

XXXX Morgan, Ohio, 1863.

+++++ Meridian Expedition,
1864.

〰〰 Red River Expedition,
1864.

||||||| Sherman, Georgia and
Carolinas, 1864-5.

➤➤➤ Hood, Tennessee, 1864

ooooo Wilson, Alabama, 1865.

ELEVATIONS

Over 2000 feet
500 to 2000 "
100 to 500 "
Sea Level to 100 feet

SCALE OF MILES
0   25   50   75   100

In fact by this time English public sentiment would not British inter-
vention. have sustained the government in a policy hostile to the North. Really, danger had been greatest in the autumn of 1862, and the decision had been due rather to domestic English conditions than to diplomacy. At that time the question of recognizing the independence of the Southern Confederacy had been seriously discussed, but the cabinet had decided to delay action. On January 1, 1863, came the definite Emancipation Proclamation, and with the adoption of emancipation by the North, the possibility of English intervention in favor of the South had passed away. England had become too thoroughly committed to that policy to ally herself formally with a slave power fight· ing to maintain slavery. The resolutions relative to the recognition of the Confederacy, laid over for consideration by the cabinet in October, 1862, were never taken up. Napoleon III, who was taking advantage of the temporary division of the United States to establish an empire in Mexico under French protection, and who hoped to maintain his hold by securing the permanence of that division, did indeed, in 1863, endeavor to force the hand of the English government. His efforts, however, were unsuccessful, and as he did not venture to act alone, the Civil War passed without breaking the relations between the Federal government and foreign powers.

Deprived of foreign assistance by the failure of its diplo- The war in
the East. matic policy, and cut off from foreign intercourse by the blockade, the South was left to encounter the three- or four-fold strength of the North. The actual contest was fought out on land. The vast bulk of the Appalachian mountains, one hundred and fifty miles wide, and crossed in the South by but a single railroad, that from Richmond to Chattanooga by way of Lynchburg, divided the field of operations. Though troops were often shifted from one side to the other, closely combined operations were impossible, and the war

in the West was almost independent of that in the East. In the latter region the two capitals, Washington and Richmond, were the objective points. The latter was better placed, for its defense actually protected the country back of it; while the Confederate forces, following the mountain valleys, several times passed to the rear of Washington. Both Washington and Richmond proved impregnable to direct attack. The Confederates, although winning battles both in 1861 and 1862 at Bull Run or Manassas, only twenty miles from Washington, failed to attack that city. Direct attacks on Richmond were defeated at Bull Run in 1861, at Fredericksburg in 1863, at Chancellorsville in 1863, and at Cold Harbor in 1864. This situation forced the rival commanders to resort to more complex strategy. The northern fleet having command of the mouths of the Virginia rivers, McClellan, the commander of the northern forces, in 1862 decided to move against Richmond by way of the peninsula between the James and the York rivers. By this move Washington and its western connections were exposed to an attack down the Shenandoah valley. Lee, who at this time was given charge of Confederate operations in Virginia, caused "Stonewall" Jackson to threaten Washington from this direction, and thereby caused the national government to retain a considerable portion of its army for the defense of the capital. Swiftly and secretly Jackson turned back and united with Lee, who fell upon McClellan and in the "Seven Days' Battles" at Mechanicsville, Gaines' Mills, Savage's Station, Frayser's Farm, White Oak Swamp, and Malvern Hill, drove him back and saved Richmond. McClellan withdrew, and Lee, following up his successes, crossed the Potomac above Washington and invaded Maryland. After a junction of the northern armies, Lee was defeated at Antietam on September 17, 1862. In 1863 Lee again invaded the North by way of the mountain valleys, some of his troops penetrating Pennsylvania to the bank of the Susquehanna opposite

Harrisburg. Again, however, all the Federal forces of the
East combined under General Meade, and Lee was defeated
at Gettysburg, on July 3, 1863. The situation thus favored
defense, and for four years neither side was able to gain
decisive advantage.

In 1864 General Grant, who was now called from the
West to take supreme command, adopted the policy of attri-
tion, based on the fact that the North could lose more men
than the South, and that fighting, therefore, even if not decisive, was of advantage to the North. With greatly superior
forces he fought Lee through the "Wilderness" between the
Rapidan and North Anna rivers, then down to the James,
and crossing that river, besieged Petersburg, which commanded the railway connection between Richmond and Wilmington, the chief port for blockade runners. In the meantime Sheridan defeated Early at Cedar Creek, October 19,
1864, and devastated the Shenandoah valley which had for so
long served the Confederates both as a granary and as a door
for their invasions of the North. With this outlet closed to
military operations, the northern forces united. By hard
fighting and by using his superior forces to extend his lines
beyond those of Lee, Grant forced the evacuation of Petersburg and Richmond on April 3, 1865. Sheridan, with the
left or southern wing of Grant's army, by rapid marching
cut Lee off from the South, securing the Danville railroad
on April 5. On April 8 he passed Lee's army and established
himself on the Lynchburg railroad just west of Appomattox
Court House, where Lee lay. On April 9 Lee surrendered
and the war in the East came to an end.

Grant and Lee.

In the West, the northern objective was the southern
transportation system, and the strategic features were the
rivers, railroads, and mountains. The first important
movement was an expedition by a combined river fleet and
army under the command of General Grant up the Cumberland and Tennessee rivers. This resulted in the capture of

The war in the West.

Forts Henry and Donelson in February, 1862. The expedition pushed on, capturing Nashville on the Cumberland and reaching northern Alabama by way of the Tennessee.

Corinth. The real objective was the little village of Corinth in northern Mississippi, which was one of the most important railroad junctions in the South, lying at the meeting point of roads to Memphis, Vicksburg, Mobile, and Chattanooga. Corinth was situated about twenty miles from the Tennessee River, and the Union army under Grant disembarked at Pittsburg Landing and encamped between the landing and Shiloh Church. Here it was attacked by a Confederate army led by Generals Albert Sidney Johnston and Beauregard in April, 1862. It maintained its position, however, and after a slow advance under Halleck captured Corinth on May 30. This capture cut the shortest route from Richmond to Vicksburg. It meant that the Union armies had penetrated almost two hundred miles into hostile territory, and for a time it seemed that the movement had been premature. The Confederates assumed the initiative all along the line during the summer of 1862. Forces under Bragg and Kirby Smith, debouching from the mountain valleys of eastern Tennessee, the one by way of Chattanooga and the other by Cumberland Gap, invaded Tennessee and Kentucky and threatened Louisville and Cincinnati. Another Confederate army threatened to retake Corinth, and all these movements were in progress while Lee was making his invasion of Maryland. The fortunes of the Confederacy were at high tide. In the early autumn, however, all these movements were checked; Lee at Antietam, September 17, Price and Van Dorn at Corinth, October 4, and Bragg at Perryville, October 8. The Union captures were thus made secure.

Vicksburg. In the meantime a movement had been going on to open up the Mississippi for the double purpose of cutting the Confederacy in two and of restoring to the northwestern states the freedom of its navigation. Joint naval and military operations had by the summer of 1862 reduced the Confederate positions on the lower Mississippi as far north as Port Hudson; on the upper river as far south as Vicksburg. The capture of this latter fortress was one of the most difficult achievements of the war. It was accomplished by Grant on July 4, 1863, the day after Lee was defeated at Gettysburg. Port Hudson fell on the ninth, and the Confederacy was split into two unequal parts. The next important position was Chattanooga, which commanded the valley of eastern Tennessee and the shortest railway route between Richmond and Atlanta. It was captured on September 9, 1863, after a skillful campaign conducted by General Rosecrans, who had won appreciation by his defense of Corinth the previous year. The capture of this key of the southwest was so serious a blow to the Confederacy that Lee sent Longstreet with one of the three corps of the Army of Northern Virginia to assist Bragg in its recovery. Bragg attacked Rosecrans, defeated him at Chickamauga, and blockaded the northern forces in Chattanooga, where they remained for a time almost in a state of siege. Grant was now sent to take command at Chattanooga and by the end of November had defeated the Confederates in the battles of Lookout Mountain and Missionary Ridge, and secured the hold on Chattanooga. *Chattanooga.*

Up to this time, Tennessee had been brought under the control of the national government and the western transportation system of the Confederacy had been crippled; but the cotton belt, the most populous and the richest region of the South, protected from attack from the coast by the pine barriers, and on the interior by the mountains and waste stretches of northern Alabama, had felt the war only indirectly. Alexander Stephens could say on March 10, 1864, "The heart of our country has never been reached by them; they have as yet been able to break only the *Atlanta.*

outer shell of the Confederacy." The next military task of the North was to penetrate the mountains and capture Atlanta, the most important railroad center left to the Confederates and the most important manufacturing city of the South. This task fell to General Sherman, as Grant was called to be commander in chief of the Union forces, with personal command against Lee. After a long, hard campaign between Sherman and General Joseph E. Johnston, Atlanta fell, September 3, 1864. This indeed broke the shell of the Confederacy, the rich central plain was open to invasion, and the nature of the country favored the largest battalions. General Hood, in command of the Confederate forces, now abandoned defense and boldly and desperately invaded Tennessee. At Nashville, on December 16, 1864, he was overwhelmed by General Thomas, known as the "Rock of Chickamauga," in the only battle of the Civil War where a large army was effectually destroyed. Sherman meantime marched boldly from Atlanta to the coast, his army spreading a path of destruction sixty miles wide through the very heart and center of the Confederacy. On December 20 he reached the coast at Savannah, capturing that city and sending notice of it to Lincoln as a "Christmas gift." Turning northward, he swept through the Carolinas, leaving a broad belt of devastation behind him. On April 26, 1865, he received the surrender of Joseph E. Johnston, who included in the terms of the capitulation all the Confederate forces still in arms. There was some fighting in May, but Johnston's surrender practically marked the end of the war.

Close of the war.

The South had contested every step and did not yield until the great army of the West had swung round to within thirty miles of the southern boundary of Virginia and ninety miles of the place of Lee's surrender.

BIBLIOGRAPHICAL NOTES

Lincoln's annual messages furnish very satisfactory accounts Sources. of activity from year to year. The *Diary* of Gideon Welles gives an intimate account of cabinet problems. The *Diary and Correspondence of Salmon P. Chase* (American Hist. Assoc., *Report*, 1902, vol. II) is also of especial value. Recollections and reminiscences are innumerable, but for the most part are valuable only when used most carefully and in combination. The annual reports of the secretaries of war and of the navy are usable.

Adams, C. F., *C. F. Adams*, chs. XI, XII, XIV–XVII. Bullock, J. D, *Secret Service of the Confederate States in Europe.* Currey, J. S. M., *Civil Government of the Confederate States.* Davis, J., *Confederate Government.* Henderson, G. T. R., *Stonewall Jackson and the American Civil War.* Long, A. L., *Lee.* Paxson, F. L., *The Civil War.* Pollard, E. A., *Lost Cause.* Rhodes, *United States*, V, ch. XXVIII. Schwab, J. C., *The Confederate States of America.*

Historical accounts. The South during the war.

Fite, E. D., *Social and Industrial Conditions in the North during the Civil War.* Hart, *Chase*, chs. VIII, IX, X, XI. Nicolay and Hay, *Lincoln*, vol. VI, chs. V–VIII, XVIII, XIX; vol. X, ch. IV. Rhodes, *United States*, vol. III, chs. XV, XVI; vol. IV; vol. V, chs. XXIV–XXVII. Weeden, W. B., *War Government, Federal and State.*

The North during the war.

Alexander, E. P., *Military Memoirs.* Dodge, T. A., *Bird's-eye View of our Civil War.* Formby, J., *American Civil War.* Grant, U. S., *Personal Memoirs.* Ropes, J. C., *Story of the Civil War.* War of the Rebellion, *Official Records, Atlas.*

Military operations.

Adams, C. F., *C. F. Adams*, 144–357, and *Studies Military and Diplomatic*, Nos. 9 and 10. Callahan, J. M., *Diplomatic History of the Southern Confederacy.* Moore, J. B., *Arbitrations*, I, ch. XIV, and *Digest of International Law*, VII, 383–390, 698–744. Woolsey, T. D., *International Law*, §§ 163–203.

Diplomacy.

CHAPTER XXIII

POLITICS DURING THE WAR

Centralizing legislation. DURING no other four years of United States history has so much important general legislation been passed as during the Civil War. The tariff schedules were based on the idea of protection instead of revenue, a comprehensive system of internal revenue was adopted, currency was brought under national control and to a large extent banking also. The policy of making profit out of the public lands was in the Homestead Act of 1862 finally abandoned for that of granting one hundred and sixty acres to actual settlers at the cost of survey. In the same year the policy of land grants to railroads was pressed to its greatest extension in the provisions for the proposed roads to the Pacific. The same year also saw the establishment of a National Bureau of Agriculture and the granting of script redeemable in public land to all the states for the establishment of colleges of agriculture.

Dominance of the North. This extension of the functions of the national government marked to a large extent the reversal of the legislative programs upon which Jefferson had been elected, which Jackson had advocated, and for which the Cotton South had more lately stood. It marked a return to many of the constructive views of Hamilton, John Quincy Adams, and Clay. The democratization of the government remained, but there was a reaction as to the policy which the government should pursue. Some of these measures were passed under the pressure of war necessity. Others were passed because the withdrawal of the southern congressmen left the North, where the majority had generally favored a stronger govern-

ment, in control. The Morrill tariff, the first step in the
new protective system, for instance, was passed on March 2,
1861, before the war began but when the secession of seven
states opposed to protection had left protectionists in control. This centralizing legislation was passed with comparatively little debate; it did not constitute the basis for
party division. The question remained open as to whether
it would be repealed when the war was over and the southern
representatives returned to their places.

In determining party alignment during this period the
most important issues were those growing out of the question of the Union, the problems of slavery and reconstruction, and the administration of the war, particularly the
exercise of executive power. As has already been pointed
out, the sentiment in favor of fighting to preserve the Union
was very general.

Just after the firing on Fort Sumter it seemed as if "Union"
the war might be conducted without the interference of party.
party politics. In the autumn elections a "Union" party
appeared in most of the states, the attempt being made to
combine every one in support of the administration. Generally the Republicans indorsed a Union ticket. The majority of the Democrats, however, preferred to keep up their
party organization, partly because the national Republican
administration was removing so many Democrats from office.
In some cases Republicans also ran independently of Unionists. The Union party failed to put an end to party
dissension, but in general it took the place of "Republican"
as the designation of the supporters of the administration,
and it enabled many to cast their influence on that side
without formally indorsing the tenets of Republicanism.

The administration party, whether it be called Union Conserva-
or Republican, was made up of men who had been identified Radicals.
with many different factions and parties, and it was a delicate task to adjust their claims and prejudices. As the war

progressed, however, old divisions became less keen, and
their place was taken by a new division between those who
were radical and those who were conservative on the question of slavery.   Chase and Sumner believed that to be the
real question at issue, and wished to declare boldly for
emancipation.   Generals in the field with strong abolitionist
views, like Frémont and Hunter, strove to force the hand
of the administration.   Seward, always apprehensive when
vigorous action was proposed, became more and more
opposed to taking any decisive measures looking to abolition, and became the leader of the Conservatives.   Lincoln
desired to free the negroes, but he realized the necessity of
placating the border states as well as the seriousness of the
negro problem apart from the question of slavery.   He,
therefore, for some time steadily maintained the rights of
the loyal slave owners.   He made the preservation of the
Union his guiding purpose.

Growth of
abolitionist
sentiment.

The progress of the war, however, was marked by a rapid
development of the antislavery sentiment.   The eighteen
hundred thousand Republicans who voted for Lincoln in 1860
were far from being abolitionists at that time.   It was against
the extension, not the existence, of slavery that they voted.
On the other hand the twenty-two hundred thousand voters in
the loyal states, who in 1860 had opposed Lincoln and thereby
expressed themselves as willing to allow slavery extension,
had so voted, for the most part, not through any friendliness
toward slavery, but because of their desire for peace.   When
peace ceased to be, a new situation confronted the country
and most men had to readjust their ideas.   In July, 1861,
Congress almost unanimously voted for Mr. Crittenden's
resolution: "That the present deplorable civil war . . . is
not urged upon our part in any spirit of oppression, nor for
any purpose of conquest or subjugation, nor purpose of overthrowing or interfering with the rights or established institutions of the states."   This very session of Congress, how-

ever, passed a confiscation act declaring forfeited the claims of owners to slaves employed against the United States. This first attack on slavery was rapidly followed up. In the spring of 1862 slavery was prohibited in the territories, — in taking which action Congress overruled the Dred Scott decision, — and emancipation with compensation for the owners was provided for in the District of Columbia. In July a new confiscation act provided for the freeing of the slaves of all those convicted of treason, and some other classes of southern citizens. Antislavery sentiment increased in volume and in insistence with every passing month. In August, Horace Greeley, the editor of the powerful *New York Tribune*, addressed to the President an article headed, "The Prayer of Twenty Millions," calling for immediate emancipation. In fact, now that war was actually in progress, practicality joined with idealism in urging action. Futile indeed would war have proved if its end saw still in existence the institution that had brought it on. The practical man who before the war had been most strongly for compromise or even surrender to southern claims, now became anxious to clear up the whole problem. This to a considerable extent accounts for the steady development of radical sentiment in the North between 1861 and 1867. Men wished to take advantage of the opportunity to accomplish more and more things which they desired, but for which they would never have thought of going to war.

Lincoln realized this growing sentiment and during the spring and summer of 1862 perfected his plan. With regard to the slaves in the loyal states he recommended emancipation by state action, the national government assisting in the compensation of the owners. With regard to slaves in the Confederate states, except certain regions already recovered by the national forces, he resolved on immediate action based on his executive power. On July 22 he read an emancipation proclamation to his cabinet, but did not make it public until

Emancipation.

September 22, when the battle of Antietam assured the safety of Washington and prevented his action from being regarded as a movement of desperation. His explanation of his decision was that emancipation had become necessary for the preservation of the Union; it was a war measure. His procedure rested upon his military authority as commander-in-chief of the army — a possibility which had been pointed out by John Quincy Adams. It took the form of a proclamation announcing that unless the states in rebellion returned to their allegiance before January 1, 1863, all slaves therein should become free. This proclamation applied only to the persons of the slaves, and not to the institution of slavery itself. The state laws remained, and, unless further action should be taken, slavery might be reëstablished. A third portion of Lincoln's plan, the colonization of the freed slaves outside the United States, proved to be a complete failure, in spite of the attempts of Seward to arrange for their reception in various semitropical countries.

Democratic position.   The issuance of the Emancipation Proclamation undoubtedly prevented the separation of the Radicals from the administration party, and Lincoln also succeeded in holding the Conservatives. The Democrats, however, maintained their opposition. This was based not only on their disapproval of emancipation, but on their criticism of Lincoln's interpretation of his constitutional power in other ways. He had suspended the writ of *habeas corpus* on his own authority, and arbitrary arrests were numerous and were not confined to districts where hostilities were in progress. On September 24, 1862, he renewed the suspension in a proclamation which made the discouragement of enlistment a crime. Promptly hundreds of men in all parts of the North were arrested for speaking and writing against the war, and were imprisoned without trial or were tried by military tribunals. To many, freedom of speech and political liberty seemed endangered. Benjamin R. Curtis, formerly of the Supreme Court, and Joel

Parker, of the Harvard Law School, attacked Lincoln as a despot. Congress later in the year authorized the suspension of the writ, but this did not silence criticism. The Democrats also attacked the policy of compensated emancipation, and the military policy of the administration. Possibly this last was the most potent cause of public dissatisfaction, for the war was lasting longer than had been expected.

Under such circumstances congressional and state elections were held in the autumn of 1862. On the whole these elections went heavily against the Union party. Horatio Seymour, a Democrat, was elected governor of New York, and the Democrats were victorious in New Jersey, Pennsylvania, Ohio, Indiana, Illinois, and Wisconsin. This success of the Democrats was not, however, sufficient to affect seriously the course of the administration, or the development of national policy. Congress continued to have a majority of Republicans and Unionists, and only in New Jersey did the Democrats obtain full control of a state government. In the other states mentioned, they controlled some branch of the government and were able to some extent to prevent action, but not to put through their own measures. Their negative influence would have been more important earlier in the war, but by this time the national administration had worked out its own machinery better and was more independent of state assistance. Their power was chiefly exerted in refusing to grant state money for bounties to encourage enlistment, in opposition, generally futile, to the national draft, and in refusing to allow soldiers in the field to vote. *Election of 1862.*

More important was the fact that the possession of power brought clearly to light the existence of two factions within the Democratic party. One faction, which was headed by Governor Seymour and to which General McClellan belonged, believed in supporting the war, but in protesting against the use of unconstitutional powers. Their protests were rather in the way of a record to be used later, than actual interfer- *Democratic factions.*

ence, though Governor Seymour actually failed to give the national government as complete support as he perhaps should have, in enforcing the draft in New York city in July, 1863, when there was dangerous rioting against the draft officers. The leader of the other faction of Democrats was Clement L. Vallandigham of Ohio. His purpose was immediate peace, without terms. His supporters came to be known as "Copperheads," and a large number of them were organized in a secret society and known first as "Knights of the Golden Circle" and after 1864, as "Sons of Liberty." This faction dictated the legislative policy in Ohio, Indiana, and Illinois, and thwarted the national administration in every way possible. In 1863 Vallandigham ran for the governorship of Ohio. He had been convicted in 1862 under Lincoln's proclamation of September 24, had been banished, and he conducted his campaign from the Canadian side of Niagara. Many of the "War Democrats" opposed him, the victories at Gettysburg and Vicksburg in the summer of 1863 strengthened the administration, and he was defeated by a hundred thousand majority.

Completion of emancipation.

The election of 1862 had little effect in checking the progress of radical ideas. Possibly it prevented the consummation of Lincoln's plan for compensated emancipation in the border states, but the movement to free the slaves there, nevertheless, went on. It was fostered by the enlistment of negro troops, which was first authorized in 1862, the law finally providing for the freeing of slaves who enlisted, with their families, and the payment of a certain sum to their masters. In 1864 the fugitive slave law of 1850 was repealed. In the same year Maryland and Missouri adopted emancipation. In January, 1865, by the necessary two-thirds majority, Congress recommended to the states a thirteenth amendment to the Constitution: "Neither slavery nor involuntary servitude . . . shall exist within the United States or any place subject to their jurisdiction." In December, 1865, the acceptance of this amendment by three quarters of the states was announced to Congress, and slavery ceased to exist.

In the meantime the problem of the reconstruction of the Union was beginning to absorb political attention. This question was presented from the beginning of the war by the case of Virginia. The western portion of that state, belonging to the Ohio valley, was thoroughly loyal and desired incorporation as the new and separate state of West Virginia. The division of a state, however, required the consent of the state as a whole. To secure such sanction, the members of the Virginia legislature from this region, with a few from districts in the eastern portion held by United States troops, met and organized a loyal government, which professed to represent the whole state. This government authorized the division of the state and the erection of West Virginia. Their action was indorsed by Lincoln and by Congress, and West Virginia was admitted in 1863. The loyal government of Virginia was thereby shorn of nearly all its territory and supporters, but since it had been recognized for one purpose, logic demanded the continuance of its recognition, and it continued to be upheld by Lincoln as the legal state government of Virginia throughout the war. Reconstruction, Virginia.

As other territory was recovered, Lincoln proceeded to organize it as rapidly as possible. In 1862 he appointed Andrew Johnson as military governor of Tennessee. This became the first step in his general policy, and he subsequently appointed military governors in Louisiana and Arkansas. In restoring civil government he operated under the confiscation act, which had created penalties for treason and rebellion that involved most men in the South. On December 8, 1863, he issued a proclamation based on his pardoning power, extending amnesty to all, with the exception of certain classes, who should take a prescribed oath of allegiance. The proclamation further set forth that when as many as one tenth the number of legal voters of a state in 1860 had taken Lincoln's reconstruction policy.

such an oath to obey and support the laws of Congress and the Emancipation Proclamation, they might organize a state government, which should so alter the state law and constitution as to abolish slavery. He would then recognize such government as the legal government of the state. Such governments were organized and recognized in Tennessee, Louisiana, and Arkansas.

The Wade-Davis plan. This plan very much displeased the growing body of Radicals. Some, such as Thaddeus Stevens, Chairman of the Committee on Ways and Means in the House and leader of the Republicans in that body, desired to punish the South, to enforce the confiscation act. Others, like Charles Sumner, less bitter, desired nevertheless to secure greater guarantees for the just treatment of the negroes. Many felt that a government based on but one tenth the voters of a state was unrepublican and should not be recognized under the clause of the Constitution guaranteeing to every state a republican power of government. A bill embodying a compromise between these views, and known from its authors in the Senate and House respectively as the Wade-Davis bill, passed Congress in 1864. To this bill Lincoln applied a pocket veto, but he offered it as an alternative to his own plan in a new proclamation. He still, however, offered to recognize governments formed in accordance with his first suggestion, although, of course, his recognition would not carry with it the reception of senators and representatives by Congress and full equality in the Union.

Election of 1864. This difference of opinion led many of the Radicals, as the election of 1864 approached, to look for some candidate other than Lincoln, whom they regarded as under the influence of Seward and as hopelessly conservative. Chase, the Secretary of the Treasury, was proposed and was not unwilling. It became evident, however, that Lincoln had been successful in gauging public sentiment, and that the great body of people had confidence in him. Many, moreover, agreed with Lincoln that it was too dangerous an experiment to substitute a new man in the midst of the war. The convention which met at Baltimore pursued a conservative course. The name Union rather than Republican was employed, Lincoln was nominated for the presidency, and for the vice presidency, Andrew Johnson, a southerner and a Democrat, was chosen, to emphasize the non-partisan character of the movement. Some of the more implacable Radicals met at Cleveland and nominated John C. Frémont as a third party candidate. This nomination met with practically no response, and opposition was actually confined to the Democrats. They attempted to unite their two discordant wings. The platform was written by Vallandigham; the nominee was General George B. McClellan, a War Democrat. Before the election, Atlanta was captured and other victories seemed to promise an early peace. This favored the Union ticket, and there can be no doubt, moreover, that Lincoln's popularity was continually growing. He was re-elected by a majority of almost half a million in the popular vote, and 212 electoral votes to 21. Just one month and five days after his reinauguration on March 4, 1865, Lee surrendered and the war was practically ended.

BIBLIOGRAPHICAL NOTES

See references for Chapter **XXII**. *Sources.*

Brummer, S. D., *Political History of New York State during the Period of the Civil War,* and Porter, G. H., *Ohio Politics during the Civil War Period,* in *Columbia University Studies,* vols. XXXIX and XL. Burgess, J. W., *Civil War and the Constitution,* II, ch. XXVIII. Dunning, W. A., *Civil War and Reconstruction,* 1–62. Hosmer, J. K., *Appeal to Arms,* and *Outcome of the Civil War.* Rhodes, J. F., *United States,* vols. III, IV, V, should be used as far as possible. Whiting, W., *War Powers.* Willoughby, W. W., *Constitutional Law,* §§ 732–738. *Historical accounts. Politics.*

Adams, C. F., *Lee at Appomatox* (essay on J. Q. Adams). Cooley, T. M., *Story's Commentaries,* §§ 1923–1927. Davis, J., *Emancipation.*

Confederate Government, II, 158–193, 460–476. Pierce, E. L., *Sumner*, IV, XLVIII–L. Nicolay and Hay, *Lincoln*, IV, chs. XXII, XXIV; V, ch. XII; VI, chs. VI, VIII, XVII, XIX, XX; VIII, chs. XVI, XX; X, ch. IV.

Biographies.   Foulke, W. D., *O. P. Morton*. Gorham, G. C., *Stanton*. Hart, A. B., *Chase*. Nicolay and Hay, *Lincoln*, a monumental work by his private secretaries, covering much of the history of the war. Pearson, G. H., *J. A. Andrew*. Seward, F. W., *Seward at Washington*. Woodburn, J. A., *Thaddeus Stevens*.

CHAPTER XXIV

RECONSTRUCTION TO 1872

THE close of the war found the country confronted with **Problems of** problems almost as serious and even more complicated than **peace.** those of the war itself. First there was the necessity of reestablishing normal conditions of government in the seceded states. Then there was the problem of readjusting the relationships of the various branches of the national government, which had been so sorely strained. Again the national finances must be adjusted to conditions of peace, with as little disturbance as possible, the diplomatic questions arising from the war must be settled, and the prestige of the United States restored. Finally the South must readjust its system of industry to meet the new labor conditions involved by the freeing of the negro.

At the very outset the most deplorable calamity conceiv- **Lincoln's** able was inflicted on the country by the assassination of **assassina-** Lincoln on April 14, 1865. In order to appreciate his loss, **tion.** it is not necessary to believe that Lincoln could have saved the country the mistakes and passions of reconstruction. Certainly his sympathetic and tolerant influence would have mitigated these mistakes, while the very manner of his death aggravated the passions of the time. It is true that the Confederate government was in no wise privy to his death; it is equally true that thousands in the North believed it to be so. Even the tender and great-hearted Phillips Brooks, in his funeral sermon, said, "Solemnly, in the sight of God, I charge the murder where it belongs, on Slavery."

Lincoln was succeeded by Andrew Johnson, who **Andrew** promptly announced that he would follow Lincoln's policy. **Johnson.**

407

In this purpose he seems to have persevered so far as in him lay. He continued Lincoln's cabinet, which had by this time grasped the details of its business, and on the whole the machinery of administration ran smoothly. In carrying out Lincoln's general policy toward the South he followed, however, too much the letter of Lincoln's precedent. One can scarcely believe that Lincoln would have pursued unchanged the policy after the war which he had evolved during it. Johnson, moreover, in action, was rough, opinionated, and narrow-minded, and policy counts for little in politics, if not joined with method. He was sure to raise up obstacles which Lincoln would never have encountered. Nor could Lincoln himself have pursued his policy without friction. Not without doubts had the Radical majority seen Congress adjourn in March, 1865, and the problem of reconstruction left for nine months, until its meeting in December, in the hands of the President. When this responsibility fell, not upon Lincoln, but upon Johnson, a southerner and a Democrat, apprehension became doubly keen and criticism was inevitable.

The President's plan.   Johnson recognized the governments established by Lincoln in Virginia, Tennessee, Louisiana and Arkansas, and on May 29 issued an amnesty proclamation, authorizing the organization of civil government in North Carolina, which was quickly followed by similar ones dealing with the other states. These followed much the same lines as Lincoln's proclamation, except that Johnson's lifelong distrust of the ruling class in the South led him to exclude all those whose taxable property was over $20,000 from his general pardon and therefore from the right to vote. The first act of the voters registered under this authority was to be the election of a constitutional convention, which was to declare the ordinance of secession null and void, abolish slavery, and repudiate all debts incurred in the support of the war. Such constitutional provisions having been ratified by popular vote, state officers were to be elected, and the Thirteenth

Amendment ratified by the newly elected legislature. This policy was acceptable to the South, and by December, 1865, nearly every state had performed these acts, had been recognized by the President as restored to its old constitutional relation, and had elected members to the ensuing Congress. The President had withdrawn all obstructions to commerce, had turned much property back to the state governments, public service corporations, and individuals, and had liberally extended special pardons to those exempted from the general amnesty. He did not, however, put an end to martial law.

When Congress assembled, it was by no means disposed to accept the President's handiwork. It was felt that so great a problem was the business of the legislature rather than of the executive. Moreover, the new southern legislatures, justly doubtful of the ability of the negro at once to adjust himself without friction to freedom, had passed and were passing codes of law designed to meet the new situation. Many of these codes of law were plainly intended to make freedom mean as little as possible; all of them were based on the principle of a distinction between the white and negro races. Except in Georgia, none of them provided for the improvement of the negro by education, which Lincoln had considered a necessary complement of freedom. Congress, therefore, refused to admit members from any of the seceded states, until it should have time to deliberate on the subject. *Attitude of Congress.*

The decision to delay the reorganization of these states was made with the almost unanimous consent of both the conservative and radical factions, and Senator Fessenden, a conservative or at least a moderate, was made chairman of a Joint Committee of Reconstruction. To the Judiciary Committee of the Senate, of which Trumbull of Illinois, another moderate, was chairman, was confided the task of providing for the negro. The first bill introduced was one to extend the life and the functions of the Freedmen's Bureau. *Freedmen's Bureau.*

During the war tens of thousands of former slaves had come into the Union lines. In dealing with them, there had been the greatest variety of authority and of experiment. Generals, the War Department, the Treasury Department, private philanthropists, and speculators had all tried a hand. They had been worked by the government, loaned to contractors, given separate land holdings, and furnished with food, medicine, and all sorts of education. To bring about some kind of harmony there had been established by Congress in March, 1865, a "Bureau of Freedmen and Abandoned Lands." This was to last for one year only. The new bill continued it, although it was still designed to be temporary, and very much enlarged the functions of its agents. They were given absolute power over contracts entered into by negroes, and the right to appeal to the military to enforce their decisions.

Break between the President and Congress. This bill was passed on February 6, 1866, and was promptly vetoed by the President. He asserted that it was inexpedient and unconstitutional. Among his grounds for taking the latter position was the fact that it was passed by a Congress from which eleven states were excluded. An attempt was made to pass it over his veto, but the Senate failed to give the requisite two-thirds majority. On February 22 the President in a characteristic and intemperate speech attacked the leaders of the majority in Congress. The President's sweeping veto and his violent speech forced the main Republican factions, the moderates and the radicals, together in opposition. The President had to rely upon the Democrats and a few "conservative" or "administration" Republicans. During March it was a question whether he could rally over a third of the Senate and so defeat the congressional plan. The crisis came over the "Civil Rights" bill, providing for the absolute equality of blacks and whites before the law. This was passed over his veto in April.

Feeling confident now of a two-thirds majority, enabling it to overrule the President, Congress proceeded rapidly. A new Freedmen's Bureau act was passed, and the Joint Committee on Reconstruction soon made its report. It declared that no legal civil government existed in the South, and that the duty of establishing such a government lay with Congress, under the constitutional clause guaranteeing a republican form of government to every state. It recommended the passage of a fourteenth amendment to the Constitution. This amendment embodied in its first section the essence of the Civil Rights bill, declaring: "All persons born or naturalized in the United States, and subject to the jurisdiction thereof, are citizens of the United States and of the State wherein they reside. No State shall make or enforce any law which shall abridge the privileges or immunities of citizens of the United States; nor shall any State deprive any person of life, liberty, or property, without due process of law; nor deny to any person within its jurisdiction the equal protection of the laws." Further clauses declared that the war debt of the South should never be paid, nor that of the Union repudiated, and barred from officeholding certain classes of southerners, unless they should be pardoned by a two-thirds vote of Congress. Finally, it provided that if any state abridged, except for crime, the right of any male citizen of proper age to vote, its representation in Congress should be reduced in proportion to the number thus deprived. Without the latter provision the late slaveholding states would gain power by the emancipation of the negro. On the old basis of representation, the seceded states had sixty-one votes in the House of Representatives; if the negroes counted as whites, they would have seventy; if the negroes counted not at all, they would have forty-five. The amendment, therefore, gave the southerners the choice of negro suffrage or reduced representation. On June 13, 1866, this amendment was sent to the states for ratification. On July 2, Tennessee

Congressional plan.

was recognized as reconstructed on the grounds that: "By a large popular vote the people have ratified a constitutional amendment abolishing slavery and have declared the secession ordinance and the war debt void, and their state government has ratified the Thirteenth and Fourteenth Amendments and has done other acts procuring and denoting loyalty." This represented the congressional plan of reconstruction.

Campaign of 1866.

The people were to choose between these two plans, that of the President and that of Congress, in the congressional election of 1866. The President appealed to nonpartisan union support. A great convention at Philadelphia on August 14 indorsed his policy. He had the assistance of Thurlow Weed, Seward's political manager, of Henry J. Raymond of the *New York Times*, and of many others who had coöperated with the administration during the war, as well as of the Democrats of North and South. He remodeled his cabinet, filling it with his friends, except for the Secretary of War, Stanton, and he used the patronage actively to advance his views. Invited to assist in laying the corner stone of a monument to Douglas at Chicago, he "swung round the circle," arranging to visit and speak at many places during his trip. This was the first time that a President had engaged in a campaigning tour, and the character of his speeches showed him at his worst. They were coarse and superficial, and undoubtedly prejudiced many against him. A riot at New Orleans about the same time, in which many negroes were killed and the police were implicated in their destruction, convinced many that the South did not intend to deal fairly with the freedmen.

Election of 1866.

The result was an overwhelming victory for the congressional plan, and the Republicans secured more than two thirds of each house of Congress. During the same period the unreconstructed southern states were considering the Fourteenth Amendment, and one after another they rejected it. They believed that the Supreme Court would overrule Congress, that the election of 1868 would reverse the position of parties in the North, and that they could then secure better terms. When Congress met in December, 1866, therefore, the North and the South were as strongly opposed as ever; the North had indorsed the plan of Congress, the South had rejected it; politically there was no sign of reconciliation.

The triumphant majority in Congress turned to the "Thorough." leadership of Sumner, the idealistic champion of equality, and to Thaddeus Stevens, the remorseless hater of the South. Sumner believed that by secession the states had committed suicide and lapsed into the condition of territories; Stevens thought they had become conquered provinces; both considered that Congress had a free hand to make them over at will. Dissatisfied with Fessenden and Trumbull's congressional plan worked out during the preceding session, they secured the passage of additional acts on March 2 and 23, and July 19, 1867, their whole policy being denominated by the title "Thorough." The existing southern state governments were disregarded; the South was divided into five districts under military rule. The military commandants were once more to register voters, excluding all whites who had ever been disfranchised for participation in the rebellion, and admitting negroes. Upon this new basis a constitutional convention was to be elected in each state, which should draw up a constitution permanently establishing negro suffrage. When this constitution had been adopted by popular vote, and the state government provided for had accepted the Fourteenth Amendment, reconstruction might be considered complete, but members elected to Congress must be able to take the "ironclad" oath, to the effect that they had not voluntarily abetted the rebellion.

The compulsory provision for negro suffrage was the Negro suffrage. most important novelty in this plan. Jefferson's philosophic statement that all men are created equal had troubled early constitution makers, who nearly always desired to exclude the negro from voting, but found this principle in their way. In the thirties, however, North Carolina and Tennessee disfranchised them, and they voted no longer in the South. At the same time the rise of abolitionism gave body to the demand for equal rights in the North, and every constitutional convention listened to discussions of negro suffrage. Often the question was referred to popular vote. Before the war, however, no state, outside of the six — New England, except Connecticut, and New York — that had allowed the negroes to vote from Revolutionary times, had adopted the practice, though popular support was growing and almost half the Republicans favored it. During the war there was a rapid growth of pro-negro sentiment. Lincoln desired negro suffrage subject to limitations, and even Johnson had at one time recommended such an arrangement as expedient. Congress adopted the policy the more easily as it applied only to the South, and was backed by the claim that the negro needed the suffrage to defend himself, and that the negro voters were needed to maintain Republican supremacy when the southern states should be readmitted to participation in the national government. The fitness of the negro for the suffrage was scarcely mentioned. Northern opinion was that the negro was naturally equal to the white man, and, in the absence of any conception of an evolutionary historic development, it was believed that he could escape the consequences of degradation in a generation at most.

"Tenure of Office" act. To intrust to President Johnson the execution of these acts, every one of which he had vetoed, seemed to many suicidal. Benjamin F. Butler of Massachusetts and others urged his impeachment. The charges that could be brought against him, however, were of such a character that it would be difficult to secure his conviction, and the majority decided that it would be sufficient to tie his hands, without removing him. To accomplish this the "Tenure of Office" act was passed, March 2, 1867. This act reversed the time-honored decision of the first Congress, that the power of removal rested with the President, and gave it to the President "by and with the advice and consent of the Senate," thus making the method of removal the same as that of appointment. The Senate had long contended that this was the correct interpretation of the constitutional provision, but only the intensity of the reconstruction conflict could bring the representatives to agree to a practice which gave so much power to the senators. The bill was intended to protect Stanton in the office of Secretary of War, but the sequel showed that this was precisely what it failed to do.

The President was anxious to have this act tested by the courts, without becoming himself personally involved. His plans to this end failed, and on February 21, 1868, he boldly produced a crisis by announcing the removal of Stanton. The radical leaders immediately took advantage of this apparent violation of a law constitutionally passed, to undertake his impeachment. The trial which followed marked the high tide of bitterness in the North.

The House managers of the impeachment held that it was only necessary to show the President's unfitness for office, and that general charges, even though not admissible in an ordinary court of law, were pertinent and sufficient. The President's legal counsel, including Benjamin R. Curtis, formerly of the Supreme Court, and William Evarts, held that he must be convicted of some direct illegal act. The President urged that his removal of Stanton, even if contrary to the Tenure of Office act, was justifiable as being the only means of bringing that act, which he regarded as an unconstitutional infringement of the executive power, before the courts. The case, however, eventually turned on a fine legal point. The law provided that cabinet officers were to hold during the term of the President by whom they were appointed and one month thereafter. After that period the President could remove

Impeachment.

them without consulting the Senate. The legal arguments
made it clear that Stanton had been appointed by Lincoln,
that Johnson was serving a term of his own in the sense of
the law, and that, therefore, the removal was legal. When
the final vote was taken seven Republican senators and all
the Democrats voted not guilty, making over one third of the
Senate, and the President was acquitted. On May 26, 1868,
he appointed General Schofield in the place of Stanton, and
for the remainder of the administration had comparatively
little trouble with Congress. The seven Republicans who
voted against the impeachment charges had been moved only
by their conviction of the President's innocence, and recent
opinion has approved their act. At the time, however, they
were read out of the party, and in most instances their political careers were ended.

Finance.   While the President and Congress were wrangling over
the reconstruction of the South, they were forced to a certain amount of coöperation with regard to financial reconstruction. The first necessity was for the reduction of expenses. This was largely the work of the several secretaries.
The volunteer army was speedily disbanded and the navy
reduced. When it came to reducing the civil establishment,
which had been expanded to meet the increased administrative needs of the war, the task was much more difficult ; the
interest on the debt, moreover, was enormous, and as a result
the national expenditure after the war was never less than
five times what it had been before. The reduction of taxes,
too, was slow. In 1866 and 1868 the internal revenue taxes
were removed from many objects, leaving, however, the
excise on spirits and tobacco. The income tax was reduced,
although it was not repealed until 1872. The main discussion arose with regard to the tariff. Many of the rates
had been raised to compensate the manufacturers for the internal revenue taxes they were obliged to pay. When the
latter were removed, it was urged that the tariff rates should

be reduced, also. In fact the repeal of the internal revenue taxes probably increased the amount of protection over what it had been during the war, but it is difficult to make an exact estimate because there was still another factor. Customs were paid in gold, and as gold became less expensive, they grew practically less heavy.

The manufacturing interests, however, had grown very strong during the war, and were now for the most part solidly with the Republican party. Congress therefore refused to lower the tariff, and in fact in 1867 increased the rates on wool and woolens by a reclassification, which was embodied in the famous Schedule K, later to become the chief point of attack in the tariff system. Financially the result was that the revenue in every year of Johnson's administration was greater than in any year of the war. With the revenue thus maintained, it was possible to reduce the debt, which at the close of hostilities stood at about three billions. During Johnson's term $271,496,000 was paid off, and other obligations were met so that the total indebtedness of the country was reduced by almost five hundred million dollars. In addition, the debt, which at the close of the war was in many forms, was, for the most part, funded into a regular series of bonds.

Payments on debt.

More controversial was the question of the currency. From 1836 to 1863 there had been no national paper money. The amount afforded by the state banks was about two hundred millions. During the war national paper began to flood the country. By 1866 national bank notes amounted to about two hundred and eighty millions. In addition there was $433,000,000 in unredeemable greenbacks, and treasury notes bearing compound interest, many of which were issued for small amounts, circulated as currency. Money was abundant, but it was cheap. At the close of the war it was worth about one half of its face value. The Secretary of the Treasury, Hugh McCulloch, urged that the first necessity was to

Currency.

restore the national credit, to raise the currency to its face value, and that the proper method of accomplishing this was to reduce the amount of paper in circulation. He retired the small treasury notes, and obtained the authority of Congress, April 12, 1866, to destroy the greenbacks as they came into the treasury to the amount of $10,000,000 in six months, and $4,000,000 in any subsequent month. By February, 1868, he had withdrawn $44,000,000, besides the $33,000,000 which was a temporary issue. In addition he had accumulated a gold reserve from the customs duties, which had to be paid in hard money. As a result, the value of the currency had been raised so that the premium on gold, while varying, averaged about thirty per cent.

The "Ohio Idea."

To many this progress did not seem desirable. The war finance had accustomed people to cheap money and high prices. Moreover, debts had been contracted when money was cheap; their face value remained the same now that money represented more actual value. A debt which represented 500 bushels of wheat when contracted, now required 700 to pay off. Senator Pendleton of Ohio devised a plan to pay the debt and again enlarge the currency simultaneously. The act providing for the issue of certain United States bonds, known as 5-20's, stipulated that the interest be paid in coin, but merely stated that the principal be paid in " dollars." He claimed that these bonds could and should be paid by a new issue of greenbacks. As these bonds were steadily becoming due and amounted to $1,600,000,000, the country would certainly be supplied with all the money it could absorb. The plan became widely popular, and this particular detail of financial reconstruction vied with the southern question in attracting public attention as the campaign of 1868 approached.

Nomination of Grant.

The Republican convention met while the impeachment trial was in progress. It indorsed the whole congressional policy with regard to the South and to the President, it stood for the payment of the whole debt in coin, and it nominated General Grant for the presidency. The nomination of Grant was due, not solely to the popularity resulting from his military successes, but also to the belief that the qualities he had shown as a general, of iron will, capacity for selecting subordinates, organizing ability, and sympathy for the southern people, were those particularly needed in the presidential office at this time. Time brought disappointment. In politics he had no clear-cut general purpose as he had had during the war ; the men to whom he was drawn had dash and ability, but too often lacked integrity of character, and his loyalty to them often sacrificed public interests; the organizing power he showed in the field unaccountably disappeared in government administration as in private business; and his sympathy for the South was counterbalanced by his soldier's conception that law must be obeyed and discipline maintained. To him a party was like an army, order was the condition of victory, and he became a partisan of a narrow type. His habitual silence, however, gave small clew to his political views, and in 1868 he was an ideal candidate in that men of divergent opinions, knowing his sterling personal honesty, could combine in his support.

The Democratic convention was torn asunder by the contest on finance between Pendleton and a conservative faction headed by August Belmont. It desired also to reassure the country as to its loyalty to the Union. The result was again a compromise, as it had been in 1864. The platform indorsed the "Ohio Idea," the candidate was Horatio Seymour, a hard-money man. The Republican policy of "thorough" was attacked. Francis P. Blair, who had supported the Lincoln administration, was selected for the vice presidency. *Democratic convention.*

The election of 1868 showed that the war issue was still overwhelmingly dominant. It revealed a more compact sectionalism than had any previous election. Grant gained *Election of 1868.*

in the Republican states and lost in the border. The Fourteenth Amendment had been declared adopted July 28, 1868,
and all the southern states had been reorganized and were
allowed to take part in the election except Virginia, Mississippi, and Texas. Six of them voted for Grant, owing
to the number of negro votes. The Republicans lost in
some districts, as Ohio, owing to the currency question.
Grant, however, was overwhelmingly elected, and the radicals
retained control of Congress.

Fifteenth   Thaddeus Stevens died before Congress met in the
Amendment.   autumn, and Benjamin F. Butler became the radical leader
in the House. A number of younger men, however, such as
James G. Blaine of Maine, Roscoe Conkling of New York,
James A. Garfield of Ohio, and William B. Allison of Iowa,
were coming to the front, so that Butler never exerted the
influence that Stevens had. These leaders were encouraged
by the result of the election to cap their reconstruction policy
by making negro suffrage universal by means of a constitutional amendment. It was certainly an anomaly that
the North should force negro suffrage upon the South,
and not allow it at home, but a constitutional amendment
had been discountenanced by the national Republican convention, and several northern states had recently refused
to grant the suffrage to negroes. Nevertheless the Fifteenth
Amendment, containing this provision, was rushed through
Congress and recommended to the states before Grant's
inauguration. Its approval was made a condition precedent
to the admission of Virginia, Mississippi, Texas, and also of
Georgia, about whose previous admission a dispute had arisen.
By a remarkable political effort, the assent of three quarters
of the states was obtained, and the amendment became part
of the Constitution, March 30, 1870.

President   The last eight years had witnessed rapid changes in the
and
Congress.   relations of the three departments of government, whose
coequal importance the framers of the Constitution had la-

bored so hard to establish. During the war the executive had assumed the real direction of political affairs, and so sane a jurist as Benjamin R. Curtis asserted, in a pamphlet entitled *Executive Power*, that the nation was practically living under a military despotism. Then followed four years when Congress became all-powerful, and only a single vote saved the executive office from permanent degradation. Grant, while not proving the active leader that was expected, yet restored to the office a reasonable degree of power. He obtained, for instance, a modification of the Tenure of Office act. Lacking the legal training which nearly all Presidents had had, he sometimes disregarded the constitutional limitations of his office in a manner more dangerous than had Lincoln, but in such cases Congress usually checked him. On the whole the equipoise between the legislature and the executive was restored.

The prestige of the Supreme Court had suffered severely during the war. Congress had ignored the Dred Scott decision, and Lincoln had disregarded the decision of Chief Justice Taney in the *Merryman* case, in which the power of the President to suspend the writ of *habeas corpus* had been denied. With the death of Taney in 1864, Salmon P. Chase became Chief Justice, and the majority of the Court had been appointed by Lincoln. With the close of hostilities the Court at once took up cases dealing with war and reconstruction. In the case of *Ex parte Milligan*, 1866, it declared that Congress had no right to erect military tribunals except in the actual locality of hostilities. In 1867, in the cases of *Cummings* v. *Missouri* and *In re Garland*, it declared unconstitutional a provision of the constitution of Missouri debarring from certain professions all who "by act or word manifested sympathy with rebellion," on the ground that it was *ex post facto* legislation. These decisions enraged the majority in Congress and threats were freely made to cut down the powers of the Court, and effect changes in its membership.

Position of the Supreme Court.

Decline of Supreme Court.

Under these circumstances the Court wisely refrained from receiving cases that the "Johnson" governors of Georgia and Mississippi endeavored to bring before it. A decision denying the constitutionality of congressional action would undoubtedly have been ignored, or the Court would have been attacked. In 1869, in the case of *Hepburn* v. *Griswold*, the Court decided, by a vote of five to four, that Congress did not possess the power of making greenbacks legal tender for debts previously contracted, and that contracts antedating the greenback law must be paid in coin. This decision was very unpopular, and, a number of changes in the personnel of the Court occurring about this time, it was reversed by decisions in the cases of *Knox* v. *Lee* and *Juillard* v. *Greeman* in 1871.

Revival of influence of Supreme Court.

In other instances the Court was more fortunate. Chief Justice Chase, presiding over the Senate in the Johnson impeachment trial, successfully maintained the dignity of his position. In the case of *Texas* v. *White* the court dealt with the vexed question of the position of the states during the war. It decided that secession had no legal effect and that they had continued to be states in the Union. "The Constitution, in all its provisions, looks to an indestructible Union composed of indestructible states." Republican governments, as understood in the Constitution, had, however, ceased to exist in them, and the duty of restoring government rested with Congress. Thus congressional reconstruction was, in general, found legal. Before Congress came together it was the duty of the President to act. Thus the governments formed by President Johnson were recognized. During the war there had been *de facto* state governments, and the Court decided that their acts, where not affecting the rights of the national government or of the other states, should be held binding. The principles here laid down continued to guide the courts in the many cases involving secession and the rights of the states which arose during the next decade. Fully as important were the "Slaughter House" cases. These arose from the widespread idea that the clause of the Fourteenth Amendment referring to the "privileges and immunities" of citizens of the United States applied to all their personal rights, and prohibited any state legislation interfering with them. The Court decided that the amendment was adopted with special reference to the negro, and was not intended to diminish the rights of the states as they had been understood. Subsequent decisions in cases involving the Fourteenth Amendment have somewhat modified the position first laid down, but it has never been given the extension claimed for it by the plaintiffs in those cases. By the end of Grant's administration it may be said that the Court had regained its position, and for thirty years it was freer from attack than ever before in its history.

While the political problems resulting from the war attracted the greater amount of attention, those of diplomacy were also pressing. Napoleon III had taken advantage of the temporary neutralization of the strength of the United States to bring about the establishment of an empire in Mexico, resting upon French support. During the war, this violation of the Monroe Doctrine had to be endured, but when the war closed there was such strong popular feeling that there was danger of a war with France. Seward handled this delicate situation with great skill, keeping the peace while he secured the withdrawal of the French troops, deprived of whom, the empire of Napoleon's tool, Maximilian, soon fell. *The French in Mexico.*

Seward's view of the Monroe Doctrine was broad and positive. He had for years anticipated the gradual, peaceful absorption of both the North and South American continents under the United States flag, and, as Secretary of State, he did what he could to accomplish this design. In 1867 he negotiated a treaty for the purchase of Alaska for $7,200,000 from Russia. Sumner, Chairman of the Senate *Expansion.*

Committee on Foreign Affairs, secured the acceptance of this treaty by the Senate, partly on the ground that the country could thus express its gratitude towards Russia for her friendliness during the war. Seward's further plans for annexing the Danish West India islands and Santo Domingo received little sympathy from Congress, which was distinctly anti-expansionist in tone, or from Sumner, who, while he shared Seward's vision, did not desire the inclusion of semitropical countries likely to strengthen the southern influence in national councils.

Grant and Santo Domingo. Grant became greatly interested in the Santo Domingo question and pressed the matter with little regard for constitutional limitations on his power, securing a treaty of annexation which he urged upon the Senate. This treaty became a matter of bitter controversy, and, when Sumner ultimately secured its defeat, his action created a breach between him and Grant that led to important consequences. Other questions of foreign affairs Grant left to his Secretary of State, Hamilton Fish, who conducted them with a conservative and calm good sense that kept peace abroad and prevented agitation at home. Throughout the administration, revolution raged in Cuba, and though a hundred threads of connection threatened to draw the United States into the conflict, neutrality was successfully preserved.

Difficulties with England. Chiefly Mr. Fish's skill was called into play by our relations with England. The victorious party in the Civil War was vindictively indignant with the people of that country, for their failure to give whole-hearted sympathy to the North during the struggle, for what was considered the premature recognition of the belligerency of the Confederacy, and for the destruction of the American merchant marine which was universally attributed to the Confederate cruisers built or fitted out in England in contravention to what the United States claimed were the accepted laws of neutrality. This bad feeling prevented the renewal of the commercial and fisheries treaty of 1854 with Canada, which expired in 1866, and controversy arose with regard to the water boundary between Vancouver Island and the United States. It was with difficulty that the action of Congress was restrained to the civility of peaceful relations. Seward's attempt at reconciliation, known as the Johnson-Clarendon agreement, was ignominiously rejected by the Senate. Sumner in attacking it asserted that England was responsible for the prolongation of the war by at least two years, and should pay damages to the extent of two billions of dollars. He hoped, with the coöperation of his friends the extreme Liberals of England, to establish this claim, and then to provide for its liquidation by the transfer of all British possessions in the western hemisphere to the United States flag. It was a fantastic conception, passing over the border from the sublime to the ridiculous, near which many of the great minds of that idealistic generation hovered. Such a proposal, coming from one so influential as Sumner, brought negotiations for the settlement of the Civil War problems to an abrupt close.

To reëstablish them was a matter of great difficulty, but it was at length brought about. The quarrel between President Grant and Sumner over Santo Domingo came to a crisis just at the critical moment, and Sumner, the chief obstacle to a peaceful settlement with England, was removed from the chairmanship of the Committee on Foreign Affairs. A joint commission representing the two countries was appointed, which drew up the Treaty of Washington in 1871. This made a new twelve-year arrangement with regard to the fisheries, granted free navigation of waterways in which the countries were mutually interested, and submitted practically all disputed points to arbitration. With regard to neutrality it laid down certain rules which were to guide the arbitration and were to govern the observance of neutrality in the future. The resulting court of arbitration at Geneva ordered the payment of about fifteen million dollars to American claimants on the ground that Great Britain had been negligent in enforcing neutrality.

Naturaliza-
tion.

Simultaneous negotiations resulted in an adjustment of the long-vexed question of the diplomatic position of naturalized American citizens. This question had been growing constantly more important with the increase of immigration, and reached a crisis in the arrests of Irish-Americans engaged in the Fenian agitation for the independence of Ireland. In 1871 Great Britain recognized the right of expatriation, and between 1868 and 1871 George Bancroft negotiated satisfactory treaties with several German states. While minor points remained unsettled, the main American contention, that five years' residence accompanied by legal naturalization constituted a change of nationality, was adopted and has since been generally accepted.

Alien
government
in the South.

In the meantime the remaining states of the South were readmitted, the last being Georgia in July, 1870; but order was far from being established. The organization of the new governments had fallen chiefly to negroes and to northerners. After the war thousands of soldiers and camp followers of the northern army had sought their fortunes in the South. Most of those who looked to the more ordinary methods of business and of farming speedily returned, defeated by the unaccustomed economic and labor conditions. The bulk of those who stayed justly deserved the opprobrious name of "carpetbaggers," and sought to rise to power through negro votes. There were, indeed, many honest, philanthropic men among them, deeply interested in the negro's welfare; but their ignorance of the character of both negroes and southern whites rendered them almost as dangerous as the unscrupulous. With the assistance of a scattering of native whites, known to other southerners as "scalawags," and in the North as "loyalists," they organized the negroes into "Union Leagues," and, with the aid of favorable registration laws, brought them very generally to the polls at the first elections. In the conventions thus elected, it was to the carpetbagger that the constructive work naturally fell; the votes were cast by negroes but the ideas came from the North, and the new constitutions, not only in the reconstructed states, but in Maryland and Missouri, were framed upon northern models, introducing in some cases the town system of local government. In some states there were clauses disfranchising thousands of whites; in others a spirit of amnesty was shown.

The governments established under these constitutions were undoubtedly the worst that have ever existed in the United States. In all the legislatures there were large numbers of absolutely uneducated negroes, few members paid taxes, and a majority of the whites were susceptible, in varying degrees, to corruption. In South Carolina, where the excesses were most picturesque, an illiterate legislature spent $128,865 for stationery in four years, and printing in one year cost $450,000; pickles, brandied cherries, a fine coffin, a fine cradle, and Colgate's fancy toilet soap figured among the legislative expenses; a few skillful strokes of the pen raised a bill of $1.88 to $6880. In addition to this crude extravagance there were more subtle financial stealings. It was a period throughout the country of disreputable politics, of speculation, of the increase of state and municipal debts. The ruin of the South tempted individuals to speculate, and rendered particularly plausible the argument that state credit should be extended to aid the work of economic restoration, especially that of the transportation system. Such legislation began before the establishment of negro governments and continued when they were overthrown, but it was most reckless in its scope and most carelessly administered during the "carpetbag" period. In South Carolina there were fraudulent overissues of bonds to the extent of six million dollars, and in four years the state debt increased nearly thirteen million. Even the educational legislation,

Governmental corruption.

commendable as introducing for the first time the free public
school system throughout the South, was unfortunate because devised upon a basis far more expensive than its
impoverished communities could stand. The war had deprived the South of its accumulated capital, reconstruction
was loading it with a burden of debt. Hundreds of thousands
of acres were sold for taxes.

The Ku-
Klux Klan.

At first the native whites were divided into two rather
bitter factions: the one following B. H. Hill of Georgia and
ignoring the new government in the hope of a change of
heart in the North; the other including Robert E. Lee and ex-
Governor Brown of Georgia, advising that the attempt be
made to guide the negro and control the new machinery.
Actual suffering and an indefinable horror of negro dominance,
however, soon united them in a fixed purpose to establish a
white man's government. The first attempt took the form
of terrorizing the negro, and was carried out by various widespread secret societies of young men, of which the most
prominent was the Ku-Klux Klan. By methods running from
mischievous intimidation to criminal violence and wholesale
election frauds, alien rule was shaken off, first by one state
and then by another. The very first legislature elected in
Virginia was controlled by native whites; in Georgia, real
alien rule lasted only from July 15, 1870, to January 1, 1871.
In Tennessee and North Carolina, with the unusually large
white loyalist population, the negro and the carpetbagger
had influence, but did not rule. In the other states violence
and disorder increased. A sense of power and of injury
incited many of the negroes to brutality, and now bloodshed was not all on one side, as had been the case in
most localities immediately after the war. Yet in every encounter it was the white man who came off victorious. It
became very soon evident that, whatever the statute books
might say, the South was a white man's country and that
home rule would in the end mean white rule.

The Republican leaders were entirely unwilling to yield either the principle or the profit of negro suffrage. Grant used his authority as President broadly to preserve the negro governments by use of military force, and Congress conferred the broadest powers upon him. On February 28, 1870, a law was passed placing elections under Federal control, and on April 20, 1871, an act giving the President great powers for the suppression of the Ku-Klux Klan. By military force, the negro governments were maintained in most southern states, which meant that the North continued to rule the South.

This condition began to create a reaction in the North. In Missouri the "Liberal Republicans" under Gratz Brown and Carl Schurz separated from the regulars and obtained control of the state, and the movement in favor of universal amnesty and the cessation of Federal interference in the South spread throughout the border states. Other elements among the Republicans, dissatisfied with Grant because of his disregard of constitutional limitations, his quarrel with Sumner, and his failure to institute a thorough reform of the civil service, and with Congress for its continuance of the war tariff, affiliated with those of the border, and, as the election approached, held a national convention at Cincinnati. It was understood that the Democrats, who, led by Vallandigham, had agreed to accept fully the results of the war and the three amendments, would indorse the candidate of the Liberal Republicans and thus concentrate all elements opposed to the administration.

The most promising candidate suggested was Charles Francis Adams, whose diplomatic prestige, derived from his English mission during the war, had recently been enhanced by his service on the Geneva arbitration. The convention, however, chose Horace Greeley, Editor of the *New York Tribune*, whose vitriolic attacks upon the Democrats extending over many years made him extremely distasteful to them. Nevertheless he was indorsed by that party, still drifting leaderless since the death of Douglas, and he began an active campaign. The Republicans renominated Grant and stood upon their record of the last twelve years. The result showed that the war issue still dominated politics. Grant was overwhelmingly elected. Even in the border states the loss of the Liberal Republicans was more than made up by the negroes, who now, under the Fifteenth Amendment, for the first time took part in a presidential election in those states.

Causes of
Republican
cohesion.

In 1860 the Republican party had been composed of many ill-fused elements, and its leadership was conservative. In 1860 the North would have fought on no issue other than that of union. The cohesion of the party, for four years in strife with President Johnson, the rise of the radicals to leadership, and its continued popular support, need explanation. Its thorough fusion was due to welding in the fiery furnace of the war, while its financial policy, especially the tariff, belted to it with bands of steel many classes of the community. It had, moreover, become synonymous in many minds with the safety of the Union. It was but necessary, in the language of the day, to "wave the bloody shirt," to rally tens of thousands to Republican candidates. While the North was ready to fight only for one supreme object, the war being joined, a constantly increasing number had a constantly growing program of other things which might as well be accomplished now that the opportunity presented itself. The great majority wanted the negro freed and wished him to have an opportunity, while a good proportion did not object if the South got a little hurt in the process. Further, the majority in the North were not content to overthrow Calhoun's theory of state sovereignty and national agency, but were opposed also to Jackson's' idea of state rights and a minimum of national activity. By the establishment of

national banking, national currency, a protective tariff, by
the extension of its functions in a multitude of ways, the
national government was making the nation a unit, and approval of this general policy made the North tolerant of
many things. It required, indeed, the distress of a great
financial upheaval to break the hold the Republican party
had obtained over the North and, through the North, over
the nation.

BIBLIOGRAPHICAL NOTES

Fleming, W. L., *Documentary History of Reconstruction*, con- Sources.
tains material gathered from many sources, illustrating conditions
in the South. For Congress: Johnston, A., *Representative American
Orations*, IV, 129–188. Macdonald, A., *Select Documents*, nos.
44–95, 99. McPherson, E. M., *History of Reconstruction*. The
Sherman letters (edited by R. S. Thorndike), ch. VIII. *U. S.
Doc. Report of Committee on Reconstruction*, 1866. For an intimate
view of the administration, see *Diary* of Gideon Welles. The
more important Supreme Court cases are the following: *Texas* v.
White (1868): 7 *Wallace*, 700. *Slaughter House Cases* (1872):
16 *Wallace*, 36, 273, 746.

J. F. Rhodes, *History of the United States*, vols. V–VII, is Historical
uniformly valuable, and excels the majority of the special studies accounts.
in their own field. Garner, J. W., *Reconstruction in Mississippi*, Executive
chs. II–IV. McCarthy, C. H., *Lincoln's Plan of Reconstruction*. plan of re-
Rhodes, *United States*, VI, 1–50. Scott, E. G., *Reconstruction* construction.
during the Civil War.

Burgess, J. W., *Reconstruction and the Constitution*. *Cam-* Congressional
bridge Modern History, VII, 622–644. Dunning, W. A., *Essays on* recon-
Reconstruction, chs. II–IV. Garner, J. W., *Reconstruction in* struction.
Mississippi, chs. V–XI. McCall, S. W., *Stevens*, chs. XIII, XV,
XVI.

Blaine, *Twenty Years in Congress*, ch. XIV. Chadsey, C. F., Struggle
Struggle between President Johnson and Congress (*Columbia Univ.* between
Studies in History, VIII, no. 1). De Witt, C. M., *The Impeach-* Congress and
ment of Andrew Johnson. Dunning, W. A., *Essays on Recon-* the executive.
struction, ch. IV. Fish, C. R., *Civil Service and the Patronage*,

ch. IX. Hart, A. B., *Chase*, ch. XIII.   Salmon, L. P., *History of the Appointing Power*, ch. II.

Conditions in the South.   F. Bancroft, *Seward*, II, chs. XL, XLII.   Adams, C. F., *Adams*, ch. XIX.   Rhodes, *United States*, VII, 74–173.   Burton, T. E., *Sherman*, 172–226.   For account of reconstruction under Grant: Fleming, W. S., *Reconstruction in Alabama*.

CHAPTER XXV

RECONSTRUCTION COMPLETED

ECONOMICALLY the histories of North and South during the reconstruction period were as different as those of two separate countries. The features of southern activity were, first, the readjustment of agriculture to the conditions of free labor; secondly, the rise of new industries. The distinctive characteristic of southern agriculture had been the plantation system. This was based on compulsory labor and the use of capital. Cultivation was by the large field system, and the slaves worked in gangs under the direct supervision of an overseer. Many northerners wished to break up this system directly by the enforcement of the confiscation act, and the distribution of the land in small holdings among the negroes. This policy failed of adoption, and the land, with the exception of a negligible amount, was left in the hands of its former owners or restored to them. The planters, who continued throughout this generation to be the governing class politically in the South, wished to preserve the plantation system as it had been. Circumstances, however, forced a gradual modification. *Divergent policies in the South.*

Realizing the difficulty of dealing with free negro labor, the planters endeavored constantly to attract foreign immigration. The foreigners landing in the United States, however, found little to attract them in the southern offers of employment, when the northern mills were offering higher wages, and the West could furnish them with individual farms at low rates. The disturbance of public order, the unwelcoming social condition in the South, the absence of *Decay of the plantation system.*

direct steamship communication with Europe, and the fact
that the southern immigration campaign was poorly organized, all combined to turn away the foreigner. The
South had to depend on its own population to an extent
rare in American history. The white population was remarkably stable, although there was some movement to
scantily populated districts, as southwestern Georgia, northeastern Mississippi, and the trans-Mississippi states. The
negroes were moved more easily than before the war, when
the planter had to pay a considerable sum for each laborer
he secured. There was, therefore, a tendency for them to
concentrate in those districts best suited to them.

Negro labor.   Forced to use the negroes, the planters started in 1865
by borrowing what they could from northern bankers, and
engaged their former slaves for money wages. This system
proved unsatisfactory, for the negroes felt no responsibility
and could not be coerced. The crop was in most districts
a failure, and in spite of the high price of cotton most planters
found themselves worse off at the end than at the beginning
of the year. In 1866 a very large number resorted to the
share system, promising the negro a certain proportion of
the net proceeds of the crop. This was more successful,
for it gave the negro a personal interest in the crop. The
negro, however, was anxious to escape from the gang system
and from supervision. In 1868 and 1869 many plantations
were divided up, and each negro family was given a separate
holding to work for itself, paying a share of the crop and subject only to a general guidance. Thus certain features of
the plantation system were very generally abandoned.

Small farms.   In the meantime a further development was taking
place. Poor crops, the heavy taxes of the negro governments,
discouragement, and other reasons led many planters to
offer their lands, or portions of them, for sale at reasonable
prices. Thus the poor whites, who had lost little during
the war, found it possible to buy small farms in the cotton

belt. The cultivation of the land in individual holdings, moreover, removed the social stigma which formerly had prevented white men from working in the cotton fields with the negroes, and many whites took up such holdings on the share system. Soon many whites began to pay a fixed rent in coin or produce, instead of dividing the crop, and became practically independent. The negroes, too, as soon as they could afford to buy the necessary farm stock, began to rent instead of share, and it was not long before many of them bought farms. The progress toward the rented or owned farm was hastened by the negro's dislike of supervision and by laws which allowed merchants to lend goods to tenants on crop liens, thus enabling the latter to start out with little or no capital. The result of these changes was twofold. Poor whites began to break down the monopoly of cotton culture which had been held by capitalists employing negro labor, and over a large area small farms independently run began to take the place of the plantations.

Undoubtedly the net efficiency of negro labor was de- Results. creased by the withdrawal of coercion and supervision. This was to some extent offset by the entry of whites into cotton growing, and by the extension of cotton growing into new regions, as a result of the use of fertilizers. It was not, however, until about 1880 that southern agricultural production reached the ante bellum totals. Under the new conditions, however, the enterprising and deserving, whether black or white, were given opportunities previously denied. Of those who still ran plantations somewhat different qualities were required than before the war, and harder work. A greater proportion of the proceeds, moreover, went to labor. Gradually the old planter class lost its grip of the cotton industry. Many of its members went into professional life, tried their fortunes in the North, or vegetated on unsuccessful plantations. Southern agricultural society became more diversified, but to a great extent the class which had played

so large a part in the history of the country, and had produced
so many of its greatest men, became a memory.

Rise of the new South.   In the meantime the South was coming to depend less
completely on its agriculture. The development of non-
agricultural industries can hardly be said to have been a
result of the war. It had been delayed in part by the existence of slavery, but it had begun before the war, and the
census of 1870 marked practically no progress over that of
1860. During the seventies, however, it secured a strong
start. The development of lumber began immediately after
the war, and furnished much of the capital which the South
so much needed. The exploitation of the iron and coal
about Birmingham in Alabama began about the same time.
Cotton mills began to spring up in the piedmont region,
where the falls of the rivers were to be found, and where the
poor white population could be reached and drawn in,
hardly any negro labor being employed in the mills. The
capital for these mills was generally furnished, half by the
neighboring community and half by northern capitalists.
The first superintendents and foremen usually came from the
North. The poor whites, however, had been accustomed
for generations to the making of homespun, and they had a
mechanical ability which soon proved itself. The manufacture of cotton so near the source of its production naturally resulted in some economies, and to these was added a
saving in the price of labor. The mills were generally located
in small villages which became economically dependent upon
them, and laborers were unable to compel as good terms as
those in the North. The southern states, too, were less
active in passing protective laws, and cheaply paid child
labor was abundant. This lowering of the labor standard
gave financial success, but prevented the production of the
finer grades of fabrics, for which skilled and therefore well-
paid workmen are required. In the meantime the southern
railroad system was changing as well as developing. The roads,

during the seventies, fell largely into the hands of northern capitalists. They, following the tendencies of that "Railroad Age," developed trunk lines running through from the South to the North, at the expense of the roads running to southern ports. Southern business tended more than ever before to concentrate at New York, and the South did less business directly with England than before the war. These tendencies were in the direction of lessening the differences between the South and the rest of the country, and bringing it into closer touch with the national economic life. The memories of the war, reconstruction, and the negro problem, however, were sufficient to hold it politically apart.

In the North the labor problem produced by the war was also serious. During the war itself it may be estimated that the labor of a million and a half men was withdrawn from industry for three years. For three years, also, America ceased to receive its customary supply of immigrants. It is not entirely clear how this loss was made good. Women worked more than previously. Many children were withdrawn from school to take jobs or work about the farm. Labor-saving machinery both in farm and factory played a part. It still remains true that one can scarcely account for the maintenance of the volume of production at the North until 1863 and its increase after that date, without the supposition that there was a general intensification of effort under the strain of the war. In spite of the scarcity of labor, wages did not at once rise to meet the increase in prices due to the depreciation of the currency. The result was the formation of labor unions of various kinds, which now began to take on their permanent shape. The close connection of the slavery agitation and the labor question secured for the laborers the championship of many of the antislavery leaders, such as Wendell Phillips. By means of strikes and other pressure, wages were generally raised, though even at the end of the war they had not risen as much as prices. At

Labor problem in the North.

the same time agitation in Massachusetts and some other states resulted in legislation favorable to labor.

Land and population.   The close of the war threw over a million soldiers suddenly back into private life, and at the same time caused a revival of immigration on a larger scale than ever before. The use of labor-saving machinery for farm and factory, moreover, continued to increase. Yet the expansion of industry was so great that even while the army was being disbanded there was a complaint of a scarcity of labor and the overemployment of children continued and became a permanent condition. The greater number of these laborers found occupation in opening up new farming lands and in the more intensive cultivation of those already broken. In the sixties the system of land distribution reached the climax of its perfection. In the older states cultivated land changed hands easily and at good prices. In Illinois and the surrounding states there were vast areas of well-located land held by railroads, land companies, and individuals, which was sold at reasonable prices and liberal terms as to payment. In Illinois, Michigan, Wisconsin, Alabama, Mississippi, and in all states west of the Mississippi River, there was public domain, which could be taken up under the Homestead Act. This latter land, however, was generally in regions not yet reached by the railroads and attracted those who had little or no capital. West of the Missouri were enormous districts not yet surveyed where the squatter could settle with no outlay, though with constant danger from the Indians. There, cattle driving and the cowboy flourished. These opportunities were temptingly displayed to the ambitious and dissatisfied all over the United States and northern Europe. States and landowning railroad companies maintained agents abroad, published advertising pamphlets in many languages, and supplied the intending immigrant with assistance.

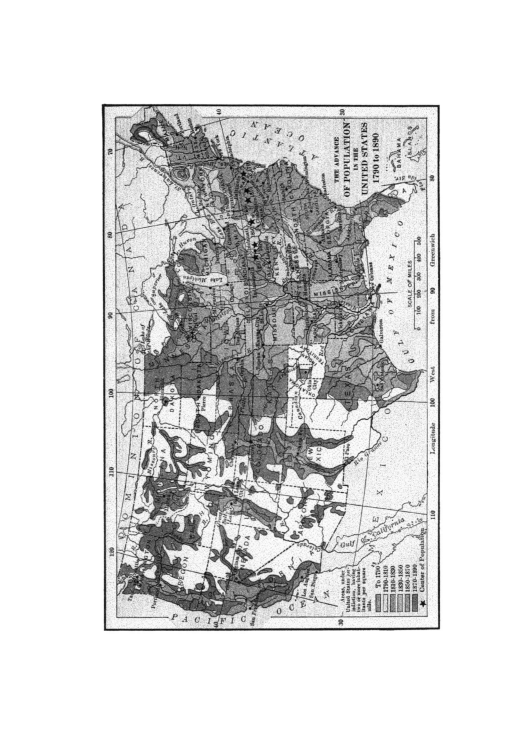

THE ADVANCE
OF POPULATION
IN THE
UNITED STATES
1790 to 1890

SCALE OF MILES
0   100   200   300   400   500

Longitude   West   100   from   90   Greenwich

Areas, under
United States jur-
isdiction, having
two or more inhab-
itants per square
mile.

To 1790
1790-1810
1810-1830
1830-1850
1850-1870
1870-1890
★ Center of Population

The whole North was in a state of flux. Native popu- *Migration.* lation was everywhere moving out toward the frontier, even from such newly settled states as Wisconsin. Its place was taken by migrants from the older states and by the European immigrants, who settled most thickly in the East, and then, leaving a comparatively small number in the intermediate region, furnished an important element in Illinois and beyond. Directly north of the Ohio, negro migration from the South was a factor. To the customary causes of movement must be added the fact that labor-saving machinery was beginning to reduce the number required for farm management, and purely agricultural counties in settled areas, even in Iowa and Wisconsin, lost population, while maintaining and increasing the volume of their agricultural production. The disbanding of the army, also, furnished a class alert to all new opportunities.

Development was greatest in the immediate valley of *Expansion.* the Mississippi — in Illinois, Wisconsin, Iowa, Minnesota, and also to a less degree in Missouri, Mississippi, and Arkansas. Between 1860 and 1870, two hundred and seven thousand farms were opened up in those states. The advance up the Missouri valley did not involve so many settlers, but the proportion of increase was even greater; the population of Kansas tripled, and it became a state in 1861, that of Nebraska more than quadrupled, and it became a state in 1867. Much of the new settlement in Missouri and Iowa was along this stream, and in all, nearly one hundred thousand farms were opened up.

A good proportion of the labor supply was employed *Exploitation of natural resources.* in the work of exploiting the natural resources of the country. The adventurous sought to renew the scenes of California in Nevada and Colorado, which became states in 1864 and 1876 respectively, and the Far West grew in population, though not phenomenally. In the upper Northwest, in Michigan, Wisconsin, and Minnesota, with their untouched forests and swift streams, the lumber industry was making rapid advances. In New York and Michigan, great fortunes were made in salt, while in Pennsylvania, Ohio, and West Virginia, the utilization of petroleum and natural gas was turning whole rural areas into populous districts, served by a network of railroads and pipe lines.

Manufactur-ing and the tariff. The development of manufacturing was prodigious. Six leading occupations employed in 1870 three hundred and sixty thousand more laborers than in 1860. In the West, flouring and tanning, being based on native products, flourished exceedingly. New machinery was invented, and great factories were erected in St. Louis, Minneapolis, Milwaukee, and other centers. In the East undertakings of all sorts grew apace, stimulated during the war by government contracts and nourished by the tariff, into a development somewhat unnatural. The tendency here was toward diversification and the manufacture of finer products and specialties. In New England the mills dotted the country wherever water power existed, for transmission of power had not yet been made possible. Many of the mill companies owned their villages, with stores and even banks, and their employees were much at their mercy. Already, however, in the seventies water power was not sufficient, and many industries were concentrating in large towns and cities on the coast, such as Fall River, to which coal could be brought by water. Here labor was more independent than in the isolated mill villages. The native population was employed to a decreasing extent in these mills, the main reliance of the New England manu-facturer being the Irish, English, and French Canadian im-migrant. The spread of manufacturing in the West strength-ened the sentiment in favor of protection, increasing the area which might be benefited. While there was constant agitation for tariff reform, the war rates were in general maintained. There was a horizontal reduction of 10 per cent in 1872, but rates were restored in 1875.

This was distinctly a railroad age. The closing of the
Mississippi during the war had developed the habit of
relying on the railroads instead of on that river, and its
tonnage decreased from 468,210.34 in 1860 to 348,201.44
in 1870. The Confederate cruisers had caused American
owners of seagoing ships to sell them, or lay them up during
the war. The advantage which the English thus gained,
coupled with the fact that the iron ships now becoming popular could be produced most cheaply in England, made a
revival of the American merchant marine difficult. Far-
sighted men like Commodore Vanderbilt turned their capital
from ships to railroads. The use of petroleum destroyed
the whaling industry by supplanting the use of whale oil.
Only on the Great Lakes did American shipping increase.
Railroad construction, on the other hand, went forward
rapidly. States, cities, counties, and individual farmers
loaned their credit to help construct lines of local utility.
Trunk lines between the Mississippi and the coast were completed and improved, and after the war the long talked of project of a transcontinental line was pressed to completion under
the fostering aid of national land grants and by Chinese coolie
labor. In 1869 the Union Pacific was completed, and, with
the laying of the first permanently successful Atlantic cable
in 1866, it marked a decided step in the binding of the world
together. Railroad building was pressed beyond the needs
of the population, with the hope of building up settlements
along the routes; 1177 miles were reported constructed in
1865; in 1870, 5525; in 1871, 7760; in 1872, 6167.

All these undertakings required capital. The occupation of new land meant tens of thousands of farmers in
debt for the land itself and for its improvements; manufacturers invested to the limit of their credit. While manufacturing was mostly carried on by partnerships, corporations were becoming more numerous. Especially railroads
were so organized. In general they were built on their bond

(margin notes: Transportation by water. Railroads. Speculation and credit.)

issues and their stock, and in many cases a part of the bonds themselves represented a capitalization of future profits rather than actual expenditure. The country was prosperous and was accumulating capital, but it was spending more than it accumulated in enterprises not immediately remunerative, and it was creating obligations far in excess of what it actually spent. Fortunes were easily made, and their possessors indulged in a riot of extravagant and ostentatious living. Imports grew more rapidly than exports. In 1860 they stood $335,200,000 to $373,100,000, in 1872 $617,600,000 to $501,-100,000. Much of this importation was of luxuries and non-productive material. To pay for it coin was drawn rapidly from the country, and although the mines were turning out great amounts of precious metals and the government was minting it rapidly, the country was forced to do its business very largely in the government's paper credit currency.

Currency.

The currency remained in a chaotic condition. The premium of gold constantly varied. It always went up in the autumn when there was a great drain upon the East for money with which to move the crops. McCulloch at such times was in the habit of selling gold from the reserve which he had established for the government, and, by supplying what the market needed, reducing the gold premium. He considered it his duty to keep the value of money as nearly constant as possible. In 1869 Jay Gould and James Fisk, two New York speculators who controlled the Erie Railroad and many other institutions and were in close connection with Tammany Hall, sought to corner gold. They brought to bear upon President Grant every resource of argument and upon his confidential advisers every temptation of bribery, to reverse McCulloch's policy and refrain from interference with the market. They seemed at first to have succeeded, and on "Black Friday," September 24, forced the premium up to war-time rates. Grant, however, was finally convinced of the dishonesty of their purposes and methods, and ordered the disbursement of enough gold to stay the threatened panic. The administration, however, failed to recommend and Congress to adopt any comprehensive plan of reform, and the currency remained a constant source of uncertainty and danger.

In 1873 credit became particularly overstrained. In September Jay Cooke and Company of Philadelphia, the most conspicuous financial house in the country, failed. It was undertaking to finance a second great transcontinental road, the Northern Pacific, a proposition perfectly sound, but the returns from which were too far in the future. This failure proved to be the signal of universal distress, and the country was soon in the throes of the worst financial disturbance since 1837. As in that case the panic but ushered in a period of economic distress from which the country did not recover for fully five years. Banks failed, great mill owners, like the Spragues of Rhode Island, went into bankruptcy, one fifth of the railroad investment of the country was sold under foreclosure, and a still greater proportion passed into the hands of receivers.

Panic of 1873.

The breakdown of the spurious prosperity which had tempted so many beyond their depth was accompanied by astounding revelations of official corruption tainting the foremost men in the nation. The most important single instance was that of the Crédit Mobilier, an organization which was formed to build and finance the Union Pacific Railroad, and which, it was now discovered, had scattered its stock at nominal prices among members of Congress to prevent any interference with its land grants. This scandal was hinted at before the election of 1872, and was made public by a congressional investigation soon afterwards. For the next four years scandal followed scandal, affecting every department of the national government, even the judiciary. The Secretary of War, General Belknap, was proved to have taken bribes, and was impeached in 1876; and in 1875 the un-

The crisis and corruption.

earthing of the notorious Whisky Ring, which in ten months defrauded the government of over a million and a half in taxes, involved General Babcock, the President's private secretary.

Indian affairs.

Perhaps the most serious maladministration was in regard to Indian affairs. The government and the tribes were alike constantly defrauded, and some portion of the difficulties with the Indians during this period must be attributed to this cause. Sitting Bull and his "Hostiles" were constantly supplied with arms and goods from the surrounding agencies, by which means they were enabled, from 1868 to 1875, to strengthen themselves. In 1875 they began war and in 1876 completely defeated General Custer in the last great Indian victory. Thus the sting of military defeat was added to the difficulties accumulating about the administration.

Election of 1874.

These revelations, combined with the financial distress, for the first time shook the hold of the Republicans on the North. In the election of 1874, the Democrats won control of the House of Representatives. This triumph was appreciated more because of the hope it excited of winning the great contest two years later, than for its intrinsic value, for the Republicans maintained their hold of the Senate and the presidency. In preparing for this contest the Democrats put aside the idea of alluring the discontented Republicans and chose for their candidate a thoroughgoing Democrat, Samuel J. Tilden, leader of his party in New York.

Samuel J. Tilden.

The reasons for the selection of Tilden emphasize the entrance of new factors into politics. His claim to recognition was based primarily on his activity as a reformer and administrator. The period of national exploitation was passing, and success would depend more and more on special knowledge, on mastery of details, on careful calculation. The population was becoming more dense, the increase of immigration was rendering it less homogeneous, and the activity of the government was of necessity being extended to many fields previously left to private initiative. The discussion of fundamental principles began to occupy less attention, and public speeches became more statistical.

Especially new to Americans were the problems of large municipalities. It was really only after the war that Boston, Philadelphia, Chicago, and San Francisco became large cities, and New York was not old enough to have solved the difficulties of a closely packed population. The questions of sewerage, of water supply, of street making and lighting, of rapid transit, of the uplifting of the slums, were all new; and the popular belief in the fundamental difference between European government and American was too strong to allow recourse to the methods of European cities. The lower class of politicians seem to have been the first to realize the possibilities of this new development. The enormous sums needed for the construction of necessary public works, and the prodigious profits that might flow from franchises to public service corporations, they looked upon as unparalleled opportunities for successful fraud; and the outgrown system of municipal government enabled them to secure the control of these new sources of wealth. In New York city there was the greatest concentration of opportunity, and the most shameless advantage was taken of it.

Municipal problems.

In that city Tammany Hall governed. Its influence was based upon the good-natured camaraderie of its district leaders, its charitable care for a dependent foreign population, a system of organization which had been developing for eighty years, and a total disregard of political and business ethics. At this time its leaders were William M. Tweed and Peter B. Sweeney. In league with Jay Gould and the Erie Railroad, they were able to control for all practical purposes the state legislature and a considerable portion of the judiciary. In 1871 this combination was at the height of its power, but during that year the iniquities of its leaders,

Overthrow of Boss Tweed.

which had long been known, were proved to the point of
legal requirement, and the gang was driven from power. So
profitable were their methods that at an early stage in the
investigation they offered a bribe of five million dollars to
secure a halt in proceedings. A leading part in the popular
uprising which brought about this result was taken by Thomas
Nast, whose biting cartoons spoke a universal language com-
prehended by native and foreigner, by literate and illiterate
alike. The planning of the campaign, however, was largely
the work of Mr. Tilden. He became identified with the
cause of good government, was in 1874 elected governor of
the state, and seemed to be a logical candidate for the presidency at a time when reform had become an issue.

National
adminis-
trative
problems.

Although the choice of a candidate because of a record
for purging municipal and state ills and a talent for the details of administration was a new idea, it was in line with the
trend of development. For more than half the time since
Tilden's candidacy the presidency has been held by men
with such a record. Many of the same problems confronted
the national, as the state and city governments. The war
had caused a sudden expansion of business, and the nationalistic policy of Congress had rendered it permanent. Never
after the war were the annual expenses of the government
less than five times as great as in any year of peace before.
Business administration became an increasingly important
function of the government.

Civil service
reform.

This increase in business was doubtless, in part, responsible for the governmental demoralization under Grant.
Already a remedy had been proposed. In the system of appointment to nonelective offices, on the basis of competitive
examinations, which had recently been introduced in England, Sumner and others of his set saw the annihilation of
the spoils system and the possibility of equipping the government with honest and efficient officers. It was, indeed, true
that the army of public servants had become so vast that

personal responsibility was not a sufficient check upon forces of favoritism. In Congress, Mr. Thomas Jenckes of Rhode Island became the leading advocate of this basic reform, and from year to year introduced bills to put it into practice. In 1871 an appropriation was passed and a Civil Service Commission was established, which introduced the new system into a few offices. Although Congress failed to continue its support, and the reform leaders and President Grant quarreled, the movement went on under the energetic direction of George William Curtis, the editor of *Harper's Weekly*. In New York and other places civil service reform associations were formed. As was true of the antislavery movement and many other projects for betterment pressed forward by that generation, the crusade was given a moral tone and was pressed with a religious conviction. In 1872 it played a part in politics, and in 1876 it became a real factor. While the Democrats failed specifically to indorse competitive examinations, they committed themselves to remedy the evils of the civil service, and it was believed that Mr. Tilden would draw the reformer vote.

The leading Republican candidate was James G. Blaine, who had been Speaker of the House, and had risen steadily in popular favor because of his sympathy with reform and his conciliatory attitude toward the South. He was opposed by several candidates supported by the President, who desired a vindication of his administration by the choice of some close friend. Just before the convention Blaine became involved in certain charges of financial dishonesty from which he could not free himself, and lost the support of the reformers within the party. To regain ground he practically reversed his attitude toward the South, and made a telling and adroit appeal to the war passions which it was still easy to arouse. After a contest, the convention chose a "dark horse," Rutherford B. Hayes, who as governor of Ohio had pleased the reform element, and who now prevented

Republican convention, 1876.

their secession from the party. The main issue that filled
the campaign speeches, however, was that renewed by Mr.
Blaine, and the Republican orators besought the voters not
to turn the country over to ex-Confederates and "Copperheads."

Election of
1876.

By this time white rule had been restored in all the
southern states except South Carolina, Louisiana, and Florida,
the administration not having ventured to carry out quite so
firm a restrictive policy after the election of the Democratic
House of Representatives as before. Excepting these three,
the southern states were carried by the Democrats. The
border states, also, for the first time since 1860, were solidly
anti-Republican. In the northern states, the political effects
of the crisis of 1873 had become modified, and the results
resembled those of 1868, except that the Democrats offset
the loss of Oregon, by the gain of Connecticut and Indiana.
Tilden received a popular majority of over two hundred fifty
thousand, but the Republicans consoled themselves with the
thought that Hayes carried the loyal states by one hundred
thousand, and that Tilden's immense majority in the South
was caused by the illegal suppression of the negro vote.

Electoral
Commission.

From South Carolina, Louisiana, and Florida, there were
double returns, and other contests arose later. If every contest were decided in his favor, Hayes would win by a single
electoral vote. The Constitution was not explicit as to
whether the President of the Senate, at the time a Republican,
or the houses of Congress, of which one was Democratic, had
the power of determining the validity of the votes, and for
a time it seemed probable that two Presidents would be declared elected and that the country might again be plunged
into civil war. With most commendable self-control, the
party leaders agreed to leave the decision to a commission
appointed in such a manner as apparently to guarantee impartiality. The Senate appointed from its body three Republicans and two Democrats, the House, two Republicans

and three Democrats, and five members of the Supreme Court were chosen, of whom two had been members of each party, while the fifth was intended to be David Davis of Illinois, who was as nearly independent as it was possible for a man in public life to be at the time. This attempt to secure a non-partisan decision was lamentably unsuccessful. Mr. Davis could not serve, and the fifth judge, finally appointed, was a Republican. Every vital point was decided by a vote of eight to seven in favor of Hayes. The Commission was hardly judicial in its attitude, but the more important result of obtaining an undisputed succession, however, was secured, and Hayes was peacefully inaugurated.

The character of this contest made a continuance of the policy of "Thorough" impossible, and Hayes gladly abandoned it, calling to his cabinet Carl Schurz, one of the Liberal Republican leaders. Federal troops were withdrawn from the South, Democratic governments quietly established themselves in the three disputed states, and everywhere control fell into the hands of the naturally dominant whites. Unfortunately, while the negro ceased to participate in politics, the negro question continued to be a determining factor. The war had brought the great majority of southern whites to act together. Reconstruction had cemented this union at a time when it might possibly have broken up, and the unified effort to regain control of their state and local governments had stamped out the last remaining political difference. It became the cardinal principle of public life that the whites must preserve their supremacy by presenting a solid front to the negro. To the bonds forged by a common struggle and by common suffering were added those produced by dread of a common danger. The instant the South became again self-governing it became "solid." Since then no Republican electoral vote has come from any state that seceded, and Republican congressmen only from those upland districts which had never been thoroughly identified with the

Restoration of home rule to the South.

The "Solid South."

southern interests. With this solidity, came loss of national influence, as under a party system of government doubtful regions have the greatest weight.

Exposition of 1876.

Nevertheless the restoration of home rule in the South meant to a considerable degree the restoration of national good will, and national feeling was undoubtedly stimulated by the great Centennial Exposition held at Philadelphia in 1876, to celebrate one hundred years of independence. Planned upon a scale of magnificence before unknown, it exhibited the wonderful material development of the country and its essential economic unity. It brought the leading spirits of all sections into harmonious coöperation, and strengthened national pride and patriotism. At the same time the hearty assistance of foreign nations and their artistic exhibits tended to break down that spirit of isolation and self-sufficiency which had been such a marked feature of American thought since the Napoleonic wars.

Factional fights.

With the positive part of his program, Hayes was less successful than with the negative. He was sincerely interested in civil service reform and earnestly endeavored to secure its extension, but he lacked the force to secure adequate support for his proposals. The Democrats controlled the House, and the Republicans were divided between the "Half-Breeds," who generally supported the President, and the "Stalwarts," led by Senator Conkling of New York, who violently attacked what he denominated the "Snivel service administration of Totherfraud Hayes."

Financial legislation.

The main object of political interest, however, had come to be the currency question. The crisis of 1873 had naturally caused serious thinking upon that subject, and the result was a conflict as to remedies. The majority of the Republicans believed that one serious cause of the disaster had been the fluctuating value of the currency, due to the failure to redeem greenbacks in coin. Still the party was divided, and in 1873 the Secretary of the Treasury actually issued

$26,000,000 additional greenbacks, to tide over the period of greatest stringency. A compromise measure, largely the work of Senator John Sherman of Ohio, was finally passed on January 14, 1875, which provided for the resumption of specie payments on January 1, 1879.

To many, particularly in those rural regions where the "Ohio Idea" had been popular, the case appeared very different. The tremendous agricultural expansion of this period was accompanied to an unusual extent by the creation of mortgage indebtedness. Capital was more ductile than it had been before. In the newer regions farmers could borrow what they needed to establish themselves, and in the older districts they went into debt to purchase the farm machinery that was becoming a necessity. Many of these mortgages had been contracted when paper money was at a heavy discount, and its gradual rise in value had meant an increase in the burden. As before the Revolution, at the time of the Shays's Rebellion, and under the Jackson régime, the more recently developed portions of the country demanded that the government use its power to cheapen capital. They believed that a generous issue of paper money would have prevented all trouble in 1873, and would now hasten recovery, which was coming but slowly. The strength of this element increased, and in 1876 a national party was formed, popularly known as "Greenback," which nominated Peter Cooper for the presidency. The ideal of this party was a money "manufactured out of material costing substantially nothing, redeemable in nothing else, inasmuch as the redemption of money is its destruction, nonexportable, deriving its existence from the will of the government, authenticated by the official stamp, and regulated as to its value by limiting its quantity." This party did not play a conspicuous part in the election of 1876, but in 1878, an "off year," when party allegiance did not bind so closely, it cast over a million votes, elected many congressmen, and pledged others to support

The "Greenback" movement.

its views. The result was that on May 31, 1878, Congress
ordered that none of the greenbacks which should be redeemed
be destroyed, but that they be returned to circulation.

Restoration of specie payments.   In spite of this agitation, John Sherman, whom Hayes
had appointed Secretary of the Treasury, very successfully
prepared the government for the resumption of specie
payments. In fact, a short time before the first of January,
1879, the premium on gold disappeared, and there was no
longer any temptation to exchange paper for it. With this
event, the financial disturbances directly caused by the Civil
War may be considered to have ended, but the fact that the
currency, and to a certain extent banking, had become
national rather than state problems remained.

BIBLIOGRAPHICAL NOTES

Sources.   On the reform movements: Curtis, G. W., *Orations and Addresses*, I, 1–36; 261–286; 313–366; II, 1–86. Tilden, S. J., *Writings and Speeches*, I, 515–606. *U. S. Doc., Fifteenth Annual Report of U. S. Civil Service Commission.*

Historical accounts.   Bigelow, J., *Tilden*, I, ch. IX; II, chs. I–III. Crawford, J. B., *The Crédit Mobilier.* Harding, S. B., *Party Struggles in Missouri during the Civil War* (Am. Hist. Assoc., *Report*, 1900, 87–103).

Grant's second administration.   Merriam, G. S., *The Negro and the Nation*, 306–361. Rhodes, *United States*, VII, 175–226. Story, M., *Sumner*, chs. XXIII, XXIV. Woodburn, *Party Politics in Indiana during the Civil War* (Am. Hist. Assoc., *Report*, 1902, 223–251).

Administration of Hayes.   Blaine, J. G., *Twenty Years in Congress*, II, 317–333, ch. XXIV. Boutwell, G. S., *Reminiscences of Sixty Years*, II, chs. XXIII, XXIV, XXVI. Burton, *Sherman.* Dewey, D. R., *Financial History*, chs. XIII–XV. Dunning, W. A., *Reconstruction*, chs. XIX–XXI. Hart, A. B., *Chase*, chs. IX, XI, XV. Haworth, P. L., *The Hayes-Tilden Disputed Election of 1876.* McCulloch, H., *Men and Measures of Half a Century*, ch. XVIII. Rhodes, J. F., *Historical Essays*, 243–264.

Reform.   Adams, C. F. and H., *Chapters in Erie*, I–III. Cary, E., *G. W. Curtis*, chs. XV–XVII, XX, XXII, XXIII. Bigelow, *Tilden*, I, ch. VIII. Fish, *Civil Service and the Patronage*, ch. X.

Ostrogorski, *Democracy and the Organization of Political Parties*, II, 539–604. Woodburn, *Political Parties and Party Problems in the United States*, chs. XIV–XXI.

On railroads: Haney, L. H., *Congressional History of Railroads*, I, 234–264. Paxson, F. L., *Last American Frontier*, chs. XI–XIII. On Indians: Paxson, F. L., chs. II, VIII, XIV–XVIII. On panic of 1873: Sprague, O. W. M., *History of Crises under the National Banking System*. On tariff: Stanwood, E., *Tariff Controversies*, II, chs. XIV and XV. Taussig, F. W., *Tariff*, 171–229. Mark Twain and Charles Dudley Warner, *The Gilded Age*. — *Economic questions.*

Illustrative literature.

CHAPTER XXVI

THE CURRENCY AND THE TARIFF, 1880 TO 1900

Period of
transition. THE period of the eighties and nineties was in many respects one of transition. The war issues had for the most
part been solved, but the memory of them continued to be
an important factor in politics. Certain results of the war,
such as the permanence of the Union and the increased
exercise of national functions, were well established. This
very fact broadened the scope of national politics, for the
currency problem which for twenty-five years before the war
had been a state affair now became exclusively national.
The war legislation, moreover, still gave shape to discussion
of the tariff, which took the form of defense of the policy then
adopted or attack upon it. In the meantime new conditions
were evolving, and new issues forcing themselves upon
public attention. In general these issues were of two kinds.
On the one side government action was demanded upon many
subjects; on the other there was an attempt to improve the
machinery of the government. This period of transition
differed from that between 1815 and 1828 in being marked,
not by the disorganization of parties, but by their stability
and effectiveness of organization. Party allegiance passed
from father to son, and independent voting was generally a
negligible factor except in the trans-Mississippi district,
where the currency moved the farmer, and the Chinese
question the Californian, to desert his party standard. The
usual tendency of national parties to compromise by adopting a policy of inaction, left the initiative on many subjects
to the states. The legislative history of most movements
begins with the states, then becomes national, and then goes

back to those states which were slow in acting. Another
noticeable feature of the period from 1875 to 1898 is that
only twice, 1889 to 1891 and 1893 to 1895, did a political
party control both houses of Congress and the presidency.
National legislation was, therefore, largely of a non-partisan
character. In this chapter, the course of national party
politics will be followed with such notice of changing conditions as seems necessary to explain them. Later, the general
unfolding of new factors in the national development will be
traced.

With the resumption of specie payments in 1879 ended   Free coinage
all important discussion of fiat money, but not the agitation   of silver.
for other kinds of cheap circulating mediums. This now
took the form of a demand for the free and unrestricted
coinage of silver. In 1873 the coinage of silver dollars
had ceased.   In 1878 the Greenback element forced a
compromise measure, known as the Bland act, through
Congress, by which silver was again made legal tender, and
the treasury department was instructed to purchase and
coin not less than $2,000,000 and not more than $4,000,000
worth of silver bullion per month. In twelve years nearly
370,000,000 silver dollars were coined, which the government credit kept in circulation at a rate considerably in
excess of the commercial value of the silver they contained.
This, however, was far from answering the demand, and
endeavor was persistent to secure the unlimited coinage of
all silver offered the government.

This demand was urged by a strong minority in both   Silver in
parties, which the party managers generally endeavored to   politics.
quiet by making some compromise.   The Democrats in
1868 nominated a strong money candidate and adopted a
soft money platform. The Republicans in 1884 declared in
favor of bimetallism by international agreement. When
such an arrangement was not forthcoming, the advocates
of free silver were able to form an independent party of no

inconsiderable proportions. In 1880 they cast over three hundred thousand votes for a Greenback candidate; in 1892, over one million for the same candidate, James B. Weaver, running on the Populist ticket.

The granger movement.
While the expansion of the currency was the chief political object of this element, other issues tended to increase its solidarity. The problem of transportation had, in the earlier period, been one of creating the means of intercourse; with the phenomenal strides in railroad construction during the fifties and sixties, attention came to be centered upon the question of rates. American foodstuffs in the European market came increasingly into competition with those from all parts of the world, and transportation rates became of vital importance. In 1865 it was calculated that the 1,062,611 bushels of wheat raised in Dane county, Wisconsin, were worth $1,188,163 at home, the railroad charge to the lake shore would bring the value to $2,125,222, and the water carriage to New York, to $2,444,005. The farmers' complaints at what they considered exorbitant charges were made effective by the rise of rural organizations. In 1867 the Patrons of Husbandry were organized. The society was secret, admitting both men and women. Its object was the general improvement of farming conditions, and its granges or local branches combined social entertainment with education and coöperative buying. Quickly attaining a large membership, the granges soon began to influence politics. In the early seventies the organized farmer became a factor to reckon with in Illinois, Minnesota, Iowa, Kansas, and Wisconsin. In Wisconsin the Grangers secured control in 1874 and passed laws fixing maximum railroad rates. This legislation was repealed subsequently, but is important because it came before the courts for review. Chief Justice Ryan of the Supreme Court of Wisconsin found it constitutional in a very able decision, and this position was confirmed by the Supreme Court of the United States in the *Granger Cases*

in 1877. In these decisions there was set forth for the first time clearly the legal doctrine that companies running railroads and performing certain other similar functions were public service corporations, and as such, were under the control of the state in which they operated.

The experience of the later seventies and eighties increased the feeling that railroads should be regulated, but it came to be realized that not rates alone were in question. The management of many railroads was both inefficient and corrupt. Fortunes were made rather by contracts for the construction of the roads and their supply than by running them. Their profits were drawn away by extravagant payments to terminal companies formed by the railroad officials. The roads were "watered" by issuing stock far in excess of the cost. It was the attempt to pay dividends on issues thus foolishly and corruptly spent or not spent at all which in many instances caused the companies to desire high rates. The rates were on a financial rather than an economic basis, and in many instances they were not charged equally to all the customers of the road. Roads by discriminating in their rates could and frequently did ruin individuals and even towns. Where two or more roads served the same territory, rates were determined not by competition but by pools or joint agreements. Roads or steamship companies refusing to agree were bought up or forced into submission by cutting off their through traffic. The question was one of great complexity, and it was one which was national in character and required national legislation. In 1866 and again in 1868 committee reports were submitted to Congress which asserted the authority of that body to legislate on the subject. In 1874 a report was made to the House of Representatives: "Upon the theory that, by reason of stock inflation, extravagance, and dishonesty in construction and management, and combinations among existing companies, the present railroad service of the coun-

Railroad rates.

National regulation of transportation.

try imposes unnecessary burdens upon its commerce."
This report advised the building of one or more roads by the
government to regulate the situation by competition. Economic causes produced a rapid lowering of rates, but a report
of 1886 asserted that this "recognized benefit has been obtained at the cost of the most unwarranted discriminations,"
and demand arose for regulations of increasing scope.

Concentra-
tion of
population
and the
labor move-
ment.

Almost at the same time that the farming interests
were becoming organized, labor was making its first important
efforts in the same direction. By the close of the Hayes administration, manufacturing had recovered from the crisis
of 1873, and began a new era of marvelous expansion. Steam
was rapidly displacing water power, bringing with it concentration at points to which coal could easily be brought, as
on the seacoast and at railroad centers. Particularly in
New England the village factories failed to recover from the
shock of 1873, and the population of many towns sank far
below what it had been a hundred years before, while cities
grew like magic. The conditions of employment changed.
The old individual relation, where employer and employee
were united by a lifetime of associations, was superseded by
one more purely economic, particularly as the native Americans tended to leave the factories to French Canadian, Irish,
and other immigrants. Corporations, often controlling many
factories, began generally to take the place of individual
owners. Laborers changed easily from one factory to
another, and from place to place, while manufacturers
settled disputes by dismissing their workmen and hiring
others, sometimes even importing them from foreign

Labor
unions.

countries. Both capital and labor felt the necessity of organization. Labor unions had been formed in the flush
times before 1837, they had been formed again and more
extensively during the war, when by strikes and other
methods they had forced up wages into some relation with the
increased prices. In 1869 the Noble Order of Knights of

Labor was founded, mainly for the purpose of securing legislation favorable to labor of all classes, and in 1881 the American Federation of Labor united many of the unions, which
had been formed by the workmen of particular trades, into a
national body. In 1872 and in 1888 some of the labor leaders
ran candidates for the presidency, and in 1892, led by the
superficial similarity of their demands to those of the agri-
culturists, they united with them in the "People's" party.
The majority of the laborers, however, clung to the two
leading parties, within which they were able to exert great
power. In this way they secured much favorable legislation.
State governments regulated the hours and conditions of
labor, and protected women and children. The national
government forbade the importation of Chinese laborers
in 1882, and in 1888 that of any labor under contract. It
is, in fact, true that during this period those movements
obtained the quickest and surest success whose leaders
worked within the old party organizations, rather than
formed independent parties.

Among the manufacturers during the war time, associa- Concentra-
tions were formed to combat the unions. During the seven- tion of
capital.
ties a much more important consolidation was beginning.
The thoroughgoing character of American democracy, which
gave such opportunity to every man, gave it as well to every
dollar. Restrictions upon the use of wealth were few, and
its accumulation, not only in the community, but particularly in the hands of individuals, was unusually rapid.
This wealth, in the hands of the most active and enterprising
men of the time, did not become, as in Europe, a conservative factor, but rather intensified the speculative attempts
to push on the development of the country. Its holders saw that the greatest opportunities now lay rather in
organization than in direct exploitation. The vast unities
of the country, physiographical, and in the customs and
needs of the inhabitants, afforded unlimited rewards to those

who sought a host of customers and but a small profit on
each sale.   To take advantage of this situation many independent establishments were united under one management,
either by agreement or by outright purchase.   In either case
the resulting organization came to be known as a trust.
The purposes of the trust were to avoid the expenses of
many separate managements and to abolish competition.
Once established, each trust sought to agree with, or to
drive out, others engaged in its particular business.   Ultimately the control of prices would be in its hands.   The
trusts were most numerous in those branches of industry
which controlled some one great national source of supply
or some universal need.   Earliest among them was the
Standard Oil Company, formed by John D. Rockefeller.
There quickly followed trusts to control sugar, whisky,
tobacco, salt, and many other things, though they were
seldom to be found in those industries depending upon a high
degree of mechanical skill.   During the same period railroad
ownership tended to consolidate, the great Vanderbilt system
being formed between New York and Chicago, and the Gould
system farther west.   The men who formed these combinations were primarily organizers and were among the ablest
of the time.

Business and politics.   The man who would rise out of the ordinary in the thirties
went into politics; in the seventies and eighties such men
went into business.   Equality of opportunity gave unlimited
possibilities to the strongest, and the "Captains of Industry"
showed the same skill in business at this time that the great
national leaders had earlier shown in political organization.
To the natural economies which organization brought about,
many of the leaders in such enterprises sought to add the
profit which might come from the overthrow of competition,
from the monopoly of basic natural resources, and from
the special favors which, as large customers or as part
owners, they might obtain from railroads and other public

service corporations. To men doing business on such a large scale the effect of public legislation on their private affairs was more evident than to the average citizen, and they were active in shaping such legislation. All their accumulated capital was drawn into political activity, both in order to obtain favorable legislation and for protection against the attacks of the agricultural and labor interests. The party managers had previously maintained themselves chiefly on the forced assessments of officeholders, and when after 1883 that source of income was reduced by the progress of civil service reform, they began to rely on the contributions of capitalists. Party leaders had to steer their course narrowly when the threats of labor leaders were on one side and the lures of capital on the other, and joyfully sought to enact any legislation upon which the two united.

The campaign of 1880 was one of the least eventful in American history. The most exciting feature was the contest for the Republican nomination. President Hayes was not a candidate, but ex-President Grant was eager for a third term, and was vigorously supported by the Stalwarts under Senator Conkling. His leading opponent was James G. Blaine, and the conflict was so bitter that, again, as in 1876, a dark horse was selected — James A. Garfield of Ohio, a friend of Blaine, and a man who stood for civil service reform. The Democrats chose General Winfield S. Hancock, a prominent Civil War veteran. The subsidence of southern issues and the failure of both parties to take a sharply defined position on the rising economic problems, made the campaign largely a struggle between the rival party organizations. The growing power of organized labor was shown by the fact that California and Nevada, resenting the failure of the Republican administration to prevent the immigration of Chinese laborers, changed from the Republican to the Democratic column. The Republicans, however, gained in the East, and Garfield was elected.

Election of Garfield.

Blaine's
foreign
policy.

Garfield appointed Blaine his Secretary of State, and the latter embarked upon a comprehensive foreign policy. He aimed to revive and extend the Pan-American policy of Clay and Adams. He endeavored to make the United States the arbiter of the disputes of Latin America, and he resented vigorously the interference of European countries in any matters concerning either American continent, and particularly with regard to the building of an interoceanic canal, which was at this time being actively pushed by a French company headed by Ferdinand de Lesseps, the promoter of the Suez Canal. Blaine was one of the few leaders of the time who conceived anything like a comprehensive foreign policy. He lacked, however, the necessary training, and the political appointees selected to carry out his schemes were most incompetent. Popular interest, moreover, did not support him, for the Americans of the time cared almost nothing for foreign affairs.

Succession
of Arthur.

In September, 1881, President Garfield died, having been shot by a disappointed officeseeker. He was succeeded by Chester A. Arthur, a friend of Conkling, who had been nominated to the vice presidency with the hope of conciliating the Stalwarts. President Arthur had the reputation of being decidedly a politician rather than a statesman. The highest position he had previously held had been that of Collector of Customs at New York. He proved to be an excellent administrator and filled his unexpected position with dignity and poise. Mr. Blaine, however, did not desire to serve under him and resigned. The President thereupon appointed, as Secretary of State, Frederick T. Frelinghuysen of New Jersey, who reversed Mr. Blaine's foreign policy in most particulars.

The
triumph of
civil service
reform.

Of much greater importance than the change in foreign policy was the impetus that the assassination of Garfield gave to the movement for civil service reform. Garfield stood for reform ; he engaged in a severe factional fight with Conkling and Platt, the New York senators, on the plea of establishing better conditions in New York, and was regarded as a martyr to the cause. The next congressional election showed a determined public sentiment behind the movement, and in 1883 Congress passed the Pendleton Bill. This provided for a Civil Service Commission which was to arrange for the classification of the government employees, and the appointment of large numbers of them on the basis of competitive examination. The President was given the power to extend these rules over other members of the civil service at his discretion. The Commission also had large power over the civil service, being particularly directed to prevent the assessment of officeholders for political purposes.

The next campaign resulted in a considerable realign- "Mugwump" campaign. ment of parties. The Republicans turned to the leadership of Mr. Blaine. They received credit for the Chinese Exclusion Act so strongly demanded by the labor interests of the Pacific coast, and as a result they recovered California and Nevada. Their platform declared in favor of international bimetallism, and consequently no soft money third party played a prominent rôle in the election. The Republican party itself, however, divided on the issue of reform. A group of able men, many of them young, opposed Mr. Blaine. He had never satisfactorily cleared himself of the charges brought against him in 1876, and was regarded as "jingoistic" in foreign policy and machine-ridden in politics. In the convention they were led by George William Curtis and prominent among them was Theodore Roosevelt, a young member of the New York legislature. When Blaine was chosen, Curtis and many others went over to the Democrats, some temporarily and some permanently. These men were known as "Mugwumps." Mr. Roosevelt, however, stayed with the Republican party.

The Democrats adopted a platform resembling that of Election of Cleveland. 1876, boldly pronouncing in favor of "honest money, the gold and silver coinage of the Constitution, and a circulating medium convertible into such money without loss." Their tariff plank was framed on the theory that the tariff should offset differences in the cost of production in this and other countries due to higher wages here. Although this is practically the Republican position at the present day, it was not regarded as so satisfactory to the protectionists in 1884 as the Republican platform, and Pennsylvania, the great protectionist state, swung from the doubtful to the Republican column for many years to come. To offset this loss and losses that might occur in the West because of their position on the currency, the Democrats declared emphatically for administrative reform, and nominated Grover Cleveland, who as mayor of Buffalo and governor of New York had made an admirable record as a reformer. The election was very close, depending upon the vote of New York state. The determining number of votes was so small, any one of a number of accidents may have been responsible for the result. It is claimed, for instance, that Mr. Blaine was defeated by an indiscreet clergyman friendly to him who described him as fighting "Rum, Romanism, and Rebellion." Cleveland carried the state by 1149 plurality in a total vote of nearly one million two hundred thousand, and was elected.

Cleveland's vetoes.

Cleveland was a man of strong character and individuality. He formed a cabinet of men for the most part not well known in public life, but who proved to be of ability and who successfully coöperated to make the administration a success. Most important among them were Thomas F. Bayard of Delaware, Secretary of State, William F. Vilas of Wisconsin, Postmaster-General, and later Secretary of the Interior, and William C. Whitney of New York, Secretary of the Navy. Cleveland made more extensive use of the veto than any other President. He vetoed a river and harbor bill, a great variety of measures of a special, local, or private character, and almost three hundred and fifty private pension bills.

In thus giving a check to the rather indiscriminate voting of public money as the result of good nature or logrolling, he contributed a distinct public service, and public opinion justified his method, in spite of a general disapproval of executive interference with legislation.

The civil service demanded all his strength of character. As first Democratic President since 1861 he found himself surrounded by subordinate officials hostile almost to a man; at the same time he was subject to terrific pressure from Democratic politicians hungry for office after so many lean years. It was impossible not to make removals, and he made many, but he did not lose sight of reform. He supported the Civil Service Commission in its recommendations, extended the rules over many branches of the service previously left open to political appointment, and took vigorous measures to enforce the laws against assessments. His administration, in fact, marks the real triumph of that reform. *Cleveland and the civil service.*

The adoption of civil service reform by the national government was followed by favorable legislation in many states and cities. Such laws, however, depend for their efficiency upon the support of responsible public officials, for many methods of evading their requirements exist. In 1881 a National Civil Service Reform Association was organized in New York city, whose object was to watch and make public all violations and to urge the extension of the system. A public sentiment favorable to the movement has been built up, and on the whole the vigor of the law has been maintained and constant progress toward the purification of public service, national, state, and municipal, has been made. During this same period a system of secret voting, known as the "Australian ballot," was widely adopted by the various states, with the result of diminishing the amount of bribery and intimidation at the polls. It remained true, however, that the selection of the holders of elective offices *Growth of the reform movement and of civic consciousness.*

was practically made by the two great party organizations. The voter at the polls could merely choose between two candidates. These party candidates were selected by organizations which were entirely unrecognized
and unregulated by the law, and were in fact nearly
always the choice of the party managers. Party caucuses
were very often held under circumstances which discouraged
the attendance of the ordinary citizens, and were often so
managed as to render such citizens powerless if they came.
Many began to urge that the parties had become actually
such an important part of the machinery of government that
their organization should be brought under government
control, that it was dangerous to leave such powerful bodies,
actually controlling the adoption of public policies and the
selection of the most important officials, entirely extra-legal.
A movement was therefore started to bring the party caucuses or primaries under legal control. Such laws were
passed in Massachusetts and some other states, but little
progress was made during this period. Nevertheless, it
may be said that, on the whole, the movement for civic
betterment, whose rise was noted during Grant's administration, became an established factor under Cleveland,
and has since that time accomplished much in the purification of politics and in making public opinion sensitive to
violations of political decency. In municipal politics many
reform campaigns have been fought and many victories
won. Although distinctly reform administrations have
seldom been long maintained, each reform victory has accomplished some definite results, and the subsequent relapse has
never meant a return to conditions quite as bad as previously existed.

Non-partisan
legislation.   Although the Republicans continued under Cleveland to
control the Senate, and no Democratic program of legislation could be carried out, many useful laws of a non-partisan
character were enacted. In 1887 the Tenure of Office Act,

which had never been literally lived up to, but under the shadow of which had grown up the custom of "senatorial courtesy," by which the senators became practical dictators of the political patronage within their several states, was repealed. In 1886 a law was passed providing that in case of the death of the President and Vice President, the succession should descend through the cabinet, from the Secretary of State downward in order of the date of creation of the several departments, instead of going to the president of the Senate as had been provided in 1791.

More important was the passage in 1887 of the Interstate Commerce Act. This was largely the result of the Granger organization in the West. The states had found that local regulation could accomplish little and demanded a national law. Bills were drawn up in the Senate by Senator Cullom of Illinois, who, as governor of that state, was familiar with the working of state laws, and in the House by Mr. Reagan of Texas, formerly Postmaster-General of the Confederacy. The final bill was framed by a conference committee and represented a compromise. It provided that all rates for interstate commerce must be reasonable and must be made public, it forbade discriminating "rebates," and "pools" for the purpose of fixing non-competitive rates by lines normally competitive, and established an Interstate Commerce Commission to enforce the act. This act is important constitutionally, as it brought into full vigor a clause in the Constitution giving Congress powers which up to this time that body had entirely neglected. Economically it has had large results in reforming the conditions of transportation, and politically it finally introduced into national politics a question which since that time has come to have the greatest significance. *Interstate Commerce Act.*

Of still greater political importance, however, was the discussion over the tariff, for during it the views of both parties became defined. During the eighties the growth of *Tariff discussion.*

the country resulted in a great increase in the revenue, and the desirability of its reduction began to attract attention. This naturally increased interest in the tariff which produced the larger part of the revenue. The natural method of reducing the revenue was by reducing the customs dues. In 1882 a Tariff Commission was appointed to consider the matter, and in 1883 the first general revision since the Civil War was enacted. While there was reduction in some duties, the new act was, perhaps, as protective as the system it repealed. The president of the Commission said: "Reduction in itself was by no means desirable to us; it was a concession to public sentiment, a bending of the top and branches to the wind of public opinion to save the trunk of the protective system. In a word the object was protection through reduction."

Defeat of Randall. The Democrats were as always divided, but a majority favored lower rates, and in 1883, when they regained control of the House of Representatives, which they had lost in 1881, they replaced Samuel J. Randall, a Pennsylvania Democrat and protectionist, who had been Speaker from 1876 to 1881, by John G. Carlisle, who favored a tariff for revenue.

Cleveland's position on the tariff. This change marked a departure from the straddling policy which that party had so long carried out with regard to the tariff. In 1887 Cleveland devoted his entire annual message to the subject and so identified his party with the policy of reduction, that only four Democrats voted against the Mills Bill, which was formed as a result of his recommendations. He urged that the tariff constituted a tax upon the people, that by it more money was raised for the government than was necessary, and that a much greater amount went directly to the manufacturers than to the government. He pointed out that under its protection, trusts were being formed which prevented domestic competition and so kept prices unreasonably high. He argued that the labor employed in the protected industries constituted but a small proportion of that of the whole country, and that even such labor would gain as much by the lowering of prices as it might lose by the lowering of wages. With a lower rate on raw materials, he predicted that American manufacturers could compete in foreign markets, and by extending their trade area, render themselves less susceptible to the influence of local financial troubles. He did not recommend free trade, but reform. "It is a condition," he said, "not a theory, that confronts us." The Mills Bill could not pass the Senate, which was Republican, but it was put forward as an earnest of what the Democrats would do if they secured full control of the government.

The Republicans also, in the Senate, framed a bill, not with a view to passage, but to exemplify their policies. They argued that the revenue might be reduced and the tariff at the same time made more protective, by concentrating the duties on articles competing with those produced in the United States, and that this should be done. They appealed for support to manufacturers and to workmen, arguing the advantages of high prices and high wages. This appeal to labor distinguishes the protectionist speeches of the Republicans from those of the Whigs, and politically it was their strongest point. The Chinese Exclusion and Alien Contract laws, protecting labor from low-priced competitors, were really portions of this protective system. With the farmer their case was less strong. The old home market argument had little weight when such a large proportion of the crop was sold abroad. The protection of wool was the strongest direct inducement they could offer this class. Their ablest leaders, such as Senator Harrison of Indiana, did not deny a connection between the tariff and the trusts, but proposed to meet this difficulty by restrictive legislation. *The protectionist argument.*

With the issue thus clearly drawn, the parties went into the election, the Republicans nominating Benjamin Harrison, the Democrats renominating Cleveland. The intense popular interest is shown by an increase of about fifteen per *Election of 1888.*

cent in the popular vote.   While Cleveland gained somewhat
the larger share of this increase, the Republicans won over
New York and Indiana, the only two states to change, and
thus gained the election.   More important still, the Republicans won the House, which they had controlled only once
since 1875, that is, between 1881 and 1883; and, retaining
a majority in the Senate, they were in a position to carry out
their policy without compromise.   Since 1875 no party had
had full control of the national government.

Republican
control.
 The Republicans had an elaborate and well-balanced program which they determined promptly to carry out, but
first it was necessary to consolidate their control.   Having
loudly attacked the election frauds common in the South,
by which negroes were prevented from voting, they unseated
a large number of Democratic members of the House,
chiefly from that section, and put Republicans in their places.
For more permanent results, they looked to an election law,
designed to protect the negro voter.   This Force Bill of 1890,
framed by Senator Lodge of Massachusetts, failed to pass,
as many within the party realized the danger of reviving Civil
War issues.   It was the last attempt to control the southern
electorate by national authority.   More successfully the
Republicans sought to render the method of doing business
in the House of Representatives less dilatory.   This was the
work of Thomas B. Reed, of Maine, the new Speaker, who so
extended the functions of his office as to earn the title of
"Czar."   He practically destroyed the power of the minority
to delay progress either by the usual motions or by refusing
to vote.   Moreover, he consolidated in his own hands the
power thus gained for the majority.   He controlled the calen-
dar which provided for bringing bills before the House, and
arranged long in advance the speakers who should be recognized.   Under his leadership, Congress was able to pass an
extraordinarily heavy program.

 For many years numbers of western states had been

clamorous for admission. In the evenly balanced conditions The "Omnibus Bill." of the parties, however, every vote was important; and in each case a new state was assumed to be of advantage to one party or the other. It had, therefore, proved impossible to authorize admission when the House was controlled by one party and the Senate by the other. Most of the states which were now ready were Republican, and Congress was glad to take this opportunity to strengthen the party, and to gain the gratitude of the West, at the same time doing something which must sometime be done. In 1889, by an "Omnibus Bill," they admitted North and South Dakota, Montana, and Washington, and in 1890, Wyoming and Idaho. By dividing Dakota, and by omitting New Mexico and Arizona, which were Democratic, they secured a decided advantage in Congress. While the first twelve new senators and seven representatives were all Republicans, however, the control of that party over the new region was soon proved to be far from stable.

With the machinery thus ready, the Republicans addressed The dispersal of the surplus. themselves, first, to the task of getting rid of the surplus. In large measure they considered it desirable to do this by increasing expenditures. Twenty millions were used in refunding the direct tax levied upon the several states during the Civil War. A still greater expenditure, and one destined to be a charge upon the treasury for many years, was involved in a dependent pension bill which raised the amount annually required for that service from about ninety million to one hundred and forty million. Increasing sums were also voted for the new navy, the beginnings of which had been made under Arthur and Cleveland, by their efficient secretaries, Chandler and Whitney.

Chief in importance, however, was the tariff. Their bill, McKinley tariff. which was passed in 1890, was popularly known by the name of McKinley, who was chairman of the House Committee on Ways and Means, but it received significant changes in the Senate, where Senator Aldrich of Rhode Island had charge of it. The principal feature of the bill was, that duties on competitive articles were raised, being in many instances placed so high as to discourage importation, and thus actually diminish the revenue. On the other hand, the duty on certain raw materials such as sugar was abolished, the sugar planters being compensated by a direct bounty. Thus protection was increased and revenue reduced. As the bill originally stood it contained little that would appeal to the farming interests or would tend to the development of an export trade. Blaine, at this time again Secretary of State, said that it did not provide a market for a single pound of American pork or a single barrel of American flour, and that he would give two years of his life for two hours on the Senate floor to oppose it. Blaine wished to amend it by providing for reciprocity with the other countries of America, a policy which was in line with his general idea of developing friendly relations with those countries and in accordance with the recommendations of the Pan-American Congress which had met at his call in 1889. His criticisms were supported by many members of Congress and much public sentiment in the northwestern states. As a result, the bill was amended by Senator Aldrich, to the effect that though sugar, molasses, tea, coffee, and hides remained on the free list, the President was to have power to impose certain prescribed duties on those articles whenever he should consider that the duties imposed by other countries on "the agricultural or other products of the United States" were "reciprocally unjust or unreasonable." This reciprocity provision was, however, made general instead of American as Blaine had proposed. Under it a number of treaties were negotiated by which "unjust and unreasonable" duties on United States products were reduced, but these were not long enough in force to show how far such a policy might ultimately be of benefit.

The Republican expedient of securing and expanding foreign markets by legislative and administrative regulation contrasted with the Democratic plan of obtaining them by freer trade and less legislation, and showed that the fundamental party differences, found in the earliest days of the republic, were still at the bottom of the respective party politics. Cleveland, like Jefferson, would leave the individual as free as possible and use government to maintain that freedom; McKinley and Blaine would have the government foster private enterprise by beneficial legislation. The same difference is noticeable in the attitude of the two parties toward the trusts. Whereas Cleveland proposed to attack them by removing their support in the tariff, the Republicans proposed preventive legislation. Already twenty-five states had passed laws against them, and now Senator Sherman brought in a bill which after much discussion and many changes passed and came to be popularly known as the Sherman Anti-Trust Law of 1890. This law declares "any contract, combination in the form of a trust or otherwise, or conspiracy, in restraint of trade or commerce among the several states," illegal, and its promoters punishable by fine or imprisonment. This was intended to appeal particularly to the western states, but it was ten years before its enforcement seriously began, and twenty years before the courts made its meaning reasonably clear.

The Republicans also repealed in 1891 the preëmption law of 1841 under the cover of which the sheep raisers of the western plains were securing vast holdings. This law had worked fairly well in regions where land had to be broken to cultivation by individual effort, but it led to fraud and monopoly in regions where exploitation at little expense but on a large scale was possible. This was a western measure, but one which while it pleased some alienated others. Another measure adopted with an eye to the West was Senator Sherman's Silver Purchase Act of 1890, which repealed the

Bland Act of 1878, and provided that the treasury purchase four million five hundred thousand ounces of silver every month, and pay for it in new treasury notes which should not be legal tender. This act was intended to raise silver to the ratio of sixteen to one with gold, which had been established by the government in 1834, but which had ceased to correspond with the actual fact. It represented rather a sop to the western cheap currency advocates and silver mine owners, than the convictions of Senator Sherman and the Republican leaders. It was a compromise intended to quiet the agitation for free coinage of silver.

Reaction. No party had ever before adopted at one time such a comprehensive system of legislation, and the politicians' feeling that action is dangerous was justified by the immediate and violent reaction that followed. The silver mining states were not satisfied with the Purchase Act, the Northwest did not regard the reciprocity and anti-trust legislation as sufficient attention to their wants, the East was alarmed at the vastly increased expenses combined with the reduction in revenue. The tariff was everywhere regarded as an extreme measure and was popular only in those districts directly favored. As happens often when defeat is approaching, local causes coöperated to weaken the Republicans. Thus, in Wisconsin a controversy regarding religious teaching in the schools worked against that party. The Democrats carried the House of Representatives by an overwhelming majority and a deadlock ensued for the last two years of Harrison's administration.

People's or Populist party. Between 1889 and 1892 a new movement of unrest had been taking shape in the West, the successor of the Granger and Greenback parties. Prosperity during the last fifteen years had driven the frontier of discontent somewhat farther west, but it had gained territory by the expansion of agricultural population into the country extending to the bases of the Rocky Mountains and the development of mining commu-

nities in the mountains. Politically its power was increased
by the admission of the six new states. In part, conditions
simply reproduced those that had always existed on the
frontier wherever it had been, but economic distress was
aggravated by the fact that in the Kansas-Nebraska region
farmers, tempted by a few exceptionally wet years, had
pressed into semi-arid regions which they did not know how
to cultivate. A number of dry seasons found them in debt
and left them bankrupt. Organizations called Farmers'

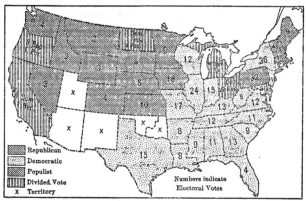

ELECTION OF 1892

Alliances and Industrial Unions were formed in 1889. These
spread rapidly, and soon found a foothold in the South,
where the farmers were continually in debt to the merchants,
who charged high rates for money. In 1891 a national
convention met in Cincinnati, the title of "People's" party
was adopted, and a comprehensive platform framed demanding the free coinage of silver at the ratio of sixteen to one, a
graduated income tax, a national paper currency to be loaned
on the security of land and crops at two per cent interest,
and government ownership of railroads and telegraphs.

This party secured control of Kansas and other states, and in 1892 nominated for the presidency James B. Weaver, the Greenback candidate of 1880.

Election of Cleveland. The Republican and Democratic parties presented the same candidates for the presidency as in 1888, and practically the same platforms. The Republicans lost heavily in the West, where the Populist party carried twenty-two electoral votes that would normally have been Republican. The election, however, was decided in the East. Here the Republicans lost nearly everywhere by the "stay at home vote." Harrison was able, and a good administrator, but he was unsympathetic and could not arouse enthusiasm, and nearly every one was still dissatisfied with some feature of the Republican program. The Democrats about maintained their figures of 1888, won the doubtful states, and elected Cleveland, together with a majority in both houses of Congress, thus attaining full control of the government for the first time since the Civil War.

Crisis of 1893. Two causes rendered this an almost barren victory. First was the severe financial and industrial panic which came upon the country in the fall of 1893. The enormous industrial advances of the past fifteen years had led to an undue expansion of credit. Suddenly public confidence became shaken, credit vanished, and tangible resources were insufficient. Thousands of enterprises were forced into bankruptcy, and nearly all others were carried on at a reduced scale. A period of hard times, with failures, and with the cities filled with unemployed, succeeded. The government was poorly equipped to deal with this situation. The radical financial changes introduced by the Republicans had made it very difficult for the congressional leaders to forecast the revenues and expenses, and as these two sides of the balance sheet are, by congressional practice, arranged by separate committees, the uncertainty of the estimates was even greater than it might otherwise have been. The expenditure for pensions proved to be greater than had been anticipated, and the occurrence of the panic reduced the revenue more than had been counted upon in framing the tariff. The result was a deficit.

The second cause was the division within the party on the silver question, which now became acute. A great increase in the production of silver was accompanied at this time by a movement on the part of many governments, particularly that of British India, to put their finances upon a gold basis and discontinue their purchases of silver. As a natural result, the market value of silver rapidly declined and that held by the United States was becoming daily of less value. As the government was bound to redeem the notes issued against this silver in either silver or gold as the holder might demand, the strain on the treasury was enormous. To meet this situation, President Cleveland, in August, called a special session of Congress, by which the silver purchase clause of the act of 1890 was repealed. This drastic method of handling the financial situation recalls the "Specie Circular" of Jackson, and, indeed, Cleveland seems to have had in mind the "hard money" policy pursued by the Democrats after the panic of 1837. This policy of adopting hard money at the very moment when the cry for soft money was heightened by the universal economic distress, not unnaturally led to a serious break between the small number of Democratic senators favorable to silver, and the majority of the party. As these silver senators, representing the newer agricultural states and those interested in silver mining, held the balance of power in the Senate, the administration having passed this measure only with Republican support, the remainder of the Democratic legislative program was endangered.

The most important feature of this program was a tariff bill, and one was at length passed, in 1894. It was obtained, however, only by a series of compromises which made it far

The silver question becomes acute.

The Wilson tariff, and the Democratic program.

from the consistent measure desired by the administration, or designed by its author, William L. Wilson of West Virginia. Duties were lowered, certain raw materials, particularly wool, were placed on the free list, and a duty was reimposed on sugar. As the estimated revenue was still below requirements, and as the sugar duty was one which would fall heaviest upon the poor, the same bill was made to include an income tax to apply only to incomes of over four thousand dollars. This law was subsequently declared unconstitutional by the Supreme Court, and consequently the government was continually embarrassed in its finances. A total deficit of over one hundred and fifty millions accumulated during the four years, and the administration, in order to maintain the practice of redemption in gold, was forced to contract a "gold loan" at a rather heavy rate, from a group of New York bankers headed by J. Pierpont Morgan.

Labor troubles.

While the administration was struggling with these difficulties it was widely held responsible for the panic itself and all its consequences, though few grounds could be urged for such a charge except that the event happened at the time. The panic had not only aggravated the distress of the West, but had hit much more severely the industrial East. Here the new labor organizations had for some years been resorting to strikes, which often endangered and occasionally broke the public peace. In 1892 much blood was shed at Homestead in Pennsylvania. In 1894 a great railroad strike, originating among the employees of the Pullman Company, was declared at Chicago, which tied up traffic at that important point, and threatened to result in serious violence. Governor Altgeld of Illinois refused to call out the state troops. Thereupon, President Cleveland sent federal troops to Chicago, on the ground that the United States mail was interfered with, and the result of his action was that the strike was broken. The President through this act appeared to the discontented industrial workers as an opponent, as his antisilver policy had made him appear to the discontented farmers and miners. In 1894 the Democratic majority in the House of Representatives was lost, further party legislation was blocked, and the President was at odds with most of his party.

Under these circumstances the campaign of 1896 began. The Republican convention met first. It nominated for the presidency William McKinley, the author of the tariff bill of 1890 and at the time governor of Ohio. The managers hoped to make the fight hinge once more on the tariff question. The convention, by a vote of $812\frac{1}{2}$ to $110\frac{1}{2}$, declared in favor of the gold standard. This led to a bolt from the party. Many of the Republican advocates of free coinage followed Senator Teller of Colorado in a secession whose goal depended on the result of the Democratic convention. That convention was strongly divided on the currency question. A vigorous minority supported the gold policy of the Cleveland administration. If the gold advocates had won, there would undoubtedly have been formed a powerful third party, for the currency question was the one of paramount public interest, and was bound to force itself into politics as had the Texas question in 1844. It happened, however, that the silver advocates captured the convention, which declared in favor of the free coinage of silver at the ratio of sixteen to one. With a platform radically new, a new leader was desirable, and was found in William Jennings Bryan of Nebraska, who captivated the convention by a remarkably dramatic speech closing with an appeal not to "crucify mankind upon a cross of gold." This convention, also, was followed by a party split, certain leaders known as the "Gold-Democrats" nominating General Palmer of Illinois and General Buckner of Kentucky on an independent ticket. This loss was fully made up by the accession of Senator Teller and his followers, while the Populists also fused with the Democrats.

Nominations in 1896.

The net result was that the issue on the currency question was plainly presented to the people. From the seventeenth century it had been a potent factor in American
politics, but never before had an opportunity been given
for a contest on it so devoid of complications. The campaign was distinctly educational. Mr. Bryan made a vigorous campaign, speaking all over the country, and the Republican campaign was admirably organized by Mr. McKinley's
friend, Mark Hanna of Ohio. The result of the campaign

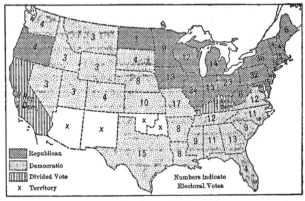

ELECTION OF 1896

was a complete change in the party alignment of the sections.
Bryan carried all those states which could be considered as
still showing frontier characteristics. He carried all the
states voting for Weaver in 1892, he won from the Republicans Nebraska, South Dakota, Washington, and Wyoming.
In the region west of the Missouri and excepting the older
communities of California, Oregon, and North Dakota, he
carried the entire forty-five electoral votes, where in 1892
the Democrats had not obtained a single one. In addition·
he carried the Solid South and the single border state of

Missouri, where the conditions producing the silver movement were still powerful. The Republicans, on the other hand, swept the entire North above the Missouri River, winning sixty-four votes Democratic in 1892, besides California, with Delaware, Maryland, West Virginia, and Kentucky, border states solidly allied with the South and with Democracy since 1872. The popular vote was enormous, reflecting the immense popular interest. Mr. Bryan received nearly a million more votes than any candidate had obtained at any previous election, and his success in uniting for the first time the agricultural and mining interests of the West with the labor interests of the East marked him as a force to reckon with in the future. Nevertheless McKinley defeated him by six hundred thousand in the popular vote, and 271 to 176 in the electoral vote.

The excessive representation of the thinly populated western states in the Senate left the silver element still powerful, and the Republicans promptly revived the coinage of silver, though to the extent of a million and a half a month, only. The rapid rise of prosperity, however, speedily contracted the area of financial discontent, and unparalleled discoveries of gold mines and the increase in gold production throughout the world caused that metal to be sufficiently abundant. By 1900, therefore, it was found possible to put the country definitely upon a gold basis by act of Congress. In the same year a slight readjustment of the national banking law resulted in an increase in bank note circulation. The end of currency agitation.

With still greater promptness the Republicans proceeded to the reëstablishment of their tariff system. Under the direction of Nelson Dingley, chairman of the Committee on Ways and Means, a tariff bill was presented to Congress at an extra session. Mr. Reed hastened its passage, and it was adopted in 1897. This returned with emphasis to the highly protective features of the McKinley tariff, but revenue needs Dingley tariff.

led to the imposition of a duty on sugar. There was provision for reciprocity, but, except within narrow limits, the assent of both houses of Congress was made necessary. In practice this provision proved sufficient to enable the administration to prevent retaliation because of the Dingley duties, but not to obtain the opening of new markets.

The Republican program of 1890 was once more in effect, but before the end of the century arrived it had become evident that a new era was at hand, and that both parties must adjust themselves to new conditions and attack new problems.

BIBLIOGRAPHICAL NOTES

Sources.   Cleveland's Message, Richardson, *Messages*, VIII, 580–591. Wallace, *Harrison and Morton*, 278–295.

Historical accounts.   D. R. Dewey, *National Problems*. Croly, H., *Marcus Hanna*. E. E. Sparks, *National Development*. Stanwood, E., *American Tariff Controversies*, vol. II. Taussig, F. W., *Tariff History*, 155–283. Dewey, D. R., *Financial History*, chs. XIX, XX. Paxson, F. L., *The Last American Frontier*. Turner, F. J., *The Contributions to the West of American Democracy, Atlantic Monthly*, Jan., 1903. U. S. Department of Agriculture, *Yearbook*, 1902, 109–113. Buck, S. J., *Granger Movement*. Ringwalt, J. L., *Transportation Systems*, 229–233, 265–269. Ripley, W. Z., *Railway Problems: Rates and Regulation*. Coman, K., *Industrial History* (rev. ed.), 354–374. Adams, T., and Sumner, H. L., *Labor Problems*.

CHAPTER XXVII

THE SPANISH WAR AND DIPLOMACY

WHEN McKinley was inaugurated few persons imagined International isolation. that the chief concern of his administration would be foreign affairs. Since the Napoleonic wars the United States had been so isolated from European complications that separation was thought of as normal and permanent. The Monroe Doctrine had for seventy-five years represented an actual condition. The annexations of the forties and fifties, moreover, had rounded out American territory, and seemed to quiet the intrigues and disputes which up to the Civil War had unsettled our relations with other American powers. Nevertheless, powerful influences were at work to draw us out of this quietude.

While the better known aspects of the Monroe Doc- Blaine and the Monroe Doctrine. trine, refraining from interference with European affairs and preventing European interference in America, had become well-accepted public policy, one side of it was far from realization. The United States had not become in any sense the leader of the American republics. England had sustained Canning's policy better than this country had supported that of Adams and Clay. England held the greater portion of Spanish-American trade, and exerted more influence than the United States. Germany, too, by trade everywhere and by colonization in Brazil, was taking second place. Mr. Blaine, as Secretary of State in 1881 and 1889 to 1892, had sought to change this condition. His policy was to make the United States the arbiter in Spanish-American disputes, whether they were between different American powers, or between any of them and European countries.

He desired also to unite the American countries by reciprocal treaty privileges, and to bind all together by means of
a Pan-American Conference which should recommend these
and other common policies to the several countries. Mr.
Blaine's projects resulted in disappointment, partly because
of mismanagement, but chiefly because of public apathy.
They were based, however, upon the growing need of the
expanding industrial development at home for foreign trade.
They represented one solution of the pressing problem of
trade expansion.

Venezuela
affair.

It is not surprising, therefore, that, although Mr. Blaine
was somewhat discredited by his work as Secretary of State,
his ideas were taken up after his death. His first line of
policy in fact received its most daring expression under
Secretary Olney, during Cleveland's second administration,
in the case of the Venezuela affair. This arose from a boundary dispute between that country and Great Britain. As a
conclusion to a protracted negotiation, Mr. Olney asserted
that the United States, in following the Monroe Doctrine,
had the right to demand the settlement of such a dispute by
arbitration, in order that it might be convinced that Great
Britain was not encroaching upon an American power.
While this might be considered a reasonable, if somewhat
far-fetched, extension of the doctrine laid down in Monroe's
message, Mr. Olney's further statements that the fiat of
the United States was law upon the American continents
and that existing European colonies on this continent were
temporary, certainly represented new aspirations rather than
established facts. President Cleveland supported Secretary
Olney with a message in 1895 so vigorous that nervous
public sentiment anticipated a war between the United
States and Great Britain. The latter country, however,
assented to arbitration, on a somewhat restricted basis, and
the matter was amicably arranged, although, of course,
Great Britain did not accept Mr. Olney's general principles.

The general popularity of the Venezuelan policy was in marked contrast with the response to Mr. Blaine's policies, and revealed a growing interest in foreign affairs.

This interest was further illustrated by the change of attitude with regard to an interoceanic canal. Interest in this project had declined for a time after the construction of the transcontinental railroads, which seemed to answer all needs. In the eighties, however, the discontent over railroad rates drew attention to the advantage of establishing a water route that might, by competition, lower them. As such a canal must be constructed through Colombia or Nicaragua, neither of them able to finance or protect it, and would be used by shipping from all the countries in the world, its international position must be settled before capital would be invested. The traditional policy of the United States had been for a canal of which the advantages should be open equally to all nations and of which the neutrality should be guaranteed by international agreement. The Clayton-Bulwer treaty of 1850 with Great Britain had placed us under obligation to that country to maintain this policy. When, however, in 1878, the formation of a French company made the construction of a canal an immediate possibility, it was found that another idea had developed. Mr. Evarts, Secretary of State under Hayes, and afterwards Mr. Blaine, asserted that such a canal must be American, and under the control of the United States government. President Hayes said it would constitute part of "the coast line of the United States." Steps were taken for the formation of an American company to use, as the French had taken the Panama route, that through Nicaragua. *Canal policy.*

This new policy was opposed by President Cleveland, and the Clayton-Bulwer treaty stood in the way. The French company, too, discovered difficulties, financial and physical, and as a result practically nothing was accomplished during the nineteenth century. The problem, how- *Failure of canal projects.*

ever, was one which could not permanently remain unsolved,·
and the attitude of the United States gave another indication of its rising interest in foreign affairs.

The Pacific.   While American problems were thus becoming more
important, a new field of interest was opening up in the
Pacific. From the time of the Confederation, American
vessels had frequented that ocean, their trade comprehend-
ing the Oregon coast, the Hawaiian Islands, and China.
These traders were followed by whalers whose chief purpose
was securing whale oil, which down to the discovery of
petroleum was widely used as an illuminant. After the
Civil War this occupation gradually died away, but for many
years it had kept the American flag in the Pacific. The
whalers were followed by missionaries who were as daring,
and whose influence, particularly in Hawaii, was more lasting. To these general influences the United States had
from 1791 added a claim by discovery to the Columbia
River and the Oregon country. This claim had become more
definite after the treaty of 1819 with Spain, which had given
us all her rights as far south as the forty-second parallel.
The treaties with England in 1846 and with Mexico in 1848
gave us a fixed hold on that portion of the Pacific coast of
America which contains the best harbors, while the annexation of Alaska in 1867 stretched out an arm toward Asia.
In the meantime the treaty of 1844, which secured the opening of "treaty ports" in China, and that of 1854, which
opened up Japan to the Western world and marks the new
birth of the Japanese nation, added prestige to power.

Samoa and   In 1878 a treaty, almost inadvertently made so far as
Hawaii.
the government at Washington was concerned, promised
our good offices to the government of the Samoan Islands.
During Cleveland's first administration that government got
into difficulties with England and Germany. The United
States interfered, and after a long and somewhat turbulent
negotiation became a party to the General Act of Berlin of

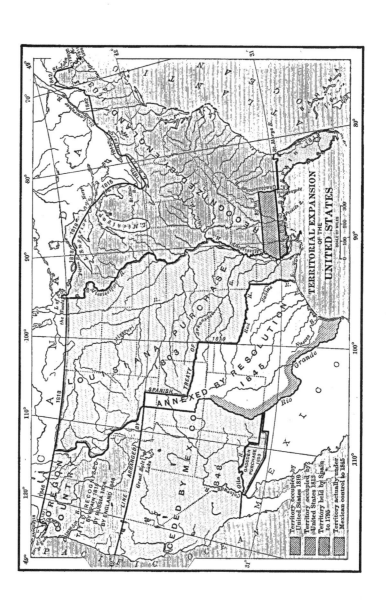

TERRITORIAL EXPANSION
OF THE
UNITED STATES

1889. By this act the independence of Samoa was recognized, but its government was to be under the tutelage of Great Britain, Germany, and the United States. Thus for the first time we were drawn into the responsibilities of a protectorate, and an "entangling alliance" with two European powers. In the Hawaiian Islands we had long taken a special interest. We had, in fact, asserted since 1842 that practically, from their position, they came under the protection of the Monroe Doctrine. In 1892 a revolution in the islands resulted in the formation of a republic there, dominated by American influence, which immediately requested annexation by the United States. This request was readily indorsed by the Harrison administration, and the matter was pressed by J. W. Foster, who had succeeded Mr. Blaine as Secretary of State in 1892. Cleveland opposed annexation, and upon becoming President in 1893, withdrew the treaty for that purpose which he found before the Senate. The question was, however, sure to be brought up again under McKinley. This gradual growth of American influence in the Pacific had been the result rather of real underlying forces and of favorable accidents than of general policy. As a result, however, the United States stood in 1898 in a position where the future control of that ocean and the development of the countries in and about it must receive its attention.

The immediate question, however, which forced foreign affairs before the public was a revolution in Cuba. The revolution there during Grant's administration had brought the United States and Spain several times to the verge of war, but a combination of the skillful diplomacy of Secretary Fish and accident had preserved the peace. In 1895 a new revolution broke out. The proximity of the island to the United States, the large investments held there by United States citizens, and the fact that many Cubans held United States naturalization papers, all brought constant annoy-

Situation in Cuba.

ance. Although President Cleveland, and after him President McKinley, endeavored earnestly to enforce the neutrality of the United States, the Spanish government was not satisfied and protested that the revolution would die out but for aid from this country. The United States asserted, as it had under Secretary Fish, that its position gave it the right to insist that the Spanish government bring the revolution to a close within a reasonable time, or grant the demands of the Cubans. American public sentiment was particularly excited by the Spanish war methods. Especially obnoxious was the *reconcentrado* policy, carried out by General Weyler, of concentrating the population in certain centers and then devastating the surrounding plantations in order to prevent the insurrectionary bands from living on the country. The most objectionable features of this policy resulted from the inability of the Spanish government properly to maintain the people in the *reconcentrado* camps, and its unwillingness to admit relief from the United States.

Negotiations between United States and Spain.

The United States would probably have intervened in the autumn of 1897, but the Liberal party in Spain came to power under Señor Segasta and promised to satisfy our government if only time were given it. Its intentions seem to have been pacific, and it is probable that it desired peace even at the expense of the cession of the island to the United States. Spanish public sentiment, however, was less yielding, and surrender might have meant the fall not only of the ministry but of the dynasty. In January, 1898, a letter of the Spanish minister at Washington, Señor de Lome, attacking President McKinley, was made public. Soon after Senator Proctor of Vermont visited the island and reported an intolerable condition of affairs. The press of both countries continually fanned the war spirit. In the midst of this high feeling, the United States battleship *Maine* was sent to Havana, ostensibly on a friendly visit, but really to show the seriousness of our intentions. On February 15, 1898, this vessel was blown up The American people believed that this was the work of the Spanish government, and public sentiment blazed into a call for war. On March 27 the United States government sent an ultimatum, demanding, together with other things, immediate amnesty, to be followed by negotiations conducted through President McKinley. The Spanish government was anxious to accede to these demands, and did so in practically all points except putting the negotiations in the hands of the President. It, however, assured General Woodford, the United States minister at Madrid, that Spain was willing to make such terms as the United States demanded. President McKinley still desired peace, but Congress was for war and was supported by public sentiment. Many of those well informed doubted whether Spanish public sentiment would allow that government to carry out its promises.

On April 11 President McKinley sent in a message recommending forcible intervention. Congress decided not only to intervene, but also to recognize Cuban independence, although no fixed government could be found to represent it. This recognition afterwards tied the hands of the United States during the peace negotiations by preventing annexation, which for a hundred years our leading statesmen had regarded as the ultimate destiny of the island. The action of Congress was immediately followed by war with Spain. *Outbreak of war.*

The war was quick and decisive. Cuba was promptly blockaded. A fleet from Spain under Admiral Cervera broke through the blockade and entered Santiago. Its attempt to leave that port, however, resulted in its defeat and capture by the American fleet under Admirals Sampson and Schley at the battle of Santiago, July 3. In the meantime an army under General Shafter had been landed near Santiago, a conspicuous portion of which consisted of the "Rough Rider" regiment, raised by Colonel Roosevelt, who resigned *War.*

his post as Assistant Secretary of the Navy to take part in the war. On July 17 the city of Santiago was captured. A fortnight afterwards an army under General Miles began the occupation of the island of Porto Rico. It happened that when the war broke out, Spain was contending also with a revolution in the Philippine Islands. An American fleet had been assembled in Asiatic waters under Admiral Dewey, and on May 1, in the dashing victory of Manila Bay, he destroyed the Spanish fleet operating in the islands. American forces were soon landed, and in coöperation with Aguinaldo, the leader of the Filipinos, attacked Manila.

Peace. On July 22 Spain indicated her willingness to treat for peace. President McKinley appointed a Peace Commission headed by William R. Day of Ohio, who in April had been appointed to succeed John Sherman as Secretary of State. The Commission met the Spanish commissioners at Paris and on December 10 a treaty was signed. Spain relinquished all its claims to Cuba, passing over the occupation to the United States, the intention of the United States being to turn the island over to its own revolutionary government. All other Spanish possessions in America were ceded to the United States, together with Guam, an island of the Ladrones group in the Pacific. In addition Spain ceded the Philippines on the payment of twenty million dollars. The cession of the West Indian islands was a natural result of the war; the fate of Cuba was determined by the action of Congress in recognizing its independence; the cession of Guam to be used as a coaling station was not surprising; but the cession of the Philippines marked a new departure in United States policy. They were remote, were well populated by peoples alien in race and language, and could not be expected to become a field for the expansion of the American people, although it was hoped that capital and trade might find openings in them. President McKinley was in August undetermined as to the wisdom of taking the archipelago. Strong pressure, both religious and commercial, was brought to bear, however, and there was a fear that if we did not take them Germany would. The treaty marked a change in American policy, not only in taking these islands, but in providing that the status of their inhabitants, as well as of those of the other cessions, be left to the determination of Congress. It had been customary to incorporate annexed territory into the United States, making its regular inhabitants citizens.

The future of these annexed territories required congressional action. The occupation of Cuba under General Leonard Wood lasted until May 20, 1901, when the control of the island was turned over to its own government. Certain conditions, however, were imposed by what is known as the Platt Amendment, which were incorporated in the treaty of 1903. These were intended to prevent the republic from falling under European influences, to provide for the sanitation of Cuban cities, from which yellow fever had so often spread to the United States, and to secure naval stations to the United States. In the Philippines the natives were as little willing to recognize United States as Spanish authority. For two years they resisted under the lead of Aguinaldo, and it was not until 1902 that peace was effectually established. In the meantime Congress had been discussing the question of civil government for the various new possessions. In 1900 a government on the territorial plan was established in Porto Rico. The Philippines were left until 1902 under the control of the President, who in 1900 appointed Judge William Howard Taft of Ohio as Governor. In the case of both regions special tariffs were established, with the difference that Porto Rico was ultimately to have free trade with the United States, while in the case of the Philippines duties were to be permanently collected on goods sent from the islands to the United States, though they were lower than those on foreign imports. The act of

Imperialism.

1902 for the permanent organization of the Philippines, moreover, though it extended the other constitutional guarantees of personal liberty to the islands and provided for a legislative assembly, did not provide for jury trial or the right to bear arms. Taking it as a whole, therefore, this legislation placed the Philippines in the rank of a colony and not of a coequal part of the United States. The action of Congress in thus making rules to govern territory abso-

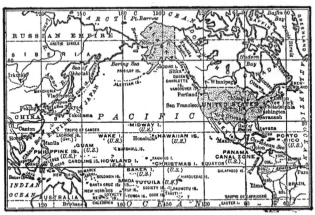

THE UNITED STATES AND ITS POSSESSIONS

lutely without regard for the restrictions placed on its power by the Constitution was contrary to the theory involved in the Dred Scott decision. In 1901 the Supreme Court, in what are known as the *Insular Cases*, sustained Congress and practically reversed that decision. In the meantime the government was promoting the development of the islands, improving the sanitation of the cities, transportation, and particularly education. So successful were the methods employed, that by 1912 English was as commonly used as Spanish had been previously. In 1899 the United States came into the possession of another colony by an agreement with Great Britain and Germany, in accordance with which the independence of the Samoan Islands was abrogated and the islands divided between Germany and the United States. In 1898 Hawaii had been incorporated into the United States by joint resolution as in the case of Texas, and numbers of small islands in the Pacific, such as Midway and Wake, were occupied as coaling and cable stations.

In the midst of these events came the election of 1900. To many the adoption of a colonial policy and the waging of war in the Philippines for conquest seemed an abandonment of the traditional principles of equality and self-government upon which our liberty was based. They not only believed that the Filipinos should be let alone for their own sake, but they feared that the extension of the power of the executive and of Congress would be reflected in this country. The Democrats took up this attack on Imperialism and again nominated Mr. Bryan for the presidency. The Republicans indorsed the policy of the administration and renominated Mr. McKinley, joining with him, as candidate for the vice presidency, Colonel Roosevelt, whose war reputation had already won him the governorship of New York. The overwhelming success of President McKinley showed that the people at large were not alarmed at the fears of the Anti-Imperialists, although it was doubtless in part due to continued distrust of Mr. Bryan's financial views. Election of 1900.

The Spanish War and the accessions of territory which it brought involved important changes in the relations of the United States with the rest of the world. The diplomacy of the five years following was more important than that of any other period after the annunciation of the Monroe Doctrine. Fortunately the direction of our foreign relations at this time fell to a man probably better fitted for the task by training and experience than any other American since John Quincy Adams. John Hay began his public life as private secretary Secretary Hay.

to President Lincoln. He had many years of experience
abroad, both in diplomatic positions and as a private citizen.
President McKinley appointed him Ambassador to Great
Britain in 1897, and in 1898 made him Secretary of State.
The holder of the latter position is usually a man of political
influence, and serves, under the President, as political head
of the administration. Mr. Hay devoted himself, however,
exclusively to diplomatic affairs. He served until 1905.
Under President McKinley he had practically a free hand in
diplomacy. After the succession of Mr. Roosevelt in 1901,
Mr. Hay continued to shape the general policy of the government, although the President assumed the direction of particular questions.

Attitude of
Europe.

The emergence of the United States as a world power at
first created alarm and dislike among the European powers,
with the exception of England. France was heavily interested in Spanish bonds, and Germany was anxious to secure
colonies and had probably expected to buy the Philippines.
Other countries were alarmed by the rapid inroads of American trade which followed the economic recovery of the late
nineties. While Americans complained because the trusts
sold goods abroad cheaper than at home, foreign countries
feared that this "dumping" would destroy their home industries. New York began to be a market for foreign bond
issues, and the financial relations of Europe and America
bid fair to become reversed. The American "invasion" was
in 1898 and 1899 a topic for international conferences, and
it seemed likely that we would become the object of international antagonism. This virulent "anti-Americanism,"
however, was short-lived. The "dumping" of American
products into the European markets was to a considerable extent a temporary phenomenon, due to the great accumula-
tions in the hands of the trusts, so many of which had
been founded in 1898 and 1899. Soon American production
and consumption reached a better balance, and the Ameri-

can invasion ceased to be so menacing. Moreover, if the
United States wished to play a part in world politics, it was
obviously able to do so. It was better policy to cultivate
friendly than unfriendly relations with it. The Emperor of
Germany in particular fostered this favorable reaction. He
sent his brother Prince Henry of Prussia to visit the United
States in 1902, ordered a racing yacht to be built in America,
which was christened by Miss Alice Roosevelt, daughter of
President Roosevelt, and made provision for a Germanic mu-
seum at Harvard University, and for exchange professorships
between German and American universities. France followed,
sending in 1902 a distinguished delegation to assist in the un-
veiling of a statue at Washington to General Rochambeau,
commander of the French forces in the American Revolution,
and in other ways promoting friendly sentiments and
intercourse.

England had been friendly throughout, welcoming the Position of
advance into world politics of a new nation of kindred blood England.
and law and speaking the same language. Her international
position was at the time described by Lord Salisbury as one
of "splendid isolation," but with the advent of the Boer
War in 1900 her isolation seemed more dangerous than
splendid. This cordiality between the United States and
Great Britain was an unusual experience, for distrust and
bickering had marked their relations for the greater part of
the time from the Revolution. It greatly facilitated the
settlement of outstanding questions between the two countries, although in many cases England was forced to insist
strongly upon her position because her great colony Canada
was involved and would brook no slighting of her interests.
English relations, however, were difficult, for many in that
country wished the friendliness between the two countries
to materialize into an alliance, and there was danger that
the United States might be drawn from its traditional
policy of avoiding foreign entanglements. By skillful diplo-

macy this danger was averted, while at the same time many long-standing problems, such as the Alaska boundary, were settled satisfactorily.

United States and Europe.

On the part of the United States an appreciation of its new position is shown by the creation in 1897 of the diplomatic grade of ambassador. Up to this time our highest representatives abroad had been ministers plenipotentiary. Secretary Hay showed a disposition to take part in all international conferences for the discussion of world-wide problems. Particularly the United States was conspicuous in the Hague Conference of 1899 for the promotion of universal peace, and in the formation of the permanent court of arbitration at The Hague. This was no new policy, for the United States had always shared in the discussion of non-political international questions, and had always been the leading advocate of arbitration and the foremost in the use of it. Its position, however, was now more powerful and its influence greater. In a note of 1902 on the treatment of Jews in Roumania, Secretary Hay indicated that the question of immigration might give the United States the right to interfere, or at least protest, with regard to European conditions. He did not, however, press the matter, and effectually maintained our traditional position of non-intervention in disputes peculiarly European.

United States and Pan-America.

The corresponding position, that European powers should keep out of American affairs, was vigorously maintained. The most serious question that arose concerned the collection of debts due by Spanish-American powers to Europeans. Professor Drago of Argentina urged the view that private debts should not be collected by national power. The United States was not willing to support this doctrine, but nevertheless feared the effects of forcible intervention by European powers. It used its influence in some cases to secure payment, in others to have claims submitted to arbitration, and in the case of the republic of Santo Domingo assumed the administration of the public revenues and the payment of the creditors. Secretary Hay did not make much progress toward the creation of Pan-American co-operation. His successor, Secretary Root, however, interested himself in this matter, and Pan-American conferences have now become regular and of increasing importance.

The acquisition of territory in the Pacific rendered the necessity for an interoceanic canal more pressing. A fleet might be needed in either ocean; without a canal two fleets would be required. Secretary Hay preferred a canal constructed under international guarantee, but the demand for an American canal had grown to be insistent. In 1901 he negotiated a new treaty with Great Britain to take the place of the Clayton-Bulwer treaty, which would allow an American canal, provided that equal rates be charged the vessels of all nations. It had by this time become evident that the building of the canal was too great a task for a private corporation, and Congress finally decided to undertake it. In the meantime the question of location arose. A long contest between the advocates of the Panama and Nicaragua routes resulted in the Spooner Act of 1902, which authorized the President to arrange with the old French company, which had begun work but had abandoned it, and with Colombia for the Panama route, if he could do so "within a reasonable time and upon reasonable terms," but otherwise to accept the offer of Nicaragua. President Roosevelt bought out the French company for $40,000,000, but Colombia refused to ratify the Hay-Herran treaty which had been drawn up at Washington, and which accorded privileges to the United States. President Roosevelt withdrew our representative at Bogota, July 9, 1903, and prepared to insist on our rights to construct the canal under the treaty of 1846. On November 3, however, the province of Panama revolted from Colombia. It was promptly recognized as independent by the United States and it as promptly

The interoceanic canal.

granted the United States all the latter required, including a
ten-mile strip of territory from ocean to ocean, for which the
United States was to pay ten million dollars in cash, and,
after 1912, a quarter of a million a year. The international difficulties in the way of canal construction, therefore,
were cleared away, and the work of sanitation in the canal
zone and of actual construction was begun.

The Far East.

The Pacific and the Far East did not fall within the scope
of the Monroe Doctrine. In that region the United States
and the great world powers met on equal terms, and Secretary Hay not only assumed an equal interest with England,
France, Russia, Germany, and Japan, in the "concert of
powers," but also in some respects the leadership. In 1900
the United States coöperated with the other powers in dealing with the Boxer outbreak against foreigners in China.
Secretary Hay also secured assent, at least professed, to the
"open door" policy of allowing all nations equal commercial
privileges in colonies, protectorates, zones of influence, and
especially in China. At the outbreak of the Russo-Japanese
war he secured the restriction of hostilities to a specified
area, and obtained guarantees of the territorial integrity and
independence of China. The war was, moreover, brought
to a close at the suggestion of President Roosevelt. During
all this period, in spite of real difficulties due to our desire to
restrict the immigration of Chinese and Japanese and the
sensitiveness of their governments to discrimination, and
difficulties less real arising from the fear of the "Yellow
Peril," friendly relations were maintained with China and
Japan. No one can doubt that the United States has
acquired a permanent interest in eastern Asia and that
American capital and enterprise will share in the awakening
of that continent. By 1905, therefore, most of the difficult
problems existing in 1898 had been solved, and new policies
had been outlined to meet the questions arising from the
Spanish War.

BIBLIOGRAPHICAL NOTES

Macdonald, *Select Documents*, nos. 109–129. Harrison, B., Sources.
Views of an Ex-President, 185–272. Howe, A. H., *Insular Cases*
(*House Exec. Doc.*, 56 cong., 2 sess., no. 509). Thayer, J. B., *Our
New Possessions.*

Latané, J. H., *America as a World Power.* Bancroft, *Seward*, Historical
II, ch. XLII. Henderson, J. B., *American Diplomatic Questions,* accounts.
137–208. Chadwick, F. E., *Relations of the United States and
Spain.* Latané, J. H., *Diplomatic Relations between the United
States and Spanish America.* McLaughlin, J. L., and Willis, H. P.,
Reciprocity. Reinsch, P. S., *World Politics.* Taussig, *Tariff
History*, 251–409.

CHAPTER XXVIII

INDUSTRIAL AND SOCIAL CHANGES

THE practical elimination of the currency question from politics by the election of 1896, with the adoption of the gold standard in 1900, and the sudden expansion of United States interests beyond its borders, which have been the main topics of the last two chapters, prepared the way for a new epoch of development. They were, however, rather the symptoms than the causes of change. In order to understand thoroughly how they and other political conditions came about, it is necessary to observe the manner in which the United States was growing.

Growth of population in the North.

In 1870 the total population of the United States was about thirty-eight and a half million; in 1910 it was over ninety-one million, excluding that of the colonies. About twenty-four millions of this increase was in the states north of the Mason-Dixon line and the Ohio, and east of the Mississippi, with Iowa. In this region the increase amounted to about one hundred and ten per cent; the additional population was occupied for the most part in manufacturing, mining, transportation, and commerce, and lived in urban communities. Although agricultural productions doubled, the population of purely agricultural regions was generally stationary, and often declined. The rapid extension of the use of agricultural machinery after 1870 enabled the farmer to dispense with some labor. The manufacture of farm products, such as flour milling and meat packing, became concentrated in large cities. The growth of railroads and, after 1900, the use of automobiles tended to centralize farm trade at favorably located towns from thirty to fifty miles apart, stunting the intermediate towns. The states in this group showing the greatest increase were: those devoted to general manufacturing, like Massachusetts, Rhode Island, New Jersey, and Pennsylvania; states not fully developed in 1870, like Michigan, Wisconsin, and Iowa; and New York and Illinois, containing the great cities of New York and Chicago.

The former slave states, excluding Florida, Texas, and Arkansas, gained about twelve million, or one hundred per cent. In certain districts, particularly in West Virginia and on the southern and eastern slopes of the mountains, iron mines and iron and cotton mills had come to employ tens of thousands, but the great bulk of the increased population was engaged in agriculture. The cotton crop increased about fourfold, and machinery was able to do little to lessen the labor of its production, while other crops had come to be raised much more extensively than before. While the average yield per acre increased, to a still greater extent the growth in production represented the occupation of the waste spaces, so abundant in the South during the plantation era. *Growth of population in the South.*

The remaining seventeen millions of increase, pouring into the outlying areas, expanded their population almost six hundred per cent. Their task was the familiar American one of extending the frontier and subduing the wilderness to civilization. They pressed agriculture to and beyond the western boundary of sufficient rainfall, about the hundredth meridian, recoiling in the nineties before a succession of dry years which caused much of the distress from which arose the Populist movement. Sheep ranches drove before them the cattle from the ranges between the hundredth meridian and the Rocky Mountains, and farms encroached upon the sheep ranches. In the mountains, miners and capitalists from the East met those from the Pacific coast, uniting the two frontiers. The Indians, not without fighting, were first confined within reservations, and later these reservations were contracted in size and subdivided. By 1910 the tribal *Expansion of the population.*

holdings of the Indians had been practically eliminated. In fact, it may be said that by 1900 the primary exploitation of the surface of the United States was complete; by 1910 the first wave was being deflected northward into Canada. By 1912 all the continental area of the United States, except Alaska, had been admitted to statehood, Utah in 1896, Oklahoma in 1907, and New Mexico and Arizona in 1912, completing the list of the states, forty-eight in all.

Disappearance of the frontier.

The existence of the frontier had been the distinguishing feature of American history. Its conquest, with the exception of a few regions like semiarid Utah, had been the work of individuals, and it had offered continuously an opportunity to the individual for economic independence. Its spirit of individualism had permeated the political as well as the economic life of the whole nation. Land was always available throughout the country. When the pioneer adventured into the wilderness, he sold the farm he had broken, often to some farmer from a still older region, who in turn sold his well-developed acres to some one with capital and the desire for a settled life. Landownership was always shifting and land opportunity was always open. Other industries had to offer high rewards to prevent men from taking advantage of the situation and becoming landowners. When the front rank found its advance barred, the recoil was felt through the whole body politic; the whole nation had to readjust itself to new conditions.

Conservation.

Realization came promptly. Up to 1900 the country exulted in its strength and its limitless resources. By 1910, it had come to dread the exhaustion of its natural resources and a well-developed movement for conservation was in progress. More careful attention to the soil was urged, in order that the fertility which for many years had been recklessly exploited might be restored by scientific farming. "Dry farming" was developed, in order that crops might be raised in the semiarid areas. Irrigation was undertaken by private enterprise, and extended by vast government projects, to open up the arid sections. Experimenters, like Luther Burbank of California, worked to discover plants that would grow in the unirrigated deserts. It was found that the enormous forests of the country had been dangerously reduced, not only by careless cutting, which took no thought of replacement, but by fires lit by sparks from railroad engines and other causes. The country was threatened, not only with lack of lumber, but with alternate flood and drought, owing to the deforestation of the regions in which the rivers rose. Geologists pointed out that the supplies of coal and iron were not limitless and that water power should be developed and preserved to take their place. To meet this situation the national government, state governments, and great corporations like the Pennsylvania Railroad, established forest reserves. The total reserves of the national government by 1910 amounted to about three hundred thousand square miles. A National Forest Service was begun in 1898, and states and corporations followed in the scientific study of forest problems, the promotion of forest growth, the prevention of forest waste, and the preservation of forests about the river heads. The use of cement as a substitute for wood and iron has somewhat lessened the demands upon the forests. Less directly connected with the movement, but practically bearing upon it, has been the development of electricity. By this means water power has been made available for many new purposes, and can be transmitted over long distances. Thomas Edison and many others are at present engaged in experiments for the production of a more perfect storage battery which would render electricity still more useful, and enable civilization to employ the forces of the wind.

Not only was there alarm lest resources should be exhausted, but also over their ownership and employment. While the public believed that the natural resources were without limit, it was not a matter of active concern how much was

Control of resources.

secured by any person or group of persons. When it came to be realized that all the anthracite coal in the country lay in one small district, the public became interested in its ownership. It was discovered that a very large amount of the natural resources upon which the future must depend were held by a comparatively small number of individuals and corporations. Thus a large proportion of the timber of the country was held by the Pacific railroads and the Weyerhäuser companies. Hence there arose a demand that the remaining resources be administered primarily for the benefit of the public and that some control be exercised over the use of those already in private hands. Thus the conservation movement became a political issue.

Specialized education.

The new task before the nation, the study and the economical utilization of its resources, demanded a new kind of training. The old type of self-sufficing "Jack-of-all-trades" which had been required in the days when men must shift for themselves and be independent of their neighbors, must give way to the expert trained to do some one thing extremely well, and willing to work in coöperation with others and under direction. The great rewards would go to those who had the ability to organize the services of others. Specialized education became necessary to furnish experts required by the national economy, and education must be freely offered to the masses if they were to continue to enjoy that equality of opportunity which the free bounty of nature no longer afforded. The problem of education was no longer merely to give inspiration and a mental training for life in general, but it must give also fitting for some special walk in life. To the old professions must be added a list of new. To retain the old spirit of education, while making an adjustment to this new need, gave rise to problems of the utmost delicacy and difficulty. The institutions of the higher education, especially the universities maintained by the various states, have responded quickly to this call. Schools and colleges of agriculture, mining, engineering, forestry, commerce, chemistry, and many other subjects turn out each year experts who are speedily absorbed into the work of the country and raise the level of its economic efficiency. On the whole the lower schools have adjusted themselves less easily. Manual training and technical high schools, and in some cities high schools to fit for some special occupation, as textile work, have been founded. Still, skilled and educated laborers are not relatively as numerous as scientific experts. To meet this need "continuation" schools are being established, where instruction is given to those who have already begun their life's work.

With this change in the character of American society, The expert there came, naturally, a tendency towards a change in po- in public litical ideals. American democracy, as it found expression life. in the philosophy of Jefferson, desired individual liberty. It looked upon government as a means of perfecting that liberty, by protecting the individual. Jacksonian democracy preserved a strong love of individual liberty, but it laid more stress on the idea of equality, acting on the supposition that all men were of much the same ability and could and should be equally trusted with the affairs as well of government as of business. There was a growing tendency, moreover, to insist upon the right of the majority to do what it liked. This latter tendency has grown steadily stronger since the Civil War. Year by year the majority has shown more disposition to regulate the life of the community for its own good. It is somewhat the old New England idea that man should have liberty to do that which is good, that is, as now interpreted, what is good in the eyes of the majority. It is also connected with a trend of thought among European peoples toward state socialism. In part a reaction against the extreme *laissez faire* doctrines of the middle of the nineteenth century, and exhibited only as a tendency to favor particular measures, it has become for many a definite program, and in 1912 a Socialist party cast over eight hundred thousand votes for Eugene Debs, its candidate for the presidency. At the same time there has developed the feeling that the real democratic equality is equality of opportunity, not the insistence on equality of ability. As the functions of government have increased, there has been an increasing willingness to trust their execution to those specially trained for the work. Democracy has become willing to carry out its purpose through experts.

Conditions of change.

Two movements have, therefore, marked the advance of democracy during this period, especially from 1890 to 1910; one that for the more direct control of government by the majority, the other for the employment of specialists. Both these movements have found expression more easily in the case of state governments than in the case of that of the nation. The American state system gives an ideal opportunity for experiment. One state may try a suggested plan ; failure means but a restricted loss, and success serves to stimulate others to adopt similar measures. This has had a corresponding disadvantage in the fact that state laws on similar subjects differ, creating great confusion, particularly in the case of the laws of marriage and divorce. Of late, however, there has been a tendency for the states to keep in touch and consciously to profit by each other's experience. Legislative reference libraries keep the legislators informed of what is being done elsewhere, and, since 1908, the governors of the several states have met regularly to discuss public policy. The field for experimental observation in government, moreover, has not been confined to the United States. Travel, study in European universities, and the growing intimacy of relationships throughout the world resulting from improved facilities of communication have rubbed off much American provincialism. We no longer regard ourselves as a peculiar people, as in fact we are less so than before the disappearance of the frontier. There has been, therefore, an increasing willingness to profit by the experience of others, particularly by that of Australia, New Zealand, and Germany.

The movement for direct control of the government by the people has included laws to control party machinery and constitutional changes to place legislation more closely in the hands of the people. Nearly all states have regulated, some more, some less completely, the primaries by which the various parties select their candidates. Several states have provided that election expenses must be made public, and some have limited their amount. To prevent undue influence being brought to bear upon members of the legislature, some states have forbidden lobbyists and some provided that they must be registered. In Oregon and other far western states the initiative and referendum of laws, and the recall of public officials, by popular vote to be taken upon petition, have been provided, and the question as to the advisability of such legislation has become everywhere an issue. A movement for woman's suffrage arising during the anti-slavery struggle began now to take effect. Massachusetts and many other states allowed women to vote on educational matters. Wyoming from its admission in 1890 included them in the general electorate. Other far western states, notably California, have of late followed this example, and the question has also come to be agitated all over the country. While nearly all state constitutions have been made over in recent years by substitution or amendment, all attempts to change the national constitution were unsuccessful until 1913. The changes then made, which will be noted in the next chapter, were not fundamental, and it remains the oldest working frame of government in the world, and, interpreted by the court decisions of over one hundred and twenty years, sometimes acts as a bar to popular wishes. Nevertheless there has been no large movement to change it, except by amendments of a not very fundamental character. Instead there has grown up a demand that the courts interpret it liber-

Direct government.

ally to meet modern conditions, and, in order to bring the courts under popular control, it has been proposed that judges be subject to recall, or that decisions of the courts, in cases involving constitutional interpretation, be liable to reversal by popular vote.

Commission government. The movement for the employment of specialists has found its most active expression in the experiments with the commission form of government. Commissions of all kinds and dealing with all varieties of questions have been largely and increasingly used. Some have merely powers of investigation. This has been true of national commissions such as the Tariff Commission, authorized by the Payne-Aldrich tariff bill of 1909, to study the relative conditions of production in this country and elsewhere, with a view to determining the tariff rates necessary to equalize them, and the Aldrich Monetary Commission, appointed to study the whole question of finance and to report a plan for the reorganization of the national banking and currency laws. Some have administrative powers, as the park commissions in Massachusetts and other states. Wisconsin has led the way in the employment of commissions which combine powers of investigation with administrative and semi-judicial powers. The Rate Commission of that state constantly passes upon questions which are really judicial. Its decisions are theoretically subject to review by the courts, but practically have proved final. Commissions with legislative power have been created for the government of cities. The first to attract attention was that which was given control of Galveston after the practical destruction of that city by the devastating tidal wave of 1900. Its success in meeting the situation aroused general public interest, and many cities have adopted the method of giving to a small elective commission the powers previously exercised by the larger councils. The idea underlying the administrative commissions has been that of confiding to experts, chosen with as little relation to politics as possible, the task of collecting information and performing non-political acts. The direction of public policy has been retained under public control and the commissions are responsible to the public. In most cases they are appointed and are removable by the executive authority; the city commissions are elected and are generally subject to recall. Moreover, the generally reliable character of the reports which they present affords a more substantial basis upon which an intelligent public opinion can be built up, than has previously existed, and the method in general makes the public will more speedily operative than heretofore.

The popular will, thus made effective, has sought both to curb the powers of corporations and to regulate the life of the individual. At the beginning of the period, corporations, deathless and powerful, and in many cases practically holding monopolies of their respective fields of business, enjoyed nearly all the advantages of individual liberty secured to the people by our form of government. In a field of free competition they seemed to be the strongest, if not the fittest, who were the most apt to survive. During the past twenty years their powers have been steadily curtailed. Laws prohibiting railroads from giving passes have somewhat diminished their influence on public opinion, while rate commissions, by making rates equal to all users, have prevented special bargains by which railroads had been able to control shippers and *vice versa*. Public utilities commissions, like those of New York and Wisconsin, have the power to see that all corporations serving the public perform their duties satisfactorily to the public. New systems of taxation have been devised, forcing corporations to contribute at least their share of the public expenses. Revelations of the scandalous conduct of certain insurance companies have brought almost universally laws for their control. The effect of these state regulative measures has been much greater than that of the

Economic legislation.

national Sherman Anti-Trust Law, and they have much aided in the work of the national Interstate Commerce Commission, but they probably represent only a broaching of the problem.

Social legislation.

Along the line of social control, laws have been passed regulating smoking and drinking, for the supervision of conditions in factories, limiting the employment of women and children, and for compulsory education. Newer in conception is the assumption by the states of the war against disease, particularly tuberculosis, and the provision for state parks. There is some tendency for the states to assume active control of the police, in order to carry out these and other measures, the authority for which rests chiefly on the police power. State assumption of power has not, however, diminished the activity of the municipal governments, any more than the increase of federal functions had reduced that of the states. Increasing density of population, its growing diversity, inequalities in wealth, decadence of certain social groups, the weakening influence of the home upon children, and the thickening problems of an aging civilization demand always more control by law, more sacrifice of individual liberty for the common good; and, with a rather remarkable adaptability, the American people have shown a prompt appreciation of this necessity and a willingness to change the form of their democracy in the hope of preserving its essence.

The foreign-born.

While these changes in the methods and purposes of government were taking place, the composition of the population was also undergoing change. In the decade between 1870 and 1880 immigration amounted to over two million eight hundred thousand, in the next to five million two hundred thousand, in the next to three million six hundred thousand, and between 1900 and 1910 to almost eight million eight hundred thousand. These totals do not accurately represent the increase in foreign population, because many immigrants return to their native countries; but in 1900 the population born abroad or of foreign parents was twenty million eight hundred and thirty-nine thousand. Only six hundred thousand of this foreign population lived in the South, and half that number were in the single state of Texas. About fourteen and a half million consisted of English, German, Irish, and Scotch, which nationalities have been coming to America from the beginning, and form the basis of the American stock. A newer element was that from the Scandinavian countries. More than half the nine hundred and ninety-eight thousand Swedes were in Minnesota and Illinois. The Norwegians numbered six hundred and eighty-four thousand, and were for the most part farmers in Minnesota and Wisconsin. Two hundred and sixty-six thousand Danes were scattered through the middle parts of western states, and Finns and Icelanders were fairly numerous along the northern border. These Scandinavians, like the British and Germans, were fitted by similarity of racial characteristics and political training to assimilate quickly the more fundamental American traditions.

More than three and a half million of the foreign-born in 1900 consisted of more alien elements, and they constituted the greater proportion of the immigration of the next ten years. The French Canadian element in 1900 amounted to six hundred and thirty-five thousand, two thirds of whom were in New England. They lived, for the most part, in groups of their own, about the cotton mills in which they worked, and, with some notable exceptions, took little part in the general life of the community. The mines of Pennsylvania drew many Hungarians, who proved to be a turbulent element, often disturbing the public peace. On the Pacific Chinese immigration became important from the time of the discovery of gold. Popular prejudice against the Chinese was strong, not only because of their alien mode of life, but also because of the low standard of wages they were

Immigration of new elements.

willing to accept; and the question of their immigration
dominated California politics during the seventies. With
the passage of the Chinese Exclusion Bill of 1881, the question
became less politically acute. The immigration of Chinese
laborers has been, on the whole, prevented since that time,
but those in the country constitute an element which has
proved as yet not assimilable. A somewhat similar problem
was presented early in the twentieth century by the immigration of Japanese, but under President Roosevelt an arrangement was reached with the Japanese government which
limited this movement. In the meantime the cities and
factories throughout the country were becoming crowded
with Russians, Jew and Gentile, Italians, Poles, Bohemians,
Austrians, and Greeks. Where these foreigners reached the
soil, with the exception of the Chinese, they speedily became
a part of the community; intermarriage was frequent and
lines of nationality tended to disappear. In the cities, however, they were inclined to live in separate quarters and to
preserve their characteristics.

New condi-
tions of im-
migration.
Much of the immigration since 1880 has been of what
may be called an unnatural character. The enforced immigration of slaves has been prohibited since 1808, the importation of coolies since the Civil War, and of laborers under
contract since 1888; Chinese and Japanese have also been
excluded. But the road to America has been made so easy
that it no longer requires any special fortitude and courage
to make the transit. The conditions which previously in-
sured that the voluntary immigrant to America was possessed
of some special qualities fitting him for success have ceased
to operate. In fact the highly colored accounts spread
broadcast through the discontented districts of Europe by
competing steamship companies have tended to draw over
many who are merely weakly restless and inefficient. These
feebler newcomers are welcomed by those great employing
interests whose factories and mines require little intelligence

from the laborer, and who are glad to supplant the highly paid and independent native workmen. In many cities, particularly in New England, New York, and Pennsylvania, these underpaid and unenlightened unfortunates live in social conditions from which America has previously been spared, separated as completely from the native population as if inhabitants of a different century. When the natural revolt against these conditions takes place, it assumes a more dangerous and revolutionary character than earlier disputes between capital and labor. The most significant attempt to organize this class has been that of the Industrial Workers of the World, and the most important crisis which has occurred has been that produced by the Lowell strike of 1912.

The enormous amount of immigration and its changing character attracted wide attention, but led to little direct public effort. The activity of the national government has been limited to preventing the coming of Chinese and Japanese, and prohibiting the entry of sick, criminal, and dependent individuals. The local governments have contributed much by their public schools systems, which have been open to all alike and have enabled practically all immigrants to acquire the English language and some knowledge of American history and habits. Quite as much has been accomplished by private efforts. Particularly "social settlements," such as Hull House at Chicago, founded and directed by Miss Jane Addams, have helped the newcomers in their difficulties and taught them American ways. The children of the immigrants seem eager to adapt themselves to American conditions, and it is to be hoped that foreign quarters will become a thing of the past, as have those of the Irish, who in the middle of the nineteenth century lived quite as much by themselves. It is plain, however, that the proportion of these newer nationalities to the whole population is so large, that when they have become assimilated, the characteristics of the whole population will have somewhat changed.

Problems of the foreign-born.

Commerce
and finance. While the United States continued increasingly to
be a receiving nation from the standpoint of migration, it
became more and more an exporting nation from the standpoint of commerce. The amount of imports in proportion to
the population did not increase nor substantially vary from
1870 to 1910, while the proportion of exports increased almost
fifty per cent. The most significant change in the character
of trade was the growing importance of exports of manufactured goods; for, while they were still in 1910 of smaller
amount than those of cotton, provisions, and other natural
products, the possibilities of their development began to
engage general attention. Reciprocity, free trade, the acquisition of colonies, and closer relations with other countries were all discussed as methods of expanding the market
for these products, which, unlike the traditional American
exports, must come into competition with those of European
factories. This interest grew rapidly between 1900 and 1910,
during which years the home demand for foodstuffs and the
active rivalry of Canada, Argentina, and Australia foreshadowed the end of the export provision trade, while the waste
of American forests threatened a future dependence upon
other nations for lumber. It became increasingly obvious
that our balance to other nations must be paid by making
better or cheaper finished articles, rather than by garnering
the fruits of nature. Throughout this period the United
States continued to be dependent on foreign nations for the
ocean transit of both passengers and goods. The great
volume of American exports, however, enabled the country
easily to pay for these services, to accumulate nearly all the
capital required for its industrial undertakings, and to enter
foreign fields, particularly China, as a lender of money.

Conditions
peculiar to
the South. While the South shared in many of these changes and was
growing into closer touch with the rest of the country, it is
still necessary to observe some special conditions there. The
South gained scarcely at all by immigration. Nevertheless,

during this period, more nearly than at any time since the formation of the government, it held its own in the increase of population. Both the white and the negro elements contributed, the gain in the whites being proportionately somewhat greater. There was some immigration from the North, partly of a leisure class seeking health and a quiet country life, and partly of business men and skilled mechanics drawn by the rapid development of manufacturing. For the most part, however, the gain came because the South was able to retain its own sons now that the diversification of industry and the breakdown of the plantation system opened more widely the opportunities for advancement. From the time of the Hayes administration, the South has been left a free hand in the solving of the race problem. This has meant white rule. At first the negroes were held from voting by force and fraud. Beginning in 1890, one state after another adopted constitutional regulations debarring the great majority of the negroes from the suffrage. These regulations were based for the most part upon educational qualifications, but, by admitting the descendants of all voters of 1860, or by some such provision, allowed illiterate whites to vote. Such "grandfather" clauses were, in 1915, declared by the Supreme Court to be in violation of the fifteenth amendment and void. For twenty-five years, however, they substituted a method supposedly legal for force. Now southern opinion seems content to apply the same tests to blacks as to whites, though election officers may favor the latter. Lynching and the crimes which caused it are on the decline, and there seems to be a general diminution in the use of "private law" and increasing respect for the law of the land. Southern state and local authorities are now doing somewhat more for negro education than earlier, though much aid is still given by the North. Negro education, moreover, as a result largely of the work of Booker T. Washington, President of Tuskegee In-

Negro problems.

stitute, has become more practical. On the whole the relations between the blacks and whites are better than ever before, and the negro of ability and skill has a good chance in life, though the negroes as a race have not as yet proved economically efficient.

Politics in the South.

The negro still influences politics. While the North has candidly left the South to treat the relation of blacks and whites as a local problem, sentiment and tradition have proved too strong in the South to allow it to give up its political unity and cease to insist on its separateness. Southern congressmen from manufacturing districts vote with those from similar districts in the North, but they retain nearly always the name of Democrat; the South remains politically solid, and its party allegiance being taken for granted, exerts comparatively little influence on national affairs. Local politics, however, have not been devoid of interest. For many years the old leaders of the planter aristocracy, known as the Bourbons, kept control, their prestige being enhanced by their success in the movement for the reëstablishment of home rule in 1876. The material foundation for their power, however, had disappeared; the planter aristocracy no longer existed as a class, its members being scattered, many into the professions, some into the North, some unable to face new conditions, and only a few retaining their old manner of life. The natural result has been that since 1890 there has been a rise to power of the poorer white farmer, in some states gradually, in some, as in South Carolina under the leadership of Senator Tillman, accompanied by a sharp fight. Among the issues upon which this fight has been made, have been temperance, currency, industrial education, and the regulation of railroads and monopolies; but the ingrained southern individualism yields slowly and has prevented adoption of any such elaborate system of control for the latter as has been provided in the states of the North. The same tradition and the unorganized condition of the labor element have allowed factory legislation to lag behind the development of the factory system.

Throughout the whole country and among all its diverse streams of population, the predominant questions of the time, in public and private life, come more and more to be immediate, practical, and complex. The general truths for which the earlier generations contended are mostly established, and their limitations realized. Equality of opportunity and equality before the law, belief in the brotherhood of man and in the sovereignty of the people, are accepted as forming the most satisfactory basis for government, but they obviously do not of themselves solve the problems of government. It is not enough to make man free, it is necessary to keep perpetual watch and ward. Many of the new issues arise on questions of detail, questions of better or worse, not of right or wrong. Continued interest and study are more important than enthusiasm. The new leaders of thought are increasingly students unable themselves to present their views to the public. The essay, the poem, the editorial, the sermon, the oration, the first-hand utterance of the leader to the people are largely supplanted by the popularized semi-scientific article in the magazine. Literature has declined in quality and in influence. Poetry has become the pleasure of the dilettante, not a real force; philosophy languishes; theology attracts interest chiefly when it offers health to the body as well as peace to the soul. Humanitarianism is more widespread, more self-devoting than ever before, but it has become, not only more practical, but more material. Ideals, however, remain potent. Foremost among the national ideals is the preservation of democracy, although there is more inequality of condition than in the time of Jackson, and more appreciation of the difficulties of making it a vital living force. Political morality rests upon a higher plane than at any time since the first period of the republic, and political interest is far more widespread than at that time. The

Ideals and public opinion.

energy and the self-reliance developed by the conquest of the continent remain as a heritage for the nation in solving its new and more humdrum problems.

BIBLIOGRAPHICAL NOTES

Historical accounts.

Hart, A. B., *Ideals of American Government.* Ross, E. A., *Changing America.* *Encyclopedia Britannica* (11th ed.), XXVII, 634–663. Bois, W. E. B., *The Souls of the Black Folks.* Brown, W. G., *The Lower South.* Caffey, F. G., *Suffrage Limitations in the South* (*Pol. Sci. Quart.*, XX, 53). Dunbar, P. L., *Folks from Dixie.* Hart, A. B., *The Southern South.* Tillinghast, J. A., *The Negro in Africa and America.* Washington, B. T., *Up from Slavery,* and *Working with the Hands.* *The South in the Building of the Nation.* Turner, F. J., *Social Forces in American History* (*Am. Hist. Review,* Jan., 1911, 217–233). Van Hise, C. R., *Conservation of Natural Resources,* and *Concentration and Control.* Addams, J., *Twenty Years at Hull House.* Riis, J. A., *The Battle with the Slum.*

CHAPTER XXIX

POLITICAL ADJUSTMENTS AND LEGISLATION

On September 6, 1901, while attending the Pan-American Roosevelt succeeds McKinley. Exposition at Buffalo, President McKinley was shot by an anarchist. He died on September 14, and was succeeded on the same day by the Vice President, Theodore Roosevelt. While the latter thus became President unexpectedly, having been elected to an office which carries with it little prestige or power, he embodied more conspicuously than any other man in the country the new forces which were coming to the front in politics.

Entering politics at the age of twenty-four as member Roosevelt's career. of the New York legislature, he speedily became interested in civil service reform. From 1889 to 1895 he served on the United States Civil Service Commission, doing much to promote its efficiency, and to spread the movement. As president of the New York City Police Board, 1895 to 1897, he showed great energy in breaking up the connection of the police force with vice and "graft" which had been exposed by various investigations. Appointed by President McKinley as Assistant Secretary of the Navy, he resigned at the opening of the Spanish War, and organized and served as Lieutenant Colonel of a regiment of "Rough Riders," enlisted largely from the "cowboys" of the western plains with whom he had become familiar by residence in North Dakota, 1884 to 1886. During the war he distinguished himself, not only by gallantry, but by an attack on the efficiency of the War Department, which resulted ultimately in the resignation of Secretary Russell A. Alger. At the close of the war he was elected governor of New York. Securing this position in opposition to "Boss" Thomas C. Platt, at that time senator from New York, he came to be looked upon as a leader by those who wished to change the old order of things. His career as governor confirmed his hold on this element, and he became a leading power in politics. In the Republican convention of 1900 he was chosen as candidate for the vice presidency, not only because of the strength he would bring to the ticket, but because Senator Platt and Senator Hanna of Ohio, the political managers for President McKinley, considered that he would be least dangerous to the established order in that position. In all the offices in which he had·served Mr. Roosevelt showed an unusual capacity for work, and a remarkable vigor and directness in urging his opinions.

Civil service and labor.

As President, Mr. Roosevelt continued his work for civil service reform, very greatly extending the number of "classified" positions which came under the examination rules, and improving the consular service, which was still left open to personal appointments. He showed great interest in the problems of labor. In 1902 a strike of the anthracite coal miners for a time caused great distress throughout the North and threatened a cessation of industry by cutting off the coal supply. The President induced both sides to submit their cases to a commission which he appointed, and whose decision brought peace. In 1903, at his suggestion, Congress created a new department of government — that of Commerce and Labor — to investigate and help remedy industrial conditions.

High finance.

During these years the movement to concentrate the control of industry went on with greater rapidity than ever before. In 1900 J. Pierpont Morgan arranged the United States Steel Company, with stocks and bonds amounting to $1,100,000,000 — the greatest corporation ever organized. Controlling ore properties, transport lines, and factories, it was able to prevent disputes between different branches of the trade, to carry out great economies, and for several years to fix the price of steel products. E. H. Harriman combined railroad with railroad, the Union, Central, and Southern Pacific, the Illinois Central, the Oregon Short Line, and smaller units, securing a firm grip on transportation within the quadrilateral formed by Chicago, Portland, San Diego, and New Orleans. His only competitors were the Santa Fe and the Gould system, consisting of the Missouri Pacific and allied lines. In New England, the New York, New Haven, and Hartford, under the initiative of Mr. Morgan, was rapidly acquiring a monopoly of transportation by land and sea, by steam and electricity. In the far northwest, James J. Hill, builder of the Great Northern, attempted to complete his hold by uniting with that road the Northern Pacific and the Chicago, Burlington, and Quincy. As the two latter were directly competing roads, a merger would be illegal, so the Northern Securities Company was formed to hold and vote a majority of the stock of both. The era of competition in transportation seemed about to end. By direction of the President, however, suit was brought under the Sherman Anti-Trust Law against the Securities Company; and the Supreme Court in 1904 ordered it dissolved as a trust within the meaning of the law. In 1912 the Court ordered the Union Pacific to give up its control of the Southern Pacific.

Before Mr. Roosevelt's becoming President, four Vice Presidents had become chief executive by the death of the elected President. All of them had desired election to the office to which they had thus accidentally arrived, but in no case had they even received the nomination of their party. Mr. Roosevelt, however, had by 1904 taken so strong a hold on the public good will that he was unanimously nominated by the Republican convention to succeed himself. In the Democratic convention the conservative wing triumphed, choosing Judge Parker of New York as candidate, and enjoining silence on the currency question.

Election of 1904.

They made their issue with the Republicans chiefly on the tariff and imperialism. The result of the election was the overwhelming victory of Mr. Roosevelt. Mr. Parker failed to call out the full Democratic strength that Mr. Bryan had developed in 1896 and 1900, while the Republicans cast an unprecedented vote. This result was not unexpected, and it had in fact been thought possible that Mr. Roosevelt might break the solid South. All thought of this, however, had been abandoned before the election as the result of southern agitation at his inviting Mr. Booker T. Washington, a negro, to luncheon.

Corporation control. Thus triumphantly elected, Mr. Roosevelt proceeded to urge, still more vigorously than before, an elaborate program. The questions of corporations, trusts, and transportation continued to attract the widest public interest. Mr. Bryan, in many respects the leader of the Democratic party, urged the public ownership of railroads as the best solution possible. Mr. Roosevelt advocated regulation. In 1905 the Interstate Commerce Act was supplemented by a provision enabling the government to secure additional information, and in 1906 a substitute act was passed giving the Interstate Commerce Commission power to fix railroad rates for interstate commerce, subject to revision by the courts. The President also ordered the Attorney-General to bring suit against a number of the trusts under the Sherman Anti-Trust Law.

Crisis of 1907. In the same year there occurred an industrial and financial crisis. This was mainly due to overspeculation in industrial securities which in many cases represented anticipated earning capacity rather than real value. It was probably hastened by the defects in the banking system, and to some extent by the destruction of property in the San Francisco earthquake and fire of 1906. While the interruption of business was not so great as in 1873 and 1893, people felt the crisis keenly, for prices of necessities did not fall so far as after those crises, and the price of meat advanced. As in 1873 and 1893 concentration of industrial and financial control was stimulated, the stronger organizations swallowing up those weakened by the disturbance of credit. To the absorption of the Tennessee Coal and Iron Company by the United States Steel Corporation, the President gave his approval, arguing that not all trusts were bad, and that in this case the advantages outweighed the disadvantages. This position was attacked by those who believed it possible to prevent trusts from holding monopolies in their respective fields, and who wished to restore competition. Discussion raged on the platform and in the press, but it was several years before the conflicting views became well defined. To improve the currency situation the Aldrich-Vreeland bill was passed in 1908, which increased the elasticity of national bank note issues. A commission to make a thorough study of currency and to report a plan for permanent relief had previously been provided for.

Some of the most notable events of Mr. Roosevelt's administration were in the field of diplomacy. In 1904 the way for the Panama Canal was cleared of diplomatic problems, as has already been pointed out. Promptly work on the canal was begun and was pushed with vigor. In 1905 Mr. Roosevelt helped to bring the war between Japan and Russia to a close, by suggesting a negotiation in United States territory. In 1906, in recognition of this service, he was awarded the "Nobel Peace" prize. In his negotiations with the Spanish-American powers, Mr. Roosevelt pursued a policy which came to be known as that of the "Big Stick," insisting on the maintenance of order and the recognition of obligations. No hostilities, however, resulted, and some progress was made towards the settlement of disputes by arbitration. Peace and "Big Stick."

While Mr. Roosevelt in practice stood for peace, he urged strongly that the United States should be prepared for war, Army and navy.

and found much support in Congress for his suggestions. The national militia law was revised, and the regular army was reorganized on modern lines with the control vesting in a general staff of which General Leonard Wood became chief. While the army was reduced from the war footing of 1898, it remained over twice as large as it had been before the Spanish War, amounting to about sixty-seven thousand men. The navy was much more largely increased, and in 1907, by direction of the President, a large portion of it cruised round the world, as a test of efficiency which it stood most commendably.

Conservation and social problems.

One of the subjects most congenial to Mr. Roosevelt was that of conservation. By executive order he withdrew large areas of public land from sale, for the purpose of investigating their natural resources, and he recommended that Congress pass legislation protecting the interests of the general public in such minerals, water powers, and forests as should be found in them. The forest service under Mr. Gifford Pinchot was reorganized by Congress and granted new powers and appropriations. Congress also, in 1902, granted the proceeds of the sales of public lands in many western states to be used for carrying out irrigation projects, a large number of which, opening up thousands of acres to cultivation, were undertaken. In 1908 the President called a meeting of the governors of the several states to discuss the whole conservation problem. President Roosevelt also gave his attention to a vast number of subjects affecting the welfare of the country, some of which were fitted to become topics of legislation and some were not. In 1906 a Pure Food Law and a Meat Inspection Law were passed, the first of which especially, actively administered by Dr. Wiley, drew widespread popular approval. Commissions were appointed to investigate a great variety of matters, such as the question of employers' liability. The labor of women and children was made a matter of study by the

Department of Commerce and Labor, and the questions of safety devices on railroads and the working hours of railroad employees were actively discussed in Congress. The President interested himself in race suicide and divorce.

While much legislation was passed during Mr. Roosevelt's presidency, much of it was passed in the form of compromise measures unsatisfactory in many respects to those whose pressure forced it through, but accepted as marking progress. A great deal, moreover, depended on the spirit in which this legislation should be administered, and many problems remained as yet untouched. The choice of Mr. Roosevelt's successor, therefore, excited the keenest interest, for Mr. Roosevelt announced that he considered that he had served two terms and would abide by the precedent set by Washington against more than one reëlection. The power of making this choice practically lay with Mr. Roosevelt himself, so strong was his hold on his party. He selected Judge William Howard Taft, who had served as commissioner and governor in the Philippines, 1900 to 1904, and as Secretary of War, 1904 to 1908. The Democrats for the third time nominated Mr. Bryan. The campaign was fought on what were known as the "Roosevelt Policies," though the hard times following the crisis of 1907 caused some emphasis to be laid on the tariff, one of the few fields of legislation upon which there had been no recent lawmaking. Both parties, however, talked of reduction, and so no clear issue was made upon it. The election again resulted in a decided victory for the Republicans, although Mr. Bryan received almost a million more votes than did Judge Parker in 1904.

President Taft announced that his administration would continue the policies of his predecessor, but changed most of the cabinet. Mr. Knox, who had been Attorney-General, succeeded Mr. Root as Secretary of State, and Mr. Ballinger was promoted from the commissionership of the General Land Office to be Secretary of the Interior. In 1910 the Interstate

Election of 1908.

The tariff.

Commerce Commission was again given more power, and a Commerce Court established to review its decisions. The latter, however, proved unpopular and was discontinued in 1913. The main interest centered upon the tariff. The agitation on this question had become so acute that a special session was called to deal with it. The result was a new act, known, from Mr. Payne, chairman of the House Committee on Ways and Means, and Mr. Aldrich, chairman of the Senate Committee on Finance, as the Payne-Aldrich law. This bill proved a bitter disappointment to those who had expected a substantial revision downward. The President shared this view, but signed the bill, building hope of relief on the fact that the law provided for a Tariff Commission. This commission was to study conditions and supply Congress with information which would enable it to frame a tariff on the basis of offsetting differences in the cost of production in the United States and other countries. The President also hoped to modify the tariff substantially by reciprocity treaties.

Both these hopes of President Taft were disappointed.

Election of 1910 and Canadian reciprocity.

Before the Tariff Commission was ready to report, the election of 1910 took place, and the disappointment of the country found expression in returning a large Democratic majority to the House of Representatives, thus breaking the control of the government which the Republicans had continuously held since the first inauguration of McKinley in 1897. In 1911 the President succeeded in securing an agreement for reciprocity with Canada. This was not universally popular in the United States, but, nevertheless, was formally approved. It, however, became at once the subject of violent controversy in Canada, and practically the sole issue in a general election there. The contest resulted in the defeat of the Liberals, led by Sir Wilfrid Laurier, who had secured the pact, by the Conservatives, who opposed it. This election, therefore, defeated the arrangement after the United States had accepted it.

The Payne-Aldrich law not only brought defeat to the Re- publicans in Congress, but also practically marked a breach between the administration and a group of Republicans in Congress known by their opponents as "Insurgents" and calling themselves "Progressives." The leader of this group was Senator La Follette of Wisconsin. In 1901 he had become governor of that state after a long fight with the established party organization. As governor he secured the passage of a primary law, the establishment of a rate commission with extremely broad powers, a law providing for the taxation of railroads on the basis of their physical valuation, and many other progressive measures. Coming to the Senate in 1906, he in general coöperated with President Roosevelt, although he expressed strong dissatisfaction because the Interstate Commerce Act of 1900 did not provide for the physical valuation of the railroads, and criticised many details of legislation and of executive action. He violently opposed the Payne-Aldrich bill, and became a constant critic of the Taft administration. A similar position was taken by Senators Dolliver and Cummins of Iowa, Clapp of Minnesota, Bourne of Oregon, Beveridge of Indiana, and others. The Progressive movement was relatively stronger in the Senate than in the House, because in most cases there had been a long state fight, and when it was won, the leader was elected to the Senate. It was not, however, without strength in the House. In the last session of the first or Republican Congress under President Taft, the Insurgent Republicans combined with the Democrats in an attack on Speaker Cannon. Chosen to that position in 1903, he had concentrated in his hands even greater powers than Mr. Reed had exercised, and had used them to a large extent in opposing legislation desired by the new element in politics. In 1911 a change in the House rules was brought about, reducing the power of the Speaker and intrusting to a committee elected by the House much of the power he had held.

Passing
of former
leaders.

The growth of the Progressive movement was marked by the retirement of many of the men who for a long time had exercised a controlling influence in national politics. In 1907 Mr. Spooner of Wisconsin resigned from the Senate. In 1911 Senator Hale of Maine, who had been a member of that body since 1881 and had become the senior member in point of service, failed of reëlection, and in the same year Senator Aldrich of Rhode Island declined reëlection. In 1912 Senator Crane of Massachusetts announced that he would not be a candidate for reëlection, and Senator Cullom of Illinois was defeated in the primary election in that state. These changes, with the deaths of Senator Hanna of Ohio, in 1904, of Senators Hawley and Platt of Connecticut in 1905, and of Senator Allison of Iowa in 1908, removed from political life more active leaders than had passed in any similarly short period except that between 1850 and 1854.

Legislative
and executive
progress.

With the Republican party divided on many issues, and the Democrats in control of the House after 1911, it was difficult to secure legislation. Yet a system of Postal Savings Banks was established by Congress in 1911, and in 1912 a Parcel Post. Postmaster-General Hitchcock, moreover, very much improved the administration of the Post Office, eliminating the deficit which had for many years existed in that department. A department of labor was established and a bureau to supervise mines, with a view to increasing the safety of the workers. Congress and the executive combined to press with vigor the construction of the Panama Canal. The splendid work of Colonel Gorgas in sanitation rendered the Isthmus safely habitable, while Colonel Goethals, of the army engineering corps, pressed the work of construction even more rapidly than planned, insuring its readiness for use in 1914. The cost bids fair to be about four hundred millions, close to the estimates of 1909. Congress also recommended to the states two amendments to the federal Constitution: one giving Congress power to impose a national income tax such as the Supreme Court had declared unconstitutional during Cleveland's administration, and the other providing for the popular election of United States senators. In 1913 these proposals were ratified by the proper number of state legislatures, and they have become respectively the Sixteenth and Seventeenth Amendments to the Constitution.

On controversial questions, however, action was blocked. The President was particularly interested in the question of the settlement of international disputes by arbitration and secured treaties with England and France which it was hoped would make war with those countries practically impossible. The Senate, however, fearing that the treaties diminished its constitutional powers over treaty making in the future, amended them in such a way as to limit their scope considerably. In 1911 and 1912 the Democratic House passed a number of bills reducing the tariff on certain classes of goods, such as woolens, which also passed the Senate by a combination of Democrats and Progressive Republicans. The President, however, vetoed them. Thus a partial deadlock existed, and public interest began to center in the next presidential campaign. *Deadlock on arbitration and tariff.*

In the meantime the executive conduct of President Taft was severely criticised, particularly with regard to the question of conservation. A controversy arose between Mr. Gifford Pinchot, Chief of the Forest Service, and Mr. Ballinger, Secretary of the Interior, with regard to what were known as the "Cunningham" coal claims in Alaska and to the opening up to public sale of certain lands on Controller Bay in the same territory. The Secretary was accused of having unduly favored certain capitalists and having allowed them to obtain a practical monopoly of Alaskan coal, and these charges were widely believed. The President supported Mr. Ballinger, and Mr. Pinchot left office in 1910. In 1911 Mr. Ballinger also resigned. A somewhat similar controversy arose in the Department of Agriculture over the enforcement *Criticism of the executive.*

of the Pure Food Law, which resulted in the resignation of Dr. Wiley in 1912.

The judicial system during Mr. Taft's administration was also subject to more severe criticism than at any other time since the Johnson administration. In 1911 the Supreme Court, on suit brought by the Attorney-General, dissolved the Standard Oil Company of New Jersey, the oldest of the trusts, holding it to be in violation of the Sherman Anti-Trust Law. While this action pleased the Progressives, the form of the decision did not. The Court held that the intent of the law was not to prevent all combinations in restraint of trade, but only those which were "unreasonable." It was argued by many that in "reading the word reasonable" into the law, the Court was amending an act of Congress, and was assuming legislative power. This decision brought to a head the dissatisfaction with the courts which had for some time been brewing, particularly because of their use of the injunction in labor troubles, and the decisions of both state and national courts declaring unconstitutional, laws representing the social, economic, and political tendencies of the time. Many began to demand that judges be subject to recall, and California adopted in 1911 an amendment to her constitution providing a method of recall. Subsequent decisions of the Supreme Court interpreting the Anti-Trust Law, such as that in the case of the Tobacco Trust in 1912, convinced many that the dissolutions ordered by the Court were not complete enough to be effective, and that the Anti-Trust Law was not, at least as interpreted, sufficient to restore an era of competition. Many others came to believe that competition could not be restored, and that combinations of capital should not be prohibited, but regulated. Attention, moreover, was attracted to the concentration of financial control in the hands of a few men, of whom J. Pierpont Morgan was the most important. It was claimed that a money trust existed, which practically held in its hands the industrial and transportation trusts by supplying or denying them money. This trust was less tangible than the others, but if such control was exercised by any group of banks or bankers, the fact was of high importance. In 1912 the House of Representatives appointed a committee, headed by Mr. Pujo of Louisiana, to investigate the facts.

Under these circumstances the election of 1912 approached. President Taft was a candidate for reëlection. The successful prosecution of several trusts by Attorney-General Wickersham, and the refusal of the Interstate Commerce Commission to approve an increase of railroad rates, were unpopular with the "stand-pat" element of the party, but its leaders, nevertheless, determined to support the President. The Progressives, however, angered by the tariff vetoes, the dismissal of Pinchot, and other acts, disapproved his candidacy. Senators La Follette and Cummins both were declared candidates, but the bulk of the Progressive support went to ex-President Roosevelt, who made a vigorous campaign for the nomination. The convention which met in June was controlled by the conservative element and President Taft was nominated. The balance of power in the convention, however, was held by delegates whose seats were contested. In practically all such contests the Taft delegates were seated by the national committee, which made up the temporary roll of the convention, and were finally recognized by the convention organized on the basis of this temporary roll. Mr. Roosevelt claimed that such action constituted a theft of the nomination. He maintained also that the bulk of Mr. Taft's strength came from states, as those of the South, where the Republican party was small and powerless to secure electoral votes. He therefore refused to recognize the nomination of Mr. Taft, and subsequently a call was issued for a new convention to meet in August. At this latter convention he received the nomination for the presidency on the National Progressive ticket. The long-

Split of the Republican party.

standing differences in the Republican party, therefore, finally resulted in a distinct split, although certain Progressives, such as Senator La Follette, distrusting Roosevelt personally, stood aloof from both candidates.

Democratic nomination. The Democratic party looked forward confidently to electing a President in 1912. The leading candidates were the men who had been brought to the front by the victory of 1910; Mr. Clark of Missouri, Speaker of the House of Representatives, Mr. Underwood of Alabama, who as Chairman of the Committee on Ways and Means had led the majority in the House, and various state governors, as Foss of Massachusetts, Baldwin of Connecticut, Wilson of New Jersey, Harmon of Ohio, and Marshall of Indiana, while many thought it possible that Mr. Bryan might be nominated for a fourth time although he was not a candidate. The Democratic party, like the Republican, was divided into Conservatives and Progressives, although the division was not so acute. Of the candidates, Governor Harmon, who had been Attorney-General during Cleveland's second administration, was regarded as most pleasing to the Conservatives. Governor Wilson was a newcomer in politics. He had been for many years well known as a writer on political and historical subjects, and in his *Congressional Government*, published in 1885, had for the first time called public attention to the method by which Congress actually did its work — that is, by the committee system. His occupation, however, was education, and he resigned the presidency of Princeton University only in 1910 to become governor of New Jersey. In that position he was instrumental in securing the adoption of a comprehensive scheme of progressive measures, and he was generally regarded as the most progressive of the candidates. Speaker Clark was regarded as standing between the extremes and for a time seemed likely to secure the nomination, receiving at one time a majority vote in the convention. The Democrats, however, adhered to the two-thirds rule as had been their custom from their first convention in 1832. Mr. Bryan attended the convention and fought to have the party declare for a progressive platform and a candidate absolutely progressive in fact and in repu‧ tation. In this fight he was successful, and on the forty-sixth ballot Woodrow Wilson was nominated.

As the campaign progressed the main issues came to be, besides a strongly felt, though somewhat vague, difference between Conservatives and Progressives, the tariff and the trusts. Both Mr. Taft and Mr. Roosevelt stood for a protective system but for a revision of the existing law, in accordance with expert advice, toward lower rates. Mr. Wilson stood for immediate, but gradual, revision downward toward a tariff for revenue. On the trusts, Mr. Taft stood for the enforcement of the Sherman Law with the idea of reëstablishing competition. Mr. Wilson believed that the Sherman Law, with additional legislation and a properly adjusted tariff, would restore competition. Mr. Roosevelt maintained his idea that not all trusts were bad, that in many cases monopolistic concentration was economically necessary, and that strong regulative measures by the national government could prevent abuses. The campaign was marked, as that preceding the nominations had been, by personal charges and countercharges, and the personal factor was unusually important in determining the result. Hundreds of thousands voted according to the confidence they felt in the one candidate or the other, rather than from a clear opinion on the points at issue. *Campaign issues.*

In the election Mr. Wilson carried forty states and 435 electoral votes, and the Democrats secured an overwhelming majority in the House and a small one in the Senate. In the popular vote Mr. Wilson, with about six million three hundred thousand, ran somewhat behind the figures previously obtained by Mr. Bryan. As many previously Republicans voted for him, the difference was somewhat greater than *Election of 1912.*

would at first appear. Probably the bulk of the Democrats who left their party voted for Mr. Roosevelt, who received a popular vote of about four million one hundred thousand, and 88 electoral votes. The states that he carried included Pennsylvania in the East and California and Washington in the West. In twenty-two states he ran second. Mr. Taft's three and a half million popular votes were inadequately represented by 8 electoral votes, those of Vermont and Utah. In nineteen he ran second. The Republicans, however, either because Mr. Roosevelt's personal popularity exceeded the drawing power of the new party, or because the short time intervening between the convention and the election prevented widespread organization by the Progressive party, won most of the congressional districts not carried by the Democrats, and upon them would fall the burden of organized opposition. As Mr. Wilson and Mr. Roosevelt were both regarded as Progressives, although many Democrats and some Republicans of conservative tendencies voted for the former, it was obvious that a very great majority of voters were dissatisfied with existing conditions and demanded an effective consideration of the new problems with which the nation finds itself confronted. While no such legislative revolution as those of 1800 and 1860 seems impending, the election probably marks the end of the recent period of hesitation and a definite launching upon a new era of national organization.

BIBLIOGRAPHICAL NOTES

Historical accounts. Allen, P. L., *America's Awakening*, containing short sketches of contemporary leaders. LaFollette, R. M., *Autobiography*. Leupp, F. E., *The Man Roosevelt*. McCarthy, Charles, *The Wisconsin Idea*. Munroe, W. B., *Initiative, Referendum, and Recall*. Ogg, F. A., *National Progress*, 1907–1917, vol. 27 of *The American Nation*. Paxson, F. L., *The New Nation*, vol. 4 of *Riverside Series*. Roosevelt, T., *An Autobiography*.

CHAPTER XXX

THE NEW DEMOCRACY

IN 1913 for the first time since 1861 the Democrats came into effective control of the government. Between 1893 and 1895 they had held the presidency and a majority in both houses, but internal divisions had prevented the carrying out of a logical program. Now harmony seemed possible. The first effect of the political revolution was to bring into administrative responsibility a new group of leaders. Naturally an unusual proportion came from the South. Of ten cabinet members, four were: J. C. McReynolds of Tennessee, Attorney-general; A. S. Burleson of Texas, Postmaster General; Josephus Daniels of North Carolina, Secretary of the Navy; and D. F. Houston of Missouri, Secretary of Agriculture. The South was still stronger in Congress. Clark and Underwood continued as speaker and floor leader respectively in the House, while in the Senate F. M. Simmons of North Carolina became chairman of the committee on finance and J. S. Williams of Mississippi the chief spokesman of the administration. Influence of the South.

It was the West, however, which furnished the new régime, with its most compelling figure in William Jennings Bryan. Thrice defeated for the presidency, and without having served in public office since his brief tenure in Congress nearly twenty years before, he had never lost the hold on the people he had established in the thrilling campaign of 1896. From a thousand political and Chautauqua platforms his geniality constantly radiated, and the magnetism of his good nature and his uprightness tied millions to him Bryan.

as to a friend. In a sense unusually real he had made Mr. Wilson President, and the latter's administration could not have accomplished a single one of its aims had Bryan been slighted; as a matter of course he was offered the principal position in the cabinet, and became Secretary of State. Yet his appointment was disapproved by many. Some, believing him to be moved chiefly by political ambition, feared he would betray the administration. Others feared his radical tendencies. Still more doubted his ability satisfactorily to administer large responsibilities and particularly foreign affairs. In practice his personal relations with the President showed his genuine good faith, while the confidence that his presence in the cabinet gave to the more radical element in the party afforded the leaders a greater freedom in handling public questions, and particularly that of the currency, than could have been attained in any other way. His management of diplomacy was more open to criticism, and particularly his choice of ministers to foreign countries showed in some instances that lack of a discriminating judgment of men which is so often the concomitant of good nature. In addition he exercised a leading influence in changing the social tone of official life at Washington, to harmonize more with that of the usual American household. His decision to serve no wine at the official banquets was criticized, but was also widely approved. The abolition of the use of wine in the navy by Secretary Daniels still further emphasized the temperance tendencies of the new order.

Social changes.

People were not long in learning, however, that the real leader of the new administration was to be the President. Woodrow Wilson came to office with less political experience than any of his predecessors except Taylor and Grant, but without hesitation he assumed the leadership, and soon demonstrated a driving force seldom before equaled. Reticent and unspectacular, he convinced the public of his complete probity and his absolute independence. His influence

Woodrow Wilson.

with Congress lay in his simple and direct expression of the requirements of public opinion and of morality as he saw them. With a scholar's disregard of tradition, he threw aside that which Jefferson had established of restricting communication between Congress and the executive to writing, and read his messages in person. With an unshakable insistence on his own views, not unlike that of Jackson, Polk, and Cleveland, he possessed something of the persuasiveness of Jefferson. He pushed through obstacles to achievement with joy in the fight and with unusual success. Whether he will prove equally successful in dealing with questions where combination, conciliation, and compromise are necessary, is yet a question.

Confronted by the not unjust demand of a party long out of power for a prompt redistribution of public offices, he nevertheless succeeded in clearing Washington of office-seekers and developing his policy in peace. In the case of officers subject to confirmation by the Senate, except those in the diplomatic and consular corps, the majority were allowed to complete their terms, at the close of which, in most cases, new men, Democrats, were nominated. The consular service was left on the whole untouched; the diplomatic service, on the other hand, was almost altogether renewed. *The civil service.*

If there was any one task which public opinion imposed upon the victorious party, it was the revision of the tariff. A special session of Congress was called, and Mr. Underwood presented a bill which had been in preparation since 1911. While to some extent a compromise like all tariff bills, it was quite obviously based on the principle of revenue rather than protection. The rates on cotton, iron, and woolen manufactures were reduced, in some cases to less than half those previously in force; to the free list were added many of our own products, chiefly raw materials such as wool and lumber; while, on the other hand, duties were *Tariff and income tax.*

imposed on certain raw materials not produced in America and free under the protective acts. It was estimated that on the whole the customs revenue would be reduced, and so, as in 1894, an income tax was added. The sixteenth amendment having settled the question of constitutionality, its proceeds could now be counted upon. It exempted incomes under three thousand dollars, or four thousand in the case of married couples, and the rate was graduated, rising with the income. The corporation tax which had been adopted in 1911 was continued, though in modified form. The bill was signed by the President October 3, 1913. Embodying as it did an almost complete revision of our revenue system, it was not without some surprise that the financial year closed July 1, 1914, with an almost exact balance of revenue and expenditure. Its economic results were less easy to gauge, and its effects on prices and on trusts were by no means certain when the next congressional election took place.

President Wilson feared that the passage of new tariff would be followed by what he subsequently called a psychological panic; that is, business depression produced not by actual adverse conditions, but by fear of such conditions aggregated by the desire of many financial leaders to prove the new policy a mistake. To prevent such an occurrence he urged that the same session of Congress which passed the tariff should pass also a currency bill. The administration measure, known as the Glass-Owen bill, was largely based upon information gathered by the Aldrich commission, although it did not follow its main recommendations. Amended vigorously in the Senate, it became a law before Congress met in regular session, December, 1913. Its purpose was to decentralize and bring under public control the banking resources of the country, and to provide a currency which should be more elastic without being less sound. In practice there had grown up a distinction between " country banks" and certain great institutions, particularly in New York. In the latter the " country banks " deposited their cash reserves, on which they received interest. It resulted that the control of bank resources was strongly centralized, and there is little doubt that during the panic of 1907 J. P. Morgan practically handled the available cash of the nation. This distinction was recognized by the creation of "Federal Reserve Banks," whose number, between the limits of eight and twelve, and whose location were left to executive discretion. The stockholders and customers of these new banks were to be banks, their directors were to represent the banks, the business community, and the government, and they were to be supervised by a Federal Reserve Board of seven government officials, including the Secretary of the Treasury, who were to be advised by a Federal Advisory Council chosen by the Reserve banks. National banks were obliged to subscribe for stock, and state banks and trust companies were permitted to do so, though it was discovered that many of them were prevented by state laws. The new banks were to hold in deposit reserve funds for the banks, to act as clearing houses, to have powers of foreign exchange, and in general to do for the smaller banks what had been done by the great institutions of New York. The established currency of the country was not disturbed, but the Federal Reserve Board was given power to issue through the Reserve banks, a new paper currency, based in part on cash reserves, though they could be at times disregarded, and in part on the ordinary instruments of credit, as short-term notes. This currency was to be receivable for all public dues, and to be redeemable in gold at Washington. It was intended that it should be issued chiefly in times of panic, when private credit was distrusted, and it was arranged that it should flow back and be destroyed when not needed.

These two laws represented the most fundamental change in the revenue, banking, and currency system which had

Trust legis-
lation.

been made since the Civil War.   During its regular session,
1913 to 1914, Congress devoted its energies largely to the
trust question.   The Clayton act amended the Sherman act
in the light of a quarter of a century of experience, and a
Federal Trade Commission was created to control corporations doing general business in more than one state, with
powers somewhat similar to, though not so extensive as,
those of the Interstate Commerce Commission over corporations engaged in interstate transportation.

Election
of 1914.

These new acts had not been long enough in operation
when the congressional elections of 1914 occurred, for the
public to have gained any distinct impression as to their
effect.   The outbreak of the Great War, moreover, so complicated the economic conditions of the whole world, that
even the closest student was at a loss in disentangling the
results of war from those of legislation.   The elections, therefore, had no great political significance.   The most important feature was the return of more than half the Progressives to the Republican fold.   The latter party gained still
further votes from the reaction that seems always to follow
a great victory in the presidential year; it carried several
states which had voted for Wilson, and sent to the House
some of its old leaders defeated in 1912, such as Mr. Cannon,
and many new members.   The Democrats, however, retained
a working majority in the House, and increased their lead in
the Senate.

Meantime the attention of the country was more or less
withdrawn from internal affairs, by a number of foreign
complications.   The chief interest of Secretary Bryan in his
department lay in the cause of peace, and he negotiated a
series of new arbitration treaties, designed to prevent the
hasty outbreak of war.   Of particular questions, that of the
rights of Japanese subjects in California was especially
troublesome, owing to the inability of the national government to control state legislation.   The desire of Congress to

exempt American vessels from tolls for the use of the Panama Canal, which was incorporated in the law of 1913 regulating its use, brought about difficulties with Great Britain, for the Hay-Pauncefote treaty of 1901 had provided that there should be no discrimination. President Wilson maintained that this was an international obligation which it was our duty to observe, and in 1914 Congress withdrew the exemption.

A more important and perplexing problem, however, involved Mexico and the Monroe Doctrine. Under the Roosevelt and Taft administrations the doctrine had gradually been extended to include the interposition of the United States in disputes between European and Spanish-American states, and our assumption of responsibility for seeing that the latter lived up to their obligations. In 1911 we asserted that no foreign corporation should be allowed to receive concessions that might prove dangerous to us at strategic points in America, though outside our jurisdiction. The colonizing activity of the Japanese began to excite some alarm, but we maintained our principles of exclusion against her also, although we did not, as in the case of the European powers, abstain from all interference with Asiatic affairs. It was still our obvious purpose to prevent the establishment of any foreign influence on American soil, which should serve as a basis for a system of balance of power such as exists in Europe, Asia, and Africa. At the same time our attention had become more and more centered about the Caribbean, that portion of South America south of the equator not being so intimately within our sphere of influence, and being also more self-sufficing, dominated as it came to be by the orderly and established governments of Brazil, Argentina, and Chile. *The Monroe Doctrine.*

Mexico, the most important country in our immediate vicinity, had long seemed quiet, and billions of dollars had been invested in her progress by Americans, English, French, Germans, Spaniards, and men of other nationalities. In 1911 her tranquillity vanished with the passing of the Diaz *Troubles in Mexico.*

régime. His successor, Madero, was overthrown by General Huerta in 1913, and was imprisoned and shot. Huerta assumed the presidency, only to face the immediate revolt of the north, under Carranza, governor of the state of Coahuila. President Wilson refused to recognize any government in Mexico, on the ground that we could not morally give cognizance to a government founded on violence and without constitutional authority. He believed that our failure to recognize Huerta would deprive the latter of credit, and that by "watchful waiting" we should see the quiet extinction of his government, and a return to peace and order. This "nonrecognition," although it seemed to many unduly passive on our part, really marked the most extreme extension of the Monroe Doctrine, for it involved us for the first time in a general supervision of the internal affairs of the American republics.

Pan-Americanism.

Unofficially we treated with Huerta, who controlled southeastern Mexico, and Carranza, who controlled the northwest. Difficulties with Huerta led in March, 1914, to the occupation of Vera Cruz by United States troops. At this point the A, B, C governments of South America — Argentina, Brazil, and Chile — offered, and we accepted, mediation, a conference being held at Niagara Falls which did much toward preventing war. In addition, it helped convince Spanish America that our policy was disinterested, and became the starting point of a new departure in Pan-Americanism, which at the meeting of the American Scientific Congress at Washington in December, 1915, developed a cordiality never before reached.

Protection of the border.

In Mexico confusion continued. Carranza overthrew Huerta, only to be attacked by his own lieutenant Villa. Our government possessed a weapon of interference in the control of the shipment of arms, which Congress had placed in the hands of the President. At first we supported Villa, but upon his defeat by Carranza, we came to pin our hopes of order upon the latter, and in November, 1915, recognized his government. Villa, however, remained at large, and in the spring of 1916 emerged from his mountain hiding places and raided our territory. The President promptly ordered General Pershing with twelve thousand regulars to cross into Mexico, on the ground that the Mexican government was not able to restrain its citizens and we were justified in taking what steps were necessary to defend our border. He also ordered out our state militia to replace the regulars along our side of the border. The whole operation was under the charge of General Funston, who had won his reputation by the capture of Aguinaldo in the Philippines. A joint commission of United States and Mexican representatives was, in the meantime, arranged, which we hoped would discuss the general problem of the regeneration of Mexico. This hope, however, proved delusive. Villa remained uncaught and grew in strength, and, this new policy having failed to produce pacification, the regulars were, early in 1917, withdrawn from Mexico, and the return of the militia, after six months of hard training, was begun.

Suddenly in August, 1914, more than half the world was involved in war. The United States was confronted by a greater world conflict than that of the Napoleonic period. While it was relatively stronger than it had been a century before, the growth of trade and intercourse had rendered the fabric of its civilization more dependent upon that of other nations, and the fact that its population was composed of immigrants from both the warring groups, suggested the possibility of a division of sentiment more dangerous than that between the French and British sympathizers under Washington. *The Great War.*

In the face of these dangers the Wilson administration determined to pursue a policy of strict neutrality based upon those precedents and agreements relating to the rights and the duties of neutrals which had developed out of our past *Administration policy.*

experience. In by far the greater number of instances these
practices were admitted by both belligerents to be the law
governing their actions.   In some cases, however, there were
disputes, and in others the belligerents claimed that modern
conditions rendered an old rule obsolete or alleged that the
disregard of some rule by the other belligerent justified a
departure from that or from some other rule on their own
part.   The disputes arising from these causes in the case of
Great Britain and her allies related for the most part to
trade; those with Germany and her allies, to the personal
safety of Americans on the high seas.   The administration
persistently asserted the American position in all such cases,
and in June, 1915, Mr. Bryan resigned from the state department on the ground that our policy should be directed primarily to the maintenance of peace rather than the maintenance of our rights.   He was succeeded by Robert Lansing,
a man of wide knowledge of international law but without
great political experience.   His appointment indicated that
the exigencies of the foreign situation were recognized as
greater than those of domestic politics.

Diplomatic   As in all similar cases, we found that neutrality had its
service.   duties.   Most of the belligerent countries requested us to
take charge of their affairs in the countries with which they
were at war.   The performance of this courtesy did not involve us in expense, but called for a greatly increased staff.
This led to reorganization and the passage of a law, February 5, 1915, which placed the entire diplomatic service, with
the exception of the ministers and ambassadors, upon a
classified basis.   To prevent the use of our territory for hostile purposes, of which there were many instances early in
the war, it was found necessary to reorganize and increase
our secret service.   Since the summer of 1915, it has been
effective.

International   As the war went on, Germany and her allies were cut off
problems.   from the outside world by the operations of Great Britain

and her allies. While this caused some industrial distress in the United States, the volume of our commerce increased enormously, owing to the demands of the British allies for war munitions and supplies of all kinds. The scope of our manufacturing expanded, and, in particular, our long languishing merchant marine revived without the national assistance which the administration at first thought would be necessary. While it was in accordance with our policy and with international law for a neutral to trade wherever possible, many German sympathizers and peace advocates urged that we put a total embargo on the export of munitions. Extremists on the other side thought we should have protested against the violation of Belgian neutrality at the opening of the war, and after the sinking of the *Lusitania*, May 7, 1915, without warning, by a submarine, and with the loss of many American lives, demanded immediate war with Germany. The administration insisted that the practice of which this was an example was intolerable, but continued the negotiations it had begun when, in February, 1915, Germany had first announced this policy. Finally, after the sinking of the *Sussex* in March, 1916, Germany agreed, May 4, to abandon its practice of sinking vessels indiscriminately without warning. As we passed through crisis after crisis, the chance that the United States might be forced to take part in the war became more evident, and attention was devoted to the problem of preparation. Upon the question of creating a permanent national volunteer force, standing between the regular army and the militia, the secretary of war, Mr. Garrison, resigned, and was replaced by Mr. Baker. Congress finally, in 1916, passed the Hay bill, a complicated measure, which provided for the strengthening of the regular army and the militia, and the creation of a corps of reserve officers. The execution of this measure was much interfered with by the high wages in industry, and a vigorous movement for universal compulsory service began to make headway. With little opposition or discussion, a great expansion of the navy was provided for.

Nominations, 1916.

Under these circumstances the election of 1916 drew near. The Democrats, without hesitation, renominated Wilson and Marshall. The Republicans, by a great majority, called Mr. Hughes from the Supreme Court, with Mr. Fairbanks of Indiana as his running mate. The Progressives, meeting at the same time, again selected Mr. Roosevelt, just before Mr. Hughes's nomination, and very possibly in the hope that he would receive the Republican nomination also. When Mr. Hughes accepted, however, Mr. Roosevelt gave him his support. The Progressive vice-presidential candidate, Mr. Perkins of Louisiana, refused to retire, and the disposition of the Progressive party became one of the chief problems of the campaign. It was a poor year for third parties. The Socialist vote decreased, the Prohibition candidate received but small support in spite of the growing popularity of that issue, and the Progressives were important only as individuals who might vote with one of the major parties, and whose good will might be secured by recognition of their principles.

Campaign, 1916.

The campaign turned chiefly upon foreign relations. Hughes and Roosevelt urged that a more emphatic policy by our government would not have brought on war but would have secured better recognition of our rights by both belligerents. The official German-American organizations supported Hughes. Wilson was attacked in the East as pro-German; in the West, as pro-British. A strong appeal was made to the women who since 1912 had secured the vote in Nevada, Montana, and Illinois; making twelve states in all, of which Kansas and Illinois alone were east of the region of the Rocky Mountains. The Republicans sent a woman's train through the country, and declared in favor of the Susan B. Anthony amendment, making woman suffrage national. Wilson declared in favor of woman suffrage by state action, and the Democratic voters called on the women especially to vote for the man "who kept us out of war." A new issue was suddenly injected into the campaign by a threatened national strike of railroad men. President Wilson, after many conferences, recommended to Congress a program granting the men their demand for an eight-hour day, and including other measures intended to prevent a recurrence of such a situation. Congress passed only the eight-hour provision, in the form of the Adamson bill. The strike was averted, but many felt that a dangerous precedent had been created in that Congress had acted under stress of an ultimatum by a single industrial interest.

The election brought out a new sectional division, long existent but not so apparent in politics, and the importance of the Far West. Hughes carried all the East and the old Northwest, except New Hampshire and Ohio, and almost nothing else. The result was uncertain for days, awaiting news from California, emphasizing in the public mind the shift of the political center, which for so many years had been in New York. While the greater number of women voters favored Wilson, their vote was not very dissimilar from that of the men in the regions where they voted, and few conclusions could be drawn from their actions. Wilson was reëlected by an electoral vote of 277 to 254, and by a popular plurality of about half a million. The Democrats retained control of the Senate, but neither party secured a majority in the House, where the balance rested with five independents and small party men. *Election, 1916.*

Assured of popular support, President Wilson initiated a more positive policy with reference to the Great War. He asked the various belligerents to state to us the terms upon which they would be willing to make peace, and, in a speech to the Senate, he urged that a world federation to enforce peace, if founded upon principles in accordance with our ideals, would not be a violation of our traditional policies, *An effort for peace.*

and asked for consideration of such a project. Before discussion had taken shape, however, a new crisis was upon us.

The Great War at the end of 1916.   In the meantime, three campaigns had brought no military decision in the Great War. The initial drive of the Germans failed to reduce France, though it won control of Belgium and the richest industrial regions of France. The Verdun drive of 1916 left the French army and spirit still intact. Germany had indeed realized for the moment her dream of Mittel-Europa, occupying Serbia, crushing Roumania, and so opening a path to the Orient. The British, however, still held its gates, Egypt and Mesopotamia, had quenched the back fires of revolt Germany had raised in India and other parts of the world, and with their allies had taken most of the German colonies. Their blockade, growing in intensity, was causing great scarcity in Germany.

Germany decides to risk war with the United States.   Under these circumstances there was a bitter struggle within the governing class of Germany, between those who thought her aggressive designs should be given up for the present and a reasonable peace concluded, and those who wished to make the final gamble: the indiscriminate, unlawful use of submarines. They believed that it was possible thus to separate Europe from America, as Russia was separated from the Western Powers; and that it would therefore be a matter of military indifference whether the United States came into the war or not. At the end of 1916, this extreme military party won the upper hand.

BIBLIOGRAPHICAL NOTES

Sources.   *Current History*, published by the New York *Times*. Gerard, J. W., *My Four Years in Germany*.

Historical accounts.   Corwin, E. S., *The President's Control of Foreign Relations*. Fish, C. R., *American Diplomacy*. Ogg, F. A., *National Progress, 1907–1917*, vol. 27 of the *American Nation*. Paxson, F. L., *The New Nation*, vol. 4 of *Riverside Series*. Robinson, E. E., and West, V. J., *The Foreign Policy of Woodrow Wilson*.

CHAPTER XXXI

THE UNITED STATES IN THE GREAT WAR

ON January 31, 1917, Germany withdrew her pledge of May 4, 1916, limiting the activity of her submarines within lawful bounds. After careful deliberation, and in the face of our protests, she announced her intention of waging war to the death against all merchant ships, enemy or neutral, in certain "zones," which included those parts of the seas where most of our ocean-going marine was employed. Germany flouts international law.

On February 3 President Wilson, personally addressing Congress, announced that he had recalled Mr. Gerard, our ambassador to Germany, and had given Count von Bernstorff, the German ambassador to the United States, his passports. Still bent on exhausting every possibility of peace, he recommended not war, but armed neutrality, such as we had employed in 1798 against France, in order that Germany might be absolutely convinced of our determination to defend our rights, and have still a chance to withhold her hand. In accordance with this recommendation, a measure for arming our merchant ships was prepared, which was supported by an overwhelming majority in both houses of Congress, but was prevented from passing at that session by "a little group of willful" senators, who "filibustered" against it, taking advantage of every technicality of the Senate rules of debate. Nevertheless the President, assured of the support of immense majorities in both houses, on March 12, proclaimed an "armed neutrality" in force. Armed neutrality.

What was in February a threat, became in April a fact. In March five American ships were sunk without warning, War exists.

and twenty American lives lost. Moreover a diplomatic
note of January 19 was made public, signed and later acknowledged by Mr. Zimmermann of the German foreign office, proposing to Mexico an aggressive alliance against us in case
we went to war with Germany, and suggesting that Mexico
take measures to bring Japan into the alliance. A flood of
evidence began to rush upon us, showing that Germany, in
violation of her professions and of international law, had
been using our territory as a base for operations not only
against her enemies, but against us also. For years she had
supported a propaganda intended to make our German-born
population loyal to her, rather than to the United States, to
whom most of them had sworn allegiance. During the war
she spent millions here to win public opinion and to influence
Congress. Her spies made their way into the centers of
government, sought to demoralize our labor system, and
recklessly destroyed American lives by blowing up factories,
docks, and ships. It was evident that Germany had been
waging war against us for nearly three years. On April 2,
1917, President Wilson recommended that Congress accept
the state of war thus thrust upon us, and on April 6 Congress
voted a declaration of war.

President Wilson pointed out that while we had not
entered the war until it was plainly evident that Germany
was actually fighting us, we sought "nothing for ourselves
but what we shall wish to share with all free peoples."
"We have no quarrel with the German people. . . . It
was not upon their impulse that their government acted in
entering this war." He reasserted his hope of world federation, but stated: "A steadfast concert for peace can never
be maintained except by a partnership of democratic nations.
No autocratic government could be trusted to keep faith
within it or to observe its covenants." He did not recommend immediate war upon Germany's allies, Austria-
Hungary, Turkey, and Bulgaria. With the enemies of

The issue.

Germany, — Great Britain, France, Russia, Italy, and many smaller nations, — he recommended the most intimate coöperation, but not alliance. His analysis of the struggle as one between democracy and autocracy had just received striking confirmation in a democratic revolution in Russia.

In entering the Great War, the United States seemed to many to be breaking away from a safe anchorage in which the wisdom of Washington and Jefferson had moored her, and John Quincy Adams, with the Monroe Doctrine, had secured her. President Wilson, however, as spokesman of the American people, made it abundantly evident that our country continued to seek the same ends and to be inspired by the same purposes as in the past. In his message to Russia, June 9, 1917, he said: "No people must be forced under sovereignty under which it does not wish to live. No territory must change hands except for the purpose of securing those who inhabit it a fair chance of life and liberty." Such self-determination of peoples, and non-intervention with their domestic affairs, has been the aim of Americans from the days of John Winthrop. In his reply of August 27, 1917, to the Pope's proposal for peace, he said: "They [the American people] believe that peace should rest upon the rights of peoples, not the rights of Governments. . . . The test, therefore, of every plan of peace is this: Is it based upon the faith of all the peoples involved?" This is the very essence of the Declaration of Independence: "That to secure these rights, Governments are instituted among Men, deriving their just powers from the consent of the governed." *American ideals.*

The means of securing these purposes have ever varied. In the Revolution we were content to secure them for ourselves alone. The experiences of the Napoleonic wars convinced us that we could not safely anticipate their enjoyment by ourselves unless they prevailed throughout the American continents. The tightening, by steam and *New methods.*

electricity, of the bonds which hold the world together **had** long caused many to think of the whole world as that house which Lincoln said "divided against itself, cannot stand." The aggressions of Germany convinced President Wilson that a world half autocratic and half free cannot be "safe for democracy."

Our leaders had never taught that we lived for ourselves alone. Lincoln believed that the fundamental issue at stake in the Civil War was democracy, that it was our duty to prove to the world, for the world, that democracy could be efficient; for if it could not govern our area, intended by nature to be one, it must yield to such form of government as could. President Wilson believed that in 1917 democracy must prove its strength against autocracy. If, through division or failure to organize its strength, democracy were to fail, the world would fall to the victor. To maintain our deep-seated ideals, it was no longer sufficient to separate ourselves and our immediate neighbors from Europe. We must recognize our neighborhood with the whole world. In his message to Russia, he said: "The brotherhood of mankind must no longer be a fair but empty phrase; it must be given a structure of force and reality. The nations must realize their common life and effect a workable partnership to secure that life against the aggressions of autocratic and self-pleasing power."

Navy and loans.

Two things only could we do at once; send our navy and lend money. Our fleet was ready for instant action, and steamed to join the navies of our associates in keeping open the lanes of traffic against the submarines. Money we had in plenty, but to lend it, we had to work out a financial system. It was decided to raise funds in part by increased taxation and in part by loans. In June, 1917, $2,000,000,000 was borrowed at $3\frac{1}{2}\%$; in October, nearly $4,000,000,000 at 4%; in April, 1918, $3,000,000,000 was put upon the market at $4\frac{1}{4}\%$. In each case popular subscription was relied on, and the "Liberty Loan" drives were made campaigns of education as to the purposes of the war.

By an act of October 3, 1917, income taxes were greatly increased, particularly in the case of large incomes, and other internal taxes were increased in amount and variety. As many industries had been stimulated by the war demands of Europe for three years, we could not use the European system of taxing "war profits," but laid a heavy general "excess profits" tax. It was estimated that these taxes would meet one third of our expenses, a very large ratio for a nation to pay by taxation in war time. Actually they produced a still larger proportion. *Increased taxes.*

The army was in much better condition than ever before, but was woefully unequal to the demands upon it. An increase of the regular army was already provided for, and in a year it almost quadrupled by volunteering. The National Guard, under the act of June 3, 1916, became at once, in war time, part of the "army of the United States." The main reliance for numbers, however, was upon a selective service draft, authorized May 18, 1917. On June 5, 9,659,382 men between the ages of 21 and 30 were registered, from whom men were called to service as the provisions for training them were created. Before the first could be called, however, it was necessary to provide trained officers. Officers' camps were established, where, under rapid and skillful instruction, thousands of young Americans were given the elements of the profession of war. On June 26, the first American troops reached France. *The army.*

The chief contributions desired from the United States, however, were food and ships. Three years of the most devastating war the world has ever seen, with the employment of tens of millions of the world's workers in the battle line and in war industries, had produced a condition in which only by changes of diet habits, and by most exact distribution, could the world be fed. At the same time the enormous toll *Food and ships.*

taken by the submarines from the world's merchant tonnage threatened to sever us from France, at the very time when we were uniting our fortunes with hers.

Shipping policy.

Already in 1916, a Shipping Board, with powers similar to those of the Interstate Commerce Commission, had been authorized. In April, 1917, the United States Shipping Board Emergency Fleet Corporation, with a capital of $50,000,000 belonging to the national government, was authorized to undertake ship construction, and a Shipping Committee of the National Council of Defense was appointed to establish full coöperation between public and private agencies. Thus organized, the United States began to be again a great shipbuilding nation.

Control of food, fuel, and transportation.

The vital matter of food production and distribution was treated in an act of August 10, 1917. This gave extraordinary powers to a Food Administrator, and the President at once appointed Herbert C. Hoover, who had made an undying record by his administration of relief work in invaded Belgium. The same act provided for a Fuel Administrator, to which position President Harry A. Garfield of Williams College was appointed. In January, 1918, the entire control of the railroads was taken over by act of Congress, and was placed in the hands of Mr. McAdoo, Secretary of the Treasury. As at the time of the Civil War, emergency meant nationalization of effort, in fact internationalization of effort. It meant, also, public control. Hosts of other acts and orders brought this subject and that, prices, quantity, quality, and disposition of products, under regulation. The United States became the purchaser for its associates, and loaned them money according to their needs.

Largely by our insistence, the control of military operations against the Germans was centralized in a Supreme War Council, and General Foch, in the spring of 1918, was made supreme commander. Under stress of emergency the forces within the United States which had been resisting the logic of national unity and world unity, collapsed. The question of the extent to which this readjustment would prove permanent was left to be determined after the war.

The sudden expansion of the functions of the national Civil service. government, and of the scope of government, national and state, made it necessary to call into public service much of the ability of the country which had previously been employed privately. In part this was done by bringing experts in all lines into the civil service, the universities contributing a remarkable percentage. Existing unofficial organizations were called in as well, such as the Red Cross, the Young Men's Christian Association, the Knights of Columbus, the American Library Association, and many others. A new form of organization was created in the semi-official Councils of Defense. In August, 1916, Congress authorized a National Council of Defense "for the coördination of industries and resources for the national security and welfare." With the outbreak of the war, every state followed this national example, and the system was soon carried into practically every city and county. Through these councils the business experience of the country was largely placed at the disposal of the government, and the mass of unaccustomed regulations was carried out and made plain to the public. To an amazing degree they carried out their work by simple explanation, without recourse to law and far beyond the limits of actual law.

This ready acceptance of the novel demands of modern Public opinion. war indicated a popular approval of the nation's course which could not be gainsaid. To no other war in which the United States has engaged, was there so little opposition. The most prominent of the opponents was Senator LaFollette, of Wisconsin, who opposed the armed neutrality, the war, and the draft. In spite of overwhelming evidence, he claimed that the war had been brought on by capitalistic influences, that "Germany had been patient with us";

and he sought to arouse distrust of the government's financial policy and of the nations associated with us. Another element of opposition came from the Socialists. This party officially condemned the war; whereupon some of the Socialists, including many of their intellectual leaders, left the party and became valiant supporters of the administration.

The German-born.

Still another body of discontent was among the German-born. For them the situation was indeed painful, torn as they were between love of kindred and the ties of their youth on one side, and their neighbors and their oath of allegiance on the other. The overwhelming majority of the German-born Americans were loyal in their obedience to the law; a majority, especially of the younger citizens, were loyal in spirit as well as in act. A few became unreconcilable traitors. By malicious rumor, by incitement to disobey the draft, by incendiary fires, by tampering with our machines, they delayed our progress, deceived our associates, and caused the death of our men.

Secret service and censorship.

To meet these acts of treason, Congress passed, in June, 1917, an espionage act, and the administration developed our secret service into high efficiency. To meet the misrepresentations of the opponents of the war, the President established, in April, 1917, a Committee on Public Information, to present the facts of the case to the American public, and to exercise also a censorship over military information.

The Wisconsin senatorial election of 1918.

As 1917 was not an election year, there was no definite nation-wide test of public opinion concerning the government's policy. National interest was high, therefore, in a special election called in Wisconsin in March, 1918, to fill a vacancy in the United States Senate caused by the death of Paul Husting, a young and promising member of that body. That state had for many years supported Senator LaFollette, and it had a greater percentage of German population than any other state in the Union. The Socialist party denounced the war, and advocated the immediate withdrawal of our army from France. The LaFollette candidate, running for the Republican nomination, counseled obedience to the law, and presented no program of action except heavier taxation. Loyalty candidates in both Republican and Democratic parties indorsed President Wilson's war policy and pledged him their full support. The results showed that the genuine Socialists had not much changed in numbers as a result of the war, constituting about 15% of the electorate. Sixty or seventy thousand Germans who voted for the LaFollette candidate in the primaries, voted in the regular election for the Socialist candidate, thus proving that racial ties counted for more with them than political views or those of religion, for most of them belonged to parties and religious bodies strongly opposed to the social doctrines of socialism. These elements, however, did not constitute a majority of the German element, and, combined, amounted to only about one quarter of the state's voters. This vote, in the state where the opposing elements seemed strongest, indicated that the nation was united as never before.

The war indorsed.

BIBLIOGRAPHICAL NOTES

The War Message and the Facts Behind It, Committee on Public Information, Washington. *First Session of the War Congress*, Ibid. *War Cyclopedia*, Ibid. Robinson, E. E., and West, V. J., *The Foreign Policy of Woodrow Wilson*, N. Y., 1917.

Sources. Historical accounts.

Every teacher should secure the various publications of the Committee on Public Information, which cover most phases of the war. They may be obtained by writing to 10 Jackson Place, Washington. *The History Teachers Magazine* has given very valuable material and bibliography on the war, since its beginning. *Current History*, published by the New York *Times*, contains important documents and articles.

CONCLUDING REMARKS

It is particularly advisable at this point to connect history with current events, to call the student's attention to the contemporary sources, and to develop the habit of using and estimating the various varieties, as the newspapers, with their news items, reports of speeches, editorials, and official records, the magazines, with their wealth of fact and opinion, and the literature of local, state, and national associations.

Contempo-
rary histori-
cal accounts.
American Year Book. McLaughlin and Hart, *Cyclopedia.* *New International Year Book. World Almanac.*

A useful test of the effect of the course in producing historical mindedness, discrimination in estimating the importance of events and their relation to past causes, and fairness in judging the actors, is to have the students bring the textbook up to date on the same scale to which it is written, that is, about fifteen hundred words a year.

INDEX

INDEX

INDEX

INDEX